ALSO BY JASON BERRY

Louisiana Faces: Images from a Renaissance
(with photographs by Philip Gould)

The Spirit of Black Hawk:
A Mystery of Africans and Indians

Lead Us Not into Temptation:
Catholic Priests and the Sexual Abuse of Children

Up from the Cradle of Jazz:
New Orleans Music Since World War II
(with Jonathan Foose and Tad Jones)

Amazing Grace:
With Charles Evers in Mississippi

VOWS
OF
SILENCE

THE ABUSE OF POWER
IN THE PAPACY
OF JOHN PAUL II

Jason Berry and Gerald Renner

FREE PRESS
New York   London   Toronto   Sydney

FREE PRESS

A Division of Simon & Schuster, Inc.

1230 Avenue of the Americas

New York, NY 10020

Copyright © 2004 by Jason Berry and Gerald Renner

All rights reserved, including the right to reproduce this book or portions thereof
in any form whatsoever. For information address Free Press Subsidiary Rights Department,
1230 Avenue of the Americas, New York, NY 10020.

This Free Press trade paperback edition May 2010

FREE PRESS and colophon are trademarks of Simon & Schuster, Inc.

For information about special discounts for bulk purchases,
please contact Simon & Schuster Special Sales at 1-866-506-1949
or business@simonandschuster.com.

The Simon & Schuster Speakers Bureau can bring authors to your live event.
For more information or to book an event, contact the Simon & Schuster Speakers Bureau
at 1-866-248-3049 or visit our website at www.simonspeakers.com.

Designed by Dana Sloan

Manufactured in the United States of America

1   3   5   7   9   10   8   6   4   2

The Library of Congress has cataloged the hardcover edition as follows:

Berry, Jason.
Vows of Silence : the abuse of power in the papacy of Pope John Paul II / Jason Berry
and Gerald Renner.
p. cm.
Includes bibliographical references (p.   ) and index.
1. Catholic Church—Clergy—Sexual behavior. 2. Homosexuality—Religious aspects—
Catholic Church. 3. Sexual abuse of children by clergy. 4. Catholic Church—Discipline.
5. Maciel, Marcial, 1920– 6. Doyle, Thomas P. I. Renner, Gerald. II. Title.

BX1912.9.B475 2004
282'.09'049—dc22   2003064249

ISBN 978-0-7432-4441-1
ISBN 978-0-7432-8706-7 (pbk)
ISBN 978-0-7432-5381-9 (ebook)

To Melanie McKay and Jacquelyn Breen Renner

for inspiration and much more

CONTENTS

CONTENTS

CATHOLIC CHURCH HIERARCHY

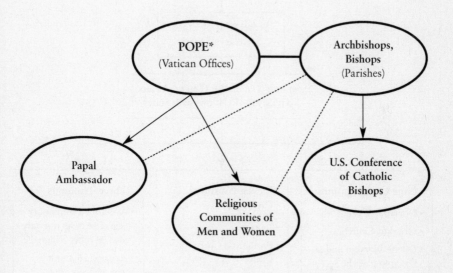

*Theologically, ultimate authority in the Catholic Church resides in the pope,
bishop of Rome, and all the bishops in concert, as at the second Vatican Council.*

M. X. Yordon, 2003

PRINCIPAL VATICAN OFFICES
(The Roman Curia)

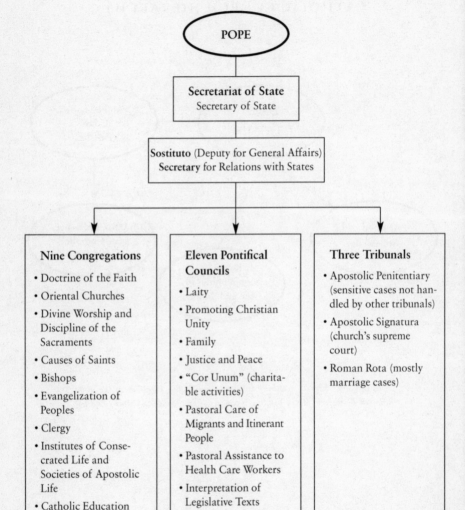

POPE

Secretariat of State
Secretary of State

Sostituto (Deputy for General Affairs)
Secretary for Relations with States

Nine Congregations

- Doctrine of the Faith
- Oriental Churches
- Divine Worship and Discipline of the Sacraments
- Causes of Saints
- Bishops
- Evangelization of Peoples
- Clergy
- Institutes of Consecrated Life and Societies of Apostolic Life
- Catholic Education

Eleven Pontifical Councils

- Laity
- Promoting Christian Unity
- Family
- Justice and Peace
- "Cor Unum" (charitable activities)
- Pastoral Care of Migrants and Itinerant People
- Pastoral Assistance to Health Care Workers
- Interpretation of Legislative Texts
- Interreligious Dialogue
- Culture
- Social Communications

Three Tribunals

- Apostolic Penitentiary (sensitive cases not handled by other tribunals)
- Apostolic Signatura (church's supreme court)
- Roman Rota (mostly marriage cases)

M. X. Yordon 2003

To get back to all the sorry Catholics. Sin is sin whether it is committed by the Pope, bishops, priests or lay people. The Pope goes to confession like the rest of us. . . . The Church is mighty realistic about human nature.

—FLANNERY O'CONNOR

PROLOGUE

THE STORY JUAN VACA told was baroque and chilling, but he wanted Bishop John Raymond McGann to understand why he had come to the diocese of Rockville Centre, Long Island. It was April of 1976. Father Vaca, thirty-nine, had dark hair flecked with silver, a fair brown face, and the discerning bishop could perhaps see the melancholy in his eyes and the sadness in his demeanor. In later years Vaca would study psychology to, as he said, "determine where sickness ends and evil begins."[1]

Vaca had joined the Long Island diocese just as McGann's predecessor was retiring. Men from the religious orders, like Jesuits or Franciscans, often serve in dioceses, but few asked to officially change status from religious to diocesan clergy. Father Vaca had impeccable credentials. In Orange, Connecticut, he had served five years as the U.S. director of the Legionaries of Christ, a religious order with headquarters in Rome.

The Legion was founded in Mexico in 1941 by Marcial Maciel Degollado. Under Father Maciel, the Legionaries built a network of schools and universities in Mexico, and branched out with prep schools and seminaries in Spain, Latin America, Ireland, and now America. With the Legion's growth, Maciel's stature rose in the eyes of the Roman Curia. By 2003 the Legion would claim eleven universities and over 150 prep schools worldwide.

Recruited by Maciel as a ten-year-old in Mexico, Vaca had grown up in the Legion, studying at the order's seminaries in Europe. Vaca told Bishop McGann that Maciel began sexually abusing him when he was twelve. He said that Nuestro Padre—Our Father, as Legionaries call the founder general—had used him in a perverse sexual relationship until Vaca was twenty-five. Maciel ran the Legion like a dictator, according to Vaca, and had dominated him by cutting him off from his family. Bishop McGann took it all in. Then he asked a classically American question: *Didn't anybody blow the whistle?*

Not that I know of, replied Vaca.

McGann's diocese encompassed Suffolk and Nassau Counties. He relied upon the generosity of Irish, Italian, and Hispanic descendants of an immigrant church, many of whom commuted into Manhattan jobs their forebears barely imagined. Nearly a third of the Fortune 500 CEOs were Roman Catholic.[2] McGann was of that generation of bishops who were builders, broadening the infrastructure of parishes, schools, colleges, and services that lifted Catholics from the margins of society to prosperity and power.

Sexual misconduct of priests was not a media topic in those days. Within the clerical world, stories occasionally circulated of priests having affairs with women, or even men. Priests were human, not without sin. In the eyes of millions of Catholics, the church nevertheless stood for moral rectitude. Father Vaca's charges went far beyond "sin." McGann had been appointed a bishop by Pope Paul VI and answered to him. McGann's priest was alleging severe moral crimes by the head of an international order. The Holy Father must be informed about this. Father Vaca had asked his bishop for *help*.

McGann was deceased when a Long Island grand jury made headlines in 2002 with a voluminous report that condemned the Rockville Centre diocese for a systemic pattern of concealing priests who molested children and lying to the families of those abused. In the case of Father Vaca, a bishop tried to do the right thing.

McGann told the Mexican cleric he would report Maciel to the Vatican. Vaca was skeptical; he thought Maciel had influence in the Curia to block an investigation. McGann insisted that they report through correct channels; he would write to the papal delegate in Washington, D.C. But a document of such gravity must be specific: Vaca had to take that next step. Over the summer Vaca settled into parish work in the town of Baldwin. On October 20, 1976, he sat down in St. Christopher's Rectory and wrote a twelve-page, single-spaced letter to Maciel. After thanking Maciel for his release from the Legion, Vaca got blunt:

> For me, Father, the disgrace and moral torture of my life began on that night of December 1949. Using the excuse that you were in pain, you ordered me to remain in your bed. I was not yet thirteen years old; you knew that God had kept me intact until then, pure, without ever having seriously stained the innocence of my infancy, when you, on that night, in the midst of my terrible confusion and anguish, ripped the masculine virginity from me. I had arrived at the Legion in my childhood, with no sexual experience of any kind. . . . It was you who initiated the aberrant and sacrilegious abuse that night; the abuse that would last for thirteen painful years.[3]

Vaca's *cri de coeur* is a riveting document, even amidst the recent tide of legal actions against priests and the media's coverage of the double lives that too many clerics have led. Vaca identified twenty men with Mexican or Spanish surnames, their place of residence in parentheses. "All of them, good and gifted young boys . . . personally told me that you committed the same sexual abuses against them, whose names I place before God as a Witness."

Vaca also impugned Regnum Christi, an organization the Legion had fostered to inspire laypeople as evangelists for the kingdom of Christ on earth. Vaca scored "the RC movement itself, with their procedures of secretism, absolutism and brainwashing systems, following the methods of secret societies rather than the open and simple evangelic methods . . . [and] through the use of subtle arrogance and vanity, [deluding members] into believing that they are the preferred beings and that they have been chosen by God." Vaca had a sister who as a "consecrated woman" had taken vows in Regnum Christi back in Mexico; he demanded that Maciel send her back to their family. Vaca wanted to be left alone to rebuild his life. Finally, "for the good of the Church," he told Maciel, "Renounce your position."

Vaca never got a reply from Maciel.

A dispassionate analysis of the letter holds three possibilities. The first is that Vaca was unstable and fabricated a defamatory picture of Maciel. The second is that Maciel was guilty and had no reason to risk self-incrimination with an answer. The third possibility—which presumably crossed Bishop McGann's mind—is that Vaca was substantially telling the truth, though perhaps not every single allegation, like brainwashing, could be proven.

Under the Code of Canon Law, McGann had a responsibility to act on the letter, or dismiss it, based on his judgment of Vaca's character and credibility. Of the twenty victims Vaca listed, one was a priest in the same Long Island diocese. The Reverend Félix Alarcón, then forty-three, had grown up in Spain and joined the Legion in early adolescence. Alarcón had opened the Legion of Christ center in Connecticut in 1965 and left the following year to join the Rockville Centre diocese. "I would have taken this to my grave," Father Alarcón said later, "but when my bishop asked me to verify what Vaca said, I was in the fray."[4] Maciel, he stated, had sexually abused him often, as a seminarian. McGann consulted with his canon lawyer, the Reverend John A. Alesandro. The canonist prepared a dossier that included a statement from Alarcón to buttress Vaca's damning letter to Maciel. Father Alesandro sent the package to the papal delegate in Washington. In vouching for the two ex-Legionaries, McGann and Alesandro were inviting a Vatican investigation into a man with an established base in the ecclesiastical power structure in Rome.

The result was—nothing. No Vatican official requested more information. The allegation that the founder of an international religious order was a pederast, and that his organization used brainwashing, met a cool Roman silence.

Two years later, in August of 1978, Vaca flew to Mexico to be with his family as his father was dying of cancer. His sister, still in Regnum Christi, resisted his pleas to leave the group. But Vaca was in a deeper crisis. He had fallen in love with a woman and felt guilty for remaining a priest. On return to Long Island he told Bishop McGann and asked to be laicized—to be dispensed from the obligations of the priesthood. Laicization required sending a petition to Rome. As part of his reason for leaving, Vaca again returned to the sexual abuse by Maciel.

Taking Vaca's troubled background into account, the bishop suggested he take a leave of absence from ministry to sort out his life. McGann also asked Vaca to see a psychiatrist. Several months into the sessions, Vaca disentangled himself from the relationship and returned to ministry. He also renewed his quest to see Maciel removed. Once again, the canonist Alesandro sent a dossier to the Holy See's apostolic delegate in Washington, D.C. On October 16, 1978, Cardinal Karol Wojtyla, the archbishop of Krakow, was elected pope and took the name John Paul II. The Sacred Congregation for Religious at the Vatican sent a receipt of the complaint. In 1997, when Gerald Renner asked Monsignor Alesandro why nothing happened, he spoke with reluctance: "All I can say is that there are different levels where people are informed about this. It was our duty to get this stuff into the right hands. I don't know why it was not acted on. . . . It's a substantive allegation that should have been acted on."[5]

"It's amazing," reflected Father Alarcón. "There are big people in Rome who are avoiding this."

Juan Vaca left the priesthood after psychotherapy and more struggle with celibacy. On August 31, 1989, he married in a civil ceremony. On October 28, 1989, Vaca wrote a seven-page letter to Pope John Paul II requesting dispensation from his vows. Although he no longer functioned as a priest, Vaca and his wife wanted their marriage blessed by the church. For a former priest or bishop, that requires the pope's approval of laicization.

Monsignor Alesandro again sent a Vaca document to the apostolic embassy in Washington. Again he received confirmation of its receipt by Rome.[6] Vaca wrote as if speaking personally to John Paul II, reflecting on his life, his failings, his marriage. He wrote of "being poorly trained" for the priesthood "because of the serious traumas I suffered for years for being sexually and psychologically abused by the Superior General and Founder, Marcial Maciel . . . in the same way I soon realized he was doing to other seminarians."

Four years later Vaca received the dispensation, one of thousands bearing the papal signature. He never heard a word about Maciel or the allegations. In 1997, in response to our questions for a report, Maciel denied the allegations, and continues to.

Why did Pope John Paul II protect Maciel?

The Vatican is under no obligation to assist investigative journalists. In the seven years since we first contacted the office of the papal spokesman, Joaquín Navarro-Valls, for comment on accusations by nine ex–Legion members that Maciel had abused them, the Vatican refused comment. No Vatican official ever told us Maciel was *innocent*. There was simply no answer to the accusations in media reports. The charges that Vaca and others filed against Maciel in a Vatican court of canon law in 1998 were shelved: no decision. Instead, Pope John Paul in 2001 praised Maciel at a sixtieth anniversary celebration of the Legion's founding. That symbolic acquittal from a pope who championed human rights under dictatorships is a numbing message on the state of justice in the church.

Our first report on Maciel, in the February 23, 1997, *Hartford Courant,* drew upon the accounts of Vaca, Alarcón, and seven other former Legionaries. Maciel refused to be interviewed. The Legion of Christ hired a blue-chip Washington law firm to try to kill the report. The Legion uses its newspapers, publicists, and apologists on its Web site to portray Maciel as a victim falsely accused. His supporters include some of the wealthiest citizens of Spain and Latin America, many of whose children attend or have studied at Legion schools or colleges. Americans who champion the Legion include George Weigel, a biographer of Pope John Paul II, and William J. Bennett, the author and lecturer on moral values. Maciel's defenders include the Reverend Richard John Neuhaus, the editor of the journal *First Things;* William Donohue, the director of the Catholic League for Religious and Civil Rights; Mary Ann Glendon, the Learned Hand professor of law at Harvard; and Deal Hudson, the editor of *Crisis* magazine.

Most Catholics in the English-speaking world know nothing of Father Maciel, the strange history of Regnum Christi, or the Legion's methods of psychological coercion. In America, Legion schools have left a trail of litigation and embittered former followers, even as the order lays plans for universities in Sacramento, California, and Westchester County, New York. In Latin America and Spain the Legionaries are a major religious movement, and in Mexico a national institution.

How do the Vatican courts treat accusations of great moral crimes by a priest close to the pope? How has the Vatican responded to the larger sexual crisis in the priesthood? These questions bear not just on Maciel and the response of many bishops to child molesters, but on eroding assumptions about clerical life. The Reverend Donald B. Cozzens, a former seminary rector, has written that the priesthood "is, or is becoming, a gay profession" [7]—echoing an issue raised in 1992 by Jason Berry in *Lead Us Not into Temptation.*[8]

Of twenty-one hundred priests identified in U.S. legal proceedings since the 1970s, the overwhelming majority preyed on teenage boys, according to Dallas attorney Sylvia Demarest, who has kept an extensive database. Therapists at a handful of institutions that specialize in treating such priests asked the bishops to fund a study that would assess the clinical findings. "The bishops voted it down," stated Dr. Leslie Lothstein, a clinical psychologist at the Institute of Living, a facility in Hartford, Connecticut, with a history of treating sex offenders. "The study people in the church don't want is comparing deviant sexual behavior among Protestant, Jewish and Catholic clergy. We've seen over 200 priests involved with teens or children. . . . Of about fifty ministers of other denominations I've counseled, the vast majority have been involved with adults—women."[9]

In June 2002, three years after Lothstein's remark, the American bishops appointed a National Review Board to gather data on clergy sex offenders in the dioceses. That study was under way as we completed this book. The bishops' denial of sexual crimes within the ranks was an unintended consequence of the celibacy law. That is not to say that celibacy causes men to abuse children, any more than marriage can be blamed for incest. Sexual behavior is rooted in personality development. The gay priest culture that arose in the last generation was another by-product of celibacy as cornerstone of a governing system. How did Pope John Paul II react to these changes tearing at the central nervous system of the church? We pose this question as products of Catholic families and schooling, with benevolent memories of priests and nuns as mentors, and priests we count as friends. Neither of us was abused, sexually or otherwise.

The most striking impact of the crisis has been in Ireland, the most culturally Catholic country on the globe, where the seminaries are now nearly barren. Studies show a deep Irish disaffection, not with faith but with the dishonesty and control mechanisms of church officialdom.[10] That disillusion spread in the 1990s as scandals beset North America, Australia, and Western Europe, hitting a critical mass in 2002 with a media chain reaction to the *Boston Globe* investigations. What happened *before* the pope summoned the American cardinals to Rome for the extraordinary meeting in April 2002? To answer that question we tracked the geography of the crisis and how lines of responsibility flowed back to Rome.

John Paul's failure on this issue stems from several factors we explore. One factor is a Vatican view of the scandal as a product of uncontrollable American courts and an anti-Catholic media. While there is certainly a pagan element in our entertainment media and a tawdry turn in news coverage toward tabloid obsessions, American reporting followed legal events. In contrast, Italy's legal system does not have the sweeping discovery powers of countries with a base in English common law, and the Italian media had far fewer civil cases to draw upon.

In Father Maciel, we confront a papal cover-up. His career is a case study in disinformation—distorting truth to gain power and fabricating a virtuous image out of pathological behavior; but the Vatican assisted this process for years by its failure to investigate serious charges. Maciel, who turned eighty-three on March 20, 2003, may be the most successful fund-raiser of the twentieth-century Catholic Church; he was very much in control of the Legion as this book went to press. Maciel's movement uses schools as a vehicle to make money and gain power within the church. The Legion claims to have five hundred priests and twenty-five hundred seminarians in twenty countries, and "tens of thousands" of laypeople as well as diocesan priests and deacons in Regnum Christi. While we do not doubt the spiritual integrity of many of those people, the evidence clearly suggests that the Legion is a Roman Catholic sect, built on a cult of personality that is centered on its founder. Maciel has fostered a militant spirituality by emulating fascistic principles he admired in the Spanish dictator Francisco Franco. More disturbing, the Legionaries use psychologically coercive techniques common to cults.

The church considers the Legion a religious order. Orders that are centuries old, like the Franciscans and the Jesuits, take vows of poverty, chastity, and obedience. Legionaries of Christ take two extra "private" vows: never to speak ill of Maciel or their superiors, and to report on those who do; and never to aspire to leadership positions. Those vows reward spying as an expression of faith.[11] As we excavated the history of Maciel and his organization, sexual behavior in clerical culture became an international news story and one of the great institutional tragedies of our time.

Pope John Paul II, his bishops, and his advisers in the Roman Curia could have arrested the crisis years ago had they heeded the warnings of a prophet in their midst. The Reverend Thomas P. Doyle, a Dominican priest, worked as canon lawyer in the Vatican embassy in Washington, D.C., in the early 1980s. No individual has played a more catalytic role in seeking justice than Father Doyle.

As a chaplain and lieutenant colonel in the U.S. Air Force, Father Doyle's career provides a prism on history. His journey—as a young seminarian during the early 1960s; as a consummate insider in the 1980s; and then as an exile—and a pariah—straddles a time in which the great promise of reforms at the Second Vatican Council of the 1960s met a backlash under the papacy of John Paul II. As the Vatican tried to muzzle theologians making honest inquiry into church teaching, a sexual underground in clerical life, concealed by ecclesiastical officials, made a mockery of enforced orthodoxy. Over a period of twenty years, Tom Doyle was *there*—writing reports, warning bishops, briefing cardinals, standing up for values of justice, then casting his lot with victims and their attorneys, helping journalists, and, in the process, rewriting the meaning of his life. He is a Catholic embodiment of the rebel, an ethos expressed by Albert Camus: "A man who says no: but whose refusal does not imply a renunciation. . . . Rebellion cannot exist without the feeling that somewhere, in some way, you are justified." The rebel "says yes and no at the same time. He affirms that there are limits and also that he suspects—and wishes to preserve—the existence of certain things beyond those limits."[12]

In 2002, while stationed at a military base in Ramstein, Germany, Doyle was besieged by reporters and TV producers from many countries as clergy sex abuse cases became an international media story. His was a rare voice of conscience, a priest speaking truth to the powers of his church.

Vows of Silence explores the Vatican's cover-up through the lives of two priests, Doyle and Maciel: one demanding justice, the other a fortress of injustice. In chronicling the major events surrounding these men, we also train a lens on the persecution of theologians and church thinkers under Cardinal Joseph Ratzinger. This latter-day witch hunt is of a piece with John Paul's refusal to confront the great crisis of the priesthood by allowing free discussion of alternatives to a male celibate clergy.

The sexual abuse of young people by clergy is not a new phenomenon in Rome. Saint Bernard of Clairvaux advised Pope Eugenius III, his fellow Cistercian monk and former pupil, how to behave after his election in the year 1145: "You cannot be the last person to know about disorder in your house. Raise your hand to the guilty, since a lack of punishment breeds recklessness that opens the door to all kinds of excess. Your brothers, the cardinals, must learn by your example not to keep young, long-haired boys and seductive men in their midst."[13] We do not share the ideological view of those who argue that the clergy crisis has been caused by "the homosexual network."[14] But neither do we share the mentality of political correctness that causes some commentators in the media and academe to shun any criticism of any dimension of gay culture whatsoever. In examining the sexual crisis of a celibate governing system, we try to heed the caution of Pascal, the French philosopher, who said that virtue is displayed not "by going to one extreme, but in touching both at once, and filling all the intervening space."[15]

Readers not familiar with the hierarchy of the church may find the charts at the beginning of the book and the glossary at the end useful references.

PART ONE

The Odyssey of Thomas Doyle

Chapter One

TO BE A PRIEST

HE WAS A FRESHMAN in a Roman Catholic seminary in upstate New York when the Second Vatican Council opened in 1962. The drama of a church gathering her bishops and best theologians was breathtaking to Patrick Doyle. His natural disposition toward authority might have sent him toward an FBI career. As a boy he hunted with his dad and at eleven joined the National Rifle Association; he remains a member to this day. But Pat Doyle, all of eighteen, wanted to help people and be close to God. The pageantry in Rome strengthened his vocation, the idea of his calling as a gift from God.

Pope John XXIII had called for "aggiornamento"—updating, or renewal—in summoning the first council since 1870. The portly pontiff exuded a benevolent, paternal grace that charmed many millions in those early years of television. He also had an instinctual approach to power; he was *furbo,* to use the Italian word: canny, sharp-witted.[1] Elected by the College of Cardinals in 1958 (a month before he turned seventy-seven) as a caretaker pope, John XXIII startled the Roman Curia in calling an ecumenical council. His sweeping, if imprecise, agenda was to "open the windows" of the church to the modern world. He died in 1963 midway through the proceedings. His successor, Pope Paul VI, a seasoned curial insider, was quite learned, yet lacked the charisma of "good Pope John."

In 1964, Pat Doyle transferred to the Dominicans, the seven-hundred-year-old Order of Preachers, and entered a seminary in

Dubuque, Iowa, named for Saint Thomas Aquinas, the medieval Dominican who grafted Aristotelian thought onto theology. Students and faculty followed Vatican II as the leaders worked to implement John XXIII's vision of engaging the church with a changing world. The Dominicans traditionally renamed their seminarians. Patrick Michael Doyle (born August 3, 1944, in Sheboygan, Wisconsin) became Thomas. With a rugged build and open Midwestern ways, Tom Doyle took the change in stride. His kin still called him Pat. "We were not a particularly churchy family," he recalls. "My parents really loved each other. They enjoyed each other's company and I guess that rubbed off. My sisters, Shannon and Kelly, have had good long marriages."[2]

Though key members of the Curia, fearful of change, wanted the council terminated, Paul VI guided Vatican II to its conclusion in 1965. The church began phasing out the Latin Mass in favor of liturgy in the local language. More than that, Vatican II proclaimed that rank-and-file Catholics were "the People of God," a great shift from thinking of the church as personified by bishops and clergy to meaning all Catholics.[3]

Tom's ancestral forebear Patrick Doyle had been born in 1830 in County Wicklow, Ireland, and sailed to America in 1850, settling in Wisconsin.[4] Tom's father, Michael Doyle, had fifteen siblings spread across the Midwest. An executive with an agrichemical business, Michael moved his wife, son, and two daughters to Cornwall, Ontario, where Pat spent his adolescence. By the time he joined the Dominicans and took the name Thomas, the family was in Montreal. When he went home for Christmas, in 1965, his mother, Doris, fifty-two, had breast cancer.

Monsignor R. J. MacDonald, the pastor back in Cornwall, made regular trips to the hospital. Kelly, then twelve, sat in her bedroom as her brother gently explained that their mother was dying.[5] After officiating at Doris's funeral, MacDonald gave Tom a rosary blessed in her memory. MacDonald was a gruff, largehearted Scotsman whose relationship to the Doyles typified the culture of American Catholicism through the mid–twentieth century. Priests developed siblinglike ties with parents in parishes. Mothers welcomed them into the home as role models for their kids. Celibacy carried a mystique of holy discipline. "The priest dealt with sacred matters in a sacred language . . . the mysteries of faith," an archbishop recalled. "To be a priest was the highest life a boy could aspire to."[6]

Irish priests molded the Catholicism of North America and Australia. To the waves of nineteenth- and twentieth-century immigrants from Ireland, priests were exalted figures in inner-city warrens, assisting people with tax forms, schools, bureaucracies, and jobs—signs said, *Irish Need Not Apply.*[7] Out of the clerical culture rose a line of cardinal-archbishops with ancestral ties to Ireland; Spellman in New York, Cushing in Boston, McIntyre in Los Angeles, Mannix in Melbourne—the list goes on of men as adroit with politicians as corporate barons.

Tom Doyle went back to Aquinas Institute and the aftershocks of Vatican II. Factional disputes were erupting over the liturgy—should guitars be used at Mass, should Latin chants be scrapped? Doyle *loved* the Latin Mass. He didn't like guys playing hootenanny licks; he felt a deep security from the bells that rang at appointed moments in the Mass, and the sweet aroma of incense burning. He believed in the order of the past. Priests and nuns in many countries were clamoring to have the law of mandatory celibacy made optional. Pope Paul VI put a lock on that talk with a 1967 encyclical that called celibacy the church's "brilliant jewel"—that which "evidently gives to the priest, even in the practical field, the maximum efficiency and the best disposition, psychologically and clerically, for the continuous exercise of a perfect clarity."[8] The pope cited no psychological studies of perfect clarity; there were none to cite.

Just before Christmas 1967, the faculty priests at Aquinas Institute went out for dinner. The prior—the priest elected to lead the Dominican community—announced he was leaving *to get married.* The gathering broke up with torn feelings. When the bell rang at Aquinas, Doyle and his fellow seminarians trooped into the common room and got the news. Feelings of betrayal by a leader darkened the festive season; some men asked why they all couldn't marry and be priests. In the months that followed, two faculty priests quit; disillusioned seminarians followed. Of the twenty-six men who began with Doyle, six would be ordained. By 2002, only three were still priests.

Had Vatican II caused a revolution? Did the council show a prophetic vision—or capitulate to a society already adrift from its moorings? The legacy of Vatican II opened a fault line in the church, widening into the new millennium.

The wrenching scandals of our day look back to those unresolved issues.

In theology classes Doyle read the ecumenical thinkers of Vatican II, the German Jesuit Karl Rahner, the Dutch Dominican Edward Schillebeeckx, the French priest Yves Congar. Their ideas of an introspective church, open to reasonable change, had made them outcasts in the 1950s under Pope Pius XII; all were rehabilitated by John XXIII.

The unrest at Aquinas continued. A religious brother who was retarded and did menial tasks disappeared. Word filtered down that he had made sexual advances to students and gone to a treatment center in New Mexico. Doyle later learned he had died in New Mexico. A theologian who studied at the Menninger Institute began speaking about homosexuality—not as sin but as lifestyle; some seminarians were spellbound. The man left the priesthood; years later he died of AIDS. Several men in Doyle's class were thrown out because they were gay.

As student protests rocked the globe in 1968, Tom Doyle sought closeness to God in the bedrock of orthodoxy. The earthquakes in the seminary seemed a test from God. He felt a greater pull to the mysteries of faith; he wanted to administer God's grace through the sacraments. "The issue of my seminary years was to *survive*," he would recall. With a voracious intellect he galloped toward a master's in philosophy. He would earn five M.A.s—adding degrees in theology, political science, canon law, and church administration.

Doyle had broken up with a high school girlfriend in Cornwall before making his choice. He wasn't indifferent to women's charms. But he saw the 1967 papal letter on celibacy as dashing any chance of imminent change in the rules.

On July 29, 1968, Pope Paul VI issued the encyclical *Humanae Vitae*, which condemned all forms of artificial contraception. Reaction to the birth control letter was awesome. Theologians in Europe and North America openly broke ranks, citing Paul's sixty-four-member advisory commission on the issue, which had overwhelmingly favored use of the birth control pill. For two years after the commission's secret report, Paul VI had read about bioethics and spoken with advisers in a Hamlet-like struggle. Should he break with a papal teaching that told couples wishing to avoid pregnancy to abstain from sex during the woman's fertile period? Or should Paul VI cross a threshold, and bless the logic of sexual intimacy without childbirth as an immediate goal?[9] He chose the past. Soon after the letter's release, an English cardinal said that Catholics using birth control devices could receive the sacraments.

As priests, nuns, and laypeople in many countries advocated freedom of conscience, a great wall of Catholic unity was cracking. Doyle learned he had cousins who used the pill. One couple became Episcopalians. At least the encyclical was not issued under a rubric of papal infallibility.

Thomas P. Doyle was ordained on May 16, 1970, in Dubuque, Iowa. Michael Doyle gave his son the wedding and engagement rings of his deceased mother; Tom had a goldsmith in Montreal implant Doris's rings, in the design of a Celtic cross, in the silver chalice he used henceforth in celebrating the Holy Eucharist. In time, he officiated at the weddings of Shannon and Kelly. If he had a mild envy of his sisters' intimacy with their spouses, and homes soon blessed with children, he led a rewarding life nonetheless. Celibacy meant sublimating the sex drive through athletics, marathon reading, intense prayer, and an array of friendships with parishioners and in the Dominican communities. He was twenty-eight when a woman in confession asked if experiencing an orgasm was a sin. On impulse he told her no—enjoy those orgasms when you have them!

In 1971 Doyle was an assistant pastor at St. Vincent Ferrer Parish in River Forest, a suburb of Chicago, when a divorced man asked his help. Could he get his first marriage annulled, and remarry in the church? Divorced Catholics were rare in Tom's parents' generation. Many Catholics believed that divorced people could never remarry within the church, though canonical proceedings did allow for annulments. Those who remarried civilly or in other churches were forbidden to receive communion. Doyle drove down to the Loop and visited the Chicago archdiocese's tribunal, where priests and lay staff dealt with the Code of Canon Law.

An annulment had stricter standards than a civil divorce; but if aberrations like spousal abandonment or systematic abuse were proven, the tribunal could deem the sacramental bond "invalid," opening the way for a new exchange of vows. Doyle helped his parishioner get an annulment and presided at the man's wedding. Suddenly, people were calling him for help on annulments. He listened as women sobbed, telling of husbands who had beaten them for years; he met kids numbed by violent and alcohol-drenched homes; he heard women talk about frigidity and being abused as girls. He saw the proud exterior of men turn brittle as they revealed sexual secrets that had plagued them for years; some were impotent, others homosexual, and though they loved their families, they wanted out of marriage. In this undercurrent of suffering, Doyle reasoned that Christ's church must help its hurting members.

"Cardinal Cody wants to see you," his Dominican provincial said one day.

The mansion of Chicago's cardinal archbishop overlooked Lincoln Park in a zone of downtown real estate called the Gold Coast. Cardinal John Cody ruled the nation's largest archdiocese with an iron fist. Cody forced many older priests out of parishes they had served for years. He would show up at a rectory unannounced, wait hours if the pastor was out, and when the man walked in order him to vacate on the spot. His decisions could be bizarre. When the psychologist Eugene Kennedy advised him that a priest on the verge of collapse should enter a therapeutic facility, Cody gave the priest money and a plane ticket to Paris. The priest flew off to a breakdown, and ended up in a New York hospital. "Who could read Cody's mind?" says Kennedy. "He wanted to control everything."[10]

As archbishop of New Orleans, Cody had overseen $30 million worth of construction in four years and championed racial desegregation. In Chicago, he had to close inner-city Catholic schools because of his poorly conceived closed-circuit TV network for parishes. He lost $2 million investing church funds in a company that crashed. But Chicago had more than 2 million Catholics whose loyalty allowed Cody to make financial gifts to members of the Roman Curia on trips to the Vatican. A fireman's son who had entered the seminary at fourteen, he took doctorates in philosophy, theology, and canon law, landing a job at the Vatican Secretariat of State in the 1930s.[11] In Chicago, his tyrannical behavior generated a river of bad press and speculation about his stability, which flowed to Rome. "As long as I'm all right with God, I don't care what my critics say," he huffed.[12] In 1978, with Pope Paul ill, the Reverend Andrew M. Greeley noted the arrival of a cardinal from the Roman Curia:

> *Sebastiano Baggio has been in our city. In a secret stop on his way to a meeting in Latin America, he visited Cardinal Cody with a*

"request" from the pope that he yield power. The cardinal is already telling people about the visit. I hear there was a fierce shouting match most of one night at the cardinal's villa on the grounds of the seminary at Mundelein, with the cardinal adamantly refusing to go along with the request. . . . [T]he cardinal often does not respond to letters from the various Roman congregations and in one case did not respond for several months to a handwritten letter from Pope Paul VI (he bragged to others about ignoring this letter, saying that "Baggio made the pope write it").[13]

Two days later the pope died. Cody flew to Rome for the funeral and conclave that selected Cardinal Albino Luciani as John Paul I. A month later Luciani, too, died. Back in Rome, Cody sat in conclave with the cardinals who chose Karol Wojtyla, the archbishop of Krakow, as the first Polish pope, John Paul II.

Well before those events, a cautious Tom Doyle had been ushered into Cody's office. The famously moody cardinal, bespectacled, with sagging jowls, inquired about his background, life in the Dominicans, his parish. Father Doyle answered politely, truthfully. Remarking on his work with the divorced, Cody asked if he knew canon law. "Not much, Your Eminence." Cody had been a scholar on the canons relating to marriage. The cold exterior melted into a strange bearish warmth as he praised the young priest for helping those who needed the church.

Thus began an odd friendship. Seasoned by the confessions of wrecked marriages, Tom Doyle saw Cody as unable to articulate his pain. He was careful not to play therapist to a cardinal. Secretaries came and went with documents to sign; Cody slept alone in the big house, surrounded by stacks of papers. With a large reach of family and friends, Doyle was upbeat about life. Cody confided about alcoholic priests he was helping financially, and support to women with out-of-wedlock children. *The fathers were priests, Father!* Doyle did not become Cody's confessor; but as Cody spoke of his compassion, Doyle saw a lonely man yearning for affections that his stormy habits barred him from finding.

Ambitious young people commonly seek out older, powerful figures they may not like, yet whom they cultivate in finding a career ladder. Cordial Tom Doyle ended up liking the old man. Cody not only encouraged his ministry with the divorced, he provided financial support for Doyle to study canon law. In 1973 Doyle went to Rome for courses in church jurisprudence. He lived at the Angelicum, the Dominican university, and took classes at the Gregorianum, the Jesuit university. He saw the Legionaries of Christ walking in pairs, like soldiers. In class they talked about orthodoxy so much as "to seem paranoid—so lacking in independent thought," he recalled. He knew little else about them.

From Rome he went to Ottawa, earning a master's in church law at St. Paul University, and then to the Catholic University of America, in Washington, D.C., for his doctorate. Catholic U—called "the little Vatican" by virtue of its founding under an 1887 charter by Pope Leo XIII—covered 144 green acres in the northeast section of Washington. At the front, on Michigan Avenue, stood the Basilica of the National Shrine of the Immaculate Conception with its brilliant blue dome. Doyle lived across the street at the Dominican House of Studies, a cavernous neo-Gothic structure with a row of steeples.

In time off from classes, he took flying lessons and got his pilot's license.

By 1978 he was back at the parish in River Forest, working on annulments at Chicago's tribunal. A group of scholars overseeing a revised edition of the 1917 canonical code enlisted Doyle to write the commentary on the canons governing marriage. He resumed his visits with Cardinal Cody, more unpopular than ever in Chicago yet on good terms with Pope John Paul II.

In 1981, a canonist working at the Vatican embassy in Washington, D.C., resigned to become a Dominican superior. The apostolic delegate, or papal envoy, was the Italian archbishop Pio Laghi. Doyle was stunned at the invitation to interview in Washington for the canon lawyer's position.

Built in 1939, the three-story building of Florentine design on Massachusetts Avenue's Embassy Row was directly across from the official residence of the vice president. In countries where the Holy See has no diplomatic standing, the papal envoy to the nation's bishops is called an apostolic delegate; a papal envoy with ambassadorial rank is called a nuncio. Pope John Paul II's secretary of state, Cardinal Agostino Casaroli, was negotiating a relationship with the Reagan administration to secure diplomatic status for the Holy See. In 1867, under pressure from Protestants, the United States had severed ties with the Vatican.

Born on May 21, 1922, in Castiglione, Pio Laghi was a peasant's son who advanced through the priesthood with doctorates in theology and canon law in Rome. He was thirty when Pope Pius XII selected him for the Vatican diplomatic corps. As befit his title, the fifty-nine-year-old Laghi had a quick mind and an elegant manner. He was a trim man with dark eyes, close-cut silver hair, and "a frustratingly consistent forehand on the tennis court," in the words of Senator John Heinz of Pennsylvania.[14] Fluent in four languages, Laghi had served in Nicaragua during the Somoza regime; then in India, Jerusalem, Cyprus, and finally Argentina, where the military regime paid the salaries of the bishops.

Laghi's tour of duty in Argentina coincided with the "dirty war" of a dictatorship that tortured and "disappeared" thousands of its own people. Laghi later called it the "most thankless" job of his career. Human rights activists accused him, bitterly, of cozying up to the regime—charges Laghi would deny as they shadowed him into the evening of his career.[15]

Doyle knew nothing of that controversy in 1981 as he sat in Laghi's large office, where a photograph of the pope hung prominently. With a prelate's gold chain draped across his chest, Laghi spoke of the need to select correct men to become bishops, reviewing qualifications to ensure that the Holy Father had a list of three candidates from whom to choose each new bishop. The topography of the church was changing. As descendants of Irish, Polish, and Italian Catholics settled into affluent suburbs of the Northeast and Midwest, the influx of Haitians, Cubans, and Nicaraguans into Florida, and of Salvadorans and Mexicans into the Southwest and California, pushed the frontiers of the church. Laghi emphasized the need for naming new bishops as Rome carved out new dioceses.

Laghi kept talking—about the need for bishops loyal to the Holy Father's vision for the church, about the Holy Father's emphasis on evangelization. Doyle had written his master's thesis in political science on Lenin's theory of social revolution. As archbishop of Krakow, Karol Wojtyla had lived through the horrors of communism. As pope, John Paul II was sending signals of disapproval to Latin America, where advocates of Liberation Theology sought an empowerment of the impoverished masses as part of their spiritual destiny. The pope saw Marxist thought as influencing such theologians. As Archbishop Laghi kept talking, Doyle, eager for a career track to become a bishop or diplomat, wondered, *Why is this guy yakking so much? Isn't he curious about who I am?*

An aide interrupted to say that the guests had arrived.

In marched Cardinal John Krol of Philadelphia, tall and gray-haired, with regal bearing (as befit his name, meaning "king" in Polish), accompanied by two newly named auxiliary bishops. Laghi showed the Americans into the dining room; French Canadian nuns served a celebratory meal with wine in honor of the two men who had joined the hierarchy. One bishop proposed "a toast to the Holy Spirit," which struck Doyle as stupid. But you can't *not* drink to the Holy Spirit when you're sitting with the apostolic delegate and the cardinal archbishop of Philadelphia. Laghi and Krol did most of the talking, ruminations on the recent shooting of the Holy Father in Rome by Mehmet Ali Agca, a Turkish terrorist. The table was charged with speculation about news on Agca's reputed ties to Bulgaria and the Soviet KGB. A plot to kill the pope was evil of the harshest form.

Cardinal Krol and the two bishops departed after lunch.

Coffee-logged, Doyle readied himself for questions.

"How soon can you come?" said Pio Laghi.

Well, replied Doyle, he would have to ask his superiors.

"Yes, fine," said Laghi matter-of-factly. "Go ask them."

And that was it—no questions, just come back when your superiors have agreed to let you work for the Holy Father. Doyle thanked Archbishop Laghi, realizing the job had been his to lose. The Vatican delegation! He flew back to Chicago on wings of joy and congratulations from his brother Dominicans.

The *Chicago Sun-Times* was investigating Cody's use of archdiocesan funds, which included generous support to a lady who had been a friend since childhood. Doyle put no stock in rumors of a sexual relationship. Cody claimed they had grown up like siblings. Still, Cody's bizarre fiscal habits had caused the U.S. attorney's office to open a probe. Cody's lawyers insisted he was protected by the constitutional separation of church and state. Lead attorney Don Reuben, a self-styled fixer in the city's power structure, called Cody "answerable to Rome and to God, not to the *Sun-Times*."[16]

Cody told Doyle that the papal delegation would be a demanding job, but he knew Doyle would handle it well. Doyle thanked him with a sad foreboding about Cody. After a round of good-byes he boxed his many books, drove to Washington, and moved back into the Dominican

House of Studies, where he would live while working as the embassy canon lawyer and for his ultimate superior, Pope John Paul II.

In Service to the Vatican

Father Doyle had voted for Ronald Reagan; he liked the administration's emphasis on a strong national defense and less government. Each day he rose for early Mass and drove to the embassy mansion for morning prayers at seven-thirty in the chapel lined with wooden carvings of the Stations of the Cross that Laghi had brought from Italy. The nuns who prepared the men's meals lived in their own quarters within the embassy. Work began with a *congresso*, or meeting, at which Laghi presided. Four Italian priests handled his correspondence, reports, and cable traffic with Rome. Doyle was among the four American priests. One wrote Laghi's speeches; another was his secretary and aide at events; a third was the *economo*, a quartermaster who issued checks, planned events, and oversaw custodial work at the embassy. Doyle dealt with some of the most important and confidential tasks, doing background checks on future bishops.

Laghi met with bishops individually and through the U.S. Catholic Conference, in northeast Washington, which served as the bishops' national support staff. (The U.S.C.C. and the National Conference of Catholic Bishops later merged, becoming the U.S. Conference of Catholic Bishops.) Secrecy was fundamental to Doyle's job. Few reporters knew who he was, which suited him fine. Laghi caused a stir in July of 1981 with a letter to U.S. bishops admonishing their diocesan newspapers for "lack of respect toward the church and the magisterium."[17] The word "magisterium" refers to the teaching authority of the pope, the church, the bishops. Laghi's letter, mentioning no journalist by name, was widely seen as a criticism of Andrew M. Greeley, the prolific priest whose column ran in many diocesan papers. Greeley, a sociologist and leading critic of the 1968 birth control encyclical, predicted the silent dissent by millions of Catholic couples who would use the pill or other contraceptives and still receive the sacraments. Laghi chided the Catholic press for "harm to the faith of the people" when articles dissented from church teaching. One editor quipped: "How can you respond to a letter that contains no specifics? You can only say: Be specific."

Doyle saw the letter as a warning shot on loyalty. Catholics constituted 24 percent of the U.S. population, some 62 million people in the richest nation on the earth. John Paul wanted them four-square on church teaching about topics that ran against the grain of popular culture. Doyle's misgivings about forbidding married Catholics the use of contraception had deepened. Those were profoundly personal decisions. Realizing he would be fired if he questioned church teaching, Doyle rationalized self-censorship as a price for securing a role of authority in a church that was bound to change. The church had tolerated slavery before the Civil War; John Paul II was speaking out for human rights. Church teachings on human sexuality gave short shrift to the social sciences. One day Rome would have to approve new theological inquiry.

Doyle had met John Paul in October of 1979 at a reception of Chicago priests during his first papal trip to America. He had arrived like some celestial superstar, handsome with his chiseled Slavic features, wide brow, and determined gaze. In the warm smile, an adoring media found a sublime persona. Most commentators ignored a subtler message, as the historian Garry Wills observed in a *Columbia Journalism Review* essay. Addressing theologians in Washington, John Paul said: "It is the right of the faithful not to be troubled by theories and hypotheses that they are not expert in judging or that are easily simplified or manipulated by public opinion for ends that are alien to the truth." Wills seized on the words as "the old defense of theological censorship. . . . The man who says that will not be quick to take questions from a press that might 'simplify' or distort the answers."[18]

The stormy years in seminary had toughened Father Doyle. Wearing French cuffs at receptions on the embassy circuit, he met Vice President and Mrs. George Bush. He had lunch with Catholic advisers in the White House. Having never imagined such a life for himself, he liked it and wanted to move up.

Doyle spent much of his time writing internal reports for Laghi's review and that of the Secretariat of State in Rome. In vetting bishops, Doyle relied on people who knew a given candidate. A questionnaire went to such people with a cover statement exactly as printed here: ANY VIOLATION OF THIS SECRET NOT ONLY CONSTITUTES A GRAVE FAULT, BUT IS

ALSO A CRIME PUNISHABLE WITH A CORRESPONDING ECCLESIASTICAL PENALTY. The questionnaire asked about the priest's attitude toward Vatican statements on "the priestly ordination of women, on the Sacrament of Matrimony, on sexual ethics, and on social justice . . . loyalty and docility to the Holy Father, the Apostolic See, and the Hierarchy; esteem for and acceptance of priestly celibacy."[19]

The prospective bishop was never interviewed, nor supposed to know he was under consideration. Doyle spoke with bishops and priests in assessing candidates. Laghi discouraged priests' councils from submitting names. The process was a "pontifical secret." Those receiving a letter from the delegate "are not to disclose this fact to anyone nor are they to discuss the content of their response with anyone."[20]

For all of the secrecy in the background checks, Doyle found it boring work. He preferred writing reports on the dioceses, fusing demographic data and internal numbers in analyzing infrastructure, state of the clergy, growth in schools, universities, and charitable services. One thing Doyle omitted from his reports was the reason behind the declining numbers of priests; some twelve hundred men were leaving American clerical life a year, most of them to marry. A similar attrition factor was emerging in Canada, Australia, and Ireland.[21] The mandatory celibacy law and the birth control prohibition were taking a toll.

Silence was a powerful force in ecclesiastical culture—things unsaid could be as important as the timely word. Under John Paul, no priest who wanted to be a bishop could speak against celibacy, or the birth control ban, or in favor of ordaining women. Doyle knew that any number of would-be bishops did not share Rome's positions. In the arc of history the church had to reckon with the *sensus fidelium*—the "mind of the faithful." Until then, he told himself, he was working for the greater good. Laghi praised his report on the Chicago archdiocese at the *congresso*.

On a trip back to Chicago he visited the seventy-four-year-old Cody in a parlor of the mansion on the evening of April 24, 1982. The cardinal, so bloated that his head seemed tiny, was dying of heart failure. Amidst the pounding *Sun-Times* reports, a federal grand jury had issued subpoenas to five archdiocesan bank accounts; Cody stonewalled the grand jury about his spending. With Doyle, the old man reminisced about happier days, until a nurse said he needed rest.

At 2 A.M. Doyle was awakened by a phone call: Cody had died.

Laghi ordered him to retrieve the cardinal's personal papers. Cody had been a voting cardinal in conclaves that had elected two popes. If investigators obtained his papers, Cody's diary might be leaked to the press. With authorities at bay, Doyle searched Cody's office and mansion. He found letters to people who were sick, and gifts from children in Cody's bedroom. A teddy bear symbolized how a man emotionally cut off found comfort in a child's gift. Doyle brought other things back to the embassy, beyond a subpoena's reach.

Cody's death ended the dismal spectacle of federal investigation. Before his death, the pope had quietly approved Cincinnati archbishop Joseph L. Bernardin to become Chicago's next archbishop. A Southerner by birth, Bernardin had shown a genteel, conciliatory manner in the early 1970s when, as general secretary, he had a shaping role at the bishops' conference in Washington. In an ironic postmortem, Cody's old nemesis, Cardinal Baggio, the head of the Congregation for Bishops, tried to block Bernardin's candidacy. Baggio had been a favorite of Pope Paul VI in seeking moderate, pastorally minded men for the hierarchy. John Paul II "was disturbed at reports that some bishops in the United States were not speaking out clearly on birth control, abortion, and divorce," wrote *Time* Vatican correspondent Wilton Wynn. Baggio's move against Bernardin backfired. Demoted by John Paul, Baggio moaned: "I am nothing in the Curia now—nothing!"[22]

When Joe Bernardin moved into the mansion in Chicago, Doyle and Pio Laghi flew in for his installation as archbishop, staying at the big house. Bernardin was the opposite of his predecessor: at ease with others, a good listener, a consensus builder. He began an address to the Chicago priests with the words "I am Joseph, your brother." John Paul would soon name him a cardinal. En route to the festivities Doyle sat with powerful churchmen in a limousine and had warm memories as Chicago glided by.

Laghi warned him about becoming too chummy with bishops after Doyle mentioned a conversation with Tom Kelly, a Dominican who had succeeded Bernardin as general secretary of the bishops' conference. Kelly (soon to become archbishop of Louisville) had told him: "You're very important to Bernardin now," meaning that the conference wanted influence over the short list of bishop candidates. Laghi solemnly told Doyle that a priest who once worked at the nunciature—as the Vatican embassy was now called—was fired for breaking confidences. The Roman Catholic hierarchy was as political as Congress or the Kremlin. Bishops dealt with various Vatican congregations, showing unity with Rome. In return they wanted collegiality, a degree of power sharing. Paul VI had changed the College of Cardinals from majority Italian to an international body, reflecting the global church's great diversity, a change that led, indirectly, to the election of the first Polish pope.

John Paul II, an actor in his youth and a scholar in philosophy, was displaying rare charisma on human rights. In 1979, Poland's communist regime begrudgingly allowed crowds to gather for his first trip home as pope. He told 250,000 people at Mass in Warsaw's Victory Square: "Christ cannot be kept out of the history of man in any part of the globe." Elsewhere on that trip, he said: "This pope has come to this place to bear witness to Christ . . . to speak of these often forgotten people and nations to the whole, to Europe and to the world."[23] He was embarking on an extraordinary foreign policy feat, a pope using the power of words, the symbol of his office, to defy tyranny. He sent underground messages to imprisoned leaders of Solidarity and monitored channels of covert aid, bolstering a national resistance movement.[24] To many Catholics, his conviction about the birth control prohibition seemed marginal, almost irrelevant.

Doyle's stock rose with the 1983 publication by Paulist Press of a revised, 1,152-page volume, *The Code of Canon Law: A Text and Commentary*. As author of the section on marriage issues, he was at the top in his field, teaching part-time at Catholic University.

In the power ties between Rome and America, theology was the dicey vocation. Theologians took risks in exploring issues of ethics and conscience. Theologians got in trouble with the Congregation for the Doctrine of the Faith, the quaint name Paul VI had given the old Holy Office of the Inquisition. Cardinal Joseph Ratzinger, a German, was prefect of the CDF. As a young priest at Vatican II, Ratzinger stood as a progressive theologian advising his national hierarchy, writing of "prophetic protest against the self-righteousness of the institution. . . . God, throughout history, has not been on the side of the institution but on that of the suffering and persecuted."[25] Back in Germany, Ratzinger became dean of theology at the University of Tübingen. As campus protests swept Europe in 1968, students occupied the classrooms of Ratzinger and his Swiss colleague Hans Küng. "Even for a strong personality like me, this was unpleasant," Küng told Ratzinger's biographer John L. Allen Jr. "For someone timid like Ratzinger it was horrifying."[26] Radicals tried to push the student parish into activism. As Allen observed: "Ratzinger later said that the Tübingen experience showed him 'an instrumentalization by ideologies that were tyrannical, brutal and cruel. That experience made it clear to me that the abuse of faith had to be resisted precisely if one wanted to uphold the will of the council.' "

Ratzinger was turning his theological concern from structural change to institutional stability when Pope Paul VI appointed him archbishop of Munich in May of 1978. A month later Paul made him a cardinal. At the conclave that August, following Paul's death, Ratzinger met Cardinal Wojtyla of Krakow, with whom he had exchanged books for several years. A month later Wojtyla became John Paul II. Ratzinger meanwhile had a publicized falling-out with Hans Küng. A theologian critical of papal infallibility, Küng was a priest committed to changing church structures. His vision of a church committed to deep structural change clashed with that of the German bishops and the Congregation for the Doctrine of the Faith, which in 1979 declared him unqualified to teach as a Catholic theologian.

Ratzinger would later say that it was not he but his former colleagues who had changed. In 1981 John Paul II chose him to lead the CDF.

When Tom Doyle met him in 1983, Ratzinger was building a case against the Reverend Charles Curran of Catholic University of America, an influential moral theologian. Curran explored the symmetry between theology and biology. How did church teachings on human sexuality, unchanged for centuries, square with the advances of science? For Rome, the unresolved issue was Curran's role in 1968 as a leader of the theologians dissenting against the birth control prohibition. Ratzinger wanted obedience to church teaching. As the CDF built a case against Curran, theologians saw Ratzinger as betraying Vatican II. Not so, Ratzinger insisted. "A progressive process of decadence," he explained, "has been unfolding under the sign of a summons to a presumed 'spirit of the Council.' "[27]

Doyle shared Ratzinger's revulsion against countercultural currents that crashed against civilized order; Doyle also liked the gentlemanly Charlie Curran and thought him no threat to the church. Ratzinger was laying the groundwork to strip him of his license to teach theology. Unlike Notre Dame, Georgetown, and other independent Catholic universities, Catholic U, with its pontifical charter, answered to Rome. Doyle had no role in the dispute and was glad of that.

At a conference in Dallas in 1983, Doyle spoke on moral values to church officials. After his remarks he sat with Ratzinger, whose silver-white hair and genteel manner shimmered with beneficence. Doyle admired his intelligence and commitment to Vatican authority, if not his views on every issue. This was a culture of power where one worked from within, sometimes slowly. Ratzinger showed a capacity to listen, as if he had all the time in eternity for what Thomas Patrick Doyle had to say. Yet Rome's battles with theologians cut against Doyle's pastoral experience of people who sought solace, not rules on sex, in response to life's burdens. He was careful not to say too much.

A sign of what Ratzinger detested landed on his desk in Rome in 1983: *A Challenge to Love: Gay and Lesbian Catholics in the Church,* an anthology of essays edited by Robert Nugent, a priest formerly with the Philadelphia archdiocese who had a master of sacred theology degree from Yale. With no whiff of personal scandal, Nugent had run afoul of Archbishop James Hickey of Washington, D.C., for his work with New Ways Ministry, a gay and lesbian outreach he had founded with a nun, Jeannine Gramick, in a suburb of Washington. Hickey forbade them from giving workshops in his archdiocese and began a long-running investigation of the pair for violation of church doctrine. In a short introduction to Nugent's book, Bishop Walter Sullivan of Richmond, Virginia, quoted a U.S. bishops' 1976 pastoral letter advocating compassion for those who "find themselves, through no fault of their own, to have a homosexual orientation." Sullivan wrote: "Some voices challenge us to love and accept homosexual Catholics; some challenge our understanding of human sexuality."[28] On a trip to Rome Sullivan visited Ratzinger. Pointing to the book, Ratzinger said: "What is the meaning of this?"[29] He ordered Sullivan to remove his name from the cover of future editions. Sullivan obeyed. The CDF requested that the Salvatorians, Nugent's order, halt future printings, which of course the order had no authority to do.

Nugent's essay claiming that the church had a substantial gay priest culture violated the logic of secrecy in ecclesiastical life.[30] In 1961 the

Sacred Congregation for Religious, in Rome, had issued a dark warning: "Advancement toward religious vows and ordination should be barred to those who are inflicted with evil tendencies toward homosexuality or pederasty for whom the common life and the priestly ministry constitute serious dangers."[31] Tom Doyle knew scattered priests who were homosexual, a few fairly up-front about it. Unless a man openly carried on, Doyle was tolerant. But he had seen religious communities torn by cliques along lines of sexual orientation. The straights wondered who the gays were screwing; the gays called homophobia a sin that created spiritual wounds. Doyle was glad too that he had no role in Hickey's investigation.

In his vetting of prospective bishops, Doyle eliminated men with sexual baggage. Yet even systems with elaborate screenings are not failsafe, as Doyle learned many years later when Arizona litigation over allegations of sexual abuse of adolescents involving one Father Robert Trupia, himself a canon lawyer, revealed that in 1980 Bishop James Rausch of Phoenix had begun paying a street hustler for sex. Rausch had advanced to the hierarchy after being general secretary of the bishops' conference in Washington. Rausch was long dead by the time the information surfaced in litigation. His background check had been done before Pio Laghi arrived in Washington, before Tom Doyle had any idea he would ever work in the Vatican embassy.[32]

Chapter Two

EVIDENCE OF
THINGS UNSAID

O F THE BISHOPS Tom Doyle met through his embassy work, none impressed him as favorably as Bernie Law.

Born in Mexico in 1931, the only child of an airplane pilot and a mother who converted to the faith, Bernard Law was elected senior class president of his majority-black high school in St. Thomas, Virgin Islands.[1] As a Harvard undergraduate he shared a dormitory suite with two Jews and a Southern Baptist. After Harvard, he spent two years at a Benedictine monastery among pastoral oaks in Louisiana, followed by six years at the Pontifical College Josephinum in Columbus, Ohio. In 1961, Law's final year in seminary, church officials learned that a faculty priest had been seducing teenage boys in his apartment, making them stand naked before mirrors, telling them, "Jesus loves you and your body."[2] The teacher was dismissed.

Law's Caribbean upbringing gave him a natural rapport with people of color. As a young priest in Jackson, Mississippi, he edited the diocesan newspaper, writing in support of civil rights, putting himself on the right side of history. In 1973, he was named the bishop of Springfield–Cape Girardeau, in Missouri, which had a small Catholic population. Tom Doyle enjoyed conversations with Law at the embassy, where bishops routinely visited to meet with Pio Laghi. Ambitious, comfortable with ideas, Law was an ardent pro-life advocate. When Doyle asked his opinion on Rome's order to have the Sisters of Mercy halt tubal ligations at their hospitals, Law opined that the surgical procedure for women who no longer wished to bear children violated Catholic birth control teaching. Though frustrated by the nuns' stall tactics, Doyle was troubled by the equating of aborting a fetus with the tying of fallopian tubes, which involved no embryo. The tubal ligations stopped at the hospitals.

With Doyle's support, the pope in 1984 made Law archbishop of Boston.

In theory, each bishop answers to the pope; but their more direct line of communication is with the papal delegate in Washington and the various congregations at the Vatican. Bishops have great latitude in running their dioceses. For all of John Paul's emphasis on loyalty, few bishops preached on birth control. They had to raise money from the pews.

A greater concern to the bishops was the agony of the church in Latin America. The Reagan administration was pouring weapons and military support into Central America. Guatemala, under a fundamentalist Christian, had a military that was slaughtering Indian peasants. Nicaragua had idealistic priests allied with the Sandinista government, the cardinal archbishop of Managua bucking the Marxist regime, and Contra guerrillas waging war on the Sandinistas. In El Salvador, Archbishop Oscar Romero had championed a "preferential option for the poor," the clarion call of a 1968 Latin American bishops conference. For exhorting his government to respect human rights, Romero was shot dead while celebrating Mass. The assassination outraged bishops, particularly Archbishop Hickey of Washington, who knew nuns in El Salvador who were raped and murdered by death squads.

Laghi was not a critic of American policy. Cardinal Casaroli, the papal secretary of state, was working to restore diplomatic ties between Washington and the Holy See. In 1984, Laghi became a full ambassador as Washington sent a representative to the Vatican. The bishops' conference, however, was emerging as a critic of the administration, with book-length pastoral letters on nuclear arms and the economy generating national debate. The 1985 economics letter, directed by Milwaukee archbishop Rembert G. Weakland, faulted Reagan policies for neglecting the poor and the working class. Most bishops were moderately left of center on domestic issues other than abortion. In 1982, as a nuclear freeze movement spread when U.S. missiles were installed in Europe, Cardinal Bernardin steered the research on *The Challenge of Peace*, which questioned the arms buildup and the morality of using nuclear weapons.[3]

Doyle, who supported administration policy toward the Soviets, watched with silent approval as Cardinal Ratzinger took aim at Bernardin for overstepping boundaries assumed by the Vatican on teaching authority in the church. Ratzinger ordered a report by the Roman Curia that admonished Bernardin and his colleagues for "opinions based on the evaluation of technical or military factors."[4] The suggestion that public stands be approved by Rome pleased political conservatives. But the work on pastoral letters stemmed from the idea of collegiality at Vatican II. Speaking out as moral teachers, the bishops wanted a greater say in guiding the church. With Pio Laghi cultivated as the bishop's link to Rome, Doyle was like a bad cop, vetting doctrinaire "conservatives" (versus more flexible, pastorally minded moderates) for the hierarchy. Avoiding the internal politics of the bishops' conference, Doyle showed himself to be following Rome's orders.

For all of the bishops' activism and internal jockeying, the issue closest to their lives was never discussed in public: the revolution in the priesthood.

Since Vatican II, the birth control letter and the antique celibacy law had driven off thousands of potential priests. The number of seminarians went into a steep slide, alongside a flood of men *leaving* clerical life. Ireland lost 35 percent of her priests and nuns between 1970 and 1995; seminary enrollment sank nearly 80 percent. The United States experienced comparable losses.[5] With the median age of a U.S diocesan cleric at sixty, the graying priesthood and the decline in seminarians was a looming problem. Shadowing the attrition rate was the rise of a gay priest culture.

In the 1970s, as roughly one hundred Americans left the priesthood every month, most of them to marry, the proportion of homosexuals among men remaining in the ministry escalated. By the mid-eighties, the cultural dynamics of a gay world took hold in rectories, religious orders, and many seminaries. Historically, the priesthood has probably always had a greater proportion of homosexuals than the overall male population. Church laws show a long history of concern about same-sex activity.[6] Saint Peter Damian in 1051 sent a famous tract denouncing homosexual activity among clergy to Pope Leo IX, who thanked him and ignored it. Leo IX "was the first pontiff to take action against marriage of priests, which the Western church had only erratically opposed."[7]

Clerical celibacy had a rationale in the example of Jesus; but some of the apostles were married, and for generations, priests and bishops married. In the late eleventh century Pope Gregory VII waged a campaign to end clerical marriage. He was especially concerned that priests' children would create dynasties by inheriting church properties. "Driven from their homes," the wives of many priests suffered greatly, "their honor ruined, their families broken."[8] Yet an institution built on sexual segregation was bound to have its fault lines. Penalties for having sex with minors run through the history of canon law.[9] The seminary experiences of Thomas Doyle and Bernard Law—in which older men left after making sexual advances on students—typify pre–Vatican II seminaries that presumed heterosexuality as the norm. When seminaries were full, rectors weeded out men who seemed unable to maintain a chaste, dignified masculinity.

In the time before "gay" had its present meaning, any number of homosexuals became priests. If a man carried on inappropriately, chances are the bishop turned to therapists. "I was in on some horrendous cases and had titanic battles with bishops over matters of my confidentiality as a therapist," said Eugene Kennedy of his years as a priest. "The hierarchy wanted homosexuality handled with compassion, and not publicly. . . . They were put back into the clerical culture, fixed up with great margins of toleration. That culture is now in shards."[10]

In 1973, the American Psychiatric Association removed homosexuality from its list of mental disorders. Catholic vocation directors began accepting men who *seemed* gay (or admitted as much), premised on an acceptance of chastity. A realization that most people do not choose their sexual orientation coincided with the clergy's embrace of psychotherapy, once deemed anathema by the Vatican. With Reform Judaism and liberal Protestant churches pulling back from the shibboleth of homosexuals as a menace to society,[11] an American bishops' 1976 pastoral letter stated that to be a homosexual was not sinful; but same-sex activity was a sin. That position of enforced chastity clashed with the ideal of full social acceptance of gay people, especially as the priesthood became a sexual closet. A glaring sign of the double standard came in 2002, when Milwaukee's Archbishop Weakland resigned after admitting to a secret payoff of $450,000 several years earlier to quiet a man from his past.

To rise in ecclesiastical culture, would-be bishops could not say that the celibacy law left the church desperate to attract new priests. The Vatican's 1961 admonition against accepting men with "evil tendencies" became a fossil record to the flood of gay men rolling into seminaries in the 1970s. "I have scores of reports from priests about affectionate or sexual approaches or responses from teachers or elders during their training," writes A. W. Richard Sipe, a psychotherapist, former Benedictine priest, and authority on celibacy. "There is no other single element so destructive to sexual responsibility among clergy as the system of secrecy, which both shields behavior and reinforces denial."[12]

The impact of gay priest culture may be disproportionate to the actual number of homosexual priests. The most extensive survey of American priests using standard polling practices was conducted by the *Los Angeles Times* in 2002. Drawing on 1854 questionnaires, the study found that two-thirds of the respondents were heterosexual celibates, that approximately 20 percent were homosexual, of whom half were celibate. Some 28 percent of priests between the ages of forty-six and fifty-five were homosexual, a reflection of the influx of gay men in the 1970s and 1980s alongside the outflow of heterosexuals who eventually married.[13] Father Donald Cozzens, a Cleveland seminary rector in those years, has stated that the priesthood is "becoming a gay profession,"[14] a concern that many priests ordained before Vatican II share about the changing image and tone of clerical life. Polls, of course, are not infallible; yet if one accepts the *L.A. Times* data that 20 percent of priests are gay, that figure is nearly three times greater than the percentage in the overall male population.

Granted that all priests struggle with celibacy, there is a crucial difference between homosexuals for whom *priest* is a primary source of identity and those for whom *gay priest* is—an agenda superseding a vocation. As gays swelled the ranks of seminaries and clergy in the 1980s, Rome largely turned a blind eye, while bishops and order superiors blinked. At Rome's Pontifical North American College, "in the mid-1980s, students . . . could be found dancing—with each other."[15] In 1990–91 a

German sociologist interviewed sixty-four gay priests or seminarians in Rome after being propositioned by a cleric outside the Vatican.[16]

Some gays entered seminary unsure of their orientation, or expecting to be encouraged in chastity. Many others flocked to religious enclaves where a homoerotic agenda cut against older patterns of assimilation into priestly life. One former seminarian called St. Peter's College in County Wexford, Ireland, "an academy of debauchery." Another labeled it "so camp they used to be running around the place like girls out of a Brontë novel."[17]

As gay liberation spilled into seminaries, the old environment shed its prohibitions and some seminarians formed cliques, having sex or acting out, while denouncing homophobia in the church. Faculty priests began coming out of their own closets, angry at the church. Gay cliques clashed with the expectations of men for whom priesthood, not sexual orientation, was the reference point. Gay cliques occur "in a fourth of seminaries and maybe more," says sociologist Dean Hoge. Some seminaries were bastions of orthodoxy. In others, like St. Francis in San Diego, a young ex-marine named Mark Brooks was booted out in 1983 for protesting promiscuity and peer pressure from gays.[18]

The New Orleans archdiocese paid a $600,000 settlement to the family of a high school boy who on a Good Friday 1986 visit to its Notre Dame Seminary was plied with liquor and sexually assaulted by an adult seminarian.[19] The Mount Calvary, Wisconsin, seminary run by Capuchin monks was riddled with lawsuits because of a ring of predatory priests who molested teenage students in the 1970s and 1980s.[20] In Baltimore, six seminarians who went on to be priests were accused of molesting youths while they were doing parish internships during their years of study at St. Mary's Seminary.[21] The changes in seminary life were not the only cause of the abuse scandals that later came to light, for many other victims were girls.

Many priests who happen to be gay lead genuine lives of Christian witness. Nevertheless, a culture of political correctness took root as the agenda of gay apologists collided with orthodox teaching. Bishops and order provincials saw the changes taking place, but assumed that ecclesiastical culture would endure, with its prestige in society very much in place—that the "inner story" would not be revealed. The "gay Catholic" story of the 1980s focused more on clashes between bishops and activists over the church's opposition to use of condoms as the AIDS epidemic spread. The paradox of a priesthood swelling with gay men got sporadic coverage. By 1990, more than two hundred American priests had HIV, including one cleric in a Chicago treatment center who claimed to have infected *eight* other priests. Catholic seminaries began requiring men to pass an HIV test before they could be ordained.[22]

The barrier to an honest reckoning of this sea change was ecclesiastical tradition itself. As the bishops failed to produce a successor generation, John Paul II was emphatic about celibacy, "the brilliant jewel," ruling out any debate over a marriage option to attract heterosexuals. The pope placed hope in such fundamentalist movements as Opus Dei, which began in Spain; the Italian group Communione e Liberazione; and the Legionaries of Christ, from Mexico.

The evidence of things unsaid shadowed assumptions of power. As Tom Doyle was learning, the great sin in ecclesiastical culture was to violate its ethos of secrecy. Cardinals take an oath to the pope to safeguard the church from scandal—to *prevent bad information from becoming public.* No bishop or nuncio wanted to get near stories about gay priests or to suggest that the church would be better if priests might marry—or be female. Most hierarchs took the long view: A church nearly two thousand years old had survived many scandals. Some future pope could make celibacy optional with a stroke of the pen.

The Turning Point

In September of 1984, a grand jury in Lafayette, Louisiana, indicted a priest named Gilbert Gauthe on thirty-four counts of sexual abuse involving nine boys. One count—rape of a child under twelve—carried a life sentence. This was Cajun country, deeply Catholic. When an attorney in a civil case *sued Pope John Paul II,* Doyle telephoned the bishop's office; a priest assured him it had been a legal technicality. Civil suits with the boys' families had been settled in negotiation. A New Orleans church lawyer had mistakenly added the Holy Father's name to the list of defendants relieved of liability. One father refused the settlement and got a new lawyer. That lawyer, in requesting a trial, cynically named the pope a defendant.[23] John Paul's name was soon dropped.

What the hell is going on down there? Doyle wondered, just when a priest from Minnesota telephoned to say that a lawyer in St. Paul was suing the church because a Father Tom Adamson had taken indecent liberties with boys. Another one! Doyle wanted to book a trip to Louisiana and Minnesota and start grilling people. But after three years of watching Pio Laghi deal with bishops, sifting information like silk between the fingers, he understood restraint. The embassy had to help bishops.

He briefed Laghi on how families could sue a diocese and the companies that held its insurance liability policies. The Louisiana negotiations had been handled privately until several parents chose to publicly file suit. Bishop Gerard Frey of Lafayette could not halt that. Father Gauthe would probably go to prison.

Laghi, ashen-faced, asked Doyle to inquire further and report back.

What drives a man to seek sexual gratification with little boys? Doyle felt a shudder of sorrow for the thirty-nine-year-old Gauthe, a year younger than himself; he said a prayer for both priests. Then he called the Reverend Michael Peterson, the founder of St. Luke Institute, a hospital in nearby Suitland, Maryland, that treated alcoholic and burned-out priests. With light brown hair and fair features, Peterson stood just over six feet. He had a stunning intellect. The two had met when Peterson sought Doyle's canonical advice about bishops demanding medical information on men in his care. Stand on doctor-patient confidentiality, said Doyle. Peterson wanted bishops to see substance abuse not in moral terms, but as an issue of biochemistry and psychology. Some men had generations of alcoholism in their families. Peterson traveled with priests leaving St. Luke to meet with the bishop or superior, emphasizing that a stressful parish or environment with drinkers would hurt Father's chances for long-term recovery.

As CEO of St. Luke, Michael Peterson lived alone in a house near the hospital, set his own schedule, and was constantly on airplanes. Prodded by Doyle on the situations in Louisiana and Minnesota, Peterson confided that other bishops were dealing with such clerics, most of them drawn to teenagers. The psychiatrist had run into conflicts with Archbishop Hickey—under canon law, his superior—over films on human sexuality that St. Luke staffers showed to priest patients. Peterson told Hickey that priests in treatment were grossly ignorant of sexuality, a big reason why they acted out. With assurances that St. Luke upheld Catholic teaching, Hickey allowed the hospital to use the films in its program.

One of the therapists' hardest tasks was getting men who had had sex with teenage boys to see their own desperately immature acts (often springing from traumas sealed away since childhood) as an abuse of power. They had to acknowledge their true sexual orientation—and then be celibate. Each man had to write a sexual history. After studying the questionnaire, one priest blurted: "I can't be a homosexual—the church forbids it!"

Bishops wanted to put priests back into ministry; Peterson told Doyle he had trouble giving assurances that a given priest would not seek more victims.

At forty-one, Peterson was a year older than Doyle. A doctor's son raised a Mormon in California, he converted to Catholicism in the 1960s as a Stanford undergraduate. After medical school at the University of California at San Francisco, he did a residency at the university hospital, where one of his patients was a man who exposed himself. Peterson wondered who was hurt more: the patient, or the women who saw him flash? Peterson's mother was alcoholic, and though he never admitted it to Doyle, he had his own addictive personality. As he focused on neurology, the young doctor decided to become a priest—an ironic choice, in light of his views on human sexuality. But Peterson, like many priests of his generation, viewed the church as greater than the sum of its theological politics. In the mid-seventies he entered Mount St. Mary Seminary in Emmetsburg, Maryland. Ordained in 1978, he became director of Marsalin Institute, a small hospital for alcoholic priests in Massachusetts. Marsalin went under after Peterson fired several therapists who had confronted him over his drinking. Straightening up, he moved the operation to Suitland, Maryland, and resurrected it as St. Luke Institute. By 1984 the place was filling up with sex offenders.[24] Doyle knew nothing of this background when he sought Peterson's help.

"So tell me about pedophilia, Mike. Are they all queer?"

No, sighed Peterson, opening a window on a world Doyle had never imagined.

Behind the term "child sexual abuse" lay a range of behaviors. True pedophiles, fixated on children, were extremely difficult to treat. They used child pornography to excite fantasies for masturbation and showed pornography to kids in grooming them for sex. Some pedophiles could achieve orgasm ten times a day—a biochemical circuitry in sexual overdrive. From a program at the Sexual Disorders Clinic of Johns Hopkins Hospital in Baltimore, Peterson had begun utilizing Depo-Provera, a synthetic hormone injected once a day, to lower the sex drive of certain priests at St. Luke.

The trauma of early sexual violation was a common factor among patients, though not every pedophile started as a victim. Narcissistic, selfish, and immature, some men literally fell in love with kids. Few pedophiles were psychopathic and violent.

Another group of abusers were "situational" offenders, seeking young people and adults alike, often while under the influence of drugs or alcohol. There was also an emergent clinical term for those who had sex with teenagers, "ephebophiles," as opposed to pedophiles, who preyed on young, prepubescent children. Many ephebophiles were regressive homosexuals who had psychosexually stunted behavior.

St. Luke's used an instrument that fit around a man's penis and measured arousal to sexually suggestive images flashed on a screen.[25] The penile plethysmograph was a gauge of sexual pathology. After a tour of St. Luke, Doyle realized that the church had to do something with these messy people: they were priests.

Sexual addiction was a strange issue on which to strike up a friendship between priests; but Michael Peterson and Tom Doyle filled a void in each other's lives.

Thinking back on the changes he had undergone in helping people get marriages annulled, Doyle was moved by Peterson's empathy for fallen priests. Michael Peterson was an emergency politician, getting bishops to confront hard facts about priests who had violated kids. Walking St. Luke's halls, Peterson would embrace a washed-out hulk, calling him "Father" with a pat on the back. He *cared* for those pathetic men, and that impressed Doyle. In Doyle, Peterson found an ally in handling the church's sickest secrets, a priest who did not kowtow to bishops. Doyle had a blunt, lawyerly approach to reality: get the facts, find a solution. As Tom gradually revealed his misgivings about work in the embassy, Michael brooded about the myopia of bishops on sexual issues.

Doyle called Lafayette, suggesting to the vicar general, Monsignor Alex Larroque, that Gilbert Gauthe go to St. Luke. Larroque explained that Father had gone to House of Affirmation, a Catholic facility near

Worcester; but Father's attorney had recently transferred him to the Institute of Living in Hartford.

When Doyle reported this to Peterson, he was surprised to hear Michael scoff at House of Affirmation as substandard. He considered the Institute of Living very solid. Doyle was careful not to involve Laghi or the embassy in his fact finding about criminal matters. Laghi could blunt a subpoena with diplomatic immunity; but the news of any subpoena would not be good for the Holy See.

Doyle wondered about the quality of his intelligence from Louisiana.

His concerns were borne out with the hurricane arrival of F. Ray Mouton Jr., the lawyer defending Gauthe on criminal charges, who flew to Washington in a January freeze in 1985 to seek advice from Peterson. A star football player in high school, Mouton, thirty-seven, was married with three children. He had prospered as a plaintiff attorney in personal injury cases; he had also defended big-time drug dealers. The Gauthe case had jolted his faith. In a civil deposition the priest admitted to having sex with *thirty-seven* boys, four times the number of victims in the indictment. Gauthe had taken photographs of young boys in sex acts, fondled them in confession, had oral sex on fishing trips and in the rectory of a rural village where he lived alone for five years until 1983, when three young brothers finally told their daddy. The father and his lawyer went to the vicar general, Monsignor H. A. Larroque, who suspended Gauthe from priestly duties and sent him to House of Affirmation.

Church officials did not inform parishioners where the priest had gone or what he had done beyond "grievous misconduct . . . of an immoral nature." As Mouton put it, if the bishop had only leveled with people, gotten the boys in therapy, *acted like the church*, they could have avoided litigation. Instead, plaintiff lawyers arranged for therapy, and a year later the boys testified to the criminal grand jury. When Mouton met his client in the fall of 1984, Gauthe was painting pictures in art therapy at House of Affirmation, run by a priest named Thomas Kane. Affirmation was about to let Gauthe go work in Mississippi as an ambulance driver. Mouton transferred him to the Hartford hospital, which had no church affiliation and barred patients from leaving the grounds. There Gauthe waited while Ray Mouton mapped strategy for a trial that was months away.

Secrets of the House

Michael Peterson and Ray Mouton had valid forebodings about House of Affirmation. In 1987, the board fired the director, Father Thomas Kane, for stealing money to buy homes in Florida and Maine. Kane repaid some of the funds but was never prosecuted. In 1989, House of Affirmation closed. In 1993, a young man sued Kane, the Worcester diocese, and House of Affirmation, charging that Kane had begun molesting him in 1968, when he was nine, in a parish church and at House. He accused Kane of passing him around for sexual pleasure with other priests who had worked at House. The victim received a $42,000 settlement in 1995. Before Kane filed for bankruptcy in the early 1990s, he transferred owner-ship of a Florida property to another staffer and Monsignor Alan Placa of the Rockville Centre, Long Island, diocese.[26] Placa had a law degree and helped orchestrate the Rockville Centre diocese's response to children abused by priests. "As attorneys, we would not be obligated to report alle-gations, but as priests we would," he conceded later.[27] In 2002, Placa was suspended following sexual accusations from two former students at a seminary in Uniondale, New York.[28] Denying the charges, he got a job with longtime friend Rudy Giuliani, the former mayor. Kane found redemption in Guadalajara, Mexico, as director of something called the World Wide Teaching Institute. Reporter Kathleen Shaw found that the university where Kane claimed to have earned a doctorate had no record of his degree.[29]

An Alliance of Three

Michael Peterson brought Ray Mouton to the Dominican House of Stud-ies to meet Doyle. His book-packed office had just enough room for two extra chairs as the Cajun dynamo filled the room with cigarette smoke and spoke in rolling phrases about the personalities. Bishop Frey drank hard and was often secluded at his family's summer home. Larroque, him-self a recovering alcoholic, ran the diocese by default and was keeper of the secrets. Gauthe had drawn complaints from parents at previous parishes; each time he was moved along, leaving a trail of victims. The bishop had removed another child molester a year before Gauthe. Lane

Fontenot had gone through House of Affirmation. *Where is Fontenot?* the priests asked. Mouton had no idea. Doyle wondered how much church officials were hiding from the lawyer who was defending their priest.

Mouton was angling for an insanity defense to plea-bargain a sentence of less than life in prison. Peterson was skeptical. Pedophilia was not a form of insanity. Gauthe molested kids every chance he got.

New Orleans insurance attorneys had negotiated quietly over a year to avoid publicity, paying $4.2 million for nine cases. Mouton reckoned the church's share was 15 percent. The insurance lawyers had not grasped the implications of Gauthe's addictive behavior. More families were filing suit. Mouton bristled about lawyers from pedigreed firms who had failed to get the bishop's deposition sealed by the judge. Why invite a media feed?

Doyle liked the way Ray Mouton's mind worked. He used common sense like a hammer. He spoke compassionately about the families Gauthe had traumatized—farmers, trappers, oil workers—who would take years to recover. In south Louisiana, old folk still spoke French. Recalling his family's years in Quebec, Doyle felt an ache for those Cajuns. He interviewed Mouton for hours. Then, with eyes smarting from the cigarette smoke, he telephoned the embassy and told a colleague to call the papal nuncio off the handball court. "I need to talk to him right away."

Later, as he briefed Laghi, Doyle realized that he had learned more in two hours with a layman than he had from Lafayette's church officials. At Laghi's behest, the Louisiana churchmen and their attorneys flew to Washington for a meeting with Peterson and Doyle. Doyle stressed the importance of getting aberrant priests into a facility like St. Luke; he also advised them to accept liability in the civil cases, stop the legal discovery, reach a financial resolution. At that meeting he learned that two other priests had left their parishes after allegations of sexual activity with boys—one was tucked away in an Alabama monastery, the other soon went to St. Luke—a total of four child-molesting priests in one diocese.[30]

The Lafayette bishop and vicar general were threatened by Ray Mouton's insistence that the church stop stonewalling. Mouton's argument that Catholics could forgive if the church were honest made sense to Doyle, though it left him stewing about a mentality in the Vatican embassy. Laghi and the Italian staff detested the news media. Doyle initially took their attitude as a response to anticlericalism in the Italian press. But there was an elitism that bothered him, a condescending attitude toward the letters from laypeople. Some were from crackpots; others raised legitimate concerns. Doyle was bothered by a mind-set that viewed concerns from the rank and file as a nuisance.

When Doyle told Laghi that Bishop Frey should go, the nuncio winced—but he did not say no.

Doyle's concerns magnified when a Lafayette attorney, J. Minos Simon, filed a discovery request naming twenty-seven priests, seeking information on homosexual and pedophiliac activities. The clerical system had no safeguards, he argued. Lane Fontenot was on the list; so was another cleric, who had gone to St. Luke for abusing boys. So were several priests who worked in the chancery or diocesan tribunal. Though their names were not revealed in the media, their sexual encounters with men were known among other priests, bolstering the lawyer's theory that the diocese, in hiding homosexual conduct, extended the shroud to child molesters. Simon had gotten his information from a lay choirmaster who knew the diocese's dirtiest secrets. The man eventually ended up in jail for molesting youths himself. He died there of AIDS.

Priests and diocesan insiders were leaking information to Jason Berry for a series in Lafayette's weekly *Times of Acadiana*. (At the time Berry was unaware of Doyle's existence.) Through his dialogue with Ray Mouton, Doyle realized that if St. Luke had ten pedophiles, their dioceses faced steep legal fees on top of their share of payments to victims. "Church needs a plan, Tom," said Mouton, like a man with field glasses gazing at troops on a ridge.

A triangle of friendships was forming. Peterson usually called Mouton at night, asking about his family, then questions to help him in briefing a bishop or religious superior. Doyle and Mouton were speaking several times a day, the canonist learning how civil discovery subpoenas could obtain personnel files, internal memos, reports from psychiatrists, seminary records, all of which could portray a devastating pattern of concealing sexual crimes.

Doyle fastened on a strategy. He would persuade Laghi to have Rome send a new bishop to Lafayette. He would also begin work with Mouton and Peterson on a report for the hierarchy on the scope of the crisis. His plan was to have the three of them speak on a panel when the bishops gathered in June.

If a bishop blundered, Rome usually sent an investigator, a "visitator," to get answers and file a report. A visitation embarrassed the bishop only if it was made public. The visitator's report is always secret and allows him to prove his loyalty to Rome. The Dominicans have an expression: *Be nice to the guys on the way up because you're going to meet them on the way down.*

As visitator, Doyle wanted A. James Quinn, a fifty-two-year-old auxiliary bishop from Cleveland. Quinn had earned a canon law degree at Rome's Pontifical Lateran University. Back in Cleveland, he worked as chancellor. When Bishop Edward F. Hoban was dying, Quinn slept in a cot by his bed, feeding and cleaning the old man. Such loyalty did not go unnoticed. Nor his intellect: Quinn had graduated second in his class at Cleveland State's law school. A canonist with a degree in civil law, the wiry Quinn enjoyed downhill skiing. He worked with the mentally handicapped. Doyle liked something else: he had a airplane pilot's license.

Jimmy Quinn had shown his no-nonsense streak in 1969, when two priests led fifty Catholics protesting the Vietnam War into Cleveland's cathedral. The pastor cut the lights; the two priests said Mass by candlelight. Quinn called the police, who cordoned off the altar. As a priest was giving out communion, two clerics tried to stop him, and in the scuffle, consecrated communion wafers spilled on the floor. The police hauled off the protestors for trespassing.[31]

Doyle's report proposing Quinn as visitator went to Cardinal Krol of Philadelphia, who was leaving for Rome. Soon thereafter the Vatican sent approval to Laghi. Quinn flew to Washington for a one-on-one with Laghi and a briefing by Doyle and Michael Peterson. In March, the visitator went to Lafayette. Bishop Quinn spent a warm evening at dinner with Ray Mouton and his family amidst his conferences with the chancery high command.

The report to the hierarchy that Doyle envisioned was also taking shape. Mouton took a blunt approach. Child molesting was a crime, he wrote. "To allow a priest to continue to function, endangering the health of children following the receipt of private, confidential knowledge that this priest victimized a child, is considered to be 'criminal neglect' (a crime in many states.)"[32] He called for open dealings with the faithful and the news media, and compliance with mandated reporting laws, whereby professionals who deal with children must tell authorities of allegations. The insurance industry would move to exclude "coverage for claims arising as a result of sexual contact between a priest and parishioner." Church losses of "ONE BILLION DOLLARS . . . over ten years is a conservative cost projection."

Doyle feared that the Lafayette debacle could replicate itself in Minnesota. He wanted bishops to stop recycling perpetrators. If an allegation had any merit, the bishop should suspend the cleric and remove him from the parish—"a statement that the man is not capable of carrying out his sacred functions or ministry until an evaluation is completed," he wrote. "How will the child be able to perceive the clergy as authentic, unselfish ministers of the gospel and the church as the body of Christ?"

Peterson distilled the clinical language and appended articles from the professional literature. Mouton, the hard-stroke realist, added: "These are lifelong diseases for which there is now much hope for recovery and control for the disorders, but NO HOPE AT THIS POINT IN TIME for 'cure.' "

Doyle was concerned that bishops, so accustomed to secrecy in their dealings with Rome, might break U.S. laws. The report hit this head-on:

> *The idea of sanitizing or purging files of potentially damaging material has been brought up. This would be in contempt of court and obstruction of justice if the files had already been subpoenaed. . . . One other suggestion regarding files has been to move them to the apostolic nunciature where it is believed they would remain secure, in immune territory. In all likelihood, such action would insure that the immunity of the nunciature would be damaged or destroyed by the civil courts.*

As they worked on the report into the spring of 1985, Mouton wondered if with their expertise, they might work as a crisis-prevention team. Doyle liked the idea; even Peterson, ever skeptical about bishops, thought an intervention team could avert disasters and help train dioceses. To make the agenda at the June bishops' meeting, Doyle needed backers, as if moving a bill through Congress. Doyle sent the canonical section to Cardinal Krol. He flew to Pittsburgh and had an encouraging meeting with Bishop Anthony Bevilacqua. Then he turned to Bernie Law in Boston. At one of his first appearances as archbishop, a Monday night in the suburbs, the fifty-two-year-old Law found two thousand

parishioners in pews and three thousand more in the aisles and outside—for evening Mass. "There's a magnetism I certainly have not wit-
nessed before, almost of a Kennedy magnitude," one parishioner told
The Boston Globe.[33]

Law had taken a large crowd to Rome for his investiture as a cardinal. When he visited Washington that spring, Doyle gave him the draft:
"Here is our report." Law proposed a subcommittee to address the
issue; he chose a Los Angeles auxiliary bishop, William Levada, to
review the report and help position its authors for a presentation. Doyle
was pleased. The wheels were moving.

And from Rome came an important visitor, Cardinal Silvio Oddi,
the head of the Congregation for the Clergy, while Doyle was working
on the report. Laghi asked him to brief the curial official. Oddi, short
and rotund, was a balding man with a strain of volatility. Oddi stayed in
the cardinals' suite on the third floor of the embassy, a lavish apartment
with a parlor and large desk. A huge cardinal's ring gleamed on Oddi's
finger as Doyle began a somber recitation of children harmed, a priest
going to prison, other priests removed, the addictive nature of child
molesting—he touched on cases in various states. Oddi's face turned
red. He forked his index and middle fingers like a scissors and made a
clipping motion. "We should find out who those priests are and *cut
them off!*" he said, meaning their testicles.

"Your Eminence, it's against the law in America to castrate men."

"They're our priests," retorted Oddi. "We can do what we want!"

"It doesn't quite work that way, Your Eminence."

Enflamed by the idea of priests molesting children, Oddi stated that
the Vatican would hold a meeting of all the congregations and issue a
decree. The idea intrigued Doyle, though how it would be done, and by
whom, was a drama within the Curia he could only begin to imagine.
But Oddi's ire was a good sign.

Cardinal Oddi asked Doyle if, when homosexuals had sex, "the one
in the passive position receives the same satisfaction as the one in the
active position."

Doyle was flabbergasted. "Your Eminence, I truly have no idea."

In early May, Doyle flew to Chicago and met with Mouton, Peterson, and Bishops Quinn, from Ohio, and Levada, from California. Bill
Levada, an astute bishop on the fast track (he would become archbishop

of San Francisco), warned against too technical a legal discussion, saying: "It is better to pose questions." Guide the bishops through the issues with questions, answers. Quinn's encouragement gave the authors added incentive. Doyle and Mouton fine-tuned the document, and delivered fourteen copies to Quinn in Ohio. As Quinn read the pages, murmuring his approval, Tom Doyle felt a wave of relief.

In late May, he was in Montreal for the baptism of a niece when Levada called with the enigmatic news that Cardinal Law's committee would not be handling the pedophilia issue—but it would be discussed at the bishops' gathering. Doyle realized the fix was in.

When the bishops met for their June 1985 gathering at St. John's Abbey in Collegeville, Minnesota, the pedophilia cases were a topic of anticipation among the gathered religion reporters. They covered most of society's hot-button issues. On June 7, the *National Catholic Reporter* had published a package of articles on pedophile-priest cases, the longest dealing with Louisiana. Tom Fox, the editor of *NCR*, had written an editorial calling for diocesan review boards with laypeople to help bishops handle accusations. At Collegeville, Fox was dismayed to learn that the discussion, featuring the general counsel, a psychologist, and a Rhode Island auxiliary bishop, was closed to the press. Eugene Kennedy, who was writing a book on the bishops, was equally glum.[34] Kennedy had seen the most troubling issues—low morale, priests leaving, the gay dynamics—barely touch the hierarchy's radar screen. Fox brooded: "Do they have any idea what this does to people when a priest molests a child?"[35]

Laghi, on returning from Collegeville, expressed surprise that Doyle had not gone. But a disillusioned Doyle had not been invited. Ironically, his loyalty to Rome—avoiding bishops who wanted information on the selection of bishops—had undercut his influence. Monsignor Daniel Hoye, the general secretary of the bishop's conference, told Peterson he had problems working with Doyle. At the moment he needed it most, Tom Doyle lacked leverage.

An added factor was tension between Mouton and Wilfred Caron, the chief attorney for the bishop's conference. Caron resented the report as an encroachment on his turf. The Pittsburgh diocese ended up implementing many of the report's recommendations. The intervention-team concept did not go down well. Mark Chopko, who succeeded Caron as general counsel, later said: "There was a feeling that those guys wanted to set themselves up for work."[36]

"There's no way we could have put out all of those fires," said Mouton. "It was killed by the politics of inertia."

Doyle understood the politics, but priests molesting kids was not an issue like nuclear arms or choosing new bishops. The shame of it hit him like hot mud when he drove Jimmy Quinn to the airport after another meeting he had with Pio Laghi. Quinn complained that Ray Mouton was a loose cannon: Lafayette officials thought he was leaking to the press. Mouton was *right*, Doyle shot back. The problem was the stupid way the church handled Gauthe and other priests! As Quinn flew away Doyle realized that the Louisiana churchmen's complaints about their own priest's attorney had struck a fraternal chord with the Ohio visitor. Don't let a layman mess with the machinery.

Still, Laghi had decided Bishop Frey must go. The search for a replacement was on. Quinn had served that end. Doyle realized that there was a crisis in a system he was only beginning to fathom. *Whom do you trust?* Jimmy Quinn and Bernie Law had sandbagged him.

Unwilling to burn a bridge, Doyle went to Boston for a meeting with Cardinal Law about a proposed institute on Catholic teachings. Law invited him to become his canon lawyer. Doyle asked why his committee had failed to act on the pedophilia report. "It went to another committee," said Law. The bishops would be taking action, he said soothingly. Doyle realized Law lacked muscle in the bishops' internal scrimmaging; the cardinal was too allied with Rome's agenda of finding bishops attuned to papal obedience rather than collegiality. Law evinced no outrage on pedophilia. Instead he grew animated as he spoke of Boston's complexities, the challenge of fund-raising. Doyle left on a cordial note, saying he'd think about the job—an offer in which he had no interest at all.

Bishops kept asking Peterson for insight on treating problem priests. In December, Peterson wrote an eight-page cover statement for the ninety-two-page manual and had St. Luke send a copy to every bishop in America. Doyle turned to Cardinal Law to pay a former parishioner in Chicago who had typed the document, and to offset the costs for three hundred photocopies. Law sent $1,000. Doyle was grateful, even as he knew their dialogue was ebbing.

Law's detachment from the 1985 manual hurt him badly years later.

In 2001, Kristen Lombardi of the weekly *Boston Phoenix* began probing Law's handling of John Geoghan, a defrocked priest. Many of his sexual victims were represented by attorneys, including Roderick "Eric" MacLeish Jr. and Mitchell Garabedian, in civil suits.[37] With dozens of cases pending, internal church documents were shielded by a protective order. Soon along, *The Boston Globe*, led by reporter Walter V. Robinson and backed by the paper's tenacious editor, Martin Baron, petitioned the court to release the documents. To that point, the archdiocese's legal strategy of bargaining money for victims' silence fitted neatly into Law's idea of power: guard the secrets. But America had changed after previous reporting on pedophile priests and in the wake of the Clinton-Lewinsky scandal. Geoghan's long career as a pedophile had ended in 1996, *ten years* after Gauthe went to prison. Why did Law allow such a man to continue functioning? Judge Constance M. Sweeney granted the *Globe*'s request to unseal the documents. An appellate court denied the archdiocese's appeal. The *Globe,* in January 2002, began excavating a sexual history of the archdiocese.

Geoghan left more than 130 victims across a string of parishes, starting in 1962, when he molested four boys in the same family. Shuffled on to new rectories (with a sabbatical in Rome along the way), sheltered from responsibility for his crimes, Geoghan held a mirror to a system that Tom Doyle was barely beginning to grasp when he met Law. In September of 1984, a woman wrote Law, warning that Geoghan, "known in the past to molest boys," was dropping boys at their homes at night. Law answered two weeks later: "The matter of your concern is being investigated and appropriate pastoral decisions will be made both for the priest and God's people." The cardinal who sent Tom Doyle $1,000 moved Geoghan to a new parish, alerting the resident monsignor to his problem. On December 7, an auxiliary bishop wrote Law about Geoghan's "history of homosexual involvement with young boys." He added that "if something happens, the parishioners . . . will be convinced that the archdiocese has no concern for their welfare and simply sends them priests with problems."[38]

The lady who had first written Law, Margaret Gallant, had several nephews who were abused by Geoghan. She had written Law's predecessor, Cardinal Humberto Medeiros, in 1982: "Regardless of what he says, or the doctors who treated him, I do not believe he is cured. . . . It embarrasses me that the church is so negligent."[39] Geoghan preyed on poor families and broken homes, going to a youth club in a blue-collar suburb before Law had to remove him, in 1989, as more victims complained. A three-week evaluation at St. Luke Institute found him a high-risk "homosexual pedophile." Law should have begun proceedings to remove him from ministry; instead the archdiocese sent him to the Institute of Living. Auxiliary Bishop Robert J. Banks was displeased with the hospital's discharge summary, which called him "moderately improved." Banks sought stronger assurances from Hartford. "The probability that he would act out again is quite low," the pressed hospital noted. "However, we cannot guarantee that it could not reoccur." Law approved Geoghan's return.

In 1994, after more complaints, he was yanked again—and put on sick leave. In a letter to Geoghan at Christmas 1996, Law verbalized the mentality of countless bishops, which inured them to the horror of children violated by priests:

> *Yours has been an effective life in ministry, sadly impaired by illness. On behalf of those you have served well, and in my own name, I would like to thank you. I understand yours is a painful situation. The Passion we share can indeed seem unbearable and unrelenting. We are at our best selves when we respond in honesty and trust. God bless you, Jack.*

That last sentence might serve as epigram to Law's statements, under oath, in a civil deposition in June 2002. Attorney Eric MacLeish represented alleged victims of another priest, Paul Shanley, whose endorsements of the North American Man-Boy Love Association in 1977 ("children may later regret having caused someone to go to prison, knowing that they are the guilty ones") had provoked complaining letters to the chancery. The documents in his church file ran *sixteen hundred pages*. As Shanley sought retirement, Law wrote: "For thirty years in assigned ministry you brought God's word and His Love to His people and I know that that continues to be your goal despite some difficult limitations."

MacLeish grilled Law. The cardinal said he had not personally seen much of the material; his aides handled these matters; office record keeping was poor: "I think that our institutional memory was faulty." Asked about the Gauthe case, Law said: "I don't have a memory of that." He didn't remember the priest fired from the Josephinum his last year of seminary. Priests abusing kids: a blank slate. He remembered Father Doyle, though, and their "good relationship, and that's why I sought him out when I needed help"—except on aberrant priests.

On June 23, 1985, the papal ambassador had sent a note to Doyle about the document he had coauthored:

> I hope Card. Law will be willing and able to support the "strategy" proposed in this "paper." I shall exchange views with him on this subject.
>
> Laghi

When MacLeish asked about the report, the cardinal said: "I do not have a recollection of having studied it."

As Law searched his memory in June 2002, he had released to Massachusetts prosecutors the files of eighty priests whose back pages showed allegations of impropriety, including abuse of minors. Some priests were furious at him for hanging such a large number out to dry. The archdiocese was hemorrhaging money in settlements estimated to reach $100 million. Both daily papers had called for his resignation; Law's once-regal confidence was sapped of joy. He would limp another six months before resigning.

Perhaps the starkest sign of Law's governing mentality came on April 24, 1989, at the funeral of Father Joseph Birmingham in Boston. Tom Blanchette saw Cardinal Law sipping coffee alone. "There's a lot of young men in the diocese who will need counseling in the wake of their relationship with Father Birmingham," Blanchette told him. He confided how the priest had molested him, his four brothers, other young men. Law drew him aside and asked him to return to the church. "Bishop Banks is handling this, and I want you to make an appointment."

Placing his hand on Blanchette's head, the cardinal prayed in silence.

Then he said: "I bind you by the power of the confessional never to speak about this to anyone else."[40]

Chapter Three

EXILE AND RENEWAL

Pio Laghi said nothing about the pope's concern, nor did he volunteer any Vatican role in changing institutional behavior. His meaning was clear: American bishops must solve their problem. By early 1986, with reports on cases in Australia and Canada, Doyle realized that recycling child molesters was rooted in a governing mentality. No bishop wanted to push the issue at the conference level, though Doyle at the behest of several bishops had given closed briefings to priests. Laghi hinted that Doyle should turn his talents to other projects. But after four and a half years at the embassy, he was disillusioned.

"Sometimes I feel ashamed to be a priest," he told Michael Peterson.

"You're doing God's work," Peterson said encouragingly.

That was Michael, always upbeat, squarely with him on a crisis that undercut Doyle's trust in men he had been taught to trust. For Peterson, the psychiatrist, walls of denial came with the territory.

On October 14, 1985, Ray Mouton negotiated a plea bargain in which Gilbert Gauthe agreed to a twenty-year term, eliminating a trial that church officials from Louisiana to Rome wanted to avoid. Doyle never met Gauthe, yet he felt great pity for him. He felt a greater sorrow for the boys whose lives he had plundered, more than one hundred of them, an evil perpetrated on many families.

At the embassy he briefed Cardinal William Baum, the former archbishop of Washington, D.C., who was the prefect of the Congregation for Catholic Education, in Rome. He was grim-faced after Doyle's presentation on the scandal. He, too, said it was terrible—the issue *must* be pursued. He, too, did little else.

On January 31, 1986, the *Times of Acadiana* reported that the Lafayette diocese had played musical chairs with seven child molesters over many years. An editorial demanded that Bishop Frey and Monsignor Larroque resign—or that Laghi remove them. But Rome would not humiliate a bishop. The tradition was to send a coadjutor bishop to serve as heir apparent, easing out, rather than demoting, a beleaguered prelate. Doyle put Monsignor Harry J. Flynn, a former seminary rector in Maryland and pastor from the diocese of Albany, New York, at the top of the candidate list.

Michael Peterson went to Rome in March, hoping to persuade Curial officials of the need for binding norms on removing child molesters. Peterson, who had been bedridden several weeks after back surgery, met with Cardinal Oddi at the Congregation for the Clergy. On return, he looked beat. "They don't get it," he grumbled. Doyle was curious about Oddi, who had reacted so dramatically after his briefing at the embassy. "They're going to issue a statement on homosexuality," said Peterson.

Doyle could not imagine Rome releasing a document on such an explosive internal matter unless Oddi had confused the distinction between pedophiles and homosexuals. Peterson said the work was being done not by Oddi's staff, but at the Congregation for the Doctrine of the Faith. Doyle understood his glumness. Cardinal Ratzinger would address theology, not sexual offenses by priests. Ratzinger's October 1, 1986, global letter to bishops, "Pastoral Care for Homosexual Persons," pronounced homosexual activity an "intrinsic moral evil" and denounced gays pressing for acceptance by the church.[1]

Peterson, gaunt and coughing, had flown too soon after surgery, putting work ahead of himself. As always, Michael asked Tom Doyle how *he* was doing.

Doyle was not doing well. At the embassy his Italian colleagues kept an emotional distance, telegraphing that he was crazy for taking on such an issue. When a colleague asked when he would have his office cleared, Doyle realized he had gotten his walking papers. No one said, *You're fired.* Laghi proposed a dinner in his honor, a formal *grazie* for nearly five years' service to the Holy See. Doyle had broken an unwritten rule of getting too close to a scandal. His idea of justice, so American, had clashed with a detached Italian style. There had been no inflammatory event, rather a problem for Doyle, that divided him from them.

The hypocrisy riled him. *"I don't want that bullshit!"* he fumed to Peterson.

"Do the dinner, Tom. Leave on good terms."

Michael was right: don't burn your bridges. Doyle provided a short list of names, including that of Father Peterson, as guests at the embassy.

He had been teaching canon law as an adjunct faculty member at Catholic U. He applied for a full-time position, but he could not put on a calm academic front in the interviews. The anger had given him an edge, and it showed. No job.

He could easily have found a pastor's job, or gone back to work within the Dominicans. But his sense of closeness to God had collided with the system. Bitter at the collapse of his career trajectory, he did not want to be under just any bishop's control. Sometimes he awoke at three in the morning, the anger so hard he could not roll back to sleep. He remembered people he had counseled, leaving a bad marriage, afraid of the unknown.

It had been fifteen years since his ordination. He loved the giving of Christ's Word in ministry, the joy of sharing the sacraments. He did not want the structure with all its byzantine conflicts and egos to wreck his vocation. There were many victims, too great a pent-up rage. Unable to persuade the hierarchy that a torrent of violations would unleash volcanic winds, he repeated words that became a prayer: *This is evil. I am going to help those who have been harmed by this evil because that's what a priest should do. This is what I believe you want. Lord, help me do it right.*

Fascinated by technology and computers, he enjoyed mastering the control panel of airplanes. The thrill of reaching high blue fields folded into a calm, settling beauty. One afternoon, following a column of whales beyond Cape Cod, he felt an almost mystical serenity. Archbishop Joseph Ryan of the Military Ordinariate in Silver Springs had asked him to assist with their tribunal. Doyle was working part-time as a tribunal judge in Scranton, flying back and forth in a rented plane. The certitude of military life reminded him of the priesthood when he had entered: obedience to just authority, individuality, and community balanced by a common good. The ordinariate was a separate archdiocese within the U.S. church. Once a priest received his posting as a chaplain, he answered to the military command. Doyle wanted a base, independent and secure, so as not to back down on his life-dividing issue.

At forty-two, he enlisted in the United States Air Force.

Requiem Days

On Good Friday 1986, St. Luke staffers rushed Michael Peterson to the George Washington University Hospital. Doyle found him in bed, sweating, shivering, and coughing. "I'm dying," he croaked. His lymphatic system had broken down. Doyle sat with Peterson and thought about the unfairness of life: that a priest, a doctor as gifted as Michael, forty-three, should go into meltdown. Fighting back tears, he realized how much of his life had changed in the two years they had been friends; his life had been altered too with Ray Mouton and the intense exchanges about pathologies of sex and power tearing at the church.

Michael Peterson, a complicated mirror of the church's contradictions, returned to his house near St. Luke, trying to work between stretches of bed rest. He had AIDS, about which a few friends and the staff were sworn to secrecy. He did not tell Doyle. Beyond the inner circle no one knew he had orchestrated the purchase of houses near St. Luke to put child molesters as the hospital ran short of bed space. Peterson thought such priests were too frightened to seek kids if they lived in a group house. It was a gross violation of the zoning permit. Neighbors thought the men were recovering alcoholics.[2]

Like Doyle, Ray Mouton was unaware of St. Luke's inner workings, though he suspected Peterson was gay. Ray had held on to his faith because of Michael. Doyle never pressed Michael on his illness, though he had his suspicions. What counted was Michael's commitment in helping priests and making bishops face the crisis. Perhaps his relentless pace had been a form of contrition, atoning for a hidden life by ministering to outcasts.

On April 28, 1986, Doyle and Mouton met in Morristown, New Jersey, to address the Eastern regional meeting of the Canon Law Society of America. Mouton asked if he had known reporters would be present. Don't worry, said Doyle; speak your piece.

"The Roman Catholic Church," declared Mouton, "cannot credibly exert moral authority externally in any area where the public perceives it as incapable of maintaining moral authority internally."[3] Prosecutors would be getting tougher—so would cops. "If we don't act now, the consequences will be catastrophic. If kids are left untreated, you have a time bomb walking in your community."[4]

More than forty priests had been reported to the embassy for abusing children. Based on the frequency of calls he was fielding, Doyle figured the numbers would triple within a year. He called pedophilia "the most serious problem that we in the church have faced in centuries." Standing before his stone-faced colleagues, Doyle urged them to level with parishioners, a cut against the conditioning of silence "for the good of the church." He stressed the need to get therapeutic help for families. "You don't send some imperious cleric out there to show them how bad they should feel about dragging the church's name through the mud."

The most serious problem that we in the church have faced in centuries—his words in *The New York Times* shot through the hierarchy. Cardinal Bernardin wrote from Chicago, chastising him for speaking publicly on the topic.

In June, Doyle organized a closed conference at the Dominican priory in River Forest, Illinois, where he had spent some of his happiest years as a young priest. Mouton joined him. Doyle wanted the selected bishops, religious superiors, Cardinal Bernardin, and his staff to see all that was at stake. But neither Bernardin's staff nor the cardinal showed up. (Unbeknownst to Doyle, Bernardin had asked psychologist Eugene Kennedy for advice. Kennedy recommended that a consultant assess the professional literature in the field as a first step in developing a policy—an idea rebuffed by the bishops' conference.)[5]

Doyle took the empty chairs of Chicago archdiocesan officials as Bernardin's backhand for his airing church laundry in the Morristown speech.

Chicago's archdiocesan lawyer did attend: James A. Serritella, a huge, shambling man who had helped stonewall the federal investigation of Cardinal Cody. Where Ray Mouton had admonished the audience to be pastoral, Serritella brayed: "What you people have to remember is that when one of these situations develops, those people"—the families—"are the enemy, and I'm on your side!"[6] Doyle was appalled. He hoped the chest beating would not influence the priests and scattered bishops in the room.

He was still living at Dominican House, working at the office of the Military Ordinariate, when priests from Allentown, Pennsylvania, asked him for help. Bishop Thomas Welsh was petitioning Rome to oust a priest accused of abuse who claimed he was innocent. After reviewing the facts, Doyle saw an issue of due process and helped with a canonical appeal. Welsh—whom Doyle considered "a sanctimonious, uncharitable man who never should have been a bishop"—complained to Laghi about Doyle's meddling. Laghi summoned Doyle.

"*Get out of this!*" snapped the Vatican ambassador.

"The priests have rights, Archbishop."

But the Allentown bishop had made his decision! Laghi, shouting at Doyle, told him he had gone too far. *Stop all this!*

"I don't work here anymore, Archbishop. You can't yell at me."

Laghi spoke paternally: "You're hurting your career, Thomas."

Doyle thanked Laghi for his concern, begging off an invitation to lunch.

Doyle had gotten through basic training with much younger guys. Standing in line to pee in a cup was a far cry from embassy receptions. He took mild pride in a stomach fairly flat. Now on an officer candidate's track, he waited for his base assignment while making visits to comfort Michael Peterson.

By April of 1987 Peterson was a shell. Doyle felt packed with sorrow. Michael had told him he had contracted AIDS through a cut while examining contaminated blood. As his life ebbed he told Ray Mouton he was gay, intimating that he had a sexual past. Doyle didn't care how Michael had gotten AIDS; he assured him that the great good of his life and ministry counted more than how he died.

"You've got to carry on," Peterson said hoarsely.

Why am I a priest? rattled Doyle's thoughts. *Why stay?* He gave Michael a rosary made in Ireland that his father had given him. Placing the beads in those shaking palms, he felt he was losing the brother he never had.

Archbishop Hickey visited Peterson with letters for him to sign, revealing his cause of illness, to circulate among bishops and priests, with public release upon his death. Hickey wanted to preempt media reports of a priest dead of AIDS. "It was like being put in a sack, beaten with a stick, and told to sign, sign, sign," Peterson groused. Doyle resented the spin control in a power structure myopic to its own hypocrisy. So much of what he believed was in a free fall.

Peterson expired on April 9, 1987, with a former nun holding his arm.

On April 13, six bishops and 144 white-robed priests filed into St. Matthew's Cathedral in Washington for the funeral. Doyle sat among them, weeping. Media coverage was sympathetic to Peterson and favorable to Hickey for his sensitivity and candor. The night before Peterson died, St. Luke's acting CEO, Steve Johnson, fired an accountant who had questioned Johnson's lavish travel expenses. Several key staffers quit or were fired by Johnson for threatening his grasp on the operation: one had questioned the policy of putting child molesters in neighboring houses. Johnson soon left in a shake-up. A year later three board members resigned, one of them complaining in a letter to the chair of "the moral tone of the Institute and its therapeutic programs . . . as an outlet for the psycho-pathology of its founder."

But bishops needed the hospital. By 1988, 135 U.S. priests had been reported to the embassy for molesting minors. A new administration eventually stabilized the place. The most troubling dimension of St. Luke was the risk assessment on patients. Bishops wanted priests back in ministry if possible. Most patients did not face criminal prosecution; their bishops or superiors never reported them to police. The hospital recommended against returning some men to ministry; St. Luke took pride in a low rate of recidivism among patients. Without an independent investigation, a full appreciation of St. Luke's role in the sexual crisis cannot be made. Most priests were diagnosed as ephebophiles. Regressive homosexuality—a narcissistic fixation on teenagers—was one strand in the complexities of a gay priest culture the bishops quietly skirted. Doyle's sensitivity toward gays had grown through his friendship with Peterson, though the culture itself often seemed to him a moral wilderness.

Soldiering On

As his ambition waned, Tom Doyle confronted a volatile line of sexual victims, a few at a time, who entered his life with harrowing stories, often told in sobs on the telephone several nights a week. He became an ironic confessor, apologizing for sins of the church. Doyle tried to imagine their faces, these voices of shattered faith, their anger changing him in ways he had only begun to fathom.

One of the early callers, in 1987, was Mark Brooks, thirty-three, who had been in a slump since his expulsion from St. Francis Seminary in San Diego. He had grown up poor in Baltimore; his father, an alcoholic, drifted away from the family. Priests were the stabilizing influences of his boyhood. His mother later moved her son and three daughters to California. Out of high school Brooks served four years in the Marines. In 1980, after working with autistic children, he entered San Diego's seminary. In another time he probably would have made a good priest; however, the seminary was in the thrall of Vincent Dwyer, a Trappist monk who had permission to travel and lecture on moral growth. Popular for his motivational lectures with priests, Dwyer spoke at many retreats.

In 1969, Dwyer had lectured in Monterey, California, at Santa Catalina, a girls' school, where he began seducing fifteen-year-old Sarah Wilgress, whose father had committed suicide when she was an infant. Entranced by his love letters (seventeen on her seventeenth birthday alone!), Wilgress was drawn into an on-and-off-relationship that haunted her long after she broke it off at twenty-eight.[7] "I really have gone through hell because of Dwyer," she reflected. "I loved being at Santa Catalina. The perfectly tended gardens, the nuns, some of them busy throwing off their veils and shortening their habits per Vatican II, gliding about, forever trying to inculcate discipline. . . . I loved the fact that it was okay to study. One was not made fun of for being serious. Dwyer's ravaging me the summer before my senior year left me completely confused. . . . And so I stayed quiet, and ran away twice my senior year, thereby sabotaging my plans for college. I stayed quiet for twenty years."[8]

In 1981, Dwyer encouraged the St. Francis seminarians to "embrace intimacy." Mark Brooks wondered if the seminarian at Dwyer's side was a lover. Dwyer was a catalyst in the hothouse environment; Brooks recoiled as teachers made advances on students, seminarians grabbed one another's buttocks standing in line for communion, and a seminarian in his thirties had a sixteen-year-old kid (not a seminarian) sharing his room.[9] As men made sexual approaches, Brooks protested to faculty members, who ignored him. The attacks on orthodoxy and the church as homophobic depressed him. He got tired of hearing gay students call themselves "wounded." He began drinking. A seminary official ordered him to enter a detox program. Brooks checked into a veterans hospital; the diagnosis was posttraumatic stress. On return to the seminary, in 1983, he was expelled.

He found a lawyer who negotiated a $15,000 settlement, basically to make him go away.[10] On February 5, 1986, he sent a fifty-six-page narrative account of his experiences, naming names, to Pope John Paul II. On January 13, 1987, he received acknowledgment from the Vatican Secretariat of State in a brief letter from Monsignor Giovanni Re, later to become a cardinal and head of the Congregation for Bishops.

Brooks was having nightmares of "being in the middle of inquisitions surrounded by priests and bishops . . . they would be in the nude and shouting accusations of all kinds at me."[11] He telephoned Doyle, fuming that liberals were wrecking the Catholic Church. "Both sides are equally to blame," Doyle replied. "It comes down to leadership and so many of them have dirty hands."[12]

Brooks was angry that the traditional order had broken down. He didn't care who was homosexual as long as they behaved responsibly. Why was the seminary overrun with promiscuous men? Doyle told him that San Diego had a history of being a clerical dumping ground. Bishop Leo Maher was known for taking in the walking wounded from other dioceses. The seminary's faculty reflected the diocese. Look to your own faith, your own values, Doyle counseled.

The *National Catholic Reporter* had given extensive coverage to the early cases, and lost several hundred subscribers after a 1985 editorial calling for independent review boards to monitor accusations: "Priests who are repeated sexual offenders must be separated from the rest of society, as any offenders should be . . . [and] prosecuted under civil law just as others should be."[13]

One spring day in 1987, a *San Jose Mercury News* reporter named Carl M. Cannon, who worked in the Washington, D.C., bureau, made a trip back to California and met with his editors. Cannon was intrigued by what he had read on a pattern of bishops covering up for child molesters. "Pattern?" said his editor, Bob Ryan. How many examples of "pattern" could Cannon prove? At least six, he said. The *Mercury News* is part of the Knight Ridder chain; an investigation carried the expectation of a series for the chain. Ryan gave him the green light.[14]

By autumn Cannon had found thirty-five priests in more than twenty-four dioceses who had been reassigned by bishops. He located Father Doyle at the Dominican House of Studies; they met for dinner at a restaurant in Georgetown. Accustomed to politicians' inflated egos, Cannon sized up a priest who had worked in the Vatican embassy and was struck by Doyle's lack of guile. The square-jawed cleric, courteous but blunt, had a what-you-see-is-what-you-get personality. Cannon, a Protestant, was amazed at how easily Catholic officials lied to parents about men who sexually assaulted their kids. Doyle asked about Cannon's background, the kinds of stories he had covered. As the talk shifted to Doyle, the reporter realized, *This guy loves the Catholic Church*. He was a classic whistle-blower: an insider unable to keep silent about corruption close by. Doyle gave him a copy of the 1985 report to the hierarchy.[15]

Cannon was struck by the authors' foresight—and how fantastically dumb the bishops had been to ignore their advice. His series ran in late December 1987 in *The Philadelphia Inquirer*, *The Miami Herald*, and the *Detroit Free Press*, among other papers. "Reluctance to address the problem is a time bomb waiting to detonate within American Catholicism," wrote Cannon with foresight of his own.[16]

Irritated by the coverage, Bishop A. James Quinn wrote to Archbishop Laghi in early 1988. His own bishop in Cleveland, Anthony Pilla, had been exposed by *The Plain Dealer* for protecting pedophiles; but Jimmy Quinn knew better. "Diocesan Bishops are doing all they can to correct procedures," he assured Laghi. Doyle and Mouton "made it appear that nothing positive is being accomplished. The truth is Doyle and Mouton want the Church in the United States to purchase their . . . expensive and incontrovertible leadership. . . . The Church has weathered worse attacks, thanks to the strength and guidance of the Holy Spirit. So, too, will the pedophilia annoyance eventually abate."

Laghi sent Quinn's letter to Doyle, with a cover letter in the language of diplomacy ("While I do not subscribe to the conclusions drawn in this correspondence") that gently said, Watch your backside, boy.

Doyle wrote Laghi, explaining that he did not seek out journalists, but spoke with those who called him. He sent Cannon's articles, and more from *The Plain Dealer*. The "negative image of the church" lay in "the manner in which certain cases have been handled." He dismissed the expertise-peddling charge: "This same line has emanated forth from the USCC general counsel office and was told to several business leaders in Cleveland who in turn put pressure on the publisher of the Cleveland *Plain Dealer* in order to prevent further coverage. . . . I do not share Bishop Quinn's opinion that this is a passing annoyance."

He wrote Quinn, disputing any desire for personal gain; media coverage was inevitable. "I am both saddened and surprised at your characterization of what we have done." In fact, he was angry at Quinn for his betrayal.

On February 9, 1988, Mark Chopko, the general counsel of the U.S. Catholic Conference, issued a statement affirming the bishops' "strong efforts to prevent child abuse, to repairing whatever damage has been done . . . [by] the healing ministry of the church."[17] Chopko routinely told journalists that bishops could not adopt a binding policy because each diocese was autonomous; each bishop answered directly to the pope. (The pastoral letters on nuclear war and the economy were teachings, not internal policy.)

On January 9, 1988—the day after Quinn assured Laghi of the Holy Spirit's guidance—an aide to Cardinal Roger M. Mahony of Los Angeles drove out to a Latino parish and confronted the Reverend Nicolas Aguilar Rivera. Parents of three different boys had accused him of molesting them. Mahony's aide told the priest he could no longer serve in the archdiocese, and offered to find him temporary living quarters. Aguilar, who had been in Los Angeles nine months, declined the offer. Two days later, he fled to his native Mexico. On April 15, Aguilar was charged with nineteen felony counts of sexually abusing ten minors. Charges were filed in Mexico. Aguilar simply disappeared.[18]

In early 1989, Philadelphia's new cardinal archbishop, Anthony Bevilacqua, asked Doyle for a background paper on laicization issues for the bishops' conference. Doyle obliged with a three-thousand-word brief. "The Holy See has made it clear that the Holy Father will not laicize a priest against his will," he wrote.[19] "For all practical purposes, the reduction of a cleric to the lay state, as a penalty, cannot be done in cases of sexual molestation."

Ecclesiastical trials faced a Catch-22 in canon law: a priest with a psychological disorder could argue that his freedom to act, his moral responsibility, was impaired. "Since most if not all clerics who become involved sexually with minors do so because of a psychological disorder, it is difficult to see how a penal trial could even be initiated." Doyle advocated an accelerated administrative process for bishops to laicize sex offenders who were "unfit for ministry," refused treatment, or would not acknowledge the harm they had done.

Rome Weighs In

In late 1989, representatives of the N.C.C.B. began discussions with the Roman Curia over a swifter means of laicizing pedophiles in accordance with canon law. Following Doyle's lead, the bishops wanted their own administrative process, without a long wait for the pope to intervene.[20] That request generated heated discussion at several Vatican congregations, whose prefects function in a rough analogy to cabinet heads of a government. The Congregations for the Clergy, for Bishops, and for the Doctrine for the Faith, as well as the Council for the Interpretation of Legislative Texts, weighed in.

"The shared sense was that what they were proposing was not the way to go," said Father X, a canon lawyer in Rome who participated in the meetings and spoke with Berry predicated on anonymity.[21] He sat in an unadorned conference room of an old building. "They were looking for special norms without submitting legislation," he continued. "The Holy See was saying, 'We have long-standing norms. *Apply these norms!*' The U.S. bishops were giving the impression that they did not have the appropriate means for dealing with these cases."

The pope at any point can halt or terminate a canonical proceeding. The norms, or rules, involved penal trials to determine whether men could be stripped of their priesthood. In these tribunals the defendant does not face his accusers before a jury. The code specifies secrecy to protect the defendant's reputation. Canonists give statements on behalf of victims to the judge or judges, typically a bishop or several canonists. Another canon lawyer, for the priest, presents a defense. There are no pitched cross-examinations with a verdict that turns on discrediting a witness. One trait the proceedings do share with civil cases is that they

How tRiαls caRRied out

can drag on for years. Many bishops saw penal trials as archaic. "The perpetrator of a violation is not exempted from penalty," states canon 1324, but "a penance [may be] substituted in its place, if the offense was committed by . . . one who had only imperfect use of reason."[22]

What did Father X think of the 1985 report by Doyle and his colleagues?

"That was a document for the American bishops," he said curtly, implying that it was not universally applicable.

Father X pointed to the 1960s as the origin of the crisis, "a time of disillusion over authority. Throughout Vatican II, there was a concern over what will change to make the code more serviceable. Many bishops embraced change." He folded his arms, like an impatient teacher. "They looked at canon law as less applicable. A social attitude that was antinomian—against the law. The attitude crystallizes in the American hierarchy's reaction to *Humanae Vitae*," the 1968 papal letter condemning artificial contraceptives.

Here was a glimpse through the Vatican lens: bishops unwilling to preach against birth control devices had betrayed canon law. From artificial contraception to pedophile priests—all of a piece, the dark legacy of dissent.

Father X was well aware of American concerns in 1989 about large monetary losses to the church. He paraphrased the bishops: "The norms are not adequate—delays are causing greater damage: we need these exceptions because we don't have qualified personnel to apply the penal procedures in the code." Father X's eyebrows rose in twin arches—as if the United States of America did not have adequately trained canon lawyers! "The Holy See's reaction to the financial damage was to consider that." He paused. "There was more concern about the scandal undermining the work of the church. In how many cases did they apply the penal procedures? Well, none."

He leaned forward, eyes intense. "The United States has the largest tribunal system in the world. To say that people were not qualified begs the issue. The U.S. tribunals violated *grandly*—terribly—the annulments of marriage."

"What do marriage annulments have to do with pedophiles?" wondered Jason Berry.

"There was a very good reason *not* to grant special norms on pedophiles," declared Father X. In the 1970s, with divorce rates escalating, the Vatican had allowed certain exceptions to the code in the U.S. to facilitate annulments. "The hope was that those norms would be incorporated in the code. Instead, just the opposite happened . . . *laxity* on annulments!" he said with exasperation.

"You need two concurring decisions on tribunals that agree in concluding an annulment case. In America the conference of bishops had a *machine* signing off on [marriage] dispensations. This was highly criticized in Rome by various respondents in these cases, canon lawyers, a wide range of people within the church." An ex-spouse can protest a tribunal's annulment decision to the Rota, an appellate court at the Vatican. The system is designed to ensure that a marriage is not dissolved for petty reasons. Father X continued: "That experience of dealing with American bishops set up a resistance to special norms for pedophiles. *We see what you've done with special norms on annulments. What are you going to do with these pedophilia cases?"*

He spoke as if lecturing the bishops: "The attitude here in 1989, at the Holy See, was that you have legal provisions. *Use them!"*

Across the Atlantic lay a vastly different reality.

In diocese after diocese, bishops confronting *numbers* of priests and expensive battles in civil cases, and trying to keep priests out of prison, were loath to launch secret canonical proceedings. Penal trials consumed time with dilatory moves that could prevent a bishop from making a swift request to the pope. Moreover, a secret trial was *not* secret: everything was subject to discovery subpoena by a prosecutor or plaintiff lawyer. What if a priest's canonist prevailed, thwarting a bishop's effort to laicize the man? The bishop was stuck with a sex offender. He could suspend the priest. Then what? Some canonists saw penal trials as limiting what a bishop could do. A savant of the code, Bishop A. James Quinn of Ohio, said in a 1995 civil deposition: "If it's true that pedophilia is a disability, then that would preclude a penalty such as reduction to the lay state. So bishops have been faced with the problem. . . . "[23]

The Vatican's refusal to accelerate an expulsion process for sexual criminals was another sign of the gulf separating Pope John Paul II and bishops in North America, Ireland, and Australia as the scandals arose. Papers from men voluntarily seeking release from their vows, typically

[handwritten in left margin: Clash w canon law]

to marry, often waited years for the pope's signature. Peter Hebble-thwaite, a respected Vatican correspondent, assessing the 1980 Norms for Laicization, wrote that the pope viewed such requests as "a disgrace and a confession of failure. The procedure has been made as difficult as possible. . . . John Paul's model priest is male, celibate, committed for life, dressed in clerical black, docile, prayerful, if need be heroic, holy and apolitical."[24]

John Paul's idea of priestly service was forged in the titanic struggle between Poland and Soviet-bloc communism; priests, like chivalrous knights, put their lives on the line and would be forgiven sins. That vision held no room for a sociopath like Gauthe, or for Shanley of Boston, who by the early 1990s was running a sex resort on the West Coast, semiretired with pension, still a priest, thanks to Cardinal Law's beneficence. A penal trial of Shanley might have made sense.

A New Arena

As Doyle's contact with victims and journalists increased, plaintiff attorneys began calling him. For a canon lawyer to assist an attorney *suing the Catholic Church* was a radical shift; the canons are premised on the pope as final authority. Ignored by the Vatican cardinals, dismissed by Laghi, and attacked by Quinn, Doyle was rewriting the assumptions of his priesthood. He had no doubt that Jesus would be with the survivors of child sexual abuse. As a pragmatist he believed in repairing a broken system. Christ said, "Render unto Caesar that which is Caesar's." If Caesar held the means to root out corruption in the church, Doyle had no doubt that Jesus would support him in gravitating to Caesar's side.

Jeffrey R. Anderson of St. Paul was in litigation against three Minnesota dioceses for the victims of Tom Adamson. It was the most time-consuming case Anderson had ever taken. Anderson absorbed the investigation costs; if the cases were settled or won a jury verdict, he took a third of what the church and its insurance companies would pay, plus his expenses. If he lost, he lost big. Jeff Anderson had a flamboyant, in-your-face quality. A member of the American Civil Liberties Union, he was politically Doyle's opposite.

In spring 1988, Doyle had moved fifty-five hundred pounds of books into his new home at Grissom Air Force Base in Peru, Indiana. His computer was set up. He was getting to know his parishioners, and at night talking on the phone to victims. He did not hang up when Jeff Anderson called. "There's a priest up here in Minnesota named Tom Adamson. They knew he was a child molester, and moved him around, and they've lied about it to me."[25]

"I've got news for you," said Doyle. "That's not unusual." He discussed the Gauthe cases in Louisiana, of which Anderson had only the sketchiest appreciation. The parallels were striking. This guy Doyle had been on the inside!

"Would you testify to these things?" asked Anderson.

"Yeah, I'd testify."

A few days later Jeff Anderson opened an envelope from the chaplain in Indiana and found the ninety-two-page Doyle-Peterson-Mouton manual. Anderson read it, greedily, struck by the wide learning in a complex field, *and all of it from the inside.* The attorney had been gathering documents through legal discovery of the Minnesota dioceses that had shuffled the priest from parish to parish, leaving a trail of sexually assaulted boys. A trial with publicity was the last thing his legal adversaries wanted. Anderson realized how much was at stake. Doyle's document suggested a national scope to a human disaster he had begun to grasp in Minnesota. Most of Adamson's sexual outlets were guys whose lives became scarred by drugs, wild sex, busted relationships, collisions with cops—the walking wounded.

Listing Father Doyle as a witness gave Anderson major leverage. The defense attorneys realized that he had a witness steeped in knowledge of the church's inner workings. Anderson negotiated an average settlement of $550,000 for the first twelve victims of Adamson. More victims started calling. As word of the settlements spread, Anderson found cases in other states. He became the leading plaintiff attorney in the field, interviewed by reporters and on network television as the scandal began to make news.

Anderson was moved by Tom Doyle's compassion, the time he spent talking to victims. An agnostic, Anderson was curious about Doyle's ability to separate his spiritual beliefs from the institutional corruption.

"I look for the light," said Doyle.

After countless phone calls and much correspondence, Anderson realized he had no invoice. He asked about Doyle's charges. "I'd just donate it," said Doyle, offhandedly. As a Dominican he had lived under a vow of poverty. As an Air Force captain he drew a salary, without a mortgage or family to support.

"I paid him ten thousand dollars on those early cases," says Anderson. "A comparable expert in complex litigation might have commanded a million dollars in fees."

As other attorneys began seeking his services, Doyle had to think about the money. He decided to take modest fees that would allow him to give financial support to victims who could not sue because the statute of limitations had expired. In the 1990s he dispensed about $100,000 to such people. He also started an account to help his nieces pay for college.

"Tom gives his money away," said attorney Sylvia Demarest of Dallas. "It's rather amazing."[26]

Geographic Reach

When the Midwest regional meeting of the Canon Law Society convened in Columbus, Ohio, on April 23, 1990, Bishop A. James Quinn lectured on pedophilia. In tape-recorded remarks he advised on record keeping. Canon law prescribes a secret archive for a bishop to file the most sensitive information. "Unsigned letters alleging misconduct should be expunged," Quinn said. "Standard personnel files should contain no documentation relating to possible criminal behavior. Serious moral questions, signed allegations, those should be a part of the secret file anyhow. But they still subpoena them . . . comb through your files."

Then came the whopper: "Now what files have been subpoenaed; they cannot be tampered with, destroyed, removed: that constitutes obstruction of justice and contempt of court. Prior, however, thought and study ought to be given if you think it's going to be necessary. If there's something that you really don't want people to see, you might send it off to the Apostolic Delegate, because they have immunity to protect something that is potentially dangerous."

By advising canon lawyers to send the Vatican embassy files *"you really don't want people to see,"* Quinn, contradicting Doyle's 1985 written warning not to draw the Holy See into U.S. legal conflicts, was telling his audience to abuse diplomatic immunity. In a brief telephone interview with Berry for a *Plain Dealer* article, Quinn dodged questions about flouting the constitutional separation of church and state, saying drily: "I suggest maybe you think about that."[27]

Doyle vented his concerns about Quinn in a letter to the Reverend Francis G. Morrisey, a leading canon lawyer in Ottawa, Canada. Morrisey wrote on July 12, 1990, saying, "It has been accepted in a number of countries to have documents 'on deposit' at the Nunciature. They have been rather willing here to keep things for the bishops. However, once a civil case has started, then this would not be acceptable, and in fact, could even be criminal."

As Morrisey was writing Doyle, a special church commission in Newfoundland was investigating the Mount Cashel orphanage in the port of St. John's, which had become the subject of hearings televised across Canada. Mount Cashel was run by the Irish Christian Brothers. Nine brothers (two of whom were lovers) had sodomized, whipped, molested, and otherwise humiliated at least thirty boys over more than two decades. A ring of pedophiles and sadomasochistic homosexuals extended to five men in the town who had grown up in the orphanage and returned to prey on boys coming up.[28] The Irish Christian Brothers, an order of educators, was plunged into legal battles in Canada, Ireland, and Australia over patterns of abuse dating to the early twentieth century.

"It goes much deeper than child abuse," Morrisey wrote in a letter to Doyle.

> I wonder if it is not the entire lifestyle of the clergy that is at stake. At times, I feel as if our entire system is even "corrupt" in the sense that at times it appears to be based more on power struggles, than on gospel values. . . . I realize that Cardinal Ratzinger, et al., might not see things in the same way. I feel that we are going to have to redo our entire structure, but no one seems able today to bite the bullet.

Morrisey, a mentor to Doyle, saw systemic decay. So did Barry M. Coldrey, an Australian scholar and member of the Christian Brothers, who wrote an internal study for his order after reports on orphanages in

Australia. In 1994, Coldrey spent six weeks in Rome doing research at the Christian Brothers' archives before handing his document to Brother Colm Keating, the superior general. "He was not thrilled that it was written, though he treated me decently," says Brother Coldrey. "I discussed it thoroughly with him and his deputy."[29] As time passed, says Coldrey, "It's fair to say I was marginalized. . . . There was a lot of bitching and bickering about what I was doing." Coldrey estimates that 10 percent of the four thousand members of the international order abused young people. In a book on the broader problem, Coldrey wrote: "The sexual abuse of minors—and general clerical infidelity to celibacy vows—has been the dark underside of the old Irish-Australian working class church, covered over many years by tribal loyalties." He continued:

> A sexual network is a small group or circle of priests, Brothers or lay workers who are living at variance with their vows on sexual matters—twos and threes who support one another by supportive silence and covering for each other. A sexual underworld is a larger, more amorphous state-within-a-state inside a diocese or Religious Congregation, where there is a substantial [number of] people who are not living their vows (or have not for periods in the past) and who cooperate to hide one another's extracurricular activities. . . . [Those] who abuse minors and commit criminal offenses have been able to hide within a sympathetic underworld of other clergy and church workers who are merely breaking their vows by having heterosexual or gay sex with consenting adults. . . . They share an unstated capacity for mutual blackmail.[30]

The term "sexual underworld" puts another slant on secret penal trials.

When an accused priest knows the sexual liabilities of those who might sit in judgment of him, how effective could a trial be? Rome never dreamed that a pathological underworld would be exposed in common-law countries—Australia, North America, and Ireland—across the 1990s. The Curia, like the blundering bishops, wanted to see such behavior as sin, human frailty. When canon law was applied, its function was not to redress great damage perpetrated on children.

Chapter Four

A TIME OF SOLIDARITY

TOM DOYLE'S odyssey took him across Indiana, Verdi operas rolling
on the tape deck, to a condominium in a Chicago suburb. There he
met regularly with a group of victims organizing a force against the
bishops. Unsure where the movement would go, Doyle went to express
solidarity—and to learn.

In late 1989, meanwhile, Charles Sennott of the *New York Post*
reported that the Reverend Bruce Ritter, founder of Covenant House for
runaway youths, was accused of sexual abuse by young men who had
gone through the program. Many well-connected New Yorkers were
dumbfounded. This was not the Father Bruce (singled out by Ronald
Reagan as a national hero) they knew.[1] After heavy *New York Times*
coverage, Cardinal John O'Connor pressured Ritter to resign. The Manhattan district attorney chose not to prosecute, because the accusers
were no longer adolescents. Ritter wrote to bishops, seeking a position
administering the sacraments, but they saw him as damaged goods. The
Vatican, through the Congregation for the Clergy, gave Ritter permission to minister in India, where a bishop agreed to receive him; but state
authorities prevented him from leaving. Sennott, who went on to
become a *Boston Globe* foreign correspondent, found that Ritter's Franciscan order had ignored complaints in 1983, and a priest who reported
three accusations to the archdiocese was told to keep quiet.[2] An investigation of Covenant House's financial irregularities forced an overhaul.

As the Ritter scandal faded, the *Times* treated clergy sex abuse as a marginal topic. Ritter conformed to a narrative sensibility of the post-Watergate era, a public figure exposed for a double life. In 1989, *The Washington Post* began coverage of the flamboyant George Stallings, who quit the priesthood rather than follow Cardinal Hickey's request to enter a treatment facility after abuse accusations by former altar boys. He, too, was never prosecuted. Stallings launched his own religion, with drums, dancing, and stem-winding sermons that bestirred a tongue-in-cheek profile by *60 Minutes*'s Morley Safer.

Stallings and Ritter were symptoms of an ecclesiastical culture run amok; yet they became ephemeral figures in a parade of tarnished celebrities. The coverage of clergy sex abuse by the major Eastern dailies was marked by a reaction to events rather than well-planned investigative work. Talk shows led by Phil Donahue and Geraldo Rivera were in the forefront of covering the issue.

The major media gave significant coverage to 1992 revelations about ex-priest James Porter, formerly of Fall River, Massachusetts. Porter's decades of assaults were exposed in a telephone conversation taped by Frank Fitzpatrick, whom he had abused as a child. A torrent of reporting and legal action followed. Cardinal Law denounced the media, singling out *The Boston Globe*. He also announced a policy to help victims and remove perpetrators. But with priests exempted as mandated reporters of abuse under Massachusetts law, Law was accountable to himself. Porter, married with children in Minnesota, was extradited to Massachusetts and sent to prison. The statute of limitations was tolled because he had left the state while some of his victims were minors. The Knights of Malta, an elite organization of lay Catholics, assisted the Fall River diocese in providing funds for a victims' settlement.[3] Attorney Eric MacLeish's work on the Porter cases set him on a path that would lead, years later, to a collision with Cardinal Law on Boston cases.

Defense lawyers commonly bargained money for silence.[4] Hush money alone does not explain why media coverage of the early 1990s ebbed. "The original problem with this story was simple skepticism that anything so horrible could be condoned by the hierarchy of a church that has done so much good in the world," wrote Carl Cannon.[5] The quick shock of a Stallings or a Ritter, a talk show or news report about bad priests, paled beneath the epic story begun in 1989 as the Berlin Wall came down and the Soviet empire began crumbling on television.

Pope John Paul II won exalted status on the global stage for his stirring speeches on human rights and support of Solidarity in Poland. As Mikhail Gorbachev told a papal biographer, Jonathan Kwitney: "Everything that happened in Eastern Europe during these past few years would have been impossible without the pope, without the political role he was able to play"[6]—a far cry from Stalin's famously cynical remark "How many divisions has the pope?"

As the Eastern bloc countries began lurching toward democracy, the pope, like a man for all seasons, criticized the excessive materialism of the West. Rarely in history has a Roman Catholic pontiff straddled politics and religion with such grace as John Paul in that heady time. Polls nevertheless showed a deep split between Catholics' devotion to the pope and their rejection of church teaching on birth control and other sexual issues.

John Paul's stature was a substantial deterrent toward a full-force newspaper investigation on clergy sex abuse. Law, O'Connor, and dozens of bishops had awful things to hide; the strategy of blue-chip defense attorneys, whenever possible, was to pay victims for their silence and seal the files. Most victims, saddled with suffering, were relieved to settle. Some wanted no publicity. Yet knowing Father would not be prosecuted left huge issues, like the role of bishops as de facto judges in letting Father carry on. Defense attorneys hoped settlements would prevent more victims from suing. Plaintiff lawyers took the best deal for the client, especially if they had more cases in the offing, or if the statute of limitations did not bode well for a seriously traumatized client.

For survivors, the church that promised a path to salvation had betrayed them twice over—first as children, when they suffered sexual invasion; then, as adults, when they saw bishops or religious superiors acting like lawyers. Hush money silenced them. As canon law bound a priest never to reveal what people said in confession, sealed agreements muzzled victims from speaking about the cleric.

Many cases *were* reported in the early 1990s, sparking the realization among trial attorneys of a criminal dimension in ecclesiastical culture. Victims who got therapy early on stood the best chance of achieving well-adjusted lives. "The first step is moving from victim to survivor," a woman from Minnesota said. "Now I am beyond the survivor stage and consider myself an advocate for others who were abused and still silent."⁷ This was the language of a dawning awareness in Ireland, Canada, and Australia about corruption in the hierarchy, though it would take years to register on public opinion. In America, the movement began through the efforts of two women whose lives intersected with Tom Doyle's.

The early meetings that Doyle attended were at the home of a woman named Jeanne Miller. They focused on documenting cases, building an organization, and prodding the media. Most survivors, struggling for a vocabulary of truth-beyond-shame, had never dreamed of attending such meetings. Justice had become the issue of their lives.

The Embattled Pacifist

Barbara Blaine was living in St. Elizabeth Catholic Worker House. The building, on S. Honore Street, which had once been a convent, was a cavernous symbol of a time when Chicago's South Side was white ethnic and nuns staffed the parochial schools. The nuns were gone. Most of the Irish, Italians, and Poles had left for more affluent environs as African Americans moved into the neighborhood. As Mass attendance dwindled, the archdiocese sold the church to a black Protestant congregation. Cardinal Bernardin gave permission for the Catholic Worker House to use the convent.

The Worker movement, founded in New York by Dorothy Day (now a candidate for sainthood), follows a gospel of living and working with the poor. The convent was a homeless shelter whose guests, as they were called, numbered about a dozen black women and twice as many children. Born July 6, 1956, Barbara Blaine was raised in Toledo, Ohio, in a large family as Catholic as they come. She was thirteen in the fall of 1969. The spirit of Vatican II infused the parish. With dreams of becoming a nun, Barbara helped prepare the altar for Mass. Her father, president of the new parish council, teased her that she would be the first woman priest. A young assistant pastor, Chet Warren, occasionally gave her rides home. One Sunday he invited her to supper at the rectory. Thrilled to be asked, showing her best manners, she dined with the priests; after the meal the priests drifted out, save for Father Chet. He closed the curtains and began kissing her. Flattered, bewildered, she began shaking. Years later she wrote:

> He asked me to promise not to tell anyone. He said if I did tell then they would put him in jail and he would not be able to be a priest any more. . . . He knew I wanted to be a sister so he proposed that we live our lives here on earth engaged to each other to be wed in heaven. From that day on my life dramatically changed. My childhood seemed over and now I felt like an adult, but not just any adult. I felt like an evil temptress. I felt cheap and dirty. The very thing that I had been taught not to do had been done to me. I felt so guilty I couldn't eat or sleep. I had caused a good holy priest to sin![8]

Brought up to idealize virginity, Blaine lacked a vocabulary of resistance; she could not verbalize what his hands and mouth were doing to her. In those days there was no abuse-prevention training in schools, the media, or many families. She grew distant from her twin sister. She went to confession. Warren said he went to confession too. He kept kissing and fondling her through high school. Migraine headaches put her in the hospital. Warren groped her there. Her grades fell. On senior retreat she broke down and told another priest. "Jesus loves you and can forgive you no matter what," he said. Barbara told Chet she couldn't see him anymore. He laughed. "You can't break away from me." She never let him touch her again.

The priest who heard her confession sank into her past, nameless. Chet Warren faded as she went off to St. Louis University. For Barbara, trusting men was a struggle; she earned a master's in social work. With a spirituality shaped by the Sermon on the Mount—"blessed are the poor in spirit, for theirs is the kingdom of heaven"—she joined the Catholic Worker. Encouraging homeless women "to strive for something better and make the most of life, I found my words speaking to myself. People who showed their woundedness made me confront my own."[9]

Her life tilted when she read about pedophile priests in the *National Catholic Reporter* of June 7, 1985. *I am not alone,* she realized. Migraines flooded back, nightmares and flashbacks. She was driving when a fit of rage came out of nowhere. All she could see was Chet's face. She ran a red light, crashing into a car. Shaken, she knew she needed help. She went back to Toledo. She confronted him: *You molested me—you're guilty for doing that!*

> *I told him now that I needed his help to be healed from what he had done to me. He apologized over and over. Suggested I pull blinds over that part of my life and that I was a saint, trying to live as a Catholic Worker, and that he would never be as faithful and committed as me and I should just forget he ever existed in my life. [I said:] "Nice but it just won't work. . . . I am going to do what is necessary for me to be healed." The following week I received a letter from him saying how nice it was to see me and how glad he was to hear that things were going so well for me in Chicago.*[10]

She approached his order, the Oblates of St. Francis de Sales, concerned he might be abusing kids. But she did not want him arrested. Living in poverty like Dorothy Day, she would not sue the church—and couldn't imagine him living any differently if she did. The Oblate provincial, the Reverend Paul Grehl, agreed to a facilitated dialogue. On January 7, 1986, Blaine and a friend, Grehl, and Warren met with psychologist Mary Morgillo. Blaine said she wanted both of them to heal. Warren denied her accusations, but when pressed by Morgillo, admitted they were true. Blaine said it was too painful to go to Mass because all priests reminded her of Warren. How many priests abused kids? She spoke of her long anger, thinking, *My body was evil, dirty, and ugly—the cause of Chet and me sinning.* What did *he* think about wrecking the close bond she'd had with her twin sister? He mumbled an apology; he seemed shattered. The meeting ended with his agreeing to more sessions with Blaine and the therapist.

After a second facilitated meeting, Chet Warren withdrew; Father Grehl sent word that he supported Warren because the confrontations were making him sick. Blaine threatened to go public. Warren went back for another session. It is common for such men to play the victim when confronted with their crimes. The women told Warren to get off the self-pity. They ended with an agreement that he and Blaine would have individual counseling and then regroup. The Oblates agreed to pay for her therapy.

Chet Warren never returned. Blaine's calls to the Oblates went unanswered. He still functioned as a priest. She saw his Oblate community circling the wagons. She believed they blamed her. As the Oblates withdrew into a cocoon, her brothers and sisters wrote the bishop, the Oblates, and Warren in her behalf. Meetings followed with the Blaines and Toledo bishop James Hoffman, the Blaines and Father Grehl. The Oblates assured the family that Warren was in therapy. He did not step down from ministry.

S.N.A.P. and Linkup

In 1988, Barbara Blaine took out a classified ad in the *National Catholic Reporter* for anyone abused by a priest to contact her. She began hearing from people. In 1990, she organized a survivors' gathering in San Francisco. Thirty people attended. An early newsletter from the Survivors' Network of Those Abused by Priests explains:

> *What is S.N.A.P.?*
> *We are a grassroots organization made up wholly of survivors of sexual abuse by priests. Our goal is to provide self-help support to others, to share resources and information, and to organize political action to challenge the Church to better deal with the problem of priests' sexual misconduct.*[11]

Blaine found an ally in David Clohessy (pronounced *Klossee*), who worked for a St. Louis political consulting firm. David and three of his brothers were molested, separately, as teenagers by their hometown Missouri pastor, one John Whiteley. David stuffed his memories. In 1988, he saw the film *Nuts*, with Barbra Streisand as a prostitute traumatized by childhood sexual abuse. "That happened to me," he told his girlfriend, leaving the movie. He wept at the rush of memories. When he confronted the priest, Whiteley said he had been treated at House of Affirmation—another family had reported him to the bishop. Clohessy asked if he had abused others in his family. Whiteley said he didn't want to violate anyone's privacy. When David told his mother, she blanched. Whiteley had been a guest on their vacations. As the brothers opened up, the family split over David's decision to sue the church. His brother Kevin had become a priest of the Jefferson City diocese, and stopped talking to him.[12]

In 1990, he stood outside the hotel in San Francisco, estranged from his parents, just crying. Finally he went in and met Barbara Blaine and a roomful of people with rocky loads of their own. As one man told his wrenching story, David Clohessy was dumbfounded. Gary Hayes was a priest who had been abused by a priest, just like his brother.

Barbara Blaine read *Assault on Innocence,* a 1988 small-press novel based on a family's struggle with the Chicago archdiocese.[13] She contacted the author, Jeanne Miller, who used a pseudonym, Hilary Stiles. Miller invited Blaine to join her burgeoning group, Victims of Clergy Abuse Linkup.

In the early 1980s, as a Eucharistic minister in Arlington Heights, Jeanne and her husband had pleaded with Bernardin's office to remove Robert Mayer, a priest who made advances on their son. The church refused; the couple took legal action to have the priest removed, and after two years were flattened by an array of stall tactics used by attorney James Serritella. When the church offered them $20,000 to drop the case, Mayer was in another parish. With their savings depleted, they took the money and swallowed another $15,000 in legal fees; their marriage broke under the pressure. In 1990, Miller was keeping files on priests, trading documents with attorneys and news clippings with journalists, casting lines to people who had gone through the legal steamroller in forming her group, which became known as the Linkup.

As a radical pacifist Barbara Blaine had no use for guys in Air Force outfits. But in Miller's living room she realized that Doyle was a priest. "Bishops have got their heads in the sand," he told the group. "They don't understand what they're up against." After reading the report he coauthored, she approached him with an Englishwoman who lived in the Catholic Worker House, who had also been abused by a priest in her youth.

"What you went through was terrible," said Doyle, with a gentleness that belied his macho look. "As a priest I want you both to know that I'm sorry. Gosh, this stuff just never should have happened to you. I'm truly sorry."[14]

The "gosh" made Barbara Blaine smile.

Jeanne Miller wanted to foster ties with Cardinal Bernardin, hoping he would adopt a pastoral policy. Blaine's group, S.N.A.P., was taking shape as a more aggressive force in confronting the bishops. News coverage was crucial to both groups . Each time Blaine was on TV or was quoted in the press, the phone at the Catholic Worker rang, with people, who spoke in halting voices, asking about S.N.A.P.

The Case That Would Not Go Away

In 1990, Doyle agreed to assist a family from the Chicago suburb of Northbrook. Husband and wife, conservative Catholics, were attorneys. A harrowing experience with their only child sent them to archdiocesan lawyer Jim Serritella. They wanted their pastor and the school principal removed. The priest was facing a lawsuit from the female principal of a previous parish for physical and sexual harassment. The couple said that their son, at seven, had been worked over, sexually and physically, by the pastor and the principal. Serritella offered to negotiate. The couple's main demand was that Cardinal Bernardin create a lay review board to deal with such priests. The archdiocese said no. Reluctantly, the couple sued the church, the pastor, and the principal.

The archdiocese immediately announced that countercharges of character defamation would be filed against the couple.

The family faced another barrier: the Cook County state's attorney had refused to prosecute. Three interrogations by an assistant prosecutor had traumatized the boy. "They think I'm lying," he sobbed in his father's arms. The parents and the child's therapist were outraged at the verbal drubbing. But with Catholic politicians entrenched in the police and the court system, priests were not prosecuted for sexual offenses. This was a tradition in many large cities with deep Catholic roots: if a priest was nabbed in a vice squad raid or with a minor, the chief usually handed him over to the bishop for discipline. Cops cynically called these "tight collar cases."

Tom Doyle went to the family's home for dinner; husband and wife impressed him as decent people confronting a system whose corruptions he knew too well. The boy was polite, if guarded. Who knew how he would act as he got older? Doyle was angry that Bernardin was letting lawyers call the shots on pastoral policy.

On February 18, 1991, in a deposition for the family, Doyle revealed that a Chicago canonist told him in 1987 that on abuse allegations, "they close ranks at the top." He spoke of Robert Mayer, the priest Jeanne Miller had reported in 1983: "I began hearing stories about him in the late seventies when I worked in the chancery. . . . Vicar General J. Richard Keating conducted the investigation." A church attorney questioned Doyle:

> *What else did [Keating] tell you?*
> *They thought the only thing the parents were interested in was money. . . .*
> *Was it your opinion that that investigation was handled improperly?*
> *Yes.*
> *Why?*
> *There seemed to be a lot of evidence that there had been misconduct on the part of this priest, a lot of stories, a lot of talk.*
> *Hearsay?*
> *On an ongoing basis. He had a widespread reputation among the diocesan priests, and, as I said, he was transferred from one parish to another.*

Mayer's blue-collar parishioners did not know Bernardin had ordered him never to be alone with anyone under twenty-one.

Andrew Greeley had also heard from the anguished father in Northbrook. Visiting their home for supper, Greeley saw them as good Catholics who had been wronged. Greeley felt the old outrage that marked his prolific output—the faith of lay Catholics in high contrast with the hierarchy's glaring flaws.

Dividing his semesters between the University of Arizona at Tucson and the University of Chicago, Greeley exerted great influence as a sociologist, using empirical data and surveys to explain the Catholic Church. Transfixed by the spiritual imagination, how the mental imagery absorbed in faith shapes human values and behavior, Greeley had published dozens of books and countless articles. He despaired of church governance. He also poured ideas into a river of novels, some of which had sex scenes that infuriated traditionalists; yet a romantic theme laced through his fiction like a Gaelic thread: human reconciliation in light of God's love. Greeley lived in a high-rise apartment in downtown Chicago, with a summer home in Michigan. (As a diocesan priest he took no vow of poverty.) With a circle of kith and kin in

Chicago, he said Mass as a guest in parishes. He credited his prolific writing to "celibacy and hard work."[15]

Bernardin and his auxiliary bishops kept a cool distance from Greeley. "I wonder if the sexual obsessions of Church leaders today will seem as absurd in years to come?" Greeley wrote in a journal. "What a terrible mess we have made out of the priesthood in the years since the Council. Horrible leadership—stupid, venal, cowardly."[16]

In his weekly *Sun-Times* column, Greeley in 1986 had scored the bishops for "pretend[ing] to believe the [pedophilia] problem does not exist."[17] In 1989, he wrote of Serritella's comments at the River Forest conference: "To make the families of the victims of priests the enemy is evil, damnable. . . . He should be fired. If the cardinal will not fire him, then Rome should appoint a bishop who will fire him."[18] Yet if anyone knew the Vatican would not intervene, it was Andy Greeley. The Roman Curia had been unable to dislodge Cardinal Cody, who died on the job. As the abuse scandal simmered, bishops resisted the secret trials the Curia wanted, and the Vatican remained passive.

Tom Doyle respected Andy Greeley but barely knew him. As his lens on church corruption widened via his encounters with survivors, the Air Force captain was becoming more radical. He saw Bernardin as a clerical politician who thrived on dealing with hierarchs from Washington to Rome. Greeley, though an outsider in one sense, commanded the respect of bishops by virtue of his scholarly writings and standing with the media.

Greeley and Bernardin had a falling-out after a fledgling journalist obtained Greeley's diaries for a book on the 1978 papal elections.[19] Greeley had given papers to a college archive under restricted access. The notes suggested Greeley plotted to have Cody ousted and Bernardin installed as his successor. The priest and cardinal denied any such plot.[20] Bad feelings worsened when Rome told Bernardin to have a committee examine the erotic content of Greeley's novels. Bernardin turned down a $1 million gift from Greeley, drawn from his fiction royalties, to Catholic inner-city schools. Bernardin refused to confront Greeley on the novels, and let the matter fizzle.

Greeley still considered Bernardin a cut above most bishops, and able to see that the greater good lay not in ham-fisted lawyering but in a policy for removing predatory priests, assisting victims, and showing integrity as a church. Apart from Greeley's columns, neither the *Sun-*

Times nor the more influential *Tribune* had given substantial coverage to the issue. After a report by Jason Berry on the Northbrook case in the May 24, 1991, *Chicago Reader*, Greeley did another column. "No one in authority in the church would talk to the author," he wrote. "Doesn't anyone tell the cardinal that to the average citizen such silence looks like an admission of guilt? Cannot the cardinal take the case out of the hands of the lawyers and intervene to end the suffering of all concerned? Can he not develop a policy that will make it unlikely that such cases will ever happen again?"[21]

Bernardin confidant Eugene Kennedy had warned him not to rely on Serritella. But for all of Bernardin's negotiating skills with bishops, he could not buck the legal strategy. Greeley's columns jolted the reputation of a cardinal who had received the Albert Einstein Peace Prize for his stance on nuclear war.

In late summer 1991, the Chicago police, responding to a neighbor's call, barged into a rectory where Mayer—nine years after the advances on Jeanne Miller's son—was sunbathing naked with a fourteen-year-old boy and a twenty-year-old man. Bernardin went to the rectory, yanked Mayer, and sent him to St. Luke Institute. When word reached Jeanne Miller, she told Mary Ann Ahern of WMAQ-TV, who reported Mayer's departure in a series on four priests accused of abusing children. Mayer's parishioners were furious. Bernardin made a public apology and dispatched aides to cool emotions at the parish.

At a parish meeting, Auxiliary Bishop Raymond Goedert did not recognize Jeanne Miller from an encounter they had had years before. People asked about previous accusations. Goedert spoke of "a mother's overreaction" to "horseplay. . . . All we found was smoke, but there was no fire." Miller, with a tape recorder, marveled at how easily he lied. A woman complained that Mayer, in a sex education class, told boys about "fisting," burrowing a fist into a lover's anus. That made Goedert uneasy. Others complained that Mayer had taken a boy to a summer cottage with a priest who had done six months in prison for child molesting. "Father Slade is from Joliet and has nothing to do with the archdiocese of Chicago," said Goedert, to moans and outcries.[22]

At the next night's meeting a fourteen-year-old girl, with quavering voice, said that Mayer had molested her. He was indicted on four counts of sexual activity with a minor and later convicted.

Greeley wrote a column calling on the state's attorney, Jack O'Malley, to appoint a special prosecutor to investigate the archdiocese for obstruction of justice. Bernardin needed "a lay review board—including at least one member of the family of a victim—to determine whether a priest ought to be reassigned," wrote Greeley,[23] voicing a demand the Northbrook couple had first made.

"I'm going to do everything I can to make sure that this kind of mistake is not made again," Bernardin announced. That "mistake" had caused Miller's marriage to break in legal battle with the archdiocese. An apologetic Bernardin called her, asking to meet. Maybe, she thought, there is a chance. He proved a sensitive listener, jotting notes; she knew he wanted *her* to halt the damage each time she spoke on television. One of Chicago's wealthiest Catholics, in sympathy with the Northbrook family, had stopped donations to the church. Bernardin named an auxiliary bishop and two prominent laypersons to a commission charged with recommending an archdiocesan policy.

He also asked Miller to visit the Isaac Ray Center, which evaluated problem priests. There, she was amazed to learn, the archdiocese refused to allow use of the penile plethysmograph as a gauge of sexual disorder. The cardinal was troubled about pictures that might cause priests to achieve orgasm! He promised her he would reconsider; he also agreed to speak at the first Linkup conference in mid-October. At Easter, he wrote: "By that time, the Commission will have completed its work. I trust that I will be able to make a constructive presentation that will clearly affirm the intention of the Archdiocese to address the problem in the most effective and responsible way possible."

In Northbrook the principal had resigned, but the priest remained on the job. Bernardin insisted that in the absence of an indictment, the priest must stay. A slight, balding man who wore large eyeglasses and spoke in cadenced traces of a South Carolina childhood, Bernardin was genteel. Still, Miller was struck by his ambivalence; his impulse to help victims/survivors was pulled back by legal forces bent on defending priests. Was he evolving?

Greeley saw Bernardin's national stature as a building block for reform. New York's Cardinal O'Connor was such a lightning rod on abortion as to seem a virtual Republican politician. Bernardin had the appeal of a philosopher prince.

"The spectrum of life cuts across the issues of genetics, abortion, capital punishment, modern warfare, and the care of the terminally ill," he had stated. "This combination of challenges is what cries out for a consistent ethic of life."[24]

"In a sense, he has the future of American Catholicism in his hands," the New York Times observed. "There is no member of the American hierarchy who is more closely watched by church leaders in the United States and abroad."[25]

He was also a target of ultraconservatives who despised him for supporting Seattle archbishop Raymond Hunthausen in a dispute with the Vatican over allowing a gay group, Dignity, to have a cathedral Mass, and for alleged permissiveness on marriage annulments. The Chicago archdiocese's AIDS education program also made Bernardin a target for the Catholic right.

Bernardin was spending a fourth of his time on a molestation scandal and getting pounded in the news. In 1991, with a $12 million deficit, the archdiocese spent $1.9 million on clergy abuse charges. Indicting Mayer was no gamble for prosecutor O'Malley, a Republican up for reelection in Democratic Cook County.

In 1992, the parents of a second boy made accusations against the Northbrook pastor, Robert Lutz. They were dragged into the litigation when the mother received a subpoena from church attorneys after the father of the first boy mentioned conversations with her in his deposition. She was questioned for two days. The parents refused to let O'Malley's staff interrogate their son, though they allowed Northbrook police and a prosecutor's designate to watch a social worker interview the boy in a hospital room with an inviewing window. The social worker believed the boy. The parents, aware of the meat grinder the first boy had been put through, refused to let police interview their child.

The second mother asked Father Greeley if she and her husband might meet with Cardinal Bernardin. Greeley jumped at the chance, hoping the exposure to parents would move Bernardin past the legal brinkmanship, the bungling by cops, and O'Malley's people. The parents of the second boy (who didn't know the other child) pleaded with Bernardin to remove Lutz. Bernardin agreed to put Lutz under a "mandate" not to be alone with children, as he had done with the indicted Mayer. But with Father Lutz proclaiming his innocence in "the case that won't go away," as an O'Malley aide called it, Bernardin said he could not remove the priest. Thus, the second family filed its own civil suit against Lutz and the archdiocese. Lutz's lawyers countersued them for defamation because they had written Bernardin and spoken to the press.

The "slap suits" outraged S.N.A.P. and Linkup members. Doyle saw the counterstrikes as an extension of Serritella's 1986 speech, casting victims' families as the enemy. With mounting losses in other states, defense lawyers were watching Chicago. Serritella's tactics were like those of industries against polluted communities: beat down opponents through litigation by ordeal. Doyle despaired over the Machiavellian strain in Bernardin, promoting a reform program while allowing bare-knuckle legal tactics.

Through the summer of 1992 the cardinal's commission culled years of personnel files. By the fall Bernardin had taken twenty-two priests out of parish work; a twenty-third followed. When the commission released its report, Bernardin opened a pastoral office to help victims, and a Fitness Review Board for priests, largely composed of laypeople—which is exactly what the first Northbrook couple originally wanted. In a perverse irony, the commission declared the Northbrook accusations unfounded—*before either case had gone to trial.* According to Jeff Anderson, attorney for the second family, nowhere else in America was a priest facing two lawsuits by children allowed to remain in his parish. Bernardin's decision was entwined in the legal defense.

The cardinal said: "I cannot change the past but I can do something about the future." Nevertheless, the archdiocese sought protection from criminal subpoenas for files of the priests Bernardin removed. O'Malley demanded the files, standing up to the church. Judge Thomas R. Fitzgerald of Cook County Circuit Court wondrously ruled that the constitutional separation of church and state gave the archdiocese "pastoral privilege" over files of accused child molesters. O'Malley appealed; the Illinois Supreme Court sided with Fitzgerald.[26]

Doyle viewed the legal scrimmaging as a mirror of Bernardin's personality—getting every side to fold toward his own solution. Privately Bernardin was also meeting with victims, trying to show compassion. When Greeley received a subpoena from defense lawyers for testimony in the Northbrook case, he was livid. He had been a priest to those families! On a blustery All Saints Day he marched up the steps of the cardinal's mansion, unannounced. Admitted to the parlor, pacing in his overcoat, Greeley seethed. Bernardin met him with a nervous face. Greeley has written:

> *I threw the subpoena at him (I did, really!) and shouted something like, "If it's a public fight you want, Joe, it's a public fight you'll get!"*
>
> *I don't remember whether he caught the papers or picked them up. "I didn't know about this till after it was sent," he said tentatively. "They are not our lawyers, after all."*
>
> *The Archdiocese maintained the fiction that the counter suits against the complaining family were being argued by lawyers hired by the defendants. I thought this was a disingenuous answer then and I still do.*
>
> *The Archdiocese was picking up the tab.*
>
> *"Don't try to sell me that," I shouted. "Your lawyer designed the strategy in this case and you're paying the bills!"*
>
> *He looked at the offending paper. "I'll see what I can do," he said softly.*
>
> *"You'd better," I said and turned to storm out, a blast of winter cold preparing to exit.*
>
> *"Don't go," he pleaded. "Sit down and let's talk for a few moments."*
>
> *So I sat down. He was my bishop after all. I knew what to expect and made up my mind how to react to it.*
>
> *"I pray every day, Andy," he said, his voice uncertain, "that we be reconciled. Can we be friends again?"* [27]

Thus began a rapprochement between two sons of the church in a maelstrom growing more volatile. The subpoena evaporated; Greeley became a back-channel adviser to the cardinal. Committed to a victims' pastoral assistance program, Bernardin was nevertheless unwilling to order attorneys to negotiate a settlement in the Northbrook cases, even as a private investigator for the defense searched people's garbage for information. Bernardin listened to Jeanne Miller, Kennedy, Greeley, and others in trying to work out of the quagmire.

In fiscal 1992 the archdiocese had a $6.4 million deficit. The annual Cardinal's Appeal had fallen $2.8 million short of its $10 million goal. An archdiocesan fiscal officer blamed the national recession, but with

$1.8 million to settle abuse cases (and $846,000 that year on legal fees), the sexual underworld was exacting its wages.[28] Bernardin said: "We will be broke in four years unless we take serious steps." The abuse scandal alone had not caused the crisis. With an aging infrastructure, the archdiocese was losing money in old neighborhoods—like the South Side, with the Catholic Worker House—because of white flight to the suburbs. Bernardin had closed two dozen old city parishes and was selling off properties to stanch the monetary hemorrhaging. With 2.3 million Catholics, Chicago was the second largest archdiocese, eclipsed by Los Angeles with its surging Latino population.

With the shocking media accounts about James Porter in New England, Barbara Blaine made a final try in Toledo. She met the Reverend James Cryan, the new Oblate superior, and told him what she had told his predecessor, Father Paul Grehl, in 1989, about Chet Warren's molesting her, even when she was in the hospital. Cryan gave no assurance that he would remove Warren. Blaine went to the hospital where Warren was a chaplain and provided documentation. The hospital got rid of him. A long *Toledo Blade* report on her struggle did not identify Warren—he had not been indicted or named in a suit.

Father Grehl, who sat in on the 1989 meeting where Warren had apologized, told the *Blade* that Blaine "needed somebody to talk to and console her, and he said every once in a while he would hug her as he would do with any other kid in the parish. Nothing was intended sexually. . . . I had no reason to doubt him."[29] Three weeks later Father Cryan admitted to the *Blade* that "a number of other women" had reported "sexual improprieties" by Warren. The priest would "resign from his duties."[30] In going to the press, Barbara Blaine forced his removal.

She was watching Bernardin with a skepticism tempered by hope. There was a lot about the cardinal she liked, though the hierarchy had been so retaliatory toward survivors that she wondered how far Bernardin's policy would go. She knew the Northbrook families and what it felt like to be bulldozed by the church. So did four hundred other people who gathered in a hotel of suburban Chicago on October 16, 1992, for the inaugural Linkup conference.

Survivors of James Porter came from New England; men and women abused as children by other priests came from California, the Midwest, and pockets of the South. So did social workers, detectives, several sympathetic priests and nuns, plus two documentary crews. Some survivors wore yellow ribbons, alerting journalists not to request interviews; most were willing to talk. Tom Doyle sensed a current of anger among people waiting to hear Cardinal Bernardin. *They are going to blast him,* he thought. This group will go after him like nothing he has ever encountered.

At the eleventh hour Bernardin canceled, sending word to Miller that he did not want to be a source of division. After all their meetings and calls she was disappointed, but she had a conference to put on and people to welcome.

In the hallway a middle-aged woman from Texas wanted to confront Bernardin from the audience, and say he must repent for raping her in a satanic ritual when she was eleven in South Carolina. (Bernardin's first parish was in South Carolina.) Jeanne Miller did not want such a confrontation; the problem was moot now. As Jason Berry spoke with the woman, who refused to let her name be used, he wondered what the media would have made of such an explosive allegation. Conference participant Kenneth Lanning, an FBI agent and authority on child abuse, disputed the existence of pedophiliac satanic cults.

A sea of emotions rocked the group over the next two days: some survivors wept and held close through the speeches; others raised their voices, demanding justice; people bonded in small groups. Many of the people meeting Tom Doyle found the priest whose voice they had known on the phone. He felt he was helping people long damaged, long alienated. Doyle was not surprised at Bernardin's cancellation; the cardinal hated bad publicity. Whoever had alerted him to the emotional volatility had done everyone a favor. Had the Texas woman made her accusation of a satanic cult, the media fallout would have been a disaster just as the survivors were finding their definition as a movement.

In a speech that Sunday, Greeley praised Bernardin for the Fitness Review Board and for removing twenty-three priests. "Priests can do anything they damn please to lay people, and feel pretty confident that they can get away with it," he bristled. "The sexually maladjusted priest has been able to abuse the children of the laity and thus far be reasonably secure from punishment." He called the priesthood a privileged class, almost immune from punishment. "We priests have lived by a different set of norms for so long that we take them for granted. . . . Any crime of one of our own must be covered up instantly and completely. Any loud criticism of our behavior by one of our own must be punished instantly for such criticism is the ultimate sin.

"Reform of clerical culture may be facilitated by financial pressure," he concluded. "Just as suits forced hospitals to impose strenuous standards on medical doctors, so the institutional church seems to have little choice but to impose appropriate behavioral standards on priests. Where virtue fails, money sometimes succeeds."

Chapter Five

POPE JOHN PAUL II
BREAKS HIS SILENCE

IN MARCH OF 1993—eight years after Father Doyle briefed Cardinal Oddi—Pope John Paul II spoke on the scandal to a group of visiting U.S. bishops following the resignation of Archbishop Robert F. Sanchez of Santa Fe, New Mexico. Three young women had revealed Sanchez's sexual encounters with them, starting in late adolescence, on CBS's *60 Minutes*. Urging prayers for "our brother from Santa Fe . . . [and] the persons affected by his action," the pope said that a person's fall, "which in itself is a painful experience, should not become a matter for sensationalism. . . . Unfortunately, however, sensationalism has become the particular style of our age. In contrast, the spirit of the Gospel is one of compassion, with Christ's saying, 'Go, and sin no more.' "[1]

Sanchez left an archdiocese in a quagmire of abuse cases that caused it to sell prime real estate to stave off bankruptcy. The Servants of the Paraclete treatment facility in Jemez Springs, New Mexico, was so deep in litigation that it was eventually forced to close. The Paracletes had let James Porter, among *twenty* patients, do weekend parish work, yielding fresh victims.[2] In contrast to his remarks on Sanchez, John Paul sounded scant sympathy for the "persons affected by his actions." This was the first in a line of papal statements that would slowly show more sorrow as a train of sexual crimes from Ireland to Australia mocked the "Go, and sin no more" standard of fraternal correction.

There was no papal statement on Bishop Hubert O'Connor of British Columbia. In December of 1991, O'Connor was in Rome for the beatification of the first Canadian-born saint when he learned he was under investigation back home. His Prince George diocese had a large population of First Nations, as Indians are called in Canada; as a young priest in the 1960s he ran a residential school at Williams Lake. Back from Rome in January 1992, Bishop O'Connor published a letter deploring the "vicious attack" and "distressful and heart-rending news" of the police investigation. "Insult added to injury . . . I was in Rome and left so helpless."[3] Two other Oblates of Mary Immaculate, his order, were charged with abusing boys during his tenure at the school.

> *I did not then or ever in my life sexually abuse any child, be it male or female. . . . The theory appears to be that since I was at the school as principal for a period of two years while [another] priest was in the area, I should have known these offences were taking place. If I didn't, then I was covering up or committing the same offences myself. . . . A very unfair and damaging assumption.*

The bishop was indicted for raping two young women under his auspices many years before. One was a seamstress for the priests, by whom he sired a child. O'Connor changed his first name on the birth certificate in arranging the child's adoption. At the 1992 trial the woman said O'Connor had given her a book to understand "the female body cycle." She was twenty-one; he had begun kissing her at a movie. She explained how it escalated.

> *I remember standing at the corner of the bed . . . it seemed like an eternity. He asked me to remove my clothes. I was feeling so scared. I had never let a man see my body naked.*
>
> *I felt I didn't have any choice but to do as he told me. So I took off all my clothes. I was feeling so ashamed, shy. . . . I turned around and saw a towel on the bed. . . . I was still a virgin then. . . . I remember feeling so scared. Father O'Connor was so big. . . . Thoughts going in my head, "He's a priest." I felt him on top of me, he was heavy. He pushed his penis inside of me.[4]*

Monitoring her menstrual cycle, O'Connor knew when it was time for her to enter a home for unwed mothers; the baby was surrendered after two days. Devastated, the mother never saw her daughter again. Yet in a society steeped in paternalism, her relationship with O'Connor stayed cordial till he left. She kept the secret thirty years; then a police detective investigating other priests approached her. A vault of shame erupted as she reckoned with how much she had lost. O'Connor resigned and hired a top-drawer lawyer. He was spared from testifying when the judge halted the trial on learning the prosecution had failed to give the defense certain evidence. At a new trial O'Connor said: "As you know, I'm a celibate man," implying that he had been seduced. The trial judge found him not guilty of rape based on inconsistencies in the woman's testimony. He was found guilty in the case of the second woman and did six months behind bars. A parole board noted, "You hold your victims in contempt." The verdict was thrown out on a technicality.[5] In the furor surrounding the aborted 1992 trial, the chief of the Assembly of First Nations wrote Pope John Paul, demanding canonical action against the bishop. Under canon law a bishop is forever a bishop, even without a diocese. The Vatican was silent on O'Connor.

In March 1993, when the U.S. bishops' delegation (including Cardinals Bevilacqua of Philadelphia and O'Connor of New York) met with John Paul, they wanted greater autonomy under canon law to remove child molesters from the priesthood. Four years after the U.S. bishops' canonists first met with Vatican authorities on the matter, the Roman Curia held fast to the use of secret trials for presenting the pope information on which he could make a decision. American bishops balked at using a ritual many thought archaic as they dealt with expensive criminal and civil cases. The Americans wanted a way to expel bad priests. "My dear bishops," said the pope. "I lived all those years under communism. I am not about to let that come into the church."[6] In viewing an accelerated way of laicizing sex offenders as akin to a totalitarian regime's trampling on clerics' rights, John Paul emphasized sin over crime, a mentality to which many bishops attributed their own mistakes, seeing the abuse of children as a moral lapse to be forgiven.[7] In Rome, the bishops spoke of financial losses from litigation; the pope told them to keep suspended priests on the payroll. "You'll get no quick fixes out of me," he declared.

On March 10, Cardinal O'Connor of New York spoke to seminarians at Rome's North American College: "It's getting increasingly difficult for some priests and some bishops to hold their heads up. Everyone is under suspicion." O'Connor admitted what some laypeople now saw. "Real damage has been done in many cases—real horrifying damage."[8] Still, he echoed John Paul in calling the attacks on the church "merciless." Bad media were hurting priests' morale and turning away men with potential vocations.

John Paul reinforced his stance in a letter to the bishops. Acknowledging the pain suffered by "the little . . . victims," he insisted that canon law provisions be applied. Offering scant analysis of the fault lines in clerical culture, the pope blamed the media:

> *While acknowledging the right to due freedom of information, one cannot acquiesce in treating moral evil as an occasion for sensationalism. . . . The mass media play a particular role. Sensationalism leads to the loss of something essential to the morality of society. Harm is done to the fundamental right of individuals not to be easily exposed to the ridicule of public opinion. Even more, a distorted image of human life is created.*[9]

John Paul's rhetoric was evasive. Scandal-battered bishops were dealing with a pope offering little leadership to resolve the crisis. Behind the high stone walls that divide Vatican City and Rome proper, who in the Curia wanted to probe the causes of an issue the pope considered marginal? Italy had no hue and cry over child-molesting priests.

Depth Charges from the Irish Diaspora

In May of 1992, Eamonn Casey, Ireland's most popular bishop, resigned his position and left for Latin America with the revelation that he had fathered a child in 1974 by a young American woman then visiting Ireland. He had suggested she place the boy for adoption. She moved back to Connecticut and raised her son with help from Irish church funds secretly allocated by Bishop Casey. "People were flabbergasted; breathless; appalled, disbelieving," writes Mary Kenny in *Goodbye to Catholic Ireland*. "This had never knowingly or openly occurred before, in the lifetime of Irish Catholics."

Bishops, whom they revered, as holy men who laid down the law on morals and doctrine, men whose respect was due because their celibacy was a personal sacrifice, were stained. . . . There was a bitterness in the common reaction. "These are the fellows who were telling us how to behave," a middle-aged woman in West Cork said to me. "These are the guys who were quizzing us, in Confession, as to whether we had entertained bad thoughts."[10]

Kenny compared the "unleashed public ire" caused by Casey's departure to "savage criticism of the Catholic clergy" in the early-twentieth-century rise of Irish nationalism. As Canadians reeled from more news of victims raised in orphanages and the O'Connor spectacle, Ireland saw the steady escalation of reports on priests who abused children or led double lives with men or women.

In Australia the greater focus was on orphanages and training schools, especially those run by the Irish Christian Brothers. In August of 1993, more than two hundred former residential students at the brothers' homes in Western Australia filed suit in New South Wales, alleging physical and sexual abuse as well as severe neglect. Facing a statute-of-limitations hurdle, the group eventually settled for $5 million.[11] In media accounts across Australia, men and women raised in such institutions spoke of lost families. "They were transported, in many cases, without the permission of parents or guardians, who by law should have been consulted," writes Alan Gill in *Orphans of the Empire*. "To modern eyes it smacks of abduction."[12]

Britain's removal of some ten thousand "orphaned" children to Australia between 1920 and 1967 rivaled Canada's "crazy quilt of adoption and fostering rules and regulations . . . [which] has not made it any easier for aboriginal children to find out who they are."[13] The Anglican Church and other denominations participated in training schools in Australia and Canada and eventually paid portions of settlement claims with the governments. The scope of abuses within the Irish Christian Brothers, from Ireland to Canada to Australia, was on another level altogether. Many brothers were untrained to care for children; some were emotional adolescents, or sociopaths. In 1935 an Australian brother had warned the superior general in Dublin: "If we do not take a determined stand with regard to this matter we are bound to have numerous scandals in the near future."[14] In 1938, the director of another Christian Brothers orphanage in Australia asked the Irish government to send children, and financial support; he was rebuffed. Throughout the 1990s, after the Canadian government paid settlements to the Mount Cashel victims, the Christian Brothers used an array of legal tactics to avoid making financial restitution.

Barry Coldrey's theory of a "sexual underworld" in clerical culture echoed in a 1998 House of Commons study on Britain's forced migrations of youths to Australia, which faulted "agencies of the Catholic Church, in particular the Christian Brothers and the Sisters of Mercy," for "the worst cases of criminal abuse."

> It is hard to convey the sheer weight of the testimony we have received. . . . Some of what was done there was of a quite exceptional depravity, so that terms like "sexual abuse" are too weak to convey it. For example . . . the account of a man who as a boy was a particular favorite of some Christian Brothers at Tardun who competed as to who could rape him 100 times first, his account of being in terrible pain, bleeding and bewildered. . . . [15]

As such information spread, a backlash was building among Irish Catholics.

Anticlericalism was nothing new to Pope John Paul; however, *Catholic* outrage toward priests in Western countries was a quantum leap from hostilities the church had weathered in the pope's lifetime. A clandestine seminarian in Poland during the Nazi darkness, and archbishop of Krakow in the long resistance to communism, his idea of church as moral opposition overrode any idea of structural change, such as moving to optional celibacy. By 1993, as various bishops made their *ad limina* trips to Rome—the every-fifth-year meeting with the pope to review life in a given diocese—John Paul was hearing about sexual abuse cases. Bishop Ronald Mulkearns of Ballarat, Australia, told the pope of his "nightmare" of eighteen months. "There has been serious hurt inflicted on many people," Mulkearns said in a pastoral letter.[16] "I admitted to the Holy Father that the past year has been by far the worst in my experience as a bishop."

> The pope was interested in and concerned about all of these issues and he reminded me of the experience of Christ and of the stress he

felt at Gethsemane and that "being in agony he prayed the longer."
I felt this was no trite response, nor pious platitude, but was the
successor of Peter confirming one of his brothers in the episcopate.

Mulkearns, who sought the laicization of a pedophile,[17] felt obliged to defend John Paul's remark about prayer. But the fall of bishops in Ireland, Canada, and New Mexico, and the requests of U.S. cardinals for quicker removal of abusers, did not move John Paul to a probing examination of *why* scandals were spreading. As papal biographer George Weigel points out, the pope in 1990 focused on the problem of vocations, insisting that seminaries be more rigorous, with a "demanding academic formation in philosophy and theology."[18] Weigel calls this a key reform, though the pope did not address psychology, or the homosexual dynamics in seminaries and religious orders, or the pervasive practices of concealing sex offenders in the ecclesiastical world.

As 1993 wore on, the church in New Mexico was jolted when a notorious priest surfaced as a secretary in an Albuquerque law firm. Lane Fontenot had left Louisiana in 1983, not laicized, for House of Affirmation in Massachusetts (which was run by a priest who was himself a child molester). From there Fontenot moved to Spokane, where he worked as a substance abuse counselor in a hospital until his 1986 arrest for abusing a teenage boy on the ward. After a year in jail, he went to the Servants of the Paraclete in New Mexico, trailed by lawsuits. After "treatment" with the Paracletes he got a job as a therapist in Albuquerque until he was sued in 1992 for making sexual advances on a client.[19]

With the Servants of the Paraclete trapped in lawsuits, some fascinating correspondence surfaced in a court file. In 1957, the Reverend Gerald Fitzgerald, founder of the order, had written Santa Fe's then archbishop, Edwin Byrne, saying he did not think it wise to "offer hospitality to men who have seduced or attempted to seduce little boys or girls."[20] Fitzgerald offered a remarkable foreshadowing of the tension in 1993 between Pope John Paul II and the American bishops over laicizing clergy sex offenders:

If I were a bishop I would tremble when I failed to report them to
Rome for involuntary laicization. Experience has taught us these
men are too often dangerous to the children of the parish and the

neighborhood for us to be justified in receiving them here. . . . They should ipso facto be reduced to lay men when they act thus.

The late Father Fitzgerald had gone so far as to purchase an empty island that he envisioned as a penitential limbo for pedophile priests; but officials in Rome forced him to sell the land. In 1966, the Paracletes opened a recovery program in Jemez Springs for alcoholics. A few years later the pedophiles began arriving.

George Weigel and Pio Laghi Weigh In

Clergy sex abuse is all but ignored in George Weigel's 992-page biography of John Paul, published in 1999.[21] Weigel was an American writer with rare access to the pope. He advised John Paul in spring 2002 when the U.S. cardinals went to the Vatican as the scandal exploded from Boston.

By then Pio Laghi had returned from Washington after a decade as papal envoy. During Laghi's years in America the bishops sent a stream of information on abusive clerics to the embassy. John Paul named Laghi prefect of the Congregation for Catholic Education, which has authority over seminaries, and made him a cardinal. What did the pope do with information in the early years of the scandal?

Laghi declined our interview request, though in a brief telephone discussion he cited the 1980s seminary investigation (conducted by Vermont bishop John Marshall, assisted by Donald Wuerl, now bishop of Pittsburgh): "I did not see those reports. They went straight to Rome."[22] That is hard to believe. The congregation monitored the visitation under its prefect, Cardinal William Wakefield Baum, the former archbishop of Washington, D.C., who was briefed on the abuse crisis by Father Doyle at the embassy. When asked about the report Doyle coauthored, Laghi snapped: "That is not my issue! Please, that's all! I cannot say anything else. . . . I was cut off."

In *The Courage to Be Catholic,* written in response to the 2002 crisis, George Weigel faults the 1980s seminary inquiry "because the visitation team included men who had been responsible for the meltdown in some seminaries in the decades immediately following Vatican II"—but he offers no names or other details.[23] Weigel writes: "The Church in the

United States expected that the Vatican was living through the American Catholic trauma of early 2002 in real-time, through adequate information from the Washington nunciature and the Internet. The Vatican wasn't, because the Vatican is simply not part of the Internet culture and the information flow from Washington was inadequate."[24]

Weigel's statement is preposterous. An "information flow" began with the 1985 report by Doyle and his colleagues. Doyle briefed Baum and the late Cardinal Oddi; Michael Peterson briefed Oddi in Rome. In 1989 canonists for the U.S. bishops began meeting their counterparts in Rome, while intelligence from far-flung papal nuncios and media coverage through the 1990s formed a river of information well before the *Boston Globe* reporting in 2002. Nor is the Vatican the poor stepchild of the digital age that Weigel would have us believe. The Holy See has a Web site; a modern press office at St. Peter's Square; a gracious staff assisting resident correspondents from the Associated Press, Catholic News Service, *Le Figaro,* and Italian and Japanese wire services; computers for visiting reporters; closed-circuit television for press conferences or coverage of the Holy Father's travels. The Vatican posts a daily digest of papal audiences and statements on the Internet. Many Vatican officials use e-mail, including sources for this book.

Rather than questioning John Paul's response, Weigel blames the bishops: "The inability of the U.S. bishops to come to effective grips with this problem in their own conference was paralleled by the evident unwillingness of many American bishops to speak openly and candidly about this problem to John Paul and the Curia."[25]

Contrary to Weigel's scapegoat theory, the crisis grew from a history of sexual secrecy demanded by the papacy. The pontifical vow cardinals take to protect the church from scandal had become an ethos of lying to the public about sexual crimes. Mulkearns of Australia (who later resigned in a swamp of bad news) was not alone in discussing child molesting with the pope. Catholic News Service reported that 1993 *ad limina* visits by Midwestern bishops "discussed a wide range of pastoral issues, including the shortage of clergy, priestly celibacy, pedophilia . . . and described the sessions as productive and encouraging—particularly their one-on-one meetings with the pope."[26] What was the result?

Journalist Robert Mickens was working at Vatican Radio in 1993 and reported on those visits. Broadcasts of that period have apparently not been preserved, according to an archival search made on our behalf. Mickens recalls that in early 1993 a Brazilian canonist at the Congregation for the Clergy, the Reverend Fernando Guimares Montera, "was collecting policies of individual dioceses for dealing with the problem."[27] Mickens never got Guimares on tape, though they spoke several times in passing. "Guimares was mystified that bishops were paying money in lawsuits," continues Mickens. "He said, 'It's a mess. All these policies around the world are different.' He couldn't believe how stupid the Americans were for paying all that money. He asked me, 'Why are they turning over records?' "—meaning church documents in civil litigation.

By then, the U.S. bishops' canonical team and Vatican counterparts had been wrangling for four years over a response beyond secret trials. John Paul knew that Sanchez was gone from New Mexico, Casey had left Ireland, and Newfoundland's archbishop had resigned amidst the Mount Cashel scandal. Canada's Bishop O'Connor stood indicted for rape. Honolulu bishop Joseph Ferrario was replaced in 1993 after a young man with AIDS—who had reported a history of abuse by Ferrario to Pio Laghi in 1986—gave public interviews. Ferrario denied the accusations.

Why did the pontiff most sophisticated in using mass media fail to resolve a crisis so damaging to the church? The most charitable answer is that John Paul saw no crisis *because he had no contact with victims*. He cared about them in the abstract; but his vision of the church's purifying truth held no room for a fearless introspection of the clerical state. He responded by demanding secret penal trials and lecturing bishops.

In March 1993, he denounced "selectivity in adhering to authoritative church teaching" and urged bishops to "rise above the clash of conflicting opinions with the forcefulness and power of truth." Those words echoed a 1989 Vatican order requiring theologians to take a fidelity oath: "I shall preserve the deposit of faith in its entirety . . . whatsoever teachings are contrary, I shall shun."[28] John Paul's insistence on obedience to truth, as defined by Rome, overrode freedom of inquiry by theologians. Dissent inside the church captured his concern and shaped his prism on clergy sexual behavior. "Under our penal process, when a priest expresses sorrow, it derails the process," Bishop (later Cardinal) Adam Maida wrote in 1990. "If he seeks reconciliation, in Canon Law we may give him absolution and say, 'sin no more.' . . . We are limited because a diocese cannot proceed to a final determination of laicizing a priest."[29]

John Paul's idealization of church truth stood out in high relief from the sinned against, the abuse victims whose U.S. numbers Andrew Greeley in 1993 estimated at one hundred thousand.[30] Ignoring abuse survivors sent a huge signal to his bishops. A meeting, even a symbolic gesture by the Holy Father, has long reverberations. When the Vatican released *Shoah: We Remember,* John Paul visited a synagogue in reconciliation. Bishops in many countries began apologizing to Jews. Several bishops in various countries have had listening sessions with clergy abuse survivors. By spring 2003 the pope had not.

Bishops had reason to be skeptical about secret penal cases. "We've been involved in one dismissal proceeding for eight years," the Reverend Mike Jamail, a Houston psychologist, said in 1993. "The man has been suspended from ministry. We're paying all his medical and salary. I told my bishop in the beginning, 'Expect it to take ten years.' He didn't believe me."[31]

The Holy See's process showed its features in a more baroque dispute.

In the same week of 1993 that American bishops were meeting with John Paul, the Apostolic Signatura—the Vatican's highest court—issued a secret March 9 ruling that *revoked* the suspension of a Pittsburgh priest facing a civil trial for sexual abuse. On March 12, a copy of the nine-page document, in Latin, rolled off a fax machine in the *Pittsburgh Post-Gazette* newsroom addressed to Ann Rodgers-Melnick, an astute religion reporter with a master of theological studies degree. The attorney representing the priest had received his copy by fax from the priest's canonical counsel in Italy. Pittsburgh was mired in a fierce snowstorm, with traffic at a standstill. Rodgers-Melnick called the bishop's office, hoping for a translation. "You have *what?*" a spokesman said.[32] The secret document was making its way from Rome to Washington by diplomatic pouch, whence it would be sent on to Bishop Donald Wuerl. Rodgers-Melnick faxed her copy to the bishop. The bishop's canon lawyer walked a mile through snowdrifts from his rectory to the bishop's house. Wuerl was anxious to confer with him on how to fight the decision.

Rodgers-Melnick, meanwhile, asked the Reverend Ladislas Orsy, a renowned professor of canon law at Catholic University, for help. He gave her an oral interpretation of the key parts of the decision. (Orsy has since moved to the faculty at Georgetown.)

The dispute had begun in 1988, when Bishop Wuerl removed the Reverend Anthony Cipolla from a chaplain's position after a nineteen-year-old man sued the priest and the diocese for childhood sexual abuse. Wuerl was initially skeptical because the accuser, a former seminarian, had made charges against others. The prosecutor refused to indict Cipolla.

Wuerl ordered Cipolla to St. Luke Institute, which recommended that he not work with children and go to a psychiatric hospital in Pennsylvania. Cipolla refused. In response, Wuerl suspended Cippola's right to administer the sacraments and forbade him to dress as a priest. Wuerl wrote the Congregation for the Clergy, in Rome: "It would be morally impossible to assign Father Cipolla, who is in need of serious psychological treatment, to pastoral care of the faithful."[33] Later the young man's attorney unearthed a police report from 1978, which stated that Cipolla had fondled a nine-year-old boy in the nude.

Cipolla was a popular speaker among followers of Padre Pio, the Italian mystic whose stigmata made him a cult figure and a saint. "Many people who know Cipolla through his Padre Pio work have written to Wuerl on Cipolla's behalf," Ann Rodgers-Melnick wrote. "The court record indicates that the Vatican also received such letters."

Cipolla went to a facility that decided he did not need hospitalization or medication. He then engaged one Count Neri Capponi, a canon law professor in Florence and a seasoned figure at the Vatican courts, to appeal the Congregation for the Clergy's acceptance of the suspension.

Canon law has a unique place in Italy. At the Pontifical Lateran University, in Rome, some seven hundred students were pursuing degrees in canon law in 2002—most of them lay men and women. According to the Lateran's canon law faculty dean, Monsignor Brian Ferme, lay canonists can earn $20,000 or more from clients in complex marriage annulments or in divorces with special property issues, a function usually done by civil attorneys in common-law countries.[34] Count Capponi in his appeal to the Apostolic Signatura challenged "a decree of His Excellency, the Bishop of Pittsburgh." The count argued that "the Rev. Cipolla is entirely sane, both in mind and body. . . . There are so many psychological and psychiatric systems which . . . [are] simply alien to any Christian anthropology." Capponi charged that the bishop misused a canon on mentally ill priests and failed to follow proper procedure. Moreover:

> The St. Luke's Institute, a clinic founded by a priest who is openly homosexual and based on a mixed doctrine composed of Freudian pan-sexualism and behaviorism, is surely not a suitable institution apt to judge rightly about the beliefs and the lifestyle of a Catholic priest. . . . This behavioristic tendency becomes all the more sinister when linked to the reigning myths of our totally secularized society and to a pan-sexualism which could only consider "abnormal" the traditional behavior of a Catholic priest.

The Signatura overruled the Congregation for the Clergy. "Father Cipolla is fully exonerated," Orsy, the scholar, told the *Post-Gazette*. "The decision is quite harsh on the bishop. It explicitly says a number of times that he did not observe procedure and he did not consider the evidence properly." Others saw a sign of Rome's distance from reality. "The Signatura has made a terrible mistake," said Andrew Greeley. "If they want to do all in their power to destroy the church in the United States, they've done it. If this becomes a precedent, they will have to reassign to parishes all these pedophile priests. I assume that all the higher powers or cardinals would go off to Rome"—and protest.[35]

Capponi's reference to the nameless St. Luke founder as a practicing homosexual six years after Peterson's funeral was a tabloid brush stroke to put frowns on Signatura judges as they read the count's strange characterization of the hospital to which bishops and religious superiors increasingly turned as the crisis grew. St. Luke's president, the Reverend Canice Connors, issued a statement:

> While we must respect the confidential nature of the records of all our patients, because Father Cipolla has chosen to make his record public, we can say that there was more than sufficient evidence according to our lengthy and scientific evaluation procedures, to recommend to the Diocese of Pittsburgh that Father Cipolla be treated at St. John Vianney psychiatric hospital.[36]

Bishop Wuerl flew to Washington, met with the papal pronuncio, Archbishop Agostino Cacciavillan, and petitioned the Signatura to reopen the case. Wuerl's request that the court allow his own canonist to rebut Capponi's petition highlighted the surreal Vatican justice system, which never told the bishop that his decision was under appeal! The seven-page verdict had made no reference to the civil lawsuit pending. "In the European legal system," Father Orsy explained, "if there are no criminal charges, you can have no civil suit. Perhaps it did not occur to [Signatura judges] that there was a civil suit. They may not have thought to ask."[37] The Signatura immediately accepted Wuerl's petition and reinstated his suspension of Cipolla.

The lawsuit against the priest and diocese was settled out of court.

Cipolla soon popped up on the Eternal Word Television Network, vested in violet, dispensing Holy Communion. "The guy was just passing through," the network president stated when told about Cipolla's status. "A poor priest has the right to say Mass, doesn't he?" In the fall of 1995 the Signatura reversed itself, upheld Wuerl's decision, and broadened the canonical definition of "psychic defect"—meaning that a priest who was not insane could be suspended for a "general mental disorder."[38]

Despite his suspension, Cipolla continued to lead retreats and pilgrimages abroad, maintaining his popularity with Catholics who considered him a victim of a hierarchy indifferent to his cry for restoring true faith.[39] In May 2002, after Cipolla was recognized saying Mass in a church in Rome, Wuerl petitioned the Congregation for the Doctrine of the Faith to ask the pope to dismiss Cipolla from the priesthood. His request was granted in November 2002.[40]

"Rome was in denial in the mid-nineties," remarked Barry M. Coldrey, the historian and Christian Brother in Australia. Coldrey routinely sent copies of his research on the abuse crisis to Vatican congregations and the papal nuncio in Australia. "People in Rome, the well-disposed ones, do have the truth and access to it. What they do with it—well, the Lord has not drawn me into that."[41]

Although Pope John Paul did not give the bishops greater authority to expel priests, he did approve an accommodation in canon law for the U.S. bishops on April 25, 1994, that modified two procedures in dealing with sexual abuse allegations. The statute of limitations in canon law was increased from five years to ten years, beginning after the victim turned eighteen; and the age of a minor was raised from anyone under age sixteen to anyone under eighteen.[42] Although the changes put canon law on a closer footing with U.S. civil law, there was no investigation of the crisis or the underlying causes.

In Canada the victims of Bishop Hubert O'Connor drew him into a healing circle, a tradition of the First Nations people. O'Connor was cleared of charges that he raped the woman who had borne the child given up for adoption. He was released on bail after serving six months for rape of the second woman, Marilyn Belleau. Belleau withdrew her charges on condition that the bishop participate in the communal rite. In a meeting hall at Alkali Lake in British Columbia, O'Connor sat with his successor, Bishop Gerry Wiesner, amidst the scent of sage smoke in a pipe-passing ceremony. Belleau, a mother of seven, spoke at length about the impact of O'Connor's violations.[42] O'Connor, who had never admitted criminal guilt, apologized for "my breach as a priest . . . which was totally wrong. I took a vow of chastity and I broke it." Belleau spoke in a choked voice of "being victimized by the courts" and her decision "to participate in this healing circle to empower myself."

Thirty-eight people spoke during the seven-hour ritual; no one was allowed to interrupt. "As a Catholic bishop I am ashamed of the violations that were actually committed by Catholic people in a school that taught Catholic values and beliefs," Wiesner said during the ceremony. "We find wisdom in aboriginal spiritual traditions for restorative justice and reconciliation."

Charlene Belleau, a sister-in-law of Marilyn, explained that in dropping the charges, "It is our preference to sit face to face with these people and let them know how they've really had an impact on our people, on our women, on our men, on our boys, on our children. Your system doesn't allow for that."[43]

Chapter Six

MEMORIES OF THE
CARDINAL

THE ROAD THAT led Steve Rubino into Tom Doyle's life began on a beach facing the Atlantic Ocean a few blocks from the lawyer's home in Margate, New Jersey. In 1987, the thirty-eight-year-old Rubino was enjoying a day on the shore when a friend asked if he would meet her sister. She had a serious problem: a priest had sexually abused her son. *This could not happen*, thought Rubino.[1]

He had litigated for plaintiffs in Superfund pollution cases and spent years on a class action representing women who had been poisoned by toxic substances in the Dalkon Shield intrauterine device. Rubino was a Republican who grew up in a working-class area of northeast Washington, D.C. His father worked as a dispatcher and mechanic in a heating oil business. Priests were dinner guests at their home. An altar boy at the National Shrine of the Immaculate Conception, Rubino was eleven when a kid tied up a cat with rope in order to torture the animal. Rubino slugged him in the face and set the cat free.

A 1967 graduate from Gonzaga, the Jesuit high school in Washington, he earned a B.A. at Mount St. Mary's College in Maryland. With a law degree from Catholic University, he became a prosecutor in Florida, building cases against drug dealers and violent criminals. Drawn to the spiraling technology of databases, he began a business in contract legal research with an expertise in environmental issues. That led to a job with a plaintiff's firm in New Jersey, which had plenty of pollution. His career was on a predictable path until he met the thirteen-year-old boy who had been assaulted sexually by Father Jack McElroy of the Camden diocese over a period of eighteen months.

The mother reported the priest to the police. Some details of the assault were so ghastly the victim could not tell his mother; he did tell his lawyer. *Priests don't do things like this,* Rubino thought. McElroy confessed, recanted, went to trial and then to prison. Rubino did a search of case law, legal literature, news articles, and sought advice from attorneys in other states. New Jersey was one of the few states with a charitable immunity law exempting churches and volunteer organizations from negligence suits. Nevertheless, Rubino sent a letter to the Camden diocese demanding $700,000 for his young client. To his surprise the church put up no fight. The diocese's insurance carriers negotiated a structured annuity with funds spread over a number of years. *They don't want to put the immunity law to a test,* he reasoned.

The agreement required a court appearance by counsel for the two parties; a short notice ran in *The Philadelphia Inquirer.* Another victim of McElroy called Rubino. In short order he wrote to the Camden diocese, this time demanding $800,000. Once again, the church agreed to settle.

Rubino was intrigued—and troubled. The church's share of each settlement, which he calculated at 15 percent, came from money that people like his parents, and well-heeled Catholics like himself, put in the Sunday basket or donated to the bishop. You don't pay large sums with the law on your side unless you have something to hide. As more victims found their way to him, Rubino the ex-prosecutor suspected that several New Jersey dioceses were shrouding a culture of sexual criminals. In 1992, when Rubino opened his own firm with a partner, Ed Ross, a fourth of the case load dealt with victims of priests. Most of the priests were not prosecuted; the victims were too old. Most cases were never filed as torts, but settled out of court as personal injury cases.

When people sought his help, Rubino said: "The only thing I can get for you is money, and that is not going to make you feel any different at the end of the case. What you've got to do is recover and learn to live well."

His clients came from broken homes and perfect homes; the parents felt huge guilt. "I haven't missed a chapter in the book of depravity,"

Rubino brooded in a 1993 interview. "There are aspects to this that still shock me because of my conservative upbringing. I had a case that involved a fistfight between two priests over a fourteen-year-old boy."[2] With his home and family in walking distance from the shore and his law office, Steve Rubino experienced clouds of horror, questions he never before dreamed. *What happened to these bishops? Why so many perpetrators? What has gone wrong with the Catholic Church?*

In late 1992, he contacted Father Thomas Doyle at his new posting, Hurlburt Field, in Fort Walton Beach, Florida. The base on the Gulf of Mexico lay in a stretch of beaches with pristine sand and emerald waters. Flying airplanes avocationally, Doyle had also discovered the wonders of scuba diving. Rubino asked if they could meet. "Anytime you want," said the voice at the other end of the line. "Come on down."

When the rental car reached the small house on the air base, Steve Rubino, with a wrestler's build and receding hairline, was torn in spirit. Like every good lawyer he wanted to know all the dirt about an opponent—and that fueled his question: Why should I stay Catholic?

Doyle, in a Hawaiian shirt, greeted him with an easy smile. Rubino was struck by the size of his library: books on church history, canon law, military history, the neat shelves mirroring a personality ruled by precision. As they became acquainted, Rubino realized he had grown up a few blocks from the Dominican House of Studies, where Doyle had lived while working at the embassy. Rubino laid out his frustration. He wasn't surprised that the defense tactics were getting tougher—corporate defendants act that way. What gnawed at his insides was the cold, imperious assumption that when a priest violated a kid, the church rallied to defend, hide, and reassign that priest. This was not the Roman Catholic Church that Steve Rubino knew.

"You've got to get something out of your head," said Doyle. "The hierarchy is *not* the church. *We* are the church—the survivors, you, and me."

"That's not the program I got growing up, Tom." Rubino was raised to see priests as extraordinary human beings who chose love of the church, under the bishops, forsaking the love of a woman and having a family. "Nobody ever told me they were a bunch of fucking corrupt thieves," he simmered.

"Get over it!" laughed Doyle.

For all of his bullish tenacity as a lawyer, Rubino could not easily get over it. Doyle liked toughness and saw that in Rubino. He also saw a man in spiritual pain, and he responded with a primer on Vatican II's visionary concept of the laity as People of God, rank-and-file believers as important as bishops in expressing God's love. Rubino's work for victims had to be done, said Doyle; he was helping people find justice and forcing the church to find its own moral bearings. The sexual crisis mirrored the calcified mentality of the Vatican and bishops who saw themselves as owners of a truth everyone else must follow.

"You don't pay money and lay down if the bishop had no responsibility," said Rubino.

"There's been a cover-up for years. That's why they're willing to pay."

"What kind of cover-up?" asked Rubino.

Doyle returned to the People of God concept. The hierarchy thought of themselves, and the priesthood, as a superior caste. The bishops were obsessed with secrecy because sexual intimacy was forbidden. "The good of the church" was a stock phrase hierarchs used in trying to keep parents quiet—in reality, trying to muzzle people so the church could conceal its corruption. As long as they could keep "scandal" quiet, they would pay—and betray the People of God. "If the bishops dealt with the problem publicly, for the benefit of victims, we wouldn't have this crisis," said Doyle. "They don't know how to be honest."

Rubino hadn't read a theology book in years, but "People of God," a familiar phrase, made sense. He wondered aloud at how much good Doyle could do the church if he weren't tucked away on an air base in the Florida panhandle.

"They shit-canned me," muttered Doyle.

Rubino had seen bitterness in cops and prosecutors who worked hard to put criminals away; but they had staffs and often worked in teams. He had never met anyone like this priest in his loud, floral shirt asking pointed questions about New Jersey dioceses, especially the bishops—a priest allied with abuse survivors against the hierarchy, a man personally standing up against evil.

Rubino wanted to understand the mentality of the bishops. As Americans, as priests, how did they morally justify reassigning a McElroy, a Porter, a Gauthe?

Doyle cited church canons that dealt with penalties for sexual abuse of minors, including a secret trial process that can lead to a priest being defrocked.

He laced his comments with barbs about the bishops—*"They damn well know what's wrong; they don't have the guts to face it."* Steve Rubino weighed his own bruised spirituality against Tom Doyle's anger. This guy should be a bishop, a cardinal, he thought. Watching the complicated soldier-priest redefine his relationship with the church made Rubino feel humble. And so, like a smart lawyer, he changed the subject. He told Doyle that in the Dalkon Shield litigation, it had taken years to unearth incriminating documents. In the Catholic Church cases, he said, "I'm seeing a pattern—obstruction of justice."

"You're doing the right thing," replied Doyle. Church law gave the bishop the option to protect a priest. Canon 1341 held that only after the bishop had ascertained that "scandal cannot be repaired" should he remove a priest. That did not stop another bishop from accepting a child molester, even if forewarned. The problem was preserving sexually dysfunctional men in a culture of clerical privilege. Clericalism—the pursuit of ecclesiastical power at the expense of laypeople—fueled the recycling of perpetrators across the geography of the surfacing scandal. Canon law had its loopholes. The concept of "fraternal correction" was riddled with abuse, as it allowed a bishop to forgive a priest with scant concern for those sinned against, the violated children and families who would reel in the aftershocks for years to come. Doyle was clear in his belief: the hierarchy's obsession with protecting priests flouted the People of God.

"Keep banging away," said Doyle. "We have got to persist in this so they will see that *we* are the church—not *them*."

Words and Acts

On June 17, 1993, after four years of secret discussions with Rome, the U.S. bishops publicly formed a committee to study procedures for removing priests and reaching out to victims. When Barbara Blaine and other survivor leaders met with a contingent of bishops, Cardinal Roger Mahony of Los Angeles called it "one of the most moving experiences I have ever known."[3] In a letter to the bishops the pope said: "I fully share your sorrow and your concern, especially . . . for the victims."[4] Back in

Los Angeles a priest named Michael Wempe was a chaplain at Cedars-Sinai Medical Center, whose officials did not know Mahony had sent him to a treatment facility after he molested two young boys in 1988. Not until news revelations in 2002 did Mahony sack Wempe.[5]

Following the 1993 news in Fort Walton Beach, Tom Doyle knew church leaders would respond only to pressure. Cardinal O'Connor, a former rear admiral in the Navy, had said: "It's long since time to get on our knees, to beat our breasts, to ask God's mercy"—yet after a New York priest pleaded guilty to sodomizing a sixteen-year-old boy, church attorneys replied to a civil suit saying that the boy "willingly consented." In Philadelphia, under Doyle's old friend Cardinal Bevilacqua, the parents of a young man abused in adolescence were countersued for failure to learn of it at the time. "Church lawyers blame plaintiffs' lawyers for trying their cases in the press," *The Wall Street Journal* noted. "Still, some can't get past the irony of the church's iron-fisted response."[6]

Doyle saw bishops using defense attorneys like codependent glue. He became friends with Rubino, sharing his outrage and admiring his tenacity. Rubino had settled twenty-five cases, with another forty under way. (He had also turned down seventy-five because of the statute of limitations.) In 1990 he had won a $2.3 million settlement for a Camden victim. In June 1993, Rubino filed a federal racketeering suit against New Jersey bishops, dioceses, and the national bishops conference in Washington. One of the plaintiffs, Gary Hayes, was a priest who had been abused as an altar boy. The suit charged that two older priests created a ring to abuse children. Rubino was hammering at the structural dynamics, how the clerical system protected criminals. Church attorneys negotiated an out-of-court settlement in the Hayes case.

In late summer of 1993 Rubino approached the Cincinnati archdiocese on behalf of a thirty-two-year-old man stricken with AIDS. Steven Cook lived outside Philadelphia. As his immune system eroded he underwent hypnosis for pain caused by dysentery. During hypnosis he began recalling sexual encounters with a priest when he was sixteen. A law student referred him to Rubino.

Cincinnati is built on seven hills. The east side has trendy coffeehouses, neighborhood names like Indian Hill, and Victorian homes that overlook a quilt of warehouses. Cook grew up in the largely blue-collar west side. Cincinnati is Ohio's archdiocese. The seminary complex called the Athenaeum sits on a hill, with Tuscan columns and breeze-ways, exuding a neoclassical aura. Steve Cook spent weekends at the seminary in 1975 as a high school sophomore, in a program to foster future priests. His parents had a printing business; he had an older sister and a grandfather he adored. At seven he had become an altar boy. At Elder Catholic High he sang in the glee club, but was largely self-effacing. Alienated from his father, who worked two jobs, he resisted telling his mother about a sixteen-year-old boy with whom he had an awakening sex life. At about that time he met Ellis Harsham.

Father Harsham taught biology at the seminary and was known for having parties with booze, pot, and pornographic films. Greg Flannery, a seminarian in 1974–75, attended a party where Harsham showed "a film of a woman having sex with a German shepherd. . . . I spent the time looking at the floor. It made me feel dirty."[7] Flannery, who never knew Cook, left the seminary in disappointment over the loose moral tone. The archbishop of Cincinnati back then was Joseph Bernardin. Rubino was curious: how much did Bernardin know about Harsham?

Cook entered the seminary in 1977 just as Harsham moved to a high school. Cook quit seminary studies in 1979, realizing he was gay. In 1980 his father was killed in a traffic accident. Graduating cum laude from Xavier University in 1981, Steven left town on a wave of sex and drugs. Arrested in 1985 for drug possession in Philadelphia, he got into recovery in lieu of a jail term, and eventually became a rehabilitation counselor.

Cincinnati archbishop Daniel Pilarczyk's 1993 *Decree on Child Abuse* called for an investigation in tandem with civil authorities, with the chancellor putting the accused on leave. In August of 1993 Rubino contacted the chancellor of the archdiocese, the Reverend Daniel Conlon. On September 1, Father Conlon had an emotional six-hour meeting with Rubino and Cook. In addition to mentioning Harsham's conduct, Cook said he had met with Bernardin at the time. Rubino subsequently wrote Conlon: "I am gravely concerned with his inability to remember some of the specifics"—what Cook believed occurred in Bernardin's private quarters. "Steven is pursuing these memories with the time that he has remaining, but as a matter of human decency, I would suggest that Father Harsham has an irrevocable duty to come forward with the truth."[8]

A month later Conlon wrote to say that the accusation against Harsham had not been "substantiated at this time." The decree would not be implemented; but the archdiocese would help with therapy costs since Harsham had admitted

> *expressing his affection with hugs but remembers no kissing. . . . Harsham acknowledges that there was much casual sexual banter between Mr. Cook and himself and that on one occasion he provided Mr. Cook with a portion of a pornographic film. . . . He denies that there was any sexual contact with Mr. Cook or that he took him to x-rated theatres or nude dancing clubs or . . . provided him with marijuana or other psychotropic drugs.*

The letter continued, a virtual invitation to be sued.

> *Father Harsham admits (and this is confirmed by others) that he was removed from the seminary faculty at the end of the 1976–1977 academic year because of an incident of sexual behavior with an adult seminarian. My investigation has shown no indication that seminary or diocesan authorities had knowledge of inappropriate sexual activity on Father Harsham's part prior to that date.*

Harsham was in counseling and would be reevaluated, the chancellor noted. But Conlon had opened Harsham's credibility to attack. Had Archbishop Pilarczyk settled with Cook, there would have been no lawsuit, and Rubino's veiled threat about "pursing memories" of Bernardin would have been sealed away. But Pilarczyk, the only prelate to call his policy a "decree," would have none of that. "Father Harsham denies ever taking Mr. Cook to visit Archbishop Bernardin in his private quarters," wrote Conlon, calling it "implausible."

Delayed memory *was* controversial—the idea that trauma victims can bury recollections too painful to cope with and realize them gradually, or in spontaneous recall years later. Most clergy cases did not turn on repressed memory; though as Dr. Bessel van der Kolk, a psychiatrist at Harvard Medical School who worked with trauma victims, noted: "A lot of the Porter victims had delayed memories."[9] Memory is always open to suspicion. Forgetting—selective remembering—happens as people age. Memories come from "bodily sensations to which you attach a story," said van der Kolk. "But the story may or may not be what truly represents these sensations."

Steve Cook was angered by Conlon's letter; he was also in despair over his advancing AIDS. Images about Bernardin washed across his thought field—sexual images, himself as victim. Was he truly remembering? Cook had a book he said Bernardin had given him. Rubino felt that for all his fragmented memories, Steven was being truthful. After years of legal battles with the church, Rubino was appalled at the ecclesiastical culture. In his AIDS-ravaged client he saw the wreckage of church crimes. After Cincinnati's stiff-arm, Rubino would not call Chicago archdiocesan attorneys to seek a negotiation. He had followed the countersuits in Chicago against the two families in litigation with the Northbrook pastor; a private detective had sifted through garbage, seeking dirt on people who had already paid hell before their day in court.

Tom Doyle was just as repulsed by the defense tactics in Chicago. He thought Bernardin was more concerned about his image than about a truthful reckoning with sexual dynamics in the priesthood; still, Bernardin had removed twenty-three priests, something no other prelate had done. His commission's report, though flawed by prejudging the Northbrook case, was more than any other diocese had done. After speaking with Cook several times by telephone, Doyle agreed to be a witness in his behalf. Convinced of Harsham's guilt, Doyle was far less certain about Bernardin. His testimony would be predicated on evidence Rubino would provide.

Doyle's ambivalence about Bernardin mirrored his doubts about the hierarchy. From his house on the air base he could walk to white sands along the Gulf of Mexico, serene with sensations of God's beauty. Doyle was a soldier now in more ways than one. Legal battles were spreading and he accepted his role in that war. In his misgivings about Bernardin, he didn't know what to believe.

Another legal situation clouded Bernardin's past. A young man in North Dakota claimed to have been abused in the early 1980s, as a seminarian, by a bishop in the Winona, Minnesota, diocese at a wild party with other bishops present, Bernardin among them. Nothing was on record; several lawyers knew about the allegations, including Jeffrey Anderson, who had declined to take the case. The young man in that case could make a powerful witness for Cook.

Rubino's lawsuit said that in October 1993 Cook "began to recall sexual abuse committed against him by defendant Bernardin when he was a minor." The complaint charged Harsham with abusing Cook as a teenager; giving him marijuana, alcohol, and pornography; and taking him into the archbishop's private quarters, where Bernardin, allegedly, had sex with him. Rubino timed the filing in Cincinnati for Friday, November 12, 1993, to coincide with the national bishops' convention the following week in Washington.

CNN had been working on a documentary about the larger scandal, to air Sunday, the fourteenth. When reporter Bonnie Anderson contacted Rubino among lawyers on her list, he offered an exclusive interview with Cook. As word of the suit leaked out, Mary Ann Ahern of WMAQ-TV, Chicago's NBC affiliate, called Bernardin, who had not seen the pleading. "There is one thing I do know," he said firmly, "and I state this categorically: I have never abused anyone in all my life, anywhere, anytime, anyplace."

The next day Harsham denied the allegations to reporters at his Dayton parish.

Cardinal Bernardin spoke at a press conference in Chicago, carried live on many stations. "Everything that is in that suit about me, the allegations, are *totally* untrue," he stated in a calm tone, standing before a reef of microphones. "I'm very comforted by the thousands of calls and faxes I'm receiving."[10] Indeed, first lady Hillary Rodham Clinton had called him expressing her support.

Bernardin asked the assembled reporters to "keep me in your prayers."

What did he think when he learned of the charges?

"I was flabbergasted. *How could this be?* I was more saddened than anything. . . . I'm more concerned about my people." He did not plan to step down until the trial, though he would abide by whatever decision the Office of Professional Fitness Review he had established should make.

"My life is an open book," said the cardinal as cameras clicked. Someone asked the inevitable: *How does it feel?* He turned to face the questioner. "I'm hurt. I'm a human being"—he put his palms on his chest—"I do have feelings. I have a heart."

Had he ever been accused before? "I've been a priest for forty-two years," he began, "and a bishop for twenty-eight years. . . . And you know, it's inevitable that anyone who is in a public position and who takes stands that are controversial is vulnerable. Accusations will be made. But it's interesting, only three accusations have been made against me, all within the current year—"

"*What were the other two?*" a journalist cut in.

He nodded, with a hard sigh. "One was from a lady outside the state trying to implicate me in a satanic rite that allegedly took place thirty-five, thirty-six years ago. The other allegation was from a young man in another state who accused me and several others of engaging in some kind of orgy with him.

"And *those*"—he gave a terse chuckle—"are *totally* false." A follow-up question began. "That's all I want to say"—he shut his eyelids momentarily—"about that."

A reporter asked if he was sexually active. He gave a faint smile. "I'm sixty-five years old. I can tell you that all my life I've lived a chaste and celibate life."

He emphasized that he could not recall meeting Steven Cook. Here was the issue, framed. Should the public believe a cardinal professing lifelong chastity, or a young homosexual dying of AIDS? Bernardin said he knew nothing of a photograph that showed them standing together. An archbishop shakes hands with countless people, he explained; he could not deny that he may have met Cook.

Bernardin handled himself brilliantly, showing grace under pressure.

Within an hour CNN was cutting between Bernardin's comments and portions of Bonnie Anderson's interview with Cook. "I remember going into his private quarters," said Cook. "We drank some Pepsis. I was given some very nice gifts, and then I was led into his bedroom and he performed anal sex on me." Cook's chin wobbled; he lowered his face. He had sandy hair, fair features, and a brown mustache. He wiped away tears. "I don't really know if you can put words to describe it, what that pain is like. It shatters your world, it shatters your soul, it shatters your life." He showed anger. "I want to see the church rid itself of this kind of vermin, this kind of evil!" He asked for others who were used "and raped by him to come forward and tell their story."

A former NBC correspondent in Beirut, Anderson asked if he would be receptive to a settlement. Cook cut her off. "I have found my voice. No one's going to buy me. I won't accept anything less than his resignation and a public apology."

In Dayton, an hour's drive from Cincinnati, Ellis Harsham was head of campus ministry at Wright State University. Students and members of his parish held a prayer vigil. His attorney called the charges "slanderous." Pilarczyk, the only bishop with a Ph.D. in classics, called the lawsuit "rubbish and deserving of nothing but contempt." Vatican Radio attacked the suit as "filthy and worthy of disdain." A S.N.A.P. statement said: "This type of hostile language serves no one—not the plaintiff, not the cardinal and certainly not the church."[11] Vatican Radio issued a clarification: it had been quoting Pilarczyk.

Jeanne Miller called on Bernardin to step aside under his archdiocesan policy, but with Cook unwilling to speak to the Fitness Review Board, it stood by the cardinal. S.N.A.P.'s David Clohessy reiterated how hard it was for any survivor to stand up against the church; Barbara Blaine praised Bernardin for his restraint. As Clohessy watched Bernardin stop to answer reporters (so unlike Porter, who had run from cameras), he thought: *The cardinal is not acting like a guilty man.*

From Ireland, where he was traveling, Father Greeley stated: "I do not believe the charges. . . . We [in the church] have protected the guilty for so long we find it very difficult to protect the innocent. . . . It's open season on priests."

"False memory" became a mantra in the media as comparisons arose with the Salem witch trials. Columnists weighed in behind Bernardin. Almost overnight, the scandal of bishops sheltering child abusers transmogrified into a media parable on memory. The mind's vagaries and quack therapists were now the issue. *Time* featured a cover with Freud's face disassembling like a picture puzzle. Buoyed by support from Rome, Bernardin entered the bishops' meeting in Washington to a standing ovation from the episcopal body he had worked so hard to build. In applauding him they were applauding themselves, shepherds who had too long been pummeled by lawsuits and bullied by the media. The tide of public opinion was turning against a tabloid culture too quick to coddle accusers.

Yet even as Bernardin took comfort in the applause and expressions of affection in his daily duties, the accusations, as his friend Eugene Kennedy wrote, "had hit him hard, had wounded him in soul and spirit."[12] To Kennedy and his wife, the cardinal confided, "I wake up in the middle of the night and I am seated in the witness box as all these spurious accusations are made over and over again"—a nightmare eerily similar to the ones of Mark Brooks, the ex-seminarian in San Diego, though in his dreams, everyone was naked.

Bernardin's attorneys asked for a quick trial; the judge complied. An accelerated discovery process began. Rubino was trying to get information from a young man in North Dakota—the ex-seminarian in Minnesota whose attorney had negotiated an out-of-court settlement said to be $70,000. A Chicago archdiocesan source told Berry that travel records proved Bernardin had not been at the Winona seminary on the dates in question. Attorney Serritella denied that the archdiocese had paid anything in resolving the dispute. This was the "orgy" charge to which Bernardin referred in his news conference.

Rubino's hopes that news coverage would embolden other victims to come forward were partially realized on November 20, when the *Dayton Daily News* reported that three men who had played football at Carroll High in the early 1970s said Father Harsham approached them sexually. After that report, three more men contacted the paper.[13] Two said Harsham "had oral sex with them in the early 1970s, after they turned to him for counseling when they were teenagers . . . [and] used pornography in his efforts to persuade them to have sex."

Harsham challenged the men, "if they believe these allegations," to report them to the archdiocese. The Decree on Child Abuse had no provision for anonymous complaints. As stories on Harsham spilled out, a church spokesman asked victims to contact Father Conlon—which Cook had done, to no avail.

With reporters digging away at Cook's past, Steve Rubino sat in a hospital, where his wife had given birth to a boy. Checking calls, he learned that WLS-TV Chicago had unearthed a 1984 physician's evaluation of Cook at the time of his Philadelphia drug arrest and court-ordered recovery program. To the question *Have there been any incidents of sexual abuse during your lifetime?* Cook had written: "At age 16, a couple of priests used to get me drunk & try to suck me off." WLS portrayed the document as a smoking gun—Cook hadn't forgotten his abuse. Rubino pointed out that Cook had said "priests," not "archbishop," on the form; but he knew trouble when he saw it. With memory at issue, if Cook remembered in 1984, how could he have forgotten by 1993?

"My heart goes out to him," said Bernardin of his accuser. "I have a great desire to meet him. I want to pray with him and comfort him."[14]

With CNN fighting a motion by Bernardin's lawyers to obtain videotapes from the Cook interviews, the cardinal's attorneys took the deposition of Cook's hypnotist. Though she had some training, she was not a licensed hypnotist and had had no idea that her two sessions to help him through dysentery pain would put her in a legal crossfire. She had not taped the sessions or documented Cook's memory before, during, and after the sessions. Her deposition was a blow to Cook's case. More devastating was the revelation that Cook had been hypnotized by a qualified therapist in Cincinnati in the late 1970s and said nothing about Bernardin. Cook withdrew the allegations against Bernardin on the last day of February 1994, telling a news conference: "I now realize that the memories which arose during and after hypnosis are unreliable. I can no longer proceed in good conscience."

Asked if he had made a mistake suing the cardinal, Rubino said, "Looking in hindsight, yes."[15]

Though Rubino made his mistakes, Cook's failure to tell his attorney full details of his past—particularly the early hypnosis sessions—would have made it difficult to name Bernardin as a defendant. The allegations against Bernardin never should have been filed; but Rubino's client was half right. The substance of the original complaint—that Harsham abused Cook—led to an out-of-court settlement with the Cincinnati archdiocese. On that, Rubino delivered for his client. Cardinal Bernardin achieved a reconciliation with Cook, celebrating Mass for his former accuser in a private gathering. Cook soon died of AIDS.

The legal drama forced many editors to wonder if the coverage of aberrant priests had gone too far. Child molesters were in many walks of life, after all. And now a cardinal had been tarnished.

Doyle realized that the survivors' movement had suffered a huge setback. For Bernardin's ordeal, however riveting and full of pathos, offered no guarantee that bishops would cooperate with authorities or help victims. The hierarchy had no coherent policy, as David Clohessy and Barbara Blaine saw from the number of survivors whose perpetrators were still functioning priests.[16]

The events surrounding Bernardin registered in other developments that received far less media scrutiny. When the suit was filed in Cincinnati, several men in Charleston, South Carolina, where Bernardin began his career as a priest, contacted attorney Denis Ventriglia. The men remembered Bernardin, who had lived in the rectory in the mid-1950s, when they were kids and were being molested by Father Frederick Hopwood. Ventriglia soon had eight clients. Charleston church officials referred him to James Serritella's Chicago law office, which handled the negotiations. "I knew we could be a thorn in their side," said Ventriglia. "My clients were seriously injured. The Chicago lawyers knew how bad Hopwood was." Bernardin's residency with Hopwood while the latter was abusing youngsters never made it into the national media coverage; perhaps it would have made no difference. On March 21, 1994, Hopwood pleaded guilty to one count of a lewd act with a minor. Ventriglia settled the cases out of court in 1995. Hopwood moved to New Jersey. The Charleston diocese lists him as "retired"—not laicized.[17]

The Chicago legal strategy of hammering troublesome plaintiffs prevailed in the summer of 1994 when the first Northbrook family lost at trial. The boy who was seven when he told his parents of being abused was now a strapping teenager, uneasy on the witness stand, his testimony challenged by an expert on "false memory." The parents, drained from a six-year legal battle, were not strong witnesses. More pivotal to the defense, the second boy alleging abuse by the pastor, Lutz, was not allowed to testify. Watching the family flattened by the church's legal steamroller—and forced to settle Lutz's counterclaims out of court—the second family withdrew its suit.

After the furor surrounding Bernardin, Doyle's friendship with Steve Rubino deepened. Whatever his mistakes, Rubino was a fighter, and so was Doyle. On November 17, 1994, Doyle was sitting in Rubino's law office when he saw the news from Ireland. Prime Minister Albert Reynolds resigned after a priest, whose extradition from Dublin had long been delayed, was convicted in Belfast and sentenced to four years in prison for sexually abusing youths.[18] Trailed by accusations for years, the priest, Brendan Smyth, was protected by his Norbertine religious order and Cardinal Cahal Daly of Dublin. Smyth's superior resigned after the trial. When the attorney general who resisted the extradition advanced to the Irish High Court, opposition parties protested; the judge resigned, so did the prime minister, and the government collapsed, forcing new elections in the republic.

This stuff is far from over, Doyle told himself.

Barbara Blaine, after years of frustration in dealing with Chet Warren's religious order, turned to Rubino, who negotiated a settlement for her. Blaine entered law school, determined to continue her struggle against church officialdom. Rubino also negotiated a settlement for

Sarah Wilgress with the Trappist order over her abuse, as a California high school student, by Vincent Dwyer. Dwyer left the Trappists—but not the priesthood—to live in Florida.

A strange coda to the Bernardin allegations surfaced in 2002. The *Boston Globe*'s reporting of hush money led reporters Stephen Kurkjian and Michael Rezendes to investigate events at the seminary in Winona, Minnesota, and the young man who was paid $70,000 to withdraw his accusations.[19] The *Globe* found that he had accused four bishops of coercing him into having sex. One of them, Robert Brom of San Diego, had been a bishop in Minnesota at the time. "Following careful investigation by many attorneys," a San Diego church statement explained, "hard facts have been brought to light which contradict [the former seminarian's] allegations. . . . he freely retracts each and every allegation and claim . . . and welcomes the assistance provided herein toward a healthy life." The Winona diocese and its seminary provided payment and the lawsuit was dropped.

How free was that retraction? Archbishop John Vlazny of Portland, Oregon, who was the bishop of Winona at the time, told the *Globe* that the retraction was a condition of the settlement. Many reporters have sought interviews with the man over the years, to no avail. The ex-seminarian did speak by phone with Mark Brooks and according to Brooks, the man called his own retraction letter "false."[20] Vlazny told the *Globe*: "I viewed this not as a matter of justice but as a matter of charity"—without explaining what happened at the seminary or why the man got the money.

In November of 1995 Bernardin was taking chemotherapy for cancer and looked "very frail" on a visit to Greeley.[21] In his final public appearances Bernardin spoke eloquently of his impending death; a journal he kept became a posthumous best seller. His funeral, in 1996, drew enormous crowds. By then Tom Doyle had shipped out to an air base in the Azores, a chain of islands off the coast of Portugal. With computer and e-mail, he was in close touch with survivors, lawyers, and a widening network of friends.

PART TWO

The Rise of the Legion of Christ

Chapter Seven

EVANGELISM BY
STEALTH

A T ONE LEVEL, Pope John Paul's detachment from the clergy sexual crisis was consistent with his style of governing. The pope who traveled more than all of his predecessors combined had a philosopher's abstract mind. No pope in modern memory has been so prolific, generating a voluminous line of works that restate Catholic moral teaching with emphasis on the church's evangelistic role in the world. Early in his pontificate the Vatican Bank became embroiled in a scandal with shadowy financiers. "When it came to money," wrote Jonathan Kwitney, "he simply never thought about it."[1] The same might be said of clerics' sexuality.

The Vatican is a city-state of 107 acres with scattered properties and universities in Rome proper. The $200 million annual budget is tiny compared to California's.[2] The Vatican draws its major support from the hierarchies of the United States, Great Britain, and Germany. Although the abuse litigation in the 1990s was sapping funds of many dioceses, the Vatican felt no hard jolt. News of these scandals was not a major focus of the Italian media.

The American bishops' parliamentary procedures in conference and the staff-researched pastoral letters had given them a new presence in the public square. John Paul was uneasy with such freewheeling debate; his greater concern was bishops who failed to correct doctrinal dissent. Division among the bishops over whether use of condoms could be condoned in public safety campaigns to prevent the spread of AIDS did not sit well with the pope. The 1968 papal encyclical forbade any use of contraceptives. On the American side, many bishops had been aghast at Cardinal Ratzinger's humiliating treatment of Father Charles Curran in ousting him from Catholic University.

John Paul called the leadership to Rome in March of 1989.

The Vatican sent a limousine to the Leonardo da Vinci Airport for Archbishop John F. Whealon of Hartford, Connecticut, a tall, slender, introspective man and accomplished biblical scholar. The prelate saw Gerald Renner gathering his bags and offered him a ride. Renner, a *Hartford Courant* reporter covering the conference, liked the no-frills archbishop. Whealon didn't bother with a spokesman. When reporters called, he spoke to them directly. He lived in a two-room apartment in an archdiocesan retirement home and drove an economy car. The years of avid handball playing had ended after hip surgery and five operations for intestinal cancer. Yet here he was, at sixty-eight, back in Rome, where he had known glorious days at Vatican II.

A native of Philadelphia, Renner graduated from Georgetown University in 1959 and went to work for a newspaper in Reading, Pennsylvania, covering organized crime. In 1965 he took a job as a press officer for the bishops' office in Washington, D.C. With Vatican II in its final session, tension arose in Washington between traditionalists, loyal to the Roman Curia, and bishops inspired by Pope John XXIII's idea of "updating." Cardinal James F. McIntyre of Los Angeles, a bullying and obstreperous man, clashed with Archbishop John Dearden of Detroit, who saw a new springtime for the church. McIntyre wanted the bishops to have closed meetings and deliver their news from the pulpit. Dearden saw Vatican II as a model: bishops and theologians would explain the church's decisions, give the gospel greater reach.[3] "What possible good would result from admitting reporters to these meetings?" grumbled the old cardinal from Los Angeles. "It would improve the caliber of the debate," a young Minnesota bishop shot back.[4]

The first meeting of the fledgling National Conference of Catholic Bishops[5] in 1966 was closed, but there were daily briefings, as at Vatican II. Subsequently the organization adopted a policy of open meetings under rules of order, although executive sessions were closed. Renner left the conference in 1967 to join the National Conference of Christians and Jews in New York as information director, and later was executive director of the NCCJ in Chicago and Baltimore. In 1976 he returned to journalism as director of Religion News Service. In 1985 he joined the Hartford daily as a religion writer.

The limousine moved through traffic on Via Aurelia, heading toward St. Peter's Square. Whealon was one of thirty-five American cardinals and archbishops arriving for the four-day meeting that began on March 8, 1989. The bishops had elected delegates, but John Paul dismissed the slate. He summoned the papally appointed leaders of the hierarchy (making an exception for the general secretary of the bishops' conference). John Paul wanted a hierarchy, as in Poland, that showed a united front and resolved differences behind closed doors. Many bishops wondered if the pope, having spent most of his life under communist rule, had a true understanding of the democratic impulses of the American hierarchy.

A number of the arriving prelates were still smarting over Cardinal Ratzinger's unprecedented stripping of some of Seattle archbishop Raymond "Dutch" Hunthausen's powers and transferring them to an auxiliary bishop. Hunthausen was charged with "lack of firmness" in 1986 for allowing Catholics and Protestants to receive communion together, permitting a Mass in the cathedral for an organization of gay Catholics, allowing sterilization procedures in Catholic hospitals, and supposed laxity on marriage annulments. Ratzinger saw a near revolt among bishops, with letters and calls to the Curia complaining of boundaries transgressed. The pope restored Hunthausen's powers after a compromise, forged by Cardinal Bernardin and several others, that allowed Hunthausen to remain as archbishop; Rome saved face by sending a coadjutor archbishop to serve alongside the Seattle prelate until his retirement.[6]

Whealon took a long view of such skirmishes. As a young scripture scholar, he had been "a respectful dissenter" on Rome's literal interpretation of the Bible. He and others had come to see the Bible as a moral and religious guide; some stories, like that of Jonah in the belly of the whale, were allegorical. Research showed that the gospels were not written by eyewitnesses, but at least a generation after Jesus's resurrection. On becoming an auxiliary bishop of Cleveland in 1961, Whealon joked to a colleague, "Maybe now I can do something to keep us all from being burned at the stake."[7] A year later, participating in Vatican II, he rejoiced at Rome's acceptance of interdisciplinary standards of scripture scholarship, religious liberty, ecumenical relations, and a reversal of centuries of anti-Jewish preaching.

Having sold his editors on a conflict in Rome, Renner was surprised at the archbishop's cheery mood. Whealon was enjoying his memories.

The limousine followed a crowded four-lane highway past apartment buildings, motels, and gas stations, when into view came a long, four-story building behind a high stone wall. A sign on the steel gate warned against trespassers: a German shepherd, teeth bared in attack mode, with the logo ATTENTI AI CANI—Beware of the Dogs. "That's the headquarters of that controversial religious order with a seminary in Cheshire," remarked Whealon. Renner frowned. Cheshire was a short drive from Hartford.

"Which religious order, Archbishop?"

"The Legionaries of Christ."

Renner made a mental note to check on the Legionaries of Christ back home. Whealon's nostalgia for Vatican II sparked Renner's sense of irony. The council was meant to open the church to the world; yet the struggle to achieve aggiornamento had become a Catholic ordeal ever since. Now on a sunny March day in 1989, he thanked the archbishop for the ride and registered at his hotel.

Gathering his credentials at the press office of the Holy See, Renner learned that the American archbishops would meet with the pope and cardinals of the Roman Curia in a subterranean Vatican room without windows.

The archbishops were bused in each morning from two religious houses, where they lodged, to a restricted area of the Vatican. The journalists waited through the sessions for briefings by a panel of bishops. The daily written summaries were couched in ecclesiastical euphemisms. Prepared texts of the speeches were more helpful. The American visitors revealed enough to amplify the record, exposing sharp differences over the tone and direction of the church.

"This historic meeting which begins today is an opportunity to give clearer expression to the bond of ecclesial and ministerial communion which unites us," John Paul explained in his opening remarks, released by the Vatican Press Office. "We shall attempt to clarify our own vision of where the Lord wishes to lead us." For the most part, the pope sat silently through the meetings, taking notes, according to those who were there.[8]

Archbishop John L. May of St. Louis, the president of the bishops' conference, pleaded for the Vatican to understand the importance of democratic values in the evolving style of the U.S. church. "Authoritarianism is suspect in any area of learning or culture," May said. "To assert that there is a church teaching with authority binding for eternity is truly a sign of contradiction to many Americans who consider the divine right of bishops as outmoded as the divine right of kings." Yet, he said, organized religion flourished because America allowed "full freedom of thought." Freedom also tolerated a dark side of the popular culture, with materialism and "hedonistic values widely disseminated among our people in some of the media."[9]

If the Americans thought that they were making any headway, Cardinal Ratzinger set them straight. Bishops must not allow theologians to dissent, he insisted. "Theologians have taken the place of the bishop as teacher, causing increasing uncertainty. . . . A bishop can be reduced to a simple administrator and moderator of theological opinion. He can lose responsibility for his teaching." Rejecting a nuanced view of tolerance, Ratzinger told them to use the power of their teaching office by "placing people at the point of decision, confronting them with the authority of truth. . . . I don't think you can compromise where truth is at stake and not just simply to maintain peace."[10]

Ratzinger held little room for the *sensus fidelium*—the mind of the faithful—and the idea that laypeople must affirm a teaching to give it authority. How many archbishops would tell a packed cathedral to obey the 1968 birth control letter, and expect affirmation?

Cardinal Edouard Gagnon, a Canadian who presided over the Pontifical Council for the Family, chastised the archbishops for not protesting enough about television shows that were a form of "subtle pornography." Moral values were eroding because of "cinema and TV shows which pretend to depict normal American life." Gagnon scored the degrading of American life by divorce, abortion, contraception, radical feminism, and school infirmaries that are "thinly disguised abortion referral clinics."

No Americans responded to Gagnon's laundry list.[11]

Cardinal Achille Silvestrini, who at the time was prefect of the Apostolic Signatura, the supreme court of the church, complained that U.S. diocesan tribunals were granting more marriage annulments than the rest of the world combined. Three out of every four annulments were granted by the United States.[12] The Curia viewed diocesan tribunals in the United States as going too easy on divorced Catholics. Before the 1983 revision of the canonical codes, annulment requests went to the Vatican. The process was cumbersome, expensive, and took too long. The recent reforms allowed local dioceses to make the final decisions. "One may deduce that various tribunals in the United States have introduced their own method," Silvestrini said tartly.

Cardinal Edmund Szoka of Detroit (later to become a curial official) called Silvestrini's argument "one of numbers and not substance." Los Angeles's Archbishop Roger Mahony said that cases were carefully screened. His archdiocese had granted one thousand the year before—and turned down thirteen thousand requests for a hearing. Whealon, confident in his tribunal at Hartford, wondered whether other countries were doing a poorer job. Was the process done "according to the norms of justice? We say that it is. Therefore, we say we are not to be criticized or held up to wonderment."

The conference ended with no formal statement. The Americans put on a good face; yet to reporters it was clear that the American hierarchy had marching orders: tone down public debate, show a united front, and use authority to criticize theologians who fail to uphold church teaching.

Six months later, as Pope John Paul rejected requests from the U.S. bishops for authority to remove pedophiles from ministry in a less cumbersome way than canon law allowed, representatives of the U. S. hierarchy went to Rome to negotiate the matter. Vatican officials balked. They said the way American tribunals mishandled marriage annulments showed that streamlining the canon law process to deal with accused child molesters could be a threat to their rights.

The Legion in Connecticut

In the files of *The Hartford Courant*, Connecticut's largest newspaper, Renner found not a single reference to the Legionaries of Christ. The Legionaries had had an almost subterranean existence since establishing their U.S. headquarters in 1965. Renner called the seminary twenty-five miles away in Cheshire, hoping to do a feature story.

"You will have to talk to Father Bannon about that, and he's not in," said the male receptionist. The Reverend Anthony Bannon was national director. Renner left his name and number. No one called back. Renner found Bannon never available. The reporter drove out to the seminary, an immense stone building in the center of 117 well-tended acres. A flustered seminarian receptionist telephoned someone else. A man in a Roman collar and ankle-length cassock appeared, did not offer his name, and told Renner he could not stay without Bannon's permission. Renner left his card.

One day in 1993 Bannon happened to answer the phone. Bannon's voice was Irish. "The Legionaries do not want any publicity." Renner said his readers would like to know about an order with its national headquarters in Connecticut. "We have had disappointing experience with the press," Bannon said. "What is said has been misquoted and distorted. Unless we can have a look at the final product we would not be interested." Renner gently replied that a right of review was journalistically unacceptable, but assured him the piece was a feature, not designed to embarrass the group in Cheshire. Bannon said no and good-bye.

What are they hiding? wondered Renner. His desk was flooded with press releases from religious groups hungry for publicity. How did the Legionaries find seminarians? And why all the secrecy?

Religion fascinated Renner the way campaigns race the pulse of political writers. He saw the church as a vast organism prone to humankind's excesses. He had done his share of reporting on cult dynamics in secretive religious groups. Beyond the mainstream beliefs lay all kinds of charismatic leaders who seized on the spiritual yearnings of their followers to gain total control, creating a personality cult. The 1978 mass suicide of Jim Jones and some nine hundred followers at Jonestown, Guyana, was the most searing example at the time.

Cults occasionally cropped up in the Catholic Church. The Benedictine Abbey of Regina Laudis in the wooded hills of Bethlehem, Connecticut, drew financial support from lay followers who visited for retreats. In the mid-eighties, critics accused the founding abbess and a Jesuit priest, the spiritual adviser at the abbey, of using psychologically coercive, manipulative practices to dominate the nuns and lay followers. They grouped people into a dozen "closed communities," with a handful of members led by "authority figures," normally a man and a woman who were not married to each other, with nuns as "spiritual mentors." At these meetings people revealed highly personal details, even about their sex lives. So found Renner for a series in the *Courant* in 1987. People were "challenged" to make radical change. One couple gave a child up for adoption so the father could be a priest and the mother a nun, leaving grief-stricken grandparents. Another couple quit when asked to surrender their baby. At Regina Laudis, families were torn apart and people milked of money for questionable enterprises.

The *Courant* exposé and other reports drew national attention to the abbey. Archbishop Whealon defended the abbey but privately asked the papal delegate in Washington for an investigation. When he got no response, Whealon ordered a priest on his staff to make personal inquiries in Rome, which produced a team of "apostolic visitors," led by Bishop Joseph J. Gerry of Portland, Maine. In 1994—seven years after the first complaints—the Vatican appointed a Benedictine monk to oversee the abbey, forced the Jesuit out and the abbess into retirement. The Reverend James J. LeBar, adviser to Cardinal John O'Connor and the Vatican on sects and cults, cited Regina Laudis as a Catholic religious community transformed into a cult.[13]

Renner began calling area priests. One pastor had accepted two Legion seminarians to teach religion to children. "I kicked them out," he said. "They seemed more interested in getting the children involved with Legion activities." An archdiocesan official called the Legionaries "a right-wing pre–Vatican II group" that cultivated traditional Catholics, particularly rich ones. "Their vocation appeal is the Marine pitch: Come with us, life is tough, we are strict, an army of Christ. Everyone in cassocks, Gregorian chant, Mass in Latin."

Tradition had its appeal. "We work for them because they are old school," said Gloria Montano of Milford, where the Legionaries first put down roots. "When they started they didn't know where the food was coming from. They needed financial help, food, everything." A Legion priest had appealed to Montano's parish in the late sixties. Parishioners stuffed envelopes, raised money, prepared holiday meals. In 1971, the Legion established its base in the adjoining town of Orange, in an old Montessori school on 12.6 acres purchased for $200,000.

The seminary in Cheshire had originally been the home of a French order, the Missionaries of Our Lady of La Salette, that had come to the United States in 1892, ministering among French Canadians in New England. By the 1970s the number of francophone Catholics was sharply declining; so were vocations. On November 5, 1982, the Legionaries of Christ bought the land and seminary for $2.9 million, with the La Salette order holding a mortgage on $2.7 million. The Legionaries fell behind in their payments. The La Salette fathers considered filing suit. Whealon, not about to allow two Catholic orders to fight in court on his turf, turned to the New Haven–based Knights of Columbus, the Catholic lay organization, rich by virtue of its insurance business. The Knights assumed a $2.3 million mortgage on the property in 1990.

Still, absent the Legionaries' cooperation, there was not a great deal to report. A group fell behind in a mortgage; there were scattered criticisms of an order that spent money it did not have to get what it wanted. In March of 1996, however, the *Los Angeles Times* reported that a group of laypeople associated with the Legionaries had bought the *National Catholic Register*, a weekly, and *Twin Circle*, a Catholic tabloid of family features, from multimillionaire businessman Patrick Frawley of Encino, California, for $500,000. The *Register* had lost circulation, from 57,000 to 22,000, in the previous decade. So had *Twin Circle*, dropping from 52,000 to 15,000. The *L.A. Times* reported the transaction without the Legion's cooperation. The newspapers were relocated to Hamden, a twenty-minute drive from Legion headquarters in Orange, in a single-story twenty-four-thousand-square-foot concrete-block building purchased for $780,000 in 1992. In 1995 the Legion transferred the title to a nonprofit corporation, Rossotto Inc., which was set up to handle the Legion's fund-raising operation, according to the incorporation documents filed with the state. Bannon and two other priests were listed as officers of Rossotto.

Renner took a shot and called the *National Catholic Register*. Joop Koopman, one of three editors who had made the move from California, was too new to the Legionaries to appreciate their penchant for secrecy. Koopman responded like a colleague, inviting Renner over. A native of Holland, Koopman spoke flawless English and cheerfully gave him a tour of the redecorated offices, in an old warehouse, with new Macintosh computers. The building also housed a fund-raising operation.

Women with headphones worked the phone lines. Buying lists of sub-scribers to Catholic magazines or contributors to church causes, the Legion was churning out letters with pleas for money to train seminari-ans or support missions to the poor in Mexico. "Lottery sweepstakes" offered cash prizes of up to $5,000 with a $5 donation for ten tickets in many of the appeals.

Koopman explained that the money to buy the newspapers came from wealthy laypeople in a New York nonprofit corporation called Cir-cle Media. "The Legionaries won't be involved in the day-to-day work-ing of the newspapers," he added. The newspapers would be independent, paying rent to the Legion. Koopman hoped the *Register* and *Twin Circle* would prosper with the infusion of money, energy, and ideas from the new owners.

Within a year, the Legion's Reverend Owen Kearns became editor and publisher, dismissing Koopman, who had worked ten years with the paper. "If you are not one hundred percent with them, they let you go," Koopman remarked later. "After the shock wore off, I was free. . . . I'm not bitter but I am certainly not a fan of theirs." He went to work in New York for Cablevision.[14]

No principals were listed in the 1995 incorporation papers for Circle Media in Albany, as allowed by state law. A Manhattan lawyer, the des-ignated agent for correspondence, told Renner: "If the fathers are not forthcoming, I cannot tell you anything else."

Renner's report in the March 25, 1996, *Courant* was the first of any substance in an American newspaper on the Legionaries of Christ:

> An order of priests styled after the military shuns publicity, but is qui-etly prospering in the state and is growing in influence in the Catholic Church. Tightly disciplined and traditional, the Mexican-founded Legionaries of Christ appeal to Catholics who yearn for the ways of the church before the reforms of the Second Vatican Council. . . . The Legionaries operate a seminary in Cheshire where 200 young men in black cassocks do preparatory studies for the priesthood before fur-ther schooling in Spain and Italy. The seminary is certified by the state Department of Education to award high school diplomas.[15]

The story portrayed the Legion, then with 350 priests and 2,000 seminarians in sixteen countries, as a growing order. The Immaculate

Conception Apostolic School in Center Harbor, New Hampshire, had seventy boys in grades seven through nine who were considering the priesthood.

People began calling Renner with more information.

Escape from Seminary

Stephen Jeffries of Bristol, Connecticut, said he had escaped from a Legion seminary when the superiors denied him permission to leave, an extraordinary claim in light of the post–Vatican II church's emphasis on free will and primacy of conscience, embedded in canon law.[16]

Jeffries, a thirty-two-year-old lieutenant in the Connecticut National Guard who was called to active duty in the Gulf War, sat across from Renner in a restaurant, matter-of-factly relating how he had plotted his escape from the Legion. He spoke of being ensnared in a closed system, with priests telling him that if he lost his vocation as a Legion priest his soul faced eternal damnation. "They tended to be more than a little bizarre," Jeffries said earnestly.

Raised in a devout, conservative family, Jeffries spent the summer of 1995 at the seminary in Cheshire with other candidates, "testing their vocations." In September they were invited to become novices, the first step in a process that can take as long as thirteen years, depending on one's age, level of education, and maturity before ordination. The Legionaries call seminarians "brothers" from the moment they enter the two-year novitiate.

As a novice Jeffries found every minute programmed, from 4:30 A.M. rising until bedtime at 10:30 P.M. The classes in religion, Latin, Greek, and Spanish were conventional; however, students had to memorize 368 verses of rules from a red hardcover book that governed everything from how to eat (never eat an apple whole, pare it on a plate) to the correct parting of one's hair (on the left). You sought permission for even taking an aspirin. You were never to ask questions, always obey orders, never speak critically about the Legion. Legion superiors read all mail: letters you wrote home had to stress positive dimensions of life. You had to write letters to seminarians you did not know, "on other fronts" (Legionaries in other countries), telling them how much you liked life in the Legion. Your only access to a telephone was through a monitored switchboard, with permission from a superior.

Some novices thrived on the discipline. Those who adapted best seemed to be the youngest, those who came from the Legion's New Hampshire boarding school for seventh- to ninth-graders. Some brothers at Cheshire were finishing high school, others were preparing for Legion seminaries in Spain and Italy.

Jeffries was sent from Cheshire to a mansion in Westchester County, New York. The hundred-acre estate sat on a hill behind a watchtower in a thickly wooded swath of New Castle, near Mount Kisco. The house with dormitory wings lay at the end of a winding half-mile private road. The Legionaries paid $3.1 million in 1994 for the property to the Unification Church of the Reverend Sun Myung Moon—the Moonies. "I got sent down to Mount Kisco and it got to be very cultish," Jeffries said. Twenty-eight brothers were living there. The Legion was seeking a building permit from the town to expand the premises. One night a priest from Orange came for dinner and told the seminarians that a committee of town officials would be visiting to gather information for the Legion's request for a zoning variance. "If they ask you how many brothers you have, say two hundred," the priest instructed the novices.

"They wanted us to lie," fumed Jeffries. He held the simple conviction that deception was wrong. When the Legion persuaded pastors to allow brothers to teach religion in their parishes, the Legion priests told the seminarians: "Your mission is to recruit three students from every class you teach into ECYD [the Legion youth program, from a Spanish acronym for 'education, culture, and sports']. Play basketball with them, get them into our programs. The object is recruitment."

An Army veteran, Jeffries did not mind the rugged training. "But in the novitiate nothing was ever explained," he said. "You were to accept everything on complete, blind faith. The will of the superior was the will of God. If you were told to jump off a bridge because it was the will of God, you jumped."

By November of 1995, Jeffries had been in the Legion six months. He still wanted to be a priest but he told his spiritual director, a Mexican priest, that he wanted out of the Legion. "He said, 'Be more generous,' " Jeffries recounted. "A week later I said it again and he said, 'Have faith, persevere.' He kept saying things like that. He was never specific."

As Jeffries persisted, the priest said: "My soul stands pure in front of the Lord, so I can be the only one who can make that decision."

Jeffries told himself, *The hell with this.*

He had a twenty-one-year-old friend named Joseph Williams, from Minnesota, who wanted to leave. "Joe Williams wanted out so badly he was in tears," Jeffries said. Their suitcases with civilian clothes were locked away in the third-floor attic. Their rooms were a floor below. How to retrieve them? In a large closet used as a boot room, Jeffries saw a door on the wall. He picked the lock, and discovered a room with machinery for an unused elevator—and a staircase to the attic. Up he went, to the suitcases. Later he showed Williams how to retrieve his bags.

The problem now was how to get the suitcases into their rooms without being seen. On the night that Jeffries had to wash dishes, as the other men were studying, he ran up to the attic, got his suitcases, and put them under his bed. His friend did the same the first chance he got. On November 11, 1995, they were assigned to pray in the chapel after lunch. With other students at athletics, the two men changed into civilian clothes, laid their cassocks on the bed, hid the bags under bushes beyond the house, and hiked three miles into Mount Kisco. In the town Jeffries called a friend. He said, "I just escaped from the seminary and I have a friend," he recalled, deadpan. "Can you pick us up?"

"No problem."

Jeffries asked that his name not be used in Renner's article. He wanted to enter another seminary and feared the publicity fallout. After a year in a diocesan seminary Jeffries decided that celibacy was not compatible with the life he wished to lead. Having since married and begun a family, he agreed to be identified for this book. His companion Joseph Williams also wanted anonymity, because he had a brother, Michael, in the Legion, and he declined to be interviewed.[17]

Hugh McCaffery tested his vocation in the Cheshire summer program and in 1995 went to the mansion near Mount Kisco, where he, like Jeffries, felt trapped by secrecy and coercion. "They laughed it off," said McCaffery. "They'd say, 'Okay, you're complaining, you're venting, but you'll get over it.' They told me to write down what you don't like and we will discuss it. I gave them a page and a half and said it was intolerable." The superiors refused to let him leave. "They are totally trained to tell you this is the fundamental option in life, and if you don't choose it you will go to hell."

One afternoon a priest told the novices, "You guys think we are brainwashing you. You think we are stealing your personalities away." *That's exactly what you are doing,* McCaffery thought. In November during an outdoor retreat he folded his cassock on the ground and walked away. "As soon as I got to the woods I started running like a deer," he recalled. "My sunglasses fell out. They cost me eighty dollars but I didn't stop to pick them up." He ran three miles into town. He used his credit card to rent a car. He drove twelve hundred miles home to Pensacola, stopping only to get gas and sleep at a motel. The homecoming surprised his parents. Glad to be free of the Legion, McCaffery was confused. "I am still trying to figure out how the Holy Spirit is supposed to be working through this group."

An American who spoke on condition of anonymity had been in a Legion seminary in Monterrey, Mexico, from September 1994 until February 1995. "I couldn't believe I had gotten myself into a cult," he said. He, too, had gone through discernment in Cheshire, and then the mansion near Mount Kisco, and from there to Monterrey. When he asked to leave, the Legionaries took weeks to honor his request. They held his money, passport, and clothes. As he explained in a letter to the *Courant*:

> *I fear retaliation if my full name is printed in your story because the Legion is a powerful, wealthy and secretive organization. I became disillusioned and left the Legion over their brainwashing, which turns people into robot-like personalities, their unrealistic expectations, their pressure on members to obey rules and accomplish tasks, their ridicule, their secrecy, their manipulating and their pressure on members to raise money for the organization.*

When the *Courant* published the story, Father Bannon faxed the newspaper a letter—nineteen days after questions had been faxed to him. "I do not consider myself free to make public comments on former seminarians," he explained. In response to complaints by Jeffries and McCaffery that the Legion still had their personal effects, Bannon stated: "I would ask you to tell anyone you know who feels I owe him anything to get in touch with me. . . . I will help any former seminarian in any way I can."[18] Several days later Bannon wrote again, acknowledging that the Legion may have made mistakes. "Since we are humans, there will no doubt be evidence of occasional error in the exercise of human reason and prudence . . . [which] we strive to correct." He complained of "many inaccuracies" but cited only "the accusation of sleep deprivation," which he denied.[19]

The Hartford archdiocese's statement said it had received no complaints about the Legion seminary. Renner had been unable to speak with Archbishop Whealon, who died on August 2, 1991. In his place the pope appointed Daniel A. Cronin, who as a young priest spent eleven years in the Vatican Secretariat of State. In contrast to his predecessor's modest asceticism, Cronin had the archdiocese try to buy a $430,000 house with twelve rooms and a swimming pool as his residence, only to back out of the sale after negative publicity amidst a $4 million fund-raising drive for Catholic Charities.[20] Cronin eventually took up residence in a mansion Whealon had sold to the Vincentian Fathers. Cronin got more bad press in December 1993, when he nixed plans for a soup kitchen in a downtown church, fearing that homeless people would have an adverse effect on downtown development, especially on church-owned property. "What can seem like a very secular investment is often what puts employment in the market place, food on the table," he stoutly insisted, "and roofs over the heads of those in need."[21]

Cronin visited Cheshire after the *Courant* reports to show his full confidence. "He even joked that he was grateful to the Legionaries for running interference because he was hoping that now that Renner was whacking them he would leave *him* alone for a while," confided one who was present.

In August of 1996 a priest whom Renner had known casually called with a tip. "There are rumors that the head of that order—Father Maciel—has a roving eye for little boys. Call Jason Berry. He knows all about it."

An Archipelago of Silences

When the first phone call came in late 1993, the author in New Orleans had never heard of the Legion of Christ. A man in California named Arturo Jurado had learned of Berry's work; he spoke of terrible things

Father Maciel had done. Berry, absorbed in the legal firestorm surrounding Cardinal Bernardin, offered to read anything Jurado sent, but as an independent writer he could not guarantee an assignment. Having invested the better part of seven years on his 1992 book, he was exhausted by the secrets of bishops who acted like gangsters. He was a Catholic because he could not find a spirituality to replace what had been his since childhood; he was embarrassed, and outraged, by the hierarchy. He was also a jazz historian, and turning his efforts in that direction when Professor José Barba, in Mexico City, telephoned, with insight on Maciel's status in Rome. Berry asked for notarized statements from all the men making accusations against Maciel, specifying details of the sexual acts, their ages, and where they happened.

With a rudimentary grasp of Spanish and a dictionary at hand, Berry over several months read the stack of single-spaced pages with a mounting sadness about Mexico. His maternal great-grandmother had grown up in Jalapa, in the state of Veracruz; her daughter, his godmother and favorite grandmother, was born there too. The two ladies had sung him a Spanish nursery rhyme when he was a child in New Orleans. Berry was riveted by Juan Vaca's 1978 letter to John Paul II, seeking dispensation from his vow, *telling the pope he had been sexually abused by Maciel*. Berry had long wondered how high the abuse of power reached. He spoke with Vaca at length by telephone to gauge his trustworthiness. He was impressed that Vaca, Barba, and the others had not filed a lawsuit.

"This is a moral issue for us," Barba told him. "We want the pope to remove Maciel." They had struggled for years with their traumatic memories and the psychological hold Maciel had on their lives. Mexico, with encrusted patterns of machismo, was not a society where men easily admit having been sexually abused as boys. "We were an archipelago of silences," reflected Barba.

Berry knew that the issue for an assigning editor would be the failure of the pope to take action. In the wake of the Bernardin case, an investigation that proposed putting John Paul II under a cloud was one hard sell. Greeley's words—"It's open season on priests"—had registered in many newsrooms. The American media was undergoing a sea change; editors wondered if the coverage had tilted unfairly against the church. Bernardin's attorneys and certain bishops had put pressure on

CNN for the editing of interviews with Steven Cook and the cardinal in Bonnie Anderson's documentary in November of 1993.

Several months after Steven Cook withdrew his lawsuit, Berry began casting lines to reporters and producers at ABC, NBC, CNN, and *Frontline*, and got nowhere. Query letters to editors at major newspapers and magazines failed. Over the next two years, he wrote about jazz and other topics, maintaining dialogue with Barba and Jurado, explaining that news moved in cycles and he thought the day would come when an editor would see the merits of an investigation. He began a file on Maciel, speaking with various priests to see who knew much about him. The last thing Jason Berry expected on a late summer day in 1996 was a call from Jerry Renner in Hartford, mentioning the name of a clerical source they both knew. Renner wanted to talk about the Legion of Christ.

Berry had met Renner at a 1989 bishops' convention in Baltimore. As distant colleagues they had spoken periodically as Renner covered abuse cases in Connecticut. Berry, who was just getting acquainted with the Internet, was unaware of Renner's reports on Legion finances and the men who escaped the seminary. When Renner asked about Maciel, Berry insisted that their conversation be off the record. He then pitched his proposal. "I don't have the authority to make an assignment," said Renner, "but this paper is very interested in Maciel. I'll go to the editors." Soon thereafter, Berry sent a memo and copies of the sworn statements. David Barrett, editor, and Clifford Teutsch, the managing editor of the *Courant*, approved a joint assignment by Renner and the freelance writer. Teutsch, with a seasoned record of investigative reporting, told Renner: "If at any point you feel these allegations can't be sustained, pull out."

On October 31, 1996, Jason Berry flew to Mexico City for interviews with Barba and six others who had sent him personal statements. Arturo Jurado flew to Mexico City from Monterey, California, where he lived.

Gerald Renner, meanwhile, got to know Juan Vaca. Vaca lived in a single-story Cape Cod home in Holbrook, a community on Long Island. He greeted Renner in a red plaid shirt and dark trousers. A trim man, with silver-streaked dark hair and gold-rimmed glasses, Vaca had a handsome face and a deep sadness in his eyes. He was nervous, saying,

"I haven't spoken to the press before." He worked as a guidance counselor in the City University of New York. Vaca had written John Paul II on parish stationery at St. Christopher's in nearby Baldwin on October 28, 1989. He was emphatic about not standing alone. Renner assured him the newspaper would quote from the interviews his colleagues were giving Berry. Still, he could see that Vaca was afraid. His living room was decorated with religious images, a picture of Our Lady of Guadalupe foremost among them. Children's toys were in the den. Vaca and his wife had a two-year-old daughter, just now with a sitter. Vaca's wife was at work. Vaca was also working toward his doctorate in psychology, seeking insight "into the way I was trapped."

"I love my church but not the humans who run it," he said. Yet he spoke warmly of Bishop James J. Daly, auxiliary of the Rockville Centre diocese, who had encouraged him to marry civilly. His wife, who had been divorced and had a son by the previous marriage, had gotten a church annulment. After Vaca received his papal dispensation, Daly officiated at their nuptial Mass.

He was the oldest of four children, raised in the town of Zitácuaro, in Michoacán, about a hundred miles west of Mexico City. Childhood photographs showed an exceptionally handsome youth with large black eyes and a trusting face, an altar boy and a Boy Scout in the troop organized by his pastor. Juan's father, an undertaker and carpenter, was president in Zitácuaro of Catholic Action, a movement of laypeople allied with the hierarchy in promoting the social teachings of the popes. Michoacán was a strongly Catholic state. When Maciel visited the pastor in 1947, Juan happened to be in the church. The Legion founder asked, "What about this one?" The pastor replied: "I think he would make a good one."

Vaca recalled Maciel's first words to him: "I am looking for boys like you."

They went home to talk to his parents, who were thrilled at the idea of Juan getting a good education in Mexico City and becoming a priest. "I wanted to be a pilot or bullfighter or priest," said Vaca, smiling over his naïveté. His mother packed a bag. Maciel drove Juan and four other new recruits over the bumpy road to the seminary at Tlalpan in Mexico City. The ease with which his parents surrendered him reflected their trust in the clergy. Sending a son to seminary was a mark of pride. "The first week I was crying, homesick," Vaca recalled. The priest who directed the school under Maciel telephoned Juan's father. Together they persuaded him to stay one week and see how he liked it. One week led to another and another.

In 1949, Maciel told Vaca's parents he had been chosen to study in Spain, a prestigious opportunity that made Juan swell with pride. On October 3, 1949, the boys boarded a bus for the port of Veracruz. From there, as third-class passengers, they made a twenty-six-day crossing on a ship called *Magallanes* to Bilbao, Spain. They were destined for the Jesuit-run Comillas University in the northern province of Santander. Comillas has since been relocated to Madrid.

In Spain, as Vaca recounted, he was twelve on the night a Legionary brother roused him just after bedtime. "Nuestro Padre wants to talk to you." In the bedroom, Maciel spoke of pains in his internal organs. "He said, 'Rub me, rub me,' and made a circle on his stomach to show me," said Vaca. "I was trembling. I was frightened, but I began rubbing. He said, 'Do it lower, lower.' Maciel got an erection. I didn't know anything about masturbation. I was on the verge of puberty. He moved my hand to his penis. I was terrified. Finally he was relieved and he faked being asleep.

"I was in shock," explained Vaca. "He was a holy man . . . a very loving man. He was my father. He did it to me at first with the lights out. Later on he did it with the lights on. Sometimes he used me as a girl. He put his penis between my legs. Once he wanted to penetrate me from behind but I did not let him do that. He had me call another one. He abused two of us together."

Vaca, who depended on Maciel for everything, felt trapped. "I told him I didn't feel right. I wanted to go to confession. He said, 'There is nothing wrong. You don't have to go to confession.' " But Vaca wasn't reassured. "Maciel said, 'Here, I will give you absolution,' " and made the sign of the cross in blessing. It was the beginning of a psychosexual relationship that Vaca said would last more than a dozen years. No one, except some of his classmates who experienced the same violations, would ever believe him—not in those days. Still, he felt "being pulled like a magnet toward the priesthood," the dream he could not abandon, the thing his parents wanted for him.

As Vaca made sandwiches for lunch, he spoke of his isolated adoles-

cence and the vow that Legionary brothers took—not just the traditional vows of poverty, chastity, and obedience, but a fourth vow. Vaca
spoke as if floating back to an anguished past. "We are not to speak or
write against the Legionaries of Christ and we are not to criticize our
superiors. If someone thinks something is wrong he is not to go outside
the Legion but to bring the complaint to the attention of superiors.
Never are we to speak to anyone outside the Legion. That's because the
devil wants to destroy the Legionaries of Christ."

Vaca had tried to get the attention of church authorities at the opening of the Second Vatican Council in 1962. The Mexican bishops were
invited to live at the Legionaries' headquarters. Vaca, then twenty-five,
directed the seminarians who waited on the bishops. Wanting to confide
in one of the Mexican bishops, he began writing an account of his life in
the Legion, including the sexual abuse. He left a dozen pages in his room.
"That was a mistake," he sighed. "No Legionary could expect privacy."
Vaca suspected Maciel had his room searched. "I was ready to be
ordained," he said. Discovery of the letter quashed that—and abruptly
ended his twelve and a half years of on-again, off-again sexual contact
with Maciel. "I saw this man looking at me with shark eyes, so hungry
and so cold. He said, 'I don't think you are ready to be ordained.' "

Maciel sent him to Spain to teach in the minor seminary in
Ontaneda, Santander. For the next six years Vaca was in exile from
Rome, first at Ontaneda and then at a new Legion novitiate in Dublin.
He moved through his twenties serving as vocational director, teacher,
dean of discipline, and dean of studies. The Legionaries were making a
big push to recruit Irish boys. "Everything was paid for by the Legionaries," said Vaca, as if recalling a promotional brochure. "My instructions
from Maciel were to get 'the prettiest and smartest kids.' "

"Why didn't you leave?" asked Renner.

Vaca closed his eyes and sighed. "I didn't know how."

In 1969, Maciel summoned him to Rome. With a good overall
record, Vaca had redeemed himself. "I guess Father Maciel figured I
would keep my mouth shut." He was ordained a Roman Catholic priest
with other Legionaries on November 25, 1969. After twenty-two years
away from his family, religious life was the only world he really knew.
Leaving it was something he could hardly picture.

He was sent to Ontaneda, this time as vice rector of that minor seminary. There, four boys complained to him that the rector was "touching" them. "I immediately telephoned Maciel in Rome," said Vaca. "Maciel ordered the rector ousted on the spot. The father of one of the abused boys was a policeman—they didn't want any trouble." Vaca said that the rector, who had himself been abused by Maciel as a boy, was transferred to Chetumal on the Yucatán Peninsula, in Mexico, known in the Legion as the "gulag" for errant priests.

In 1971, Maciel sent Vaca to Connecticut to serve as president of the Legionaries of Christ in the United States and rector of the seminary then in Orange. Vaca considered the promotion a reward for his covering up the abuse by the rector at Ontaneda. He opened satellite Legion houses in Camden, New Jersey; Larchmont, New York; Silver Springs, Maryland; and Haddonfield, Michigan, near Detroit. But as guilt burrowed inside him, Vaca knew that one of his predecessors in Connecticut, Father Félix Alarcón, had also been molested by Maciel during his seminary years. Alarcón had left the Legion less than a year after his arrival in America in 1965 and was serving as priest in the diocese of Rockville Centre. In 1976 Vaca decided he was ready to follow Alarcón in that path.

Chapter Eight

MYTH OF THE FOUNDER

ON JANUARY 26, 1979, John Paul II made his first foreign trip as pope. He flew to Mexico, the world's second largest Catholic country (after Brazil). On the plane a reporter asked what favor he might ask the Virgin of Guadalupe, the national saint. "I shall ask her to pray for the Mexican people, who have suffered a lot, just like the Polish people," replied the Holy Father.[1]

Sixteenth-century clerics who helped colonize Mexico for the Spanish crown followed the bloody tracks of conquistadores in building a feudal empire that ignored the material needs of the Indian masses. By 1800 all of Mexico—then encompassing Texas and a piece of the U.S. Southwest—had but ten primary schools.[2] Following Mexico's eleven-year war of independence from Spain, which culminated in 1821, the Mexican church endured a long, violent backlash. Graham Greene's *The Power and the Glory,* a classic portrait of the 1930s, is set in Tabasco. The governor of that state had his staff greet him each day with the cry *"God does not exist!"* to which he barked, *"Nor has he ever existed!"*[3]

Despite Juan Vaca's letter of accusation to the pope in October 1978, Father Maciel flew on the plane in the pope's inner circle, a reward for his advance work. Maciel had made careful inroads with President José López Portillo. At Los Pinos, the presidential residence in Mexico City, a Legionary priest, Father Carlos Mora Reyes, was the spiritual director of López Portillo's mother and celebrated Mass at her private chapel on the grounds. This was a far cry from the suffering church to which the pope alluded. Still, Mexico had no diplomatic ties with the Holy See. López Portillo kept a calculated distance from the church. Maciel got the president's mother and sisters to smooth the way for the trip. "López Portillo overrode the protests of his anti-clerical interior minister and issued the invitation, stipulating only that the Pope would not be received as a head of state and would have to have a visa like any other visitor," writes George Weigel.[4]

Such a groundswell was building that López Portillo went to the airport. After John Paul kissed the ground, the president of a country where priests in living memory had been stalked and killed greeted him with a warm smile and words of irony: "Welcome to your home." A million people lined the five-mile stretch into Mexico City.

John Paul saw the Legionaries of Christ as a knightly order allied with a resurgent national church. As Protestant evangelicals siphoned off middle-class Catholics in Guatemala and other Latin countries, Mexico seemed a regional model—a church that would not cling to Liberation Theology, a movement allied with the poor, especially in the Christian base communities of Brazil. Although John Paul would champion human rights, often and eloquently, he wanted theological movements conforming to Vatican authority. As Cardinal Ratzinger began an investigation of Liberation Theology advocates who claimed scriptural inspiration for alternatives to poverty and persecution, the Legion cultivated officials in Argentina and Chile, where torture was a part of political strategy.[5]

Maciel pitched the Legion's appeal to Catholics uneasy with the church's "preferential option for the poor." Many orthodox intellectuals view the Legionaries as a sign of renewal in the restoration church of John Paul. Yet even well-heeled Mexicans aware of their role as educators of upper-class children call the order "millionaires of Christ."

Maciel is a case study in disinformation and a cult of personality.

The story of Marcial Maciel Degollado begins on March 10, 1920, in Cotija de la Paz, a town in the state of Michoacán, 220 miles west of Mexico City. Maciel's birthplace is known as "the town of the cassocks" for the many priests it has produced.[6] In Cotija stands a statue of Bishop Rafael Guizar Valencia, an uncle of Maciel's. In 1995 Bishop Guizar was put on the path to sainthood when Pope John Paul II declared him "blessed," an act that registered Maciel's influence with the pope.[7] The stone house where the bishop was born in 1878 is a tourist attraction.[8] The house where Maciel was born has been expanded into a retreat center and Legion museum. Above the town sits an expansive retreat center for the Legionaries' "consecrated women," who take vows of poverty, chastity, and obedience, though they are not formally an order of nuns.

Maciel's father, Francisco Maciel Farías, "made his fortune little by little" with a sugar mill and a ranch.[9] In a recent oral memoir, *Christ Is My Life,* Maciel reflected on his father as "an honest man, faithful to his personal and Christian commitments, very much a man of conscience."[10] Cotija's inhabitants at the time of Marcial's birth were "generally not of mixed blood"—the town founded by ten Spanish families, maintained a racial purity unblemished by Indians.[11] Marcial (nicknamed Güerito, meaning a boy with fair hair and light skin) was one of seven boys and four girls; former Legionaries say he was so attached to his mother, Maura Degollado Guizar, that he seldom spoke of his father. He has introduced her cause for sainthood at the Vatican, interestingly, under her maiden name.[12]

A Legion booklet portrays a boy who rises early to milk cows and in the afternoons cares for the poor and sick. Sometimes "he has arrived home barefoot after giving his shoes away, Mama Maurita finally has to forbid him to do it again."[13] On one occasion Mama finds him shivering from the cold, having given away all his clothes.

The campaign that put Maciel's uncle and mother in line for canonization should be seen as groundwork for his own posthumous candidacy for sainthood. At a 1992 beatification ceremony, Maciel told close aides, "Don't start my canonization process until I've been dead thirty years."[14] He evidently was not eager to have his life examined for saintliness too soon, while people with long memories were still around. The stories that fill out his official biography are of such exaggerated heroism and questionable humility as to exceed the slickest script for a plaster saint.

Glenn Favreau, an American born in 1964, entered the Legion in 1984 and left in 1997, after his ordination as a deacon. Favreau says he was not abused sexually, though he felt his personality was being stripped away by control tactics.[15] He recalls how impressed he was at the outset of his Legion years when a priest instructor told him how Father Maciel, back in the early forties, had gone door to door, begging for money. At one home, a man spit in his face and Maciel coolly rejoined, "All right, that was for me. Now how about something for my seminarians?" Favreau later discovered the story was identical to one told of Saint Philip Neri, the sixteenth-century founder of the Oratorian fathers.[16]

Maciel's mother shielded him from his father's harshness. Don Francisco thought his son too soft. The Reverend Rogelio Orozco, a parish priest in Cuernavaca who lived as a youth with the Maciel family for two years, said that Marcial's "relations with his father were not good. He didn't think Marcial was very intelligent." Orozco saw one of his older brothers beat Marcial and suspects his father did so too.[17]

Many child molesters were abused as youngsters. "His father wanted him to be a hard man, not a sissy boy," said Juan Vaca. "He let him sleep with the men in cottages in the fields. [Maciel] said that once when he was asleep he was molested by one of the men. He told me this when I was about eighteen or nineteen during one of those incidents, you know, that I had with him."[18]

Maciel has said: "One thing that stood out in my education at home, especially under the careful eye of my mother, was a great respect and veneration for the position of the priest."[19] Four of his close relatives were bishops and a dozen other relatives priests or nuns.[20] They endured anticlerical persecutions that traumatized Mexican society in the early twentieth century. Maciel's militant faith has its taproot in this embattled history.

It began when Spanish troops who claimed Mexico in the early sixteenth century opened a vast mission territory where "the clergy were virtually members of the royal bureaucracy. After the viceroy the archbishop was the most important figure in the country."[21] As soldiers subjugated the Indians, Spanish priests were divided between those allied with the military and the landholding aristocracy, and the Franciscans and other religious order priests who protected the Indians. Catholicism entered the imagination of Indians in a profound way. Missionaries in Mexico "allowed the Indians to sing and dance before the Christian images as they had before their gods. They gave them sacramental theater, music and choirs, mural paintings, elaborately impressive church facades and altar pieces," wrote historian Enrique Krauze.[22]

A common spirituality drew on the widely reported apparition in

1531 of the Virgin of Guadalupe to an Indian named Juan Diego on the site where Aztecs had once worshiped Tonantzin (mother of the gods). Although Juan Diego's existence has been disputed by some historians,[23] the Virgin of Guadalupe has become so ingrained in the Mexican religious sensibility that "Guadalupians" and "Catholics" are often used interchangeably. The banner of Guadalupe was raised in the cause of Mexican independence from Spain.[24] The hierarchy was so enmeshed with colonial rule that when Mexico won independence in 1821, the Catholic Church was stripped subsequently of significant wealth, land, and facilities. But politics could not uproot the faith among the Indians, the great hacienda owners, or the growing mestizo, or mixed-blood, society in between.

Throughout the nineteenth century and into the first half of the twentieth, amidst bloody revolutions and counterrevolutions, persecutions against the church waxed and waned. A new constitution in 1917 outlawed Catholic schools, expelled foreign priests, stripped clerics of their voting rights, banned monasteries, and shut down Catholic newspapers.

The Cristero Revolt and Maciel's Uncles

Two of Maciel's uncles and two other close relatives became bishops in a time when many priests, like the character in Graham Greene's novel, led clandestine lives, saying Mass in private homes. Maciel was four when the fanatical president Plutarco Elías Calles came to power. Calles exceeded his constitutional authority by banishing bishops and fining clerics or nuns who publicly dressed as such. A Knights of Columbus hall in Mexico City hatched a National League for the Defense of Religious Liberty, known by its Spanish acronym LNDLR (for Liga Nacional Defensora de la Libertad Religiosa).[25]

On July 31, 1926, the bishops closed the churches in protest of Calles's decrees. In Guadalajara, four hundred men barricaded themselves in the Sanctuary of Our Lady of Guadalupe and fired at federal troops until their ammunition ran out. Thus began the Cristero Revolt, which spread through the west central states of Jalisco, Colima, Michoacán, Zacatecas, and Nayarit. The hierarchy, most of whom went into hiding, were split over the LNDLR's tactics of armed revolt. Campesinos who resented government intrusion into religious life in the villages rallied behind landowners under the cry *"Viva Cristo Rey"* (Long Live Christ the King). Maciel was six when the Cristero Revolt began, and he lived at its epicenter. His mother's brother Jesús Degollado Guizar, a pharmacist of thirty-five in 1927, became a general of the rebel forces, drafted by the LNDLR. Writes historian Jim Tuck:

> *Degollado lost his first three battles and in one engagement suffered the humiliation of seeing his troops break and run. But the mild-mannered druggist persevered. He stiffened discipline and proved to be a natural military leader. Degollado did so well as commander of the Cristero's Division del Sur that he ended the war as leader of all rebel forces . . . the most humane and chivalrous of the Cristero chiefs. With the exception of a brutal [enemy] leader, he refrained from shooting prisoners.*[26]

The United States wanted economic stability and had Ambassador Dwight Morrow broker a deal between the Mexican government and the Roman Catholic hierarchy. The 1929 truce had the specific approval of Pope Pius XI, who wanted an end to the bloodshed. Morrow had the help of Monsignor John J. Burke, general secretary of the National Catholic Welfare Conference (now the U.S. Conference of Catholic Bishops), and the Reverend Edmund A. Walsh, S.J., the vice president of Georgetown University, founder of its School of Foreign Service and a papal adviser.[27]

No Cristero leader participated in the negotiations. When General Degollado learned of the settlement on June 21 he protested in a telegram to Pius XI, saying that "liberties such as life, property, legitimate right of those engaged in this struggle . . . have not been considered."[28] He implored the pope to reconsider "and not forget faithful sons." There is no record of a reply. Emilio Portes Gil, who had become interim president in 1928, assured the bishops he had no wish "to destroy the identity of the Catholic Church" and promised that churches, rectories, and seminaries would be restored, with amnesty for the Cristero fighters. Degollado, disguised as a poor ranchero, traveled by train to Mexico City to meet with LNDLR directors.[29] It fell upon him to arrange the surrender terms. The government had taken Degollado's wife hostage while he was fighting. He demanded her release before a laying down of arms. Portes Gil agreed to a no-reprisals guarantee for Cristero officers, soldiers, and civilian supporters of the rebellion—among the promises he did not keep.

In an emotional farewell, General Degollado praised his troops for their courage and loyalty. Embittered toward the bishops, he told his men that they had not lost, but had been abandoned by "those who were to have been the first to receive the worthy fruits of [our] sacrifices." Degollado did not apply for amnesty. He stayed undercover for several years while other Cristeros and LNDLR leaders were stalked and murdered. On September 29, 1932, Pius XI protested the persecution of the church in Mexico.

> *Bishops, priests, and faithful Catholics continued to be penalized and imprisoned, contrary to the spirit in which the modus vivendi had been established. To Our great distress We saw that not merely were all the Bishops not recalled from exile, but that others were expelled without even the semblance of legality. . . . Notwithstanding explicit promises, priests and laymen who had steadfastly defended the faith were abandoned to the cruel vengeance of their adversaries.*[30]

Another uncle on Marcial's mother's side was Bishop Rafael Guizar Valencia of Veracruz, the man memorialized in the town statue. He opposed the Cristeros' use of force. Pope John Paul II beatified Rafael Guizar—the last step before sainthood—for "heroic charity towards the poor" on January 29, 1995.[31]

Born in 1878, Guizar was one of ten brothers. Ordained in 1901, he spent most of his life under persecution, even fleeing Mexico with a price on his head. Exiled to Cuba in 1919, he was named bishop of the diocese of Veracruz by Pope Benedict XV and consecrated in the Havana cathedral. Guizar returned to Mexico in 1920, the year Maciel was born, and rebuilt a seminary in Jalapa to replace one the government had closed. "A bishop can do without a mitre, crosier and even a cathedral, but he can never do without a seminary," said Guizar. "The future of his diocese depends on the seminary."[32] When the government seized the new seminary, Guizar moved to Mexico City. Disguised as a junk dealer, he reestablished his seminary. An obese man, saddled with diabetes and other ailments, he gained a reputation for holiness by selling what he could—even his pectoral cross and episcopal ring—to help others. The Calles persecutions drove him into exile again, helping with seminary formation in Cuba, Colombia, and Guatemala. In 1929, with the Cristero war at an end, Guizar returned to his clandestine seminary in Mexico City. Through the 1930s priests who functioned without government authorization were subject to being hunted down.[33]

Maciel has made many references to a childhood memory of men hanged in the Cotija town square for defending the faith. In such an environment it is hard to believe that his protective mother would allow the nine-year-old to accompany the town physician "caring for soldiers of both sides who have fallen in the Cristero war."[34] The Legion's previously mentioned booklet also has a photograph of Maciel as a boy, clearly posed, wearing a cowboy hat with a gun in a holster and a belt of bullets, and flashing a sweet smile. It is supposed to add to the Legion's story of Maciel following the heroic path of his uncles, as warrior and priest.

Bishop Rafael Guizar trained seminarians at a safe house in Mexico City. Maciel was sixteen when he joined his uncle's group in 1936. He claims not to have considered himself worthy to be a priest while growing up, until a revelation in 1934:

> One day in May, in the town where I was born, returning from my parish church, where I had said the rosary, going towards home, I met two nuns, who my family knew, and who because of the religious conflict lived outside of the convent. When they stopped to say hello to me, one of them was surprised to see me because she thought that I had gone to the seminary that my uncle Rafael Guízar y Valencia, Bishop of Veracruz, had in Mexico City. She asked me why I hadn't become a priest. I responded, "I, too, can be a priest?" She answered, "Yes, you can." . . . God used what we call "confusion" to make me understand that he was calling me. It was then strikingly clear to me that God had set his eyes on me, that he chose me as his priest, despite my unworthiness and wretchedness.

Humility as he expressed here is expected in the lives of saints. For a teenager raised by a devout mother with close relatives serving as bishops and priests, seminary would seem a natural choice rather than an epiphany borne of some chance encounter.

Life in his uncle's secret seminary was hard. "Students did not drink milk or eat meat."[35] The youth who so recently felt unworthy of a calling had a revelation at Mass on June 12, 1936, a "call from God to form a group of priests who would enthusiastically and generously devote themselves to spreading the kingdom of Jesus Christ."[36] Maciel states that he "argued with God" about starting a religious order as an inexperienced sixteen-year-old. What a leap from his bashful encounter with the nuns. His objections "were all worthless before the Lord. . . . It was like a second calling."

Maciel's "inner voice" follows him to the state of Veracruz for winter break. Riding horseback at night through a deep canyon he talks with God, "so absorbed in the conversation that he loses all notion of time and distance, confident the horse knows the way."[37]

The booklet (by J. Alberto Villasana, a Legion priest) places Maciel on February 11, 1937, in Orizaba, a city in Veracruz. A near riot erupted after the shooting death of a woman in a police raid on a home where a priest said Mass. The booklet includes photographs of demonstrations—but no identifiable image of Maciel. Villasana writes that the sixteen-year-old marched with a crowd led by priests to the municipal palace to demand the reopening of churches. In a passage reminiscent of Maciel's uncle the Cristero general, Villasana writes:

> From the balcony Marcial calms the crowds, thus demonstrating the organization and cohesion of the movement. Then he climbs onto the top of an army truck in the middle of the square and tells the people that their requests have been heard.
>
> Some praise him, and others threaten him, thinking that he has sold out to the government. When he arrives at the parish he shows the truth of his words by bringing the keys out from the rectory and opening the church. Once the multitude of the faithful has entered they pray the rosary.[38]

The source for these events (a scrapbook kept by a priest in 1937) provides no quotation or confirmation of Maciel's involvement. The passage cites no article, diary, interview, or academic works, *yet tries to seem scholarly* by acknowledging the Legion of Christ archives and taped reminiscences by Maciel. In actuality, we read what Maciel told Father Villasana.[39] With a leg wound from a bayonet, arrested in Jalapa on orders of the governor, young Marcial is taken to Tierra Blanca. "Frightened? No. On March 13 we once again find him organizing, together with the other leaders of the movement, the third and definitive uprising."[40]

Freed in late March, he returns to Mexico City, is arrested again, and is bailed out of jail at a cost of twenty pesos by one of his aunts. Under orders of his uncle Bishop Guizar, he returned to the seminary in Mexico City in June.

The booklet is disseminated among members of Regnum Christi, the organization of lay Catholics who support and draw spiritual nour-ishment from the Legion. Strangely, the Legionaries' fiftieth-anniversary history book makes no mention of Maciel's heroism as he moved through his seventeenth year, in 1937.

Bishop Guizar died on June 6, 1938. The Legion history says that "misunderstandings" arose. "Marcial had to leave the seminary."[41] Villa-sana reports that two months after the "holy death" of his uncle, "the vicar-general of the vacant see and the new provisional rector expel from the seminary *'the Bishop's spoiled nephew who is planning a foun-dation'* "—a religious order. The italics are Villasana's; the quotation is clearly Maciel's interpretation of what the two churchmen of his uncle's diocese thought of him.[42] The self-absorbed Maciel misses the implica-tion of two church superiors, in a persecuted land, washing their hands of a seminarian from an influential family. "Spoiled" begs the larger question: what in his character made them recoil?

An even darker explanation may underlie the expulsion. The day before Bishop Guizar died, he had been heard shouting angrily at Maciel. He was giving his eighteen-year-old nephew a dressing down after two women had come to the bishop's house to complain about Maciel, who was their neighbor. Father Orozco, who was among the original group of boys to form the Legion in 1941, said he heard the women had complained about the "noise" Maciel was making with chil-dren he had brought into his home to teach religion. He said that the seminary officials blamed Maciel for his uncle's having had a heart attack.[43]

Maciel's constructed acts of heroism—the boy tending to wounded Cristeros, the teenager leading antigovernment protests—put him in his uncles' footsteps. Maciel is making his persona: a heroic, saintly mask to cover his worldly genius at pulling money from the rich while hiding sex with boys in the closet of church secrets. Spurned by his own father, Marcial Maciel Degollado will remake himself as Father, triumphant.

In 1937, the American bishops opened a seminary for Mexicans in Montezuma, New Mexico, with instruction by Jesuits. The seminary functioned for thirty-five years, until Mexico was able to restore its seminaries. Maciel, at eighteen, entered in 1938 with the help of another uncle, Bishop Antonio Guizar Valencia of Chihuahua.

Villasana writes that Maciel made a special trip to Mexico to raise scholarship funds for thirty young men. Back at Montezuma, "his rich personality" ingratiates him with other seminarians. "He follows the custom of giving away everything he has to others" (hardly the mark of a spoiled nephew). "His mind works like a laboratory, translating everything in terms of the mission he is undertaking."[44] Nevertheless, before Christmas in 1939, Maciel says, he was warned by Bishop Guizar that he would have to give up the idea of forming a new congregation if he wanted to continue at Montezuma.[45] Maciel turned yet again to a family relation, Bishop Francisco González Arias, who agreed to sponsor him as a seminarian at Montezuma for his diocese of Cuernavaca.[46] But he still finds no welcome there.

On June 17, 1940, a Jesuit knocks on his door and tells him to leave. "He gives Marcial half an hour to prepare his things. He tells him that a car is already waiting for him at the door." Marcial asks to see the rector. No. Leave on the spot.[47]

Even if the rector felt it "not prudent" for him to be planning a religious order in a diocesan seminary, that does not explain the humiliation of getting kicked out on thirty minutes' notice, without so much as a farewell or God bless. Two years of study—raising scholarship funds for thirty seminarians to boot!—and out you go.

The Legion says he left because of "misunderstandings."

"He was kicked out because he was not considered apt for the priesthood," said a Mexican Jesuit who studied at the seminary and requested anonymity. "He wasn't smart enough, and he was not emotionally or psychologically balanced—that's what I was told by his professors."[48]

He returned to Mexico on June 17, 1940, and made his way to Cuernavaca and his sympathetic sponsor, Bishop González. Over the next several months, Maciel and the bishop wrote or visited several seminaries. Like a row of falling dominoes, rectors in Puebla, Morelia, San Luis Potosí, and Mexico City said no. Maciel concluded that Jesuits in his last school were sending reports to "all the seminaries in the country . . . so that they will not accept him." He goes to San Antonio; a Franciscan provincial agrees to accept him. "But a short time later he too receives a letter from Montezuma. They had found out." Again, he is turned down.[49]

"Found out" what? The narrative logic is fascinating. Maciel wants the readers—Regnum Christi members who donate money to the Legion—to see the depths of his struggle, the barriers he had to surmount in founding the Legionaries. "How much moral suffering he carries within him! At twenty [sic], they expel him from a second one, and he is the object of many calumnies and slander by religious."[50]

Now the misunderstandings are clouded by "calumnies"—and a new pattern arises: clerical conspiracies to thwart Maciel's quest, the founding of a religious order.

Why would seminary officials in New Mexico blackball an aspirant who wanted to form a religious order? Derailing his vocation makes no sense unless he had grossly offended priests at Montezuma. Why else would churchmen in a Mexico desperate for vocations, with priests being killed, refuse him for seminary?

Bishop González assigned him private professors. Free from the nagging judgments of seminary superiors, Maciel began to search out adolescent recruits for his unnamed religious order. He found accommodations in the three-room basement of an old house at 39 Calle Turin in Mexico City. He is said to have used newspapers for a mattress, a towel for a blanket, his shoes wrapped in pants as a pillow. Like Francis of Assisi, he should be seen in this phase as a wellborn youth choosing the grace of poverty.

At twenty, without a full education, he starts teaching others. The example of his bishop uncles and the natural pride of a nephew of a Cristero general strengthened his confidence as Maciel gathered thirteen boys to train.[51] The house owner gave them access to the dining and living rooms in the upper floors as a chapel and study hall. She also gave money. Bishop González installed one of his priests, the Reverend Daniel Santana, as rector; the bishop appointed Maciel "permanent director" of the new religious order. Santana celebrated Mass at their first formal meeting on Friday, January 3, 1941, which the Legion commemorates as the date of its founding.[52]

The basement seminary became imperiled as word leaked out about its purpose, making the house subject to government seizure. Maciel showed his flexibility, and genius for fund-raising, by finding the money to buy a small house with a garden on the south side of Mexico City, at 21 Victoria Street, adjacent to the diocesan seminary. The boys set up tents for a dining room, washing utensils, eating in shifts. Sometimes dinner was just bread and sardines.

> The young founder rose at 3:00 in the morning to milk the cow and go out to sell some of the milk to buy eggs, bread or fruit. Then he would wake his boys, prepare them breakfast and direct their morning meditation. After that he gave them some classes and talks. He was with them for recreation, always looking after their spiritual and human formation. He frequently went out begging from door to door for what the brothers needed. Other times he went out to seek new vocations for the Congregation. In the evening, in front of the picture of the Blessed Virgin, he gave them a few spiritual reflections to enthuse them before they went to bed; he spoke of worldwide apostolic projects . . . and when the house was at last in silence, Marcial would go off to study for a few hours. He had to prepare himself for his theology exams. Then, at three o'clock the next morning, the day began again. [53]

He had come far from the two seminary expulsions.

Father Santana stepped down, for reasons not given. Maciel had conflicts with a new rector appointed by his uncle—for reasons unstated. On November 26, 1944, Marcial Maciel Degollado, at twenty-four, was ordained by Bishop González Arias in the Basilica of Our Lady of Guadalupe. He had had far less training than the average diocesan priest or member of a religious order in most countries of the world.

He made up for that with good connections. From various benefactors he obtained two hundred thousand pesos, a considerable sum at the time,[54] and called his order the Missionaries of the Sacred Heart. He stamped the group with what he had learned growing up in the years of persecution and the Cristero Revolt: a militant religiosity.

We must decisively advance the interests of Christ's kingdom, leaving aside our toys and using real weapons to cut off the enemy who is so well equipped, and turn the enemy's weapons against him. We have to defend the rights of Jesus Christ and conquer for Him the mind of science, the fire of youth, and the workers' strength.[55]

The child with toy weapons in the cowboy picture will become the man fighting for the church, with the "fire of youth" central to his quest.

"Maciel had this incredible charisma," said a man who was among the first group of Legionaries.[56] "He is a magician with money, and impresses the richest people, who are not always very clever." His charisma was heightened by Catholic memories of the civil war and the Mexican church's years of terror. Maciel admired the Spanish dictator Francisco Franco. In 1936, Franco led nationalist troops against the democratically elected left-wing government. A three-year civil war followed in which Franco drew support from Hitler and Mussolini, while Franklin Roosevelt and leaders of other Western democracies stayed neutral. Franco's Catholicism was wrapped in fascism and fixed on restoring the Spanish monarchy, an agenda with great appeal to Latin American conservatives. Franco kept Spain neutral in World War II.

Wealthy Mexicans, Venezuelans, and Spaniards in Mexico were impressed by Maciel's plan for a corps of priests trained as educators in a quasi-military environment. Alfonso Torres Robles chronicles Maciel's web of financial contacts in *La prodigiosa aventura de los Legionarios de Cristo*. Maciel patterned his order on the Jesuits; however, the Legionaries' learning was not akin to the Jesuits' stress on rigorous questioning and analytical thinking. Maciel created a cult of adoration to himself, Nuestro Padre. In raising funds he stressed the order's obedience to the pope. In building his network of benefactors Maciel presented Legionaries as a bulwark against communism in nations to the south. His early support came from some of the most powerful men in postwar Mexico. They included Miguel Alemán Valdés, the president of Mexico (1946–52); the textile manufacturers Guillermo and Luis Barroso; and Jorge Pasquel, well known to baseball fans for his efforts with the Mexican League.[57] In 1948 the Legion moved out of rented quarters into the suburb of Tlalpan, redeeming a mansion previously owned by Luis Napoleón Morones, leader of the communist-influenced Revolutionary Confederation of Mexican Workers, a legendary character known for diamond rings and wild parties with beautiful women.[58] Maciel called the school Quinta Pacelli, after Pope Pius XII, Eugenio Pacelli.[59]

Maciel's mystique drew on a bizarre incident in June of 1949. Several seminarians heard sharp pops; moments later Maciel entered through a window, looking frightened, holding his hat—pierced by a bullet. Communists had tried to kill Nuestro Padre! His escape was miraculous: from the position of the bullet hole, he should have been shot in the temple. At a subsequent reception for benefactors a priest patted a gun in the belt beneath his cassock, saying, "Just in case something happens like before."

Many years later, two former Legionaries, Vaca and Barba, in separate conversations, learned that Maciel had one of his followers in the order shoot the hole in the hat to impress donors. To boys steeped in the lore of Mexican martyrs, Nuestro Padre's brush with an assassin exalted him as a crusader sent by God. In 1951, when José Barba, then twelve, left Tlalpan for the seminary in Spain, he recalls: "We were going to fight against our personal enemy, communism, drawing on stories of atrocities against priests and nuns and Catholics in the Spanish Civil War."[60]

Selected seminarians were shown a photograph of Nuestro Padre as a youthful Cristero—the photograph in the cowboy outfit—and told how Maciel had ridden horseback into the mountains to meet with priests who gave him consecrated hosts for campesinos in the villages. That happened in Veracruz in 1937, the Villasana booklet says.

A Bridge from Mexico to Spain

With the end of World War II, Maciel's ambition to build an international religious order began to take wing. He found "the hand of God" in a chance meeting with the rector of the Pontifical Comillas University in Spain, where diocesan priests were trained by the Jesuit fathers.[61] The Reverend Francisco Javier Baeza, S.J., was traveling in Latin America with the Spanish government's offer of scholarships to worthy students. Maciel wanted the scholarships; he also had a love-hate complex about the Jesuits since his expulsion from the New Mexico seminary. He told benefactors that the Jesuits had rebelled against the pope—his order was totally loyal. He had his seminarians call him Nuestro Padre, just as the Jesuits' founder, Ignatius Loyola (a Basque soldier), had been called.[62] In Madrid, he wangled a meeting with the foreign minister, Alberto Martin Artajo, who told him scholarships were possible if his order had the pope's approval.[63]

For an obscure Mexican priest, not yet thirty, to meet with Pius XII was a major undertaking. He found lodging in Rome at the Pio Latinoamericano College and learned that a private audience was impossible without a letter of recommendation, and even then could take weeks.[64] In June of 1946 the ascetic, reed-thin pope was one of the world's most revered, sought-after men.[65] Newspapers praised Pius's holiness and his "heroism" for refusing to leave Rome and his "implacable defenses of the rights of men in the face of threats from Hitler and Mussolini."[66] Such was the public view of the fastidious pontiff who habitually cleaned his hands with medical lotion to extinguish germs from human contact.[67] (His reticence on the Nazi atrocities became an issue in 1963 with the controversy surrounding the publication of Rolf Hochhuth's play *The Deputy*.) To secure a papal audience, Maciel had the names of two uncle bishops worth mentioning; yet Maciel's story is that all by himself he circumnavigated the curial gatekeepers. As "Pius XII celebrated a solemn Mass of beatification in St. Peter's," Maciel waited till the ceremony was over with a surplice folded over his arm. As Pius XII went down a greeting line, Maciel said: "Holy Father, I am a Mexican priest and I have something important to tell you, but I don't have anyone to recommend me to you."[68]

Pius reportedly turned to his secretary and said: "Tomorrow at noon."

But the story is problematic. There is no record of Pius XII saying "a solemn Mass of beatification" in June 1946.[69] In fact, through his entire pontificate he beatified only six people.[70] Perhaps the horror of a war in which millions died left him in no mood for making saints. He conducted only one canonization in 1946: of Mother Francis Xavier Cabrini, on July 7. A charitable interpretation is that Maciel fabricated the point to enhance his proximity to a saint being made. In any event, Pius would have been interested in hearing what a Mexican priest had to say. Fluent in Spanish, Pius had recently named cardinals from Chile, Cuba, and Peru.[71]

Maciel reports that in his audience on June 12, 1946, Pius was animated by his plans for the new congregation and encouraged him to petition the relevant offices of the Roman Curia for canonical approval. Armed with the pope's encouragement and letters of recommendation, he returned to Spain, got the scholarships and more. The foreign minister referred him to the count of Ruisenada, Sir Claudio Güell Churruca, a banker and entrepreneur, who arranged free passage for the Mexican seminarians aboard a vessel of his Spanish Transatlantic Company.[72]

On August 20, 1946, Maciel's kinsman and protector Bishop González Arias of Cuernavaca died at seventy-two. On September 2, he took thirty-four of his young charges from Mexico City to Havana, where they boarded a ship for a twenty-eight-day voyage to the port of Bilbao. From there it was ninety miles to Comillas, a beautiful town overlooking the Bay of Biscay. The count allowed Maciel to use his father's summer mansion as a seminary. In early December they were ordered out.[73]

As with the "misunderstandings" behind his seminary expulsions, the reason given for the eviction is nebulous. A Spanish count gives a priest and thirty-four boys passage on his ship, donates use of a family resort home—and then kicks them out? The Legion states that their dutiful spiritual formation had caused "envy"—presumably among Jesuits who taught at Comillas. That is hard to believe.

Maciel found a house outside Comillas; they converted the stables into dormitories. Later they found quarters at a Cistercian monastery in nearby Cobreces. The students were transported to the university in a bus that Maciel had bought as war surplus in New York.[74] Maciel began traveling back and forth to Mexico, setting the pattern that would mark his life. "In the 1950s," reports Alfonso Torres, "then–Mexican president Miguel Alemán Valdés, one of the great protectors of Maciel, sent sacks of beans, coffee, sugar and other products to the young seminarians."[75]

Meanwhile, reports about Maciel were sent to Rome "laced with calumnies of every kind," according to the Legion history, which does not say who made the reports, nor to whom in Rome they were sent.[76] Maciel himself says the accusations "branded me as a liar and a drunkard and a thief, and declared that I was practically holding the seminarians prisoners, not letting them go to confession with anyone except me." They were proven false, he said.[77] The pattern of conspirators darkening his reputation has shadowed Maciel's career. The Legion's vague reasons for such treatment make no sense; the "calumnies" do make sense if other churchmen learned about his sexual abuse of seminarians. What "misunderstanding" could be so grave?

The Congregation of Religious was the presumable destination for complaints, the office responsible for religious orders. The Legion history states that Maciel "had foreseen that his young age was bound to stir up objections, but he had never thought there would be people so determined to block the approval" with slanderous reports to Rome.[78] Those reports, if they have not been destroyed, would be in the congregation's archives. In early May of 1948 Maciel went to Rome. He wrote back, saying, "Humanly speaking there is no hope" of the order gaining canonical approval—quite a fall after his meeting with Pope Pius XII two years earlier.

Maciel turned to a powerful figure he had cultivated, Cardinal Nicola Canali, the seventy-three-year-old governor of Vatican City State, who had a reputation as a financial genius. Canali had supported Eugenio Pacelli—Pius XII—at the conclave that elected him pope in 1939.[79] "Corpulent, bewigged and by temperament cantankerous," Canali was a leading fascist sympathizer in the Vatican during the war.[80] Such sympathies would have made Maciel, with his adulation of Franco, a political soul mate. According to the Legion history, Canali arranged an audience with Pius XII. This presumably was in May 1948, though no date is given. Maciel outlined his plans for the religious order. Pius reportedly told him: "Leaders, Father Maciel; we must form the leaders of Latin America and the world and win them over to Christ. . . . You must be 'sicut acies ordinata,' an army in battle array."[81] Maciel decided to rename his order (originally registered as Missionaries of the Sacred Heart and Our Lady of Sorrows). His original thought was to name his group Legionaries of the Pope, but several prelates thought it presumptuous to identify an order with the pope. He settled on the Legionaries of Christ.

"I approve and bless the forms of apostolate you propose," Pius wrote in a letter dated May 12, 1948. The Congregation of Religious approved the Legionaries as a congregation of the diocese of Cuernavaca. The Code of Canon Law required formal establishment under the authority of the new bishop of Cuernavaca, Alfonso Espino y Silva.

Maciel flew to Mexico and arranged with the bishop for a June 29 ceremony. He was at the apostolic school in Tlalpan on June 13 when "an interior voice" told him: "Today. The foundation has to be today." He left for Cuernavaca, revealing his message to Bishop Espino.[82] The Legion states that on the same night "the bishop signed the decree that gave life to the new congregation in the bosom of the Church." Maciel, as superior general, received the vows of the first two Legionaries.

The Legion states that "negative reports" from Maciel's unnamed, if persistent, enemies in Rome went to Cuernavaca, telling the bishop to rescind his approval—too late. Why would functionaries at the Roman Curia try to halt the final step of a founding that the pope had supposedly approved? Nothing got in the Legion history that Maciel did not dictate or approve. The story is either disinformation to show Maciel triumphant over his unnamed enemies, or a signal that his sexual past nearly caught up with him.

In 1950, authorities at Comillas University forced Maciel's seminarians out of the university.[83] Maciel was away most of that summer, according to Juan Vaca; any number of seminarians could have told Jesuit confessors or counselors about his sexual advances. The Legionaries studied for a time at a monastery in the neighboring town of Cobreces. In 1952, Maciel found a permanent location in a former four-story hotel at Ontaneda, in the province of Santander. No Jesuits would meddle with the life Maciel had in mind for his students.

In 1949, a twenty-two-year-old Comilllas seminarian named Federico Dominguez switched allegiances and joined the Legionaries.[84] Dominguez found Maciel "an extremely charismatic man." He left the Legion after seven years. In 1996 he was a Spanish studies teacher in Los Angeles. "I believed the devil was after this man because he was so saintly," said Dominguez. But soon he realized Maciel "was poorly educated. He made many spelling mistakes." Dominguez became Maciel's de facto secretary, taking dictation. "I got to know how he wanted his letters. But the thing that started bothering me, he was always exaggerating." In letters to patrons in Mexico "he was practically lying. He would say we had three hundred students but there were only one hundred. To women, the letters were always florid. I had to invent half of it to make them see how marvelous he was. I began to have my doubts about him."

Dominguez saw Maciel's genius, though. "Maciel really had an uncanny way of getting money from people. He came across as a man driven by an idea."

One night Maciel excused himself from dictation, saying that he had to read the breviary, the text priests were expected to read an hour each day. Dominguez needed clarification of a figure in a letter; he went to Maciel's room. "It was dark," he explained. "He was already in bed. Juan Vaca was there. Why couldn't [Maciel] tell me, 'I was terribly tired'? I got the figure and got out of there."

But the sight of the Mexican boy, on the cusp of adolescence, alone in Maciel's room made him wonder. He had no evidence of sexual contact. But Dominguez told himself: *This man lies too much*.

Federico Dominguez's suspicions about Maciel grew when he went to Mexico to assist in recruiting students for the apostolic school in Tlalpan. "Maciel told me that we were trying to get smart kids, not Indian-looking," said Dominguez, echoing remarks with a dozen former Legion members who say Maciel had an obsession with boys of fair complexion—a narcissistic projection, or a view of Indians as inferior to European stock. Said Dominguez: "The thing that put a great deal of suspicion in my mind was that he was always surrounded by the kids who were very good looking."

Chapter Nine

THE WAR AGAINST
INTERNAL ENEMIES

THE VATICAN would eventually hear reports from nine men that Marcial Maciel sexually abused them in their seminary years, but only after an odyssey shadowed by fears of retaliation from the Legion and its founder. Juan Vaca, supported by Father Alarcón, made his appeals in 1976, 1978, and 1989. The leader of the larger group was Professor José de Jesús Barba Martin.

Of the many youths who entered seminary in the 1940s at Tlalpan, José Barba brought an intellect of exceptional promise. Barba spent thirteen years as as a Legionary, leaving at twenty-four. In 1978 he earned a doctorate at Harvard in Latin American studies. He returned to Mexico City and in the early 1980s worked at the Legionaries' University of Anáhuac North. As part of the benefits package, his two children attended a Legion primary school. José Barba never forgot Maciel's abuse; the logic of survival worked against a confrontation with Maciel, whom he rarely saw in later years. His silence mixed with a hunger for justice that grew as he got older. In 1989 he became a professor at ITAM (Instituto Tecnológico Autónomo de México). As he amassed a personal library of twenty thousand books, Barba matched his passion for Spanish with an eloquence in English, Italian, and French.

Documenting Maciel's abuses was a slow, painful process of reconnecting with some men he had not seen in years. They had no legal recourse in Mexico; Maciel had abused them in Spain and Rome. Civil litigation was not their goal anyway.

The 1993 news coverage of North American clergy scandals stirred a torrent of emotions in Barba's group. *How does he get away with it?* they wondered about Maciel. On December 5, 1994, a half-page advertisement in *El Universal* and six other major dailies in Mexico City featured a photograph of Maciel kissing the ring of John Paul II and an open letter from the pope, celebrating Maciel's fiftieth anniversary as a priest, calling him "an efficacious guide to youth."[1]

José Barba got sick to his stomach on seeing the ad. The pope's words were too profane to let pass and strengthened his resolve to act. But the scandals that sent tremors through Catholic communities of North America, Ireland and Australia had barely touched Latin America. The Legionaries were a national institution in Mexico. Maciel had raised enormous sums in Spain, establishing the Francisco de Vitoria University in Madrid through a coalition of benefactors, including the wealthy Oriol family, of whom four sons became Legionary priests. Maciel cultivated the opera tenor Placido Domingo to perform at fundraisers. As Chile emerged from the bloody Pinochet dictatorship, the Legion had two universities, two private schools, and a radio station in that country.[2] The Legion seminary in Ireland was on a rolling spread in Foxrock, a village south of Dublin, where wealthy Mexicans sent their sons to learn English. In 1998 the order sold off twenty acres for 25 million Irish pounds.[3] In 1996 the Legion bought a 264-acre office complex in Mount Pleasant, New York, from IBM for $33 million, for use as a religious center. A spokesman said the Legion had substantial debts.[4] Maciel, however, thought nothing of paying $9,000 a ticket to fly the Atlantic aboard the supersonic Concorde and renting a helicopter to appointments in Mexico, Colombia, and Connecticut.[5]

Excavating the Past

In agreeing to on-the-record statements in November of 1996, Barba and his cohorts knew they were setting themselves up for denunciation by the Legion and possible ridicule in Latin societies. But they wanted the pope to acknowledge what Maciel had done to them and investigate the Legion.

Of the nine men, one had died in early 1995: Juan Manuel Fernán-dez Amenábar, a former rector of the University of Anáhuac. As his health deteriorated, Amenábar, as he was called, told a number of peo-ple about Maciel's sexual abuse and dictated a personal statement. Amenábar was born in Spain. So was Félix Alarcón, the only man among the nine to remain a priest. He was doing parish work in Venice, Florida, when Renner opened the dialogue. The other seven accusers, all Mexican, came from middle-class or well-to-do backgrounds and had done well professionally. Most had children; four of them had divorced. None had taken legal action against the Legion or the church.

"The pope has reprimanded Germans for lack of courage during the Nazi era. We are in a similar situation," said Barba. "For years we were silent. Then we tried to reach authorities in the church. This is a state-ment of conscience."[6]

José Barba was born in the state of Jalisco, in western Mexico, on April 16, 1937, the sixth of eight siblings. His parents came from Span-ish stock; his father traced his ancestry to Castille. The civil war forced the couple to leave for Mexico City in 1918. In Tabasco and Veracruz, where the fighting was fierce, people were mutilated and beheaded.[7] By the 1930s, the family had recovered its land. José's father had fifty men working his farm. "I took pleasure in riding horses as a boy, and seeing the older men, my uncles, who enjoyed horses and cockfights," Barba recalled.

José was four when they took a second home in Mexico City to give better schooling to the children. Mexico followed the calendar of Spain, with a December–January vacation of parades for the saints and piñatas for the children. But Mexico's leftist governments had no diplomatic relations with Spain. The Franco dictatorship had an elaborate network of police spying. Nevertheless, Pius XII agreed to a 1953 concordat that gave Franco final say in the appointment of bishops and new dioceses. After Vatican II, Pope Paul VI halted the agreement.[8] Yet to many Mexi-cans, Spain was a land of faith restored. The Mexican clergy had exalted status for believers who remembered the government persecu-tions. Barba's mother wanted her second youngest, a voracious reader who enjoyed piano lessons, to enter the Society of Jesus; but the Jesuits did not take children.

In the fall of 1948 José Barba went with his mother and a sister to visit the Legion seminary at Tlalpan, on a trolley-car route on the southern outskirts of Mexico City. Behind the wall, shaded by the cedar trees, the place seemed like paradise, with a swimming pool, lake, ball field, shooting range, bowling alley, and horse stables. José, eleven, had a cousin who had joined but would soon leave. "I was anguished," recalls Barba. "I loved my sister Nina—she was like a mother to me—but I did not want to hurt my mother, who wanted a priest in the family."

He entered on December 3, 1948, five months before his twelfth birthday.

By custom a new seminarian was greeted by one close to his age. The boy who welcomed Barba had large black eyes and an open, trusting face. He was holding a golf club. His name was Juan Vaca.

Families visited on the first Sunday of each month. "I felt my father was sad," reflected Barba. "But he seemed resigned to the situation, and I repressed my feelings." He cried in bed, missing his family. But as the days passed on the beautiful estate, with an academic regimen he enjoyed, José Barba made friends and felt good in the crimson sweater, blue pants, and white shirt with the other apostolic schoolboys.

A large photograph of Maciel—thin brown hair, blue eyes, clear Gallic features—hung in the receiving room. In the tradition of French religious orders, the young seminarians at that point referred to him as Mon Père. Maciel was twenty-eight in 1948. Barba's first impression came one February morning in 1949; the boys quickened with excitement: Mon Père had come! "He played marbles with us, surrounded by a new group," recalled Barba. "I remember it was the day Arturo Jurado arrived."

Arturo Jurado Guzmán, a month shy of his eleventh birthday, had grown up in the colonial town of Salvatierra in the state of Guanajuato, nestled in the north central mountains. Father Maciel had come to town looking for boys with vocations. Arturo's father worked for the state as manager of the income tax office in town; his mother was a lay activist; he had an older brother in seminary in the state of Michoacán. The pastor recommended his favorite altar server to Maciel. For some reason, his mother refused to give permission for Arturo to leave. "What did she see behind Maciel's appearance?" wondered Jurado, looking back years later. "I do not know. My mother is dead now."[9]

Maciel berated her in the living room, telling her the wrath of heaven would rain down on her soul if she refused to let the boy obey

God's call. Conditioned to show obedience to priests, his mother relented. When Arturo piled into the car with several other recruits for the five-hour ride to Tlalpan, he had no earthly idea of what lay ahead.

Spain—a World Away

As "an apostolic schoolboy" in Spain, Barba discovered a deepening spirituality in the land where his language began. He loved the lyricism of Enrique González Martínez and the "somber fountains" of Antonio Machado's verse. "Those wonderful days were also lively, full of walks and mountain climbing," Barba recalled. "Nearby, the bells of the Cistercian Abbey of Santa María de Via Caeli—white and gentle as a lamb—tolled across the rolling green valley."[10] Yet for all of the epiphanies of a mind awakening, Barba and his colleagues were slowly losing touch with their families. The letters they wrote and received were read by Maciel or his underlings; the boys were told to write favorably of the seminary. They had no access to telephones.

At Maciel's behest certain youngsters corresponded with people who gave money to the Legion. Using seminarians in that way is unheard of in the Dominicans, Franciscans, Jesuits, and other religious orders. One of the important early supporters of the Legion, Flora Barragán de Garza, the wife of an industrialist, lived in Monterrey, in the state of Nuevo León, Mexico. A 1952 letter from Colegio Mayor, in Santander, Spain, by a young Legionary to Señora Barragán, addresses her warmly as "Mamacita"[11] and explains: "Our very dear Father Maciel, after being with us a short time, had to go to Rome . . . but promised he would return in the beginning of May. He was in good health. . . . Through our young veins we feel the flow of passion to devote ourselves totally to [the Lord] . . . with ardorous, virile, saintly love."

Irish seminarians recruited later followed the model. Paul Lennon, who entered the Legion in Dublin in 1961 and left in 1984, wrote to Flora Barragán and Maciel's mother. "We would write our *madrinas*, godmothers, and thank them for the help they were giving us financially, supporting our vocation," explained Lennon. "Sometimes you might write to a benefactress for a year or several years and then you might change over to another. You were never told why. Some of the most famous or wealthy *madrinas* came to visit and at least we could see what they looked like."[12]

The erosion of family ties happened so gradually that the students did not understand their vulnerability. "We had this adoration for Father Maciel," reflected Arturo Jurado. "What he said was for the glory of God."

The teachers called Nuestro Padre a "living saint," a man on a mission against communism, purifying the church with a spiritual army. To teenage boys removed from sheltered families, Maciel was a Big Brother in the Orwellian sense, supreme and overguarding. Most of their families lacked the means for overseas travel; five years might pass without direct parental contact. An ethos filtered into their minds through films they saw celebrating General Franco's heroics, and in churches with memorials to priests and nuns killed in the Spanish Civil War. "We were like soldiers, Legionaries of Christ," said Jurado. "We were *not* allowed ever to even think that our superior was wrong, and, certainly, never question any order from the superior."[13]

The boys were told that to desert the Legion meant their souls would go to hell: *"Lost vocation, sure damnation"* was the mantra that caused many to remain long after they wanted to leave, spawning guilt that led to therapy years later.

Maciel's cult of personality turned on the fourth vow—never to speak ill of Nuestro Padre and to inform on anyone who did. Religious orders take vows of poverty, chastity, and obedience. The Legion's fourth vow meant that spying on one another was rewarded as an expression of faith. The vow provided Maciel with deeply personal information on those who might reveal his behavior. (Some years later the Legion added a fifth vow, a pledge never to seek positions of leadership and to tell on those who express such ambitions.)

"They brainwashed us," said Alejandro Espinosa Alcalá. *"Lost vocation, sure damnation . . .* terrorized me."[14]

Alejandro Espinosa, fifty-nine in 1996, a rancher living near Brownsville, Texas, was one of six brothers and two sisters raised in Maciel's home state of Michoacán. He entered seminary at Tlalpan in 1950, "extroverted and totally restless, a loving boy missing my parents," he chuckled ruefully. "The [priests] were keeping me apart from others. . . . If I was expelled I would be condemned to hell."

Espinosa received whippings from one of the priests for disciplinary infractions. Such punishment was common at the seminary, though none of the men interviewed considered it an overly sadistic environment.

By the early 1950s all of the boys had made the transition to Spain.

In the seminary at Ontaneda, the young males entering puberty were expected to maintain their sexual purity. Faculty priests told them women were temptresses to be avoided. Masturbation was a mortal sin, punishable by eternal damnation, unless one repented in confession. Even today, the official teaching of the Roman Catholic Church holds masturbation to be a mortal sin, though few serious theologians consider it a cause for the loss of heaven. In the 1950s other Catholic seminaries took a misogynistic view of women; but the Legion was a culture of extremes. Encyclopedia plates of Botticelli's *Venus* and other works depicting nude women in classical art were blocked by dark paper Scotch-taped over the page.

To police their consciences the boys were given whips. At night the dormitory silence was broken by the thrashings of leather on the legs and backs. The other tool of self-punishment was the *cilicio*, a leather strap studded with chain hooks and wrapped around their thighs. The practice of self-flagellation was an ascetic practice that began with ancient monks but became common in the Middle Ages as expiation for one's sins and the sins of others. Flagellation was done in pious emulation of Christ, who was scourged with a whip before he was crucified. Many religious orders, the Jesuits among others,[15] followed the discipline but it has been suppressed or abandoned in most places since the Second Vatican Council (1962–65).[16]

"The needles entered my flesh and caused great pain, yet my bad thoughts would pursue me still," reflected Fernando Pérez Olvera, an engineer, who was sixty-two in 1996.[17] With infected wounds, Pérez listened to Maciel give a sermon "that made us tremble in a darkened church, with just a candle." Maciel portrayed God "as an implacable being who will throw us into the flames of hell if we died in mortal sin."

Seduction Rituals

Fernando Pérez was fourteen when Maciel invited him to sleep on a floor mattress by his bed. He did so for a month. One night, he said, Maciel "was lying in bed, naked, covered with a blanket, writhing in pain. He told me to massage his stomach. 'The pain is lower, under my stomach.' I touched with my hand his penis that was erect."

To a Catholic seminarian with dawning sexuality, the betrayal of chastity by his idealized Nuestro Padre was crushing. For most of the men affected, Maciel's grooming rituals triggered traumatic memories that lasted years. Fernando Pérez decided to leave "because I did not have the power to overcome my temptations." He rebelled—in order to get expelled. Maciel "locked me in a room with one bed and a night table, and one window that had to remain closed . . . it was very hard in that jail"—solitary confinement for a month. "For a longer period I would have lost my mind." He was still unruly. Maciel ordered him to pack and walk to the railroad station in town. He left at ten in the morning "and reached the station at 7 P.M., very tired, very hungry," without a cent. By eleven that night he was alone and desperate when Maciel appeared with another student and drove him back.[18]

Fernando Pérez returned to Mexico by boat in 1950, one of several youths who left at the time when Jesuits were suspicious of Maciel's sexual activity. "After being a happy child, I became an introverted, negative young man," he reflected, "with fears, feelings of guilt, constantly depressed . . . reminding me of Maciel's threats of hell." He credited the woman he later married with helping to restore his life.

His younger brother, José Antonio Pérez Olvera, had also been in the novitiate in Spain and advanced to studies in Rome. A broad-shouldered lawyer of fifty-nine in 1996, José Antonio said that he never knew until years later why his older brother had left. While at Mass one morning, José Antonio was summoned to Maciel's room, where the founder expressed concern for his sibling gone back to Mexico. "He said my brother masturbated frequently and it was urgent to take him away from sin . . . to save him from vice. I didn't know what to think. I had not spoken of this with my brother."[19]

Maciel needed a sample of his semen to send to a famous doctor in Madrid who would help remedy his brother's problem. José Antonio, sixteen, believed "chastity was the number one virtue," yet he submitted as the priest took down his pants, fondled him to orgasm, and put the semen in a flask. Maciel said soothingly: "The purpose was right." He told the youth to receive Holy Communion and "never tell anyone of this heroic act."

For José Antonio, "This act, coming after six years of strict formation, was devastating . . . like being deflowered.

"As sons of the Christian family, as Mexicans, we had been taught
that the father should be obeyed. Leaving seminary meant eternal
damnation. . . . It was a vindictive God." The sexual encounter made
him feel "like an accomplice." From then on he avoided Maciel. With his
brother gone, José Antonio suffered chronic insomnia, anxiety, and
stress. "I kept praying to God, *If I have to become mad, I will stay here,
provided I get salvation.*" He finally left at twenty-six, after a Spanish
priest he trusted told him if he was unhappy he should leave and not
worry at all about his soul. He went on to earn a law degree but shame
shadowed his ties to the possessive Legion culture. Unburdening the
guilt took years.

José Antonio Pérez Olvera considered the flagellation by seminarians "a form of psychological transference"—punishing themselves for
Maciel's sexual pathology. "There is little appreciation for double personalities in Latin cultures."

As excuses for his advances, Maciel told some that his doctor had
ordered him to release a buildup of semen; to others, that he had a
swollen prostate, a statement that betrayed the ignorance of seminarians
too young and naïve to know that a swollen prostate causes impotence.
He also told them that Pope Pius XII had given him a special dispensation for sex due to chronic pain.

Grooming rituals are common to pedophiles. Calling boys to his
room, portraying himself as pain-ridden, seeking their healing touch
were techniques of the lure. Some resisted; others molested a few times
fell out of favor. Those who participated regularly were given more privileged status. "We joked about Vaca sleeping all the time," said Barba, not
realizing that Vaca was exhausted from the nights with Nuestro Padre.

Alejandro Espinosa, the restless one whipped for his hyperactivity at
Tlalpan in Mexico, was frequently molested by Maciel in Spain.[20] "The
general of this army—it was strictly an army, we were the Legionaries—
was telling me that he had a lot of hopes for me in his strategy for the
kingdom of God," he explained. "I wrote him two times a week. I
received several letters from him. It was a sign of prestige. . . . I was
called to his room. He spoke about his pain: *It is the cross that Jesus
Christ is putting on my shoulders.* I spent the night in his room."

The strapping Alejandro was called to Maciel's room often. "It was very repulsive to me but I believed my problem was nothing compared to his. I had to be brave. . . . I considered myself like a nurse and accepted as a great distinction that he trusted me."

One who resisted Maciel's advances was Saúl Barrales Arellano, known as "the charitable one" by his peers. They thought his kindness would make him a natural priest. Sitting in his home in Mexico City, Barrales, a schoolteacher for many years, was a man of calm dignity. He revealed that Maciel "asked me to manipulate him sexually five or ten times and I refused."[21] But Maciel kept summoning him.[22] "On a daily basis I fervently asked God not to permit this kind of activity to take place. . . . How many times did I have to endure sleeping on the cold floor of a room in almost total darkness, where he called me, close to the bed in which he was lying, in order to prevent other young men from entering into this temptation?"

Saúl Barrales could only block people from Maciel's room on the nights he slept on the floor. Maciel quit calling him.

Vaca and Espinosa were like incest victims, sons with natural longings for paternal love twisted into sexual service to Nuestro Padre's narcissistic tyranny. Many years later, Vaca recalled Maciel's words as they were driving in Spain: "Juan, I know you love me very much now, but a time will come when you will hate me."[23] Vaca was confused at the remark, though it lodged in his thoughts as if surgically implanted.

The Eternal City

In Rome, where Maciel established the Legion's house of major studies, the Mexicans were told they must no longer address one another in the familiar *tú*. Henceforth, they would use the formal *usted*—or *carissime frater*, "dearest brother," in Latin. Collegio Massimo, at 677 Via Aurelia, was several miles from the Vatican. "Everything I had learned so enthusiastically about Imperial and Christian Rome came together as in a dream at the sight of St. Peter's dome," José Barba has written in *L'espresso*, the Italian newsweekly. "This is what I was seeking: Rome, art, virtue and holiness."[24]

They were ordered to avoid men from the Colegio Español and the Pio Latinoamericano College—in other words, Spanish-speaking semi-

narians. As José Barba explained: "These seminarians—we were told—
were lacking in the social graces typical of a Legionary; nor did they
have the 'style of Christ' we were to put on. We Legionaries were supposed to be 'distinguished as princes and, at the same time, humble servants of all.'" The Legionaries were not prohibited from talking to
American or Canadian seminarians; but most had not studied English.
Latin was the lingua franca in classes at the Jesuit-run Gregorian University, just up the street from the fabled Trevi Fountain, yet it hardly
suited conversational purposes. The young Legionaries were driven several miles to and from their classes like a military regiment, largely unto
themselves.

Steeped in a militant spirituality and an environment of punitive
chastity, they still had little concept of themselves as sexual beings.

For Félix Alarcón, the Legion seemed a salvation after childhood
trauma. The youngest of six children, Alarcón was born February 3,
1934, in Madrid. He was barely two when the Spanish Civil War began
and his father and an eighteen-year-old brother were taken out of their
home by communists and executed on the street. Church became ever
more a sanctuary for his distraught mother and siblings. Growing up
with such a horrific loss, he wanted to be a priest, yet wondered if he
could afford it. "I was serving Mass one day when I got a tap on the
shoulder," said Alarcón. There stood the seminarian Federico
Dominguez, then functioning as Maciel's secretary. His invitation to
visit the Legion novitiate seemed like the hand of God.

Alarcón entered the Legion with "the desires to become a priest,
faithful and totally dedicated; but very soon Father Maciel would force
me into . . . fondling, masturbations, oral sex." The abuse threw him
"into a total psychological and spiritual confusion . . . until all options
were finally reduced to a single one—to *escape* . . . to save as much as
could be saved."[25]

Maciel would never give him a favorable reference to another seminary. *Lost vocation, sure damnation.* Alarcón had to be ordained before
he could escape, or sacrifice his dream of the priesthood. In 1966, sent
to Connecticut to establish the Legion's U.S. headquarters, Father Félix
Alarcón, at thirty-two, left the Legion for the diocese of Rockville Centre, Long Island. He had spent more than half of his life in the
Legionaries. In a letter to Barba after the *Courant* report, he reflected:

*I frankly believed that in my years there with all of you it was me
who had to endure the experience worse than anybody else. I regret
that in my innocence and isolation I was not in a position to help
anybody else. I did not know that the abuse reached so many of
you. . . . I admire your courage and your integrity. As far as I am
concerned, I should have preferred to remain silent, but it is clear
now that my only choice is to make common cause with our suffering. Our lives may be considered little or insignificant, but we are
telling the truth, without hatred, without seeking gain, embracing
the Cross of our Lord Jesus, in whose faith we want to live and die.
I hope a reborn Church might emerge from all this turmoil, more
coherently sensible, humbler, less arrogant.*[26]

Barba turned eighteen in the spring of 1955. The stories of Maciel's
heroism and saintliness had become enmeshed with another reality: his
fragile health. Nuestro Padre was often in the infirmary at Collegio Massimo, or secluded in his room, when not traveling. Late one morning, Barba
was summoned by a Legion brother to see Maciel. As he entered the room
a boy was leaving with a look of panic on his face. Maciel lay in bed with
the window blinds shut. He motioned to Barba, *Come closer.* A pillow
rested on the bed between priest and novice. Barba was sweaty from working outside. As Maciel revealed the special permission from Pope Pius XII
to masturbate him, he guided Barba's hand to his organ and reached for
Barba's. "I became erect," said Barba. "I had never masturbated before. . . .
He pushed my hand aside. *You don't know how to do it!* I was doubly
ashamed"—for not knowing what Maciel wanted, and because he had just
committed a mortal sin. "It was the first time I had an ejaculation."[27]

Barba began crying. "I felt defeated. I stood up to leave. He said,
'Stay here.' . . . I went to the bathroom and cleaned myself. When I went
back he was in a white robe. *Come.* We were walking out. *Don't say
anything to Father Arumi* [the head of novices]. *The Spaniards do not
understand any of this.* . . . So we went outside and had lunch. He
rubbed his hands and blessed the food and chatted in good humor."

Maciel made another attempt on Barba on Holy Saturday 1955, the
day before Easter. In the afternoon, Barba was about to join novices in
preparing the grounds for a ceremony, the blessing of the first stone for a
church to Our Lady of Guadalupe. Maciel decided to build the church

after observing the number of Mexicans visiting Rome in those years. "Accompany me," said Maciel, taking his hand. "I'm not feeling well." This time, according to Barba, they spent all afternoon in a private room of the infirmary. He watched another Legionary inject him in the buttock with a painkiller. When they were alone, Maciel began caressing his legs and buttocks, "as if I were a woman," forcing kisses upon him, until he realized that Barba was unwilling. They heard Gregorian chant in the chapel. "Go join the community," Maciel said.[28]

Two days later, Cardinal Clemente Micara, the vicar of Rome, blessed the cornerstone of the new Our Lady of Guadalupe Church before a distinguished gathering.

Days of Dolantin

The boys were told, repeatedly, that Pius XII had encouraged Nuestro Padre to found their order. As they moved through adolescence they saw Maciel receive injections for chronic pain in the infirmary, in private quarters, in hotels. "I saw him injecting two times, three times a day," said Alejandro Espinosa. "His arm was pocked with blue spots from needle marks and his buttocks looked like a pincushion. . . . I saw him furious when he didn't get the drug. One time when Saúl returned with one little case, he took it at once."

Saúl Barrales, "the charitable one" who had slept on the floor of Maciel's room, was sent by car to the hospital on Isola Tiberina, a small isle in the Tiber River, to obtain the narcotic Dolantin. Better known as Demerol in the United States, it was highly addictive.[29] If one hospital refused, the driver headed to another. "We were living in a world with a lack of knowledge," said Barrales. "I would go to drugstores to ask for the drugs but they wouldn't give them to me because they were forbidden. When I went to hospitals run by nuns, some of them would give me the drugs to take to Maciel."

Arturo Jurado was sixteen when Maciel summoned him to his bedside, moaning with abdominal problems. He spent a week watching him suffer. "At that time I was awfully innocent," said Jurado. "We had a great veneration for him."

Arturo Jurado, slight of build with thinning black hair, was fifty-eight in November of 1996. With a doctorate in Spanish from the University of Illinois–Urbana, Jurado was teaching soldiers and diplomats at the United States Defense Department School of Languages in Monterey. In the modus operandi he described, Maciel gathered boys to witness his suffering, then weeded them out individually for sex. "He taught me and forced me to masturbate him. I got an order from a holy man and I obeyed that order without any question."[30] As the encounters increased, he said, "Maciel told me that King David had a lady in the Bible. David called for her to sleep with him, therefore, it was okay [for me] to sleep with Maciel." Jurado estimated that Maciel abused him on forty occasions over several years.

> I was like a nurse. On many cases I injected him, regular injections and intravenous injections. . . . At some point he said, "You don't like my body, do you?"—more or less in the same manner as a woman would mention to her partner except a woman usually uses the question in an affirmative way, "Do you like my body?" I was speechless.

In Rome, Jurado said, he was dispatched to Salvator Mundi Hospital on at least a dozen occasions to obtain Dolantin for Maciel.

"For me the psychological torture which had its origin in his abuse of drugs was by far much worse than all the rest of the things," Father Alarcón reflected.

> I remember by heart the formula of that drug as good as I know the Lord's Prayer: "Ester-etilic chlorhydrate of methyl-phenyl-pipheridin carbonic acid." Those years would become a perennial interaction of sex and drugs. Trying to obtain the "Dolantin" was a real drama— through hospitals, and doctors, searching even in telephone books, traveling outside the city of Rome with the car drivers Tarsicio [Samaniegro] and I think [Guilermo] Adame, too. One time I even had to fly in a TWA Constellation plane from Rome to Madrid to obtain the "Dolantin." . . . He was supposed to be good, an elected man, and a saint, while at the same time there was also in him this dark side which began to become impenetrable and self-contradictory.

In Spain, Maciel's behavior got so out of hand that they were kicked out of a hotel in San Sebastián, said Alarcón. "We escaped in a Pullman train towards Salamanca."

They had grown up believing Maciel was a spiritual warrior. In his narcotic dazes and punctured flesh they saw the suffering of a man who was leading them to become figures of Christ. His flawed humanity, so powerful, overrode a realization of what he was doing to *them*.

According to the Legion history, reports "laced with calumnies of every kind" were sent to Rome during the order's early years.[31] But the Legion insists that there were no complaints of sexual misconduct, and, as we explain in chapter 10, emphatically denies Maciel's drug use.

The Vatican Steps In

The Legion's 1991 history omits any reference to the Vatican investigation between 1956 and 1958. Within the Legion, that time is called "the War." Maciel more recently calls it the "Great Blessing." Indeed it was a war: a war against internal enemies.

Federico Dominguez, the Spanish seminarian who handled Maciel's correspondence, had watched his injections of painkilling drugs and knew the man was in trouble.[32] On a trip to Mexico in 1955, Dominguez became alarmed at Maciel's constant contact with young boys at the seminary in Tlalpan. He confided his suspicions to Father Luis Ferreira Correa, the Legion's director of the school. Ferreira had heard confessions of the seminarians. Canon law forbids a priest from disclosing anything he hears in confession, but Ferreira could encourage such youths to speak with a superior. Dominguez sought the counsel of a Benedictine priest, Gregorio Lemercier, at the Monastery of the Resurrection in Santa Maria Ahuacatitlán near Cuernavaca, in late December of 1955. Lemercier then met with Ferreira and told both men to write the Vatican. In the meantime, an older Legion seminarian in Rome was passing information to the Curia.[33] The complaints landed at the Congregation of Religious, headed by Cardinal Valerio Valeri, a frail, scholarly man and a Vatican diplomat before receiving the red hat in 1953.

In October of 1956, Maciel tearfully told his seminarians in Rome that he had taught them to be obedient to the pope, and now he must show obedience by stepping aside, even though Vatican officials were mistaken. He did not specify how the Vatican had erred. Confusion spread in the community. Those excluded from Maciel's advances wondered why Pope Pius XII, who had approved the Legionaries' status, should suspend Father Maciel from his duties. He left for a hospital outside Rome, forbidden to enter the Vatican or the seminary.

Cardinal Valeri and the more powerful Cardinal Alfredo Ottaviani, secretary of the Holy Office, had grave doubts about Maciel's integrity. Valeri had seen Maciel in the Salvator Mundi Hospital in the spring of 1956, according to Vaca. The cardinal "walked in his room at 7 A.M. with a secretary and saw him in a drug state."[34]

At least two apostolic investigators—visitators—entered the scene: the Reverend Anastasio Ballestrero, an Italian, the superior general of the Carmelite Order, and the Reverend Benjamin Lachaert, a Belgian, the order's vicar general. Ballestrero in later years became the cardinal archbishop of Turin. Both men are now deceased. The Legion, in a December 20, 1996, letter to *The Hartford Courant,* said Ballestrero was dead. The authors accepted the statement at face value; they subsequently learned that the cardinal did not die until June 21, 1998.[35]

A third priest, Monsignor Alfredo Bontempi, was an official observer of the seminary, the oversight for which he passed to Father Antonio Lagoa of the Legion. The investigation was done with considerable concern for the students. Monsignor Bontempi introduced himself to the assembled college. "He said that he had been appointed as a supervisor of the *rectoria* and had, in turn, redelegated the position to Father Lagoa, but that he would be seeing us once or twice a month," recalled José Barba, who kept a diary. "Our communications with him were always as a group."

At Collegio Massimo more than fifty seminarians were questioned. The pressure on them was enormous. As Legionaries of Christ they had sworn to uphold the fourth vow—never to speak ill of Father Maciel or the Legion, and to inform on those who did. Suddenly they had to choose between vow and visitators—outsiders of high authority. To the older students, admitting sexual activity of any kind might abort the priestly life for which they had spent years preparing. As in countless studies of incest, the temptation to seal away dirty family secrets was like a magnetic force. Who had brought them from the fields and villages of distant Mexico to the steps of ordination in Rome? *Our Father.*

Father Lagoa told them the Vatican visitators were "evil people, of bad intentions," remarked Arturo Jurado.

"We were told there are these enemies of God, out to get Maciel," said Juan Vaca. "I denied [his] drug abuse. I made a big defense and praise of Maciel."

The Carmelite visitors apparently did not ask each person the identical set of questions. Some were asked about sexual activity, others were not. Each student placed his hand on the Bible and swore to tell the truth, lest he be excommunicated. Asked what he thought of Maciel, José Barba replied: "He is a saint." *Why?* "Because I have seen him suffering in the infirmary."

Under more pointed questioning, Barba retreated. "I was scared. . . . I didn't tell him about my experiences. I lied."

Arturo Jurado also lied. "For me it was obedience," he said in explaining why he did not reveal the sexual abuse.

José Antonio Pérez Olvera said he was asked one question: "At any point did Father Maciel do anything improper to you and ask you not to tell anyone, not even under confession?" *No*, he replied. Reflecting on a lie told under oath, Pérez, a lawyer, said: "I sacrificed myself for him. Internally, I feel I was excommunicated." After years of working through the past, Pérez considered himself "Catholic enough."

"I knew he was on the wrong side," Alejandro Espinosa said of Maciel. "But I didn't dare to judge him. . . . My vow was not to say anything bad and report anyone who did." He, too, lied.

For eighteen months Maciel floated in an ecclesiastical limbo between the outskirts of Rome, Spain, and Mexico. Three Legionary priests— Lagoa, Rafael Arumi, the superior of novices, and Ferreira, the vicar general—oversaw daily operations in Rome, assisted by Federico Dominguez. "None of my old friends would talk to me," said Dominguez. "It was circle the wagons. . . . The Carmelite was not getting any information from the people there. Father Ferreira and I were personae non gratae."

Each morning Vaca and a comrade dissolved laxative tablets in Ferreira's coffee. He sought medical help but nothing did any good. After three months Ferreira returned to Mexico. Daily oversight fell to Lagoa and Arumi; both priests were in Maciel's corner.

Maciel still pulled the strings. Seminarians were summoned from Rome to confide with Maciel on personal issues. He punished or got rid of those he suspected of disloyalty. In 1957, he ordered Saúl Barrales, "the charitable one," sent to the Canary Islands to prevent him from being questioned by the Carmelites. Barrales spent nine months in exile.

Then Maciel expelled him and shipped him back to Mexico. He was so depressed that it took more than a year before he could tell his parents, who had been planning a trip to Rome for his ordination ceremony.

As the investigation wore on Vaca received a call from Maciel, in Spain, in May of 1957, telling him to get money from Lagoa and fly to Madrid. When Vaca arrived Maciel wanted a briefing. He also needed Dolantin, Vaca said. Wary of Franco's sharp-eyed police, they set out for Spanish Morocco, where drugs were notoriously plentiful and law enforcement lax. Vaca spoke at length of their visit to Ceuta and two other towns on the Mediterranean. At Tetuan, they stayed in a hotel, where Maciel passed out in the bathtub. "He would have drowned if I had not gone in," said Vaca. Only twenty, he was starting to feel "all cut up inside." For nearly half his life Maciel had been father, lover, religious overseer.

Maciel sent Arturo Jurado to the seminary in Spain in 1958, forestalling his ordination. Jurado believes that his resistance, at twenty, to allowing Maciel to penetrate him sexually challenged Maciel's control. With *Lost vocation, sure damnation* drumming in his thoughts, Jurado announced he was quitting, and told Maciel sarcastically: "Don't worry, you're not responsible."

The Carmelites concluded their investigation in the latter part of 1958. Although the Legion claims that the investigation cleared Maciel, in keeping with Vatican policy, the report has never been made public. Marcial Maciel Degollado returned to his position of authority four days after the death of Pope Pius XII, on October 9, 1958, and fifteen days before the October 28 election of his successor, Pope John XXIII.

In a document provided by the Legion, dated February 6, 1959, Cardinal Clemente Micara—who had been Pius's vicar of Rome—said that he was carrying out orders for the Sacred Congregation of Religious on October 13, 1958, to reinstate Maciel.[36] It is not unusual for a document from the Holy See to be released well after the date on which it takes effect. However, the Legion does not provide the October 13 document ordering the reinstatement. Micara had blessed the first stone at Our Lady of Guadalupe Church, for which Maciel had raised the money. Now Micara did Maciel the biggest favor of his life.

Maciel regained power in a rare interlude without a pope.

"All the cardinals in charge of departments in the Roman Curia, including the secretary of state, lose their jobs when the pope dies," writes Thomas J. Reese, S.J., in *Inside the Vatican*.[37] There are three exceptions. One is the camerlengo, or papal chamberlain, who organizes the funeral, the conclave of cardinals, and the enthronement of the new pope. Then there is the major penitentiary, who deals with highly sensitive confessional matters. Finally, the vicar of Rome remains pastor of that diocese. The Congregation of Religious was theoretically inoperative with Pius dead but would have honored any commitment the pope had already made. Unless the Vatican has an archival document bearing Pius XII's seal that restores Maciel, one has to wonder how he persuaded Micara to use his powers in that interstice to salvage his career.

Vatican officials were undoubtedly concerned about Maciel's drug use. Although addiction was not an issue in society as it is today, the Carmelite visitators and Cardinals Valeri, Ottaviani, and Micara surely wanted assurances that his problem was under control. But Maciel's drug dependency did not end when Micara's signature put him back in the cockpit. In 1961, he sent Vaca and two other Legionaries to Mexico to visit major benefactors. That summer, stated Vaca, he accompanied Maciel to a medical complex in Temple, Texas. "I went with him to the hospital but he was there all by himself with a doctor. We stayed in a hotel, paid cash. He always paid in cash. He never used credit cards. . . . The next day he went back to the hospital for the return of his tests. He said the doctor gave him something to clean up his system. It was very painful for him to stop taking drugs. He used other medications to ease his reactions.

"He tried to stop many times. I know he was using through seventy-three or seventy-four. He went through many medical checkups. He would stop using drugs for two, three months, and then go back again. He used to go to hospital for a cleanup of his blood." Vaca said that Maciel used insulin at one point, not for diabetes. Insulin has been used for shock therapy on patients with drug addictions; it induces a short coma that changes the body's metabolism, supposedly improving the chance for shaking off the addiction.[38]

Seeds to the Wind

Maciel celebrated Christmas 1958 with his seminarians in Rome. Father Ferreira left the order; he served as a pastor in Mexico until his death in

2001. Federico Dominguez was transferred during the investigation from Rome to Maynooth Seminary near Dublin. When Maciel was reinstated, Dominguez left the Legion. He took classes at University College, Dublin, where he met the woman who became his wife. They settled in Los Angeles, where he taught high school.

In 1958 Maciel sent José Barba to Mexico as a teacher at the seminary in Tlalpan. Back on the lush estate he had entered at eleven, Barba, twenty-one, renewed ties with his family. Confused about Maciel's sexual advances, Barba had no idea what had befallen Vaca, Jurado, and others. In the fall of 1959, Barba met a middle-aged British widow of deep spirituality for conversations to improve his English. Janet Collin was being cultivated by the Legion as a *madrina*. She was a cerebral woman who found a palliative to the grief for her recently deceased husband in the writings of the Spanish mystic Saint John of the Cross. Barba felt a beauty in the language that mirrored an essence of the woman. He did not fall in love with her; but as she exposed him to the works of Rilke and other poets, Barba realized it was possible to love God and have a joyful view of life. As books began filling up his room, one of his superiors scolded him for being pretentious—you do not need all those books! The Legion submissiveness cut against a welcoming world of ideas opened by the lady who became a kind of mentor. One day he realized he no longer wished to be a priest.

In a polite exchange, Maciel said that he would welcome Barba back should he change his mind. Barba left on October 24, 1962. "They will never change," Janet Collin told him, creating her own distance from the order.

Barba became a freelance translator and in the early 1960s began teaching Spanish literature and culture in San Miguel Allende, a colonial town and tourist mecca. In 1964, an old Legion classmate, Alejandro Espinosa Alcalá, visited him in San Miguel. Alejandro, who came from a ranching family, had the rugged quality of a *charro*—a man of silent strength. In Rome, Alejandro and José Barba had not been particularly close. Barba was stunned when Alejandro revealed how Maciel had engaged in masturbation with him and another seminarian, and fumed over Maciel's supposed papal dispensation for sexual relief.

I was not the only one! José Barba realized.

The idea of speaking out as a victim of sexual abuse by a priest was unthinkable in the mid-sixties, especially in Mexico, with its resurgent Catholicism and culture of machismo. Barba himself wrote Maciel three cordial letters from graduate school. For those who left, the Legion was a reference for education or work. The men also feared Maciel. Those realities retarded the long struggle of the men to make public statements. The first hurdle was understanding themselves as psychological prisoners and victims of sexual assault.

In 1967 Barba was riding a trolley in Mexico City with José Antonio Pérez Olvera, who had been a year ahead of him in Rome and was attending law school. Barba remembered the day José Antonio had appeared at his room with a baleful expression to say that his twin sister back in Mexico had died. There had been no service for her at the seminary. As José Antonio told Barba about what Maciel had done to him, the scholar wondered how many others had been targets of Nuestro Padre.

In time Barba was reunited with Arturo Jurado. Sharing a fluency in many languages, they reflected on the weight of silence that was warping them. By the early 1990s, as they were reading Juan Vaca's 1978 and 1989 letters to the pope, their determination grew.

They wanted John Paul to break his own silence.

Chapter Ten

THE LEGION'S DEFENSE
OF FATHER MACIEL

"THEY ARE out to assassinate my character," brooded Juan Vaca. He got no argument from Gerald Renner and a newsroom colleague as they sat in Vaca's tidy living room in early 1997. Reliving a painful past, responding to the many fact-checking calls, providing letters he once thought only Vatican officials would see, Vaca was nervous. He did not want the life he had made with his wife and child jeopardized by an attack by the Legion.

The Hartford Courant had a proud tradition, though it was not known for crusading. Founded in 1764, the oldest continuously published newspaper in America, the *Courant* (pronounced *current*) had once run an ad from George Washington trying to sell some land in Virginia. The *Courant* was the most influential daily in Connecticut. In 1978 the Times Mirror Company bought the newspaper, giving it free reign on local news and editorial decisions.[1] In 1992 the paper won a Pulitzer Prize for reporting on flaws that plagued the Hubble space telescope, which had been built by a Connecticut company.

With a circulation of three hundred thousand Sunday readers, the *Courant* editors approached the Maciel exposé with careful tenacity. More than half of Connecticut's 3.3 million population were Roman Catholic.[2] The attitude in the national media toward the clergy abuse phenomenon in the late nineties was essentially "old story." Many print and broadcast media *had* done such stories, some of them exceptionally well reported. But the national magnitude of sexual concealment in clerical culture had never gotten the scrutiny it warranted, especially since the criticism of CNN for its coverage of Cardinal Bernardin. In his reporting on litigation in Bridgeport, Renner had been frustrated by a court order sealing church documents from view. Questions shadowed the way Bishop Edward Egan, a canon lawyer with long experience in Rome, had handled child molesters. The pope later named Egan archbishop of New York, then cardinal.[3]

In late November 1996, Renner wrote Maciel a two-page letter summarizing the accusations, naming the accusers, and requesting an on-the-record interview; he sent the letter by facsimile to Legion headquarters in Rome. The response came in a four-page letter on December 6, 1996, from attorney James F. Basile of the Washington, D.C., office of Kirkland & Ellis. Founded in Chicago, the law firm was one of the largest in the nation, with a senior partner in Kenneth W. Starr, special prosecutor in the investigation of President Clinton.

"Father Maciel and the Legionaries completely deny these allegations," wrote Basile. His client "wishes to provide more than a blanket denial"—though Basile said nothing about an interview. He requested all statements by the men, any pertinent documentation, the specific allegations the paper intended to publish, and a response time of one week. To deny that, wrote Basile, would be "evidence of bias and malice and creates the risks of falsehoods and misstatements being published." The shot across the bow—"malice"—warned of a possible defamation lawsuit.

"Many of the same individuals who are currently making allegations against Father Maciel made *unrelated* false allegations against him in 1956 and on several other occasions since that time," Basile advised. In other words, Barba's group, who were mostly teenagers in 1956, were now accused of making false accusations to the Vatican investigators—even though they sheepishly admitted in our interviews to having lied back then in order to *defend* Maciel.

Basile sent copies of his letter to the editor and publisher at the *Courant* and the general counsel of Times Mirror in Los Angeles, a clear signal that Maciel wanted the story killed. Basile sent more letters, demanding documents per the rules of discovery in a civil lawsuit. But Maciel had filed no suit. The newspaper would give him a fair opportunity to rebut allegations and would weigh that response in deciding what to publish. On December 20, Basile sent a nineteen-page rebuttal by the Reverend Owen Kearns, the Legionary spokesman in Connecticut and editor and publisher of the *National Catholic Register*. Father Kearns included a forty-four-page appendix of letters, documents, and statements to discredit the accusers. The newspaper began an exhaustive fact-checking effort.

An Irishman who had joined the Legion in 1960s, Kearns had a two-pronged defense. The nine men were lying as "part of a coordinated campaign to smear Father Maciel," "to teach him a lesson" and "punish him for his pride." Secondly, the Vatican had exonerated Maciel after a two-year investigation in 1958. Having failed then, the old enemies were raising *new* allegations of sexual abuse. Kearns conceded that Maciel had been accused in the 1950s of drug abuse—and cleared.

Any conspiracy requires a motive and a goal. The goal—getting the pope to acknowledge Maciel's abuse and act accordingly—was clear. What was the motive? Was "pride" sufficient fuel for a conspiracy "to teach [Maciel] a lesson"?

Kearns derided Vaca as "a proud, status-conscious man angered and disappointed at his professional failures," who wanted "greater power in the Legion." Kearns ignored the fact that Vaca had *resigned* in a letter to Maciel with graphic accusations in 1976 sent to Rome by the Rockville Centre canon lawyer.

"This is the way they work," muttered Vaca. He said he had turned down Maciel's offer to make him vicar general of the order to stop him from quitting. Stephanie Summers, a *Courant* deputy managing editor, had joined Renner to question Vaca about the Legion's rebuttal and make her own assessment of his credibility. "They try to destroy their enemies any way they can," Vaca continued. "People who leave the Legion are considered traitors—treated as nonpersons. You are not allowed to mention the name of someone who left." He admitted the years of sexual abuse had affected him. He looked at Summers with moist eyes, and apologized for the details of his life. He reflected on his psychiatric counseling after leaving the Legion. *How hard it must be for him to talk about this,* Summers thought.[4] In the documentation asserting Maciel's innocence, the accounts of another man once enmeshed with Maciel became singularly important.

Accusation from the Grave

Juan Manuel Fernández Amenábar, a Spaniard, had entered the Legion at Santander in the 1950s. As a young priest he was an assistant to Maciel. In the 1970s he became the director of the Legionaries' Irish Institute near the upscale Los Lomas district in Mexico City. Amenábar was a natural orator much loved by those he served. The superrich of Mexico City sent their children to the Irish Institute; some arrived in cars driven by bodyguards.

"The family names of the Irish Institute were like a Who's Who of Mexican high society," recalled Paul Lennon, an ex-Legionary with a therapy practice in Arlington, Virginia.

> But some of the families were trying to buy class. El Negro Durazo, the corrupt police chief, sent his sons there. Maciel entrusted Amenábar to cultivate rich families who could "help" the Legion. Amenábar enjoyed those special missions; but he was such a likeable guy that those of us less privileged forgave him his good times. He admired the way we foreigners loved the Spanish language and culture. He was not afraid to talk to outsiders—a Legion taboo.[5]

Molested by Maciel as a seminarian, Amenábar by midlife was trying to break from his control.[6] The turning point was Pope John Paul's 1979 trip to Mexico. As the pope flew to Oaxaca, Amenábar joined the entourage. He was struck by John Paul's joyousness in greeting the people. In the months that followed, Amenábar felt haunted by his knowledge of Maciel's secrets. Nevertheless, in 1982, Anáhuac North, the Legion's flagship university in Mexico City, named him president. Amenábar's popularity in rich precincts of Mexico City would be a boon to fund-raising. But finally, in 1984, he asked Maciel to transfer out of the Legion. Summoned to Rome, Amenábar confronted Maciel about the moral conflict he felt in continuing as a priest "without serious harm to my soul," as he recounted in a written statement. The same document states that Maciel offered him money to remain in the order.[7]

Amenábar quit his college presidency, quit the priesthood, left Mexico and found work in a suburb of San Diego, California. He married; the relationship foundered. He suffered two strokes. In 1989 he returned to Mexico City, hobbling into the city's Spanish Hospital, his fingernails uncut, hair bedraggled, unable to speak. In 1990, during a long rehabilitation, Amenábar received a papal dispensation from his priestly vows.

A young physician, Gabriela Quintero Calleja, was doing her internship at the hospital as an ear, nose, and throat specialist. Though he was only fifty-two, half of Amenábar's body was paralyzed. Dr. Quintero was impressed by his will to recover. One of six children in a large Catholic family, she was a generation younger than Amenábar. With her help his speaking improved. She began visiting him after making her rounds; sometimes she read him the poetry of García Lorca. "I was the person closest to him his last three years of life," she said in a long interview in Mexico City.[8] Amenábar showed her his diary, recounting what Maciel had done.

Because he had been in California so long, many of Amenábar's friends were unaware he was back in Mexico City. Word slowly spread. "Some of the wealthiest men in Mexico were good friends of Juan Manuel," she continued. After the wife of Televisa, the head of the leading television network, visited and sent flowers, Father Maciel got concerned.

José Barba, who had been a colleague at the university, began reading to Amenábar. Barba's friends visited, giving moral support to a fellow survivor. Another visitor, the Reverend Alberto Athié, came at the behest of several wives of Legion school alumni. As executive secretary of the Mexican Bishops' Commission on Reconciliation and Peace in Chiapas, the poverty-ravaged southern state, the scholarly, white-bearded Athié had done mediation work with Indians in revolt against the government. He was also vice president of Caritas, the bishops' relief organization. Father Athié was shocked at what Amenábar, disillusioned in faith, told him about Maciel. But his goal was not to investigate the truth of the allegations but to listen to Amenábar "as part of a process of reconciliation," he later remarked.[9] He only wanted Amenábar to be at peace with God, himself, and others.

In July of 1994, Father Maciel visited. As the Legionary general sat with Amenábar in a garden pavilion, Dr. Gabriela Quintero joined them. She took note of Father Maciel's elegant manners, his handsome looks.

"Ah, you are the doctor," he said.

"Ah, and you are the Father Maciel," she replied. He met her sarcasm "with a gaze of competition—like when two women meet," she recalled.

Maciel had come with a psychologist named Raul de Anda Gómez, who had visited Amenábar previously. "I believe Maciel wanted to learn through other people about his condition," she continued. She considered de Anda a spy for Maciel. The Legionaries "didn't care for Juan Manuel—they only wanted to take him away when people started coming to see him."

By her account, Raul de Anda told Maciel: "The doctor wants to go to Spain for postgraduate work."

The Legion had a house of studies in Salamanca, replied Maciel. "We could help you both go there."

"Maciel's idea was not crazy—taking Juan Manuel and me away from here," she said. "His voice was very relaxed as he made the offer. He told me to think it over. 'You would be near the Legion. You would have an apartment.' "

She told him no on the spot.

When the visitors left, Amenábar said of Maciel: "Watch him. He is a fox."

"The pope's joyousness [in 1979] was a catalyst in his decision to leave," she continued, "because the pope was a sort who did happily what he did and Juan Manuel wasn't happy. Many times he said the pope was being deceived by Maciel. *The day the pope finds out . . .* and then he would move his hand in a my-goodness gesture, as if to say there would be a great scandal."

On January 6, 1995, Amenábar signed his statement with Barba and several ex-Legionaries as witnesses. He cited Maciel's drug use, his own sexual abuse, "other religious men and novitiates who were his victims," and mentioned Maciel's ruse that Pope Pius XII had sanctioned his sexual activity.

In the final days, Father Athié, concerned for Amenábar's soul, suggested that to die in peace, he must in his heart forgive Maciel. Amenábar was weeping. "I pardon Father Maciel *but at the same time I ask for justice!*" he croaked. Then he made his confession. Athié absolved him of sin and gave Amenábar the sacred wafer of the Eucharist. Amenábar asked him to celebrate his funeral Mass; Athié promised he would. Juan Manuel Fernández Amenábar died on February 7, 1995, at fifty-seven, in the Spanish Hospital.

The next day an unidentified priest entered his room and stole his personal papers.

At the funeral Mass, Father Athié spoke of his death with forgiveness in his heart—and said that he had also asked for justice, without going into details. After the ceremony, José Barba introduced himself to Athié. A dialogue began.

The Legion's Attack on Amenábar's Story

Father Owen Kearns wrote that Amenábar was unable to speak, write, or make any rational judgment because of his stroke. Kearns sent the *Courant* a letter from a man identified as Amenábar's "physician"—Raul de Anda Gómez, who suggested that the dying man "was a possible victim of persons without principles." But de Anda was a psychologist, not a physician—and a former Legionary. Amenábar was never de Anda's patient, according to Dr. Gabriela Quintero. She told Jason Berry that Amenábar "made his declaration [against Maciel] in full use of his mental faculties." Dr. Quintero and Father Athié—who barely knew Maciel—would have to be alpine liars by the Legion's lights.

Francisca Toffano del Rio, a psychologist and friend of Amenábar who visited him often, supported Quintero's evaluation in a notarized statement to the *Courant*. Quintero said it was her "desire to reveal the truth that has been kept hidden for so many years, since so many members of the Catholic Church as well as the society as a whole seem ignorant of the moral character of Father Marcial Maciel Degollado."

In trying to debunk the "deathbed confession," the Legion's strategy of disinformation became a mirror on new lies and more leads about Maciel.

There was, in November of 1996, a tenth accuser, Miguel Diaz Rivera, a sixty-two-year-old professor of philosophy of law and former Legion priest in Oaxaca. In a two-hour telephone interview with Jason Berry, Diaz detailed his sexual encounters with Maciel and pronounced him "a divided personality." Diaz backed up his interview with a sworn affidavit in January 1997.

Less than a month later, as the *Courant* was going to press with the long report for Sunday, February 23, 1997, Maciel's lawyer tried a final roadblock. A *new* affidavit from Miguel Diaz—retracting his earlier statements—arrived in the newsroom by facsimile from Washington that Saturday. Compared to his interview, with details of a wrenching experience, Diaz's eleventh-hour retraction rang hollow. He did not return Renner's telephone call to his home. The editors made a deadline decision on one revision—the number of accusers was dropped from ten to nine. Renner added Diaz's retraction to the story.[10]

"Which one of his affidavits can we quote from?" asked Renner.

"Both of them," advised Ralph G. Elliot, a veteran First Amendment lawyer and the newspaper's counsel. "In one or the other he committed perjury."

The Legion sent affidavits from four other men who said they had been asked to join the conspiracy, and refused.[11] Two of them turned out to be on the Legion's payroll in Mexico City; a third worked for Maciel's brother; the fourth was a businessman with children in a Legion school. One of the men in a telephone interview could not remember details of the supposed meetings to hatch a conspiracy—though he insisted, with a rather amazing leap of logic, that he stood by his assertions of meetings that he could not recall.

As the conspiracy accusations crumbled, Cliff Teutsch, the managing editor, said of Barba's group: "I have no doubt these guys are telling the truth."

The Legion and the Vatican

The Vatican investigation of the 1950s is airbrushed out of the Legion's history. Ironically, Kearns cited those missing events in claiming that Maciel was never accused of sexual abuse, but "of drug abuse, financial mismanagement and rebellion against the Holy See."[12] The Vatican's silence on Maciel allows no corroboration of Kearns's claim. Maciel's attorney sent *The Courant* a copy of a letter, undated, without letterhead, seemingly written in 1958 by an "apostolic visitor," the Reverend Polidoro Van Vlierberghe, to the papal nuncio in Mexico. Because his last name was difficult to pronounce, the Belgian-born Franciscan was known as Polidoro. He became the bishop of Illapel, Chile.[13] Polidoro was not one of the visitators in Rome; he interviewed Legionaries in Spain and Mexico. The undated letter that the Legion attributes to Polidoro states:

During the visitation, which was carried out with detail and rigor, I was able to confirm that in addition to being a complete exaggeration of the facts, the accusations raised against Father Marcial Maciel and his work were based on calumnies and on the personal ambitions of the Vicar General [Ferreira] of the Institute [Legionaries], and supported—for unspeakable reasons—by two members of the Mexican Episcopacy and by the Society of Jesus. . . .

In view of the fact that Maciel's fledgling Legion had been thrown out of the Jesuit university at Comillas—with the Legion's own history referring to "calumnies" sent from Spain to Rome—Polidoro's "unspeakable reasons" suggest that some accusations *were* sexual. His reference to two Mexican bishops harks back to Maciel's checkered early years, when he was shunned by Mexican seminaries. Polidoro's purported letter asked the nuncio to intercede with the Sacred Congregation of Religious, in Rome, to exonerate Maciel.

When I realized how unfounded were the accusations raised against Father Maciel and I saw for myself that the Legion of Christ is a fervent Institute with great vigor in the spiritual, intellectual and economic spheres, I set forth with a clear conscience that the Holy See ought to end, once and for all, the present situation of the Institute, reinstating Father Maciel. . . .

Polidoro wrote of visiting Cardinal Valeri, prefect of the Congregation of Religious, "so the good wine would not turn into vinegar . . . [or] deprive the Church in Latin America of a source of aid . . . an enormous hope." Maciel had been suspended after Valeri saw him in Salvator Mundi Hospital in a drugged state. Polidoro praised the Legion's seminarians as "a very select group that is producing magnificent fruits" and criticized "two members of the Institute [who] express disagreement and even outright hostility—all the more suspect considering the virulent and unspeakable motives which inspire it. . . . "

The unnamed members were Federico Dominguez, the Spanish seminarian, and Father Ferreira, the men who filed the complaint with the Congregation for Religious. *Polidoro never interviewed the nine men who made the accusations.* One of those nine—Fernando Pérez Olvera—

left the Legion several years before Maciel's suspension and was never interviewed by the Holy See. The letter suggests Polidoro bought Maciel's story of a conspiracy. But the bishop's position was clouded by a second document the Legion produced. This letter, dated December 12, 1996, from Bishop Polidoro, in Santiago, Chile, stated: "Many charges were raised against Fr. Maciel during the 1950s but . . . at no point in our extensive and searching interviews about the character and deeds of Father Maciel did a single allegation of sexual impropriety ever surface."

Polidoro was eighty-seven in 1996. The letter says Maciel was now "accused of sexual abuse by some of the same individuals who did not hesitate to accuse him in the 1950s of so many other faults and grave crimes that were proven totally false."

The man who triggered the investigation, Federico Dominguez, left the Legion in 1958 and by 1996 was teaching in California.[14] He insisted that sexual abuse was central to the charges he discussed with Father Ferreira, who sent the complaint to the Congregation of Religious. José Barba, the scholar with bulldog tenacity, and Arturo Jurado, who taught at the U.S. Defense School of Languages, suspected that the Polidoro letters were fakes, and set out to prove that. To their displeasure, the newspaper reported Polidoro's claims as part of the defense of Maciel.

Rebutting Drug Abuse

The newspaper weighed statements the Legion provided from three physicians to support the charge by Owen Kearns and the Washington attorney that the drug abuse accounts were spurious and part of a plot.[15]

The first letter—an undated, handwritten note by Dr. Ricardo Galeazzi-Lisi—said he examined Maciel at his seminary in Rome and "found nothing whatsoever in his organism which might indicate a medicinal dependency. His constitution is healthy and normal and therefore he has no need of any therapy in order to carry out his normal occupations. I release the present document for legal use." Quite aside from the dubious merits of a letter "for legal use," Galeazzi-Lisi, trained as an eye doctor, was a money-grubber who in 1958 peddled articles and photographs of the dying Pope Pius XII. The Vatican declared him persona non grata. Italy revoked his license to practice medicine.[16]

The second letter, by Dr. Luigi Condorelli, dated October 5, 1956, states:

> I certify that today I have visited the Rev. Father Marcial Maciel: he is a man in good health with a totally normal psychological attitude, a determined character, and no stigma which might indicate an hereditary neurosis. His family history in this regard is also completely negative.
>
> A general and specific physical examination fails to demonstrate even the slightest sign which might indicate an actual chemical dependency, or more specifically, a toxic state induced by morphine or barbiturate-related drugs. There is no presence of any element whatsoever indicating a psychological predisposition, in the form of a disorder manifesting a toxic state, which would lead one to believe that the Rev. Marcial Maciel suffers from chemical dependency . . . his internal organs are functioning normally (although it seems that he has a previous history of abdominal difficulties caused by colic).

The language of this letter is questionable. A patient's "determined character" has nothing to do with a medical diagnosis. The reference to Maciel's family history is also irrelevant; the doctor had no way of gaining such information, save from the patient.

The final letter, dated October 10, 1956, from Dr. Enrico Gambini at the Villa Linda clinic in Rome, said that Maciel "has been submitted to daily medical examinations since the fifth day of the present month and has been found to be in perfect physical and psychological health."

The two dated letters—within a five-day period—say Maciel was drug free in October of 1956, which was just when the Vatican suspended him. Maciel presumably used the letters to try to persuade the Vatican that he was fit for ministry. They suspended him anyway. In light of the detailed accounts of his drug abuse by Vaca, Arturo Jurado, and others, before and after the suspension, the question arises of how reliable the testing was—and whether he passed such tests.

"In the nineteen fifties drug abuse was hardly studied as a problem," explained Michael Massing, a MacArthur fellow who spent years researching drug issues and policies for his book *The Fix*. "There was little done in the way of chemical testing. It was not until the late nineteen sixties that testing really began. Even today the state of knowledge among practitioners is so small that people in the drug field are trying to make physicians aware of how to look for drug abuse."[17]

José Barba contends that the Gambini letter is a fake because Maciel was in the community from October 5 until October 10, the day the letter is dated. On that day Maciel appeared before the assembled Legionaries at 9 P.M., "emotionally distraught, weeping," explained Barba.[18] "He said he had to prove his obedience to the Vatican by stepping aside. He asked, 'How can the trunk of the tree be bad while the fruits can be good?' We were just beginning the Spiritual Exercises of Saint Ignatius and it caused a great emotional chaos. The next day I went to see Father Arumi [the director of novices] and said I wanted to quit. If the leader was expelled, what was our fate? 'You are a coward,' Arumi said. But the only way I would continue was to speak with Nuestro Padre."

Arumi took him by car to Villa Linda clinic, said Barba. As Arumi paced the hall, Barba entered the room. Calling him "my son," Maciel said that three cardinals had visited him that morning. Maciel seemed lucid, saying not to worry, the Legion would carry on, he would be back. Barba left with a feeling of relief.

Girding for the Attack

With *The Hartford Courant* still researching, Maciel's minions girded for attack. In Rome, the Legion community was summoned to a special meeting. Glenn Favreau, an American who was studying as a Legionary at the time, said that the Reverend Luis Garza, the vicar general of the Legion—and Maciel's designated heir apparent—rose to speak. Garza grew up in Monterrey, a scion of one of Mexico's richest industrial families. A graduate of Stanford University, Garza had been assiduously recruited by Maciel; Garza's parents had been major contributors. Garza told the assembled Legionaries that the media was about to publish accusations against the character of Nuestro Padre—the product of a conspiracy. The Legion had investigators working to determine who was behind it. Those present were told that should they come across an article or if anyone sent them material, they must give it to their superiors without reading it.

Favreau, from upstate New York, was thirty-one at the time. "We were told to tell people who mentioned [the report], *This is just another attack against the Legion because we are faithful to the church and to the pope,*" he recalled. "We were never to discuss this subject with other Legionaries and those who did were to be reported to the superiors immediately."

In late 1997, Favreau, who was having doubts about his vocation, met privately with Maciel. Favreau had not read *The Courant* report; Maciel raised the subject. "He said, 'Even at my age they make these accusations against me. Why did they never bring them up earlier? All during the years of the Great Blessing [Maciel's novel term for the Vatican investigation when he was suspended] many accusations were made against me, but none of this type. Cardinal O'Connor of New York had a private investigation conducted and found out that the Jesuits were behind the accusations and their release to the media. But these kind of things, after so much in my life, don't affect me anymore.' "

On Sunday February 23, 1997—nearly six months after Renner first telephoned Berry—the *Courant* report began on page one, continuing with six thousand words covering two pages inside the paper and part of a third, with a sidebar on the Legion's attack on the accusers and their alleged conspiracy.

Much to the dismay of Vaca, Barba, and the others, the report had little impact on the U.S. news media. Although the *Los Angeles Times* syndicated news service moved a tightly condensed version on its wire, the Associated Press in New York did not put the story on the international wire, despite the reporting of the Vatican investigation and refusal to comment. An AP editor told Renner it was a Connecticut story!

Five years later, when *The Boston Globe* ignited a chain reaction of investigative reports, *The Courant* story drew wide comment. At the time of its publication, the major American media had marginalized the church's crisis.

"This effort to smear a distinguished Catholic leader is reminiscent of the fake accusations against the late Joseph Cardinal Bernardin," Owen Kearns stated in a letter published in *The Courant*. "To any impartial observer the evidence eliminated the credibility of the allegations."[19] Maciel, after months of refusing direct comment, sent his own letter, which the newspaper published.[20]

I wish to state that in all cases [the accusations] are defamations and falsities with no foundation whatsoever, since during the years these men were in the Legion never in any way did I commit those acts with them, nor did I make any such advances to them nor was the suggestion of such acts ever mentioned. During the time that these men were in the Legion of Christ and even after they had left, I spared no sacrifice to help them as much as I could as I have always done with every person the Lord has put under my care. I do not know what has led them to make these totally false accusations 20, 30, 40 years after leaving the congregation. I am all the more surprised since I still have letters from some of them well into the 1970s in which they express their gratitude and our mutual friendship.

Despite the moral suffering that this has caused me I bear no ill will toward them. Rather I offer my pain and prayers for each one of them, in hope that they will recover their peace of souls. . . .

The *National Catholic Reporter* published the longest independent account with focus on the accusers.[21] Catholic News Service, a self-sustaining division of the U.S. bishops' conference, keyed on the denials of Maciel and Kearns in reporting the allegations to its network of diocesan papers and magazines.[22] *The New York Times, Washington Post, Boston Globe* and TV networks ignored the story until the events of 2002.

In Mexico, the major news media laid off the story at first. In April, *La Jornada*, a left-wing daily, ran a four-part series by Salvador Guerrero Chiprés that drew on *The Courant* report in profiling Barba and company, with new information.[23] When the reporter sought comment from the prelate of Mexico City, Cardinal Norberto Rivera Carrera snapped: "You must tell us how much they paid you!" *La Jornada*'s series spurred coverage in smaller Mexican papers. In May, Channel 40, an independent television station, aired a documentary with interviews of Barba and others, but not, of course, Maciel. In a matter of days a major corporation withdrew its advertising budget in the hundreds of thousands of dollars. In the next month twenty-five major advertisers withdrew. Channel 40 would have gone bankrupt had another station not provided interim financial help.[24]

The AP's failure to put the story on its international wire all but killed *The Courant* findings in Europe. In Italy, as best we can determine, the first examination of Maciel appeared two years later in *L'espresso*, the weekly newsmagazine, in an article by the respected religion writer Sandro Magister.[25]

The Courant never heard again from the Kirkland & Ellis law firm. The Legion did hire a public relations consultant. After entering the World Wide Web, the Legion resumed its attack on Amenábar's "deathbed confession" with a Web-site-linked site. Only, now Raul de Anda's comment disappeared. In a December 6, 2001, letter, Dr. José Manuel Portos Silva, a cardiologist, states that he was Amenábar's physician from 1978 to 1995 and his patient had totally lost the ability to speak or write in the last six years of his life, ignoring everything said by Dr. Gabriela Quintero, who helped him regain speech, and by his confessor, Father Athié.

Prominent conservative Catholics rallied to the Legion's cause with testimonials that today appear on the Web site.[26] Deal W. Hudson, in an open letter in *Crisis* magazine, which he edited, called on *The Courant* to "withdraw its false article and apologize to Father Maciel, the Legionaries of Christ and faithful Roman Catholics who support his many charitable and fruitful apostolates in the United States and around the world."

William Donohue is president of the Catholic League for Religious and Civil Rights in New York, which presents itself as a monitor of anti-Catholic bias in the news and entertainment worlds. Donohue appears often on television. He wrote to *The Courant* on March 3, 1997: "To think any priest would tell some other priest that the pope gave him thumbs up to have sex with another priest—all for the purpose of relieving the poor fellow of some malady—is the kind of balderdash that wouldn't convince the most unscrupulous editor of the weekly tabloids."

Donohue's statement was a blatant distortion of what the men said. Maciel's ruse about getting permission for his sexual urges from Pope Pius XII was not, of course, told to "some other priest," but rather to bewildered seminarians, some barely past puberty, in order to sexually abuse them and satisfy himself.

The Reverend Richard John Neuhaus, editor of the magazine *First*

Things, weighed in with a March 8, 1997, letter complaining of "the scurrilous charges that have been lodged against Father Maciel." He had "come to know and respect most highly the work of the Legionaries, both in this country and in Rome," and prayed that Maciel's "apostolate will survive and flourish long after these terrible attacks have long been forgotten."

Neuhaus has lectured at the Legion seminary in Rome, Regina Apostolorum. Later, in *First Things,* he published an essay attacking us for purveying scandal. He called Maciel "a man who combines uncomplicated faith, gentle kindness, military self-discipline, and a relentless determination to do what he believes God has called him to do . . . a virile holiness of tenacious resolve that has been refined in the fires of frequent opposition and misunderstanding."[27] Neuhaus explains that "after a scrupulous examination of the claims and counter-claims, I have arrived at a *moral certainty* that the charges are false and malicious."

Neuhaus achieved "moral certainty" without meeting any of the men who made the accusations. He never spoke to Dr. Gabriela Quintero, who treated the dying Amenábar; the psychologist Toffano; or his confessor, Father Athié. In his moral certainty Neuhaus resembles the many bishops who for years shunned abuse victims and rewarded child-molesting clerics.[28]

Maciel drew support from Mary Ann Glendon, the Learned Hand professor of Law at Harvard, in a May 23, 2002, letter that accepts Owen Kearns's position with no factual findings of her own. Glendon, strangely for a legal scholar, bases her analysis on feelings, a personal impression of Maciel as a man of "radiant holiness." She explains: "That irresponsible journalists keep dredging up old slanders is perhaps best viewed as a tribute to the success of Regnum Christi and the Legionaries of Christ in advancing the New Evangelization."

George Weigel and William Bennett were more cautious.

Weigel, the papal biographer who advised Pope John Paul during the cardinals' meeting in Rome in April 2002, provided his letter on June 24 of that year. Weigel lavishes praise on the Legion without saying outright that he believes Maciel innocent.

I have been deeply impressed by the work of the Legionaries of Christ in the United States, in Mexico and in Rome. . . . In Mexico, the Legion's universities are helping prepare the Church for a role in Mexican public life that hasn't been possible in over a century. . . . If Father Maciel and his charism as a founder are to be judged by the fruits of his work, those fruits are most impressive indeed.

William Bennett, the former education secretary, drug czar, and author, was earning $50,000 per speech as a commentator on values and virtue before the revelations of his $8 million in losses from casino gambling.[29] Bennett gave a speech to a Regnum Christi conference in Baltimore, shortly after his April 30, 2002, letter that endorsed the Legion—without mentioning Maciel.

As the sexual abuse scandal continues to rock the Catholic Church, one of the things faithful Catholics need to be able to do is trust the priests whom they know. I am fortunate enough to know and trust the priests of the Legionaries of Christ. They do excellent work with the young men in my community, providing them with role models who are exemplars of Christian life. And they do similar work around the world, calling Catholics to live a better life by their example. The flourishing of the Legionaries is a cause for hope in a time of much darkness.

Pope John Paul II gave his answer in the fall of 1997 by naming Maciel one of twenty-one papal delegates to a Synod for America, held in Rome that November and December.[30]

The synod—where both Mary Ann Glendon and Father Neuhaus sat near Maciel—involved 250 church leaders from North and South America in talks about evangelization, economic justice, and church cooperation. Most participants were bishops elected by their peers; there were also cardinals, several leaders of religious orders, and the group the pope picked.

Maciel's appointment was devastating news to Barba and his comrades after the long struggle to get their accusations into the public square. Barba went to work on a formal statement to the pope, which reached nearly five thousand words and was published, as an open letter by the group, in the weekly magazine of the newspaper *Milenio*, two weeks before Christmas 1997, in Mexico City.[31]

"We have seemed so insignificant to the Catholic hierarchy, Holy

Father," the letter began. "In spite of the enormous gravity of facts we have revealed, then and now, we have not received any answer, bureaucratically at least. . . . "

> *If there has been a conspiracy . . . it hasn't been from our part because we consider our action a difficult and risky service to the church and society. It is rather a conspiracy from people constituted with authority within the Legion of Christ and the church hierarchy . . . a conspiracy of shameless covering up and a new most unjust victimization of us on behalf of persons in the Roman hierarchy, of people already informed in the Vatican.*

The words stamped on the page registered the character of Barba, the courtly professor unwilling to retreat from his moral outrage: one could visualize him, several inches less than six feet tall, looking up at robed ecclesiastical justices, at the the power and history of the church, insisting as he wrote: "For if truth is not searched and if the new justice not made, a much larger scandal will expand and the credibility of the church's magisterium will remain in doubt forever in the minds of many people."

Chapter Eleven

IN THE VATICAN
COURTS

THE PALAZZO DEL SANT' UFFIZIO—Palace of the Holy Office—is a rust-colored stone building several stories high that stands with a power of its own behind the sweeping colonnade at St. Peter's Square, just to the left of the great basilica. The ground-floor windows with protective grills span the front of the palace, five on each side of the massive wooden door. A line of smaller windows frames the porch and balcony. Expansive apartments serve as living quarters for key members of this agency. The workaday entrance is beyond a cobblestoned parking lot on the side nearest St. Peter's Basilica, past Swiss Guards in Renaissance outfits of red, blue, and yellow stripes. At the archway leading into the courtyard, a man behind a window calls the appointed party before sending you on to the elevators.

Constructed in the 1540s, the Supreme Sacred Congregation of the Holy Office was the seat of the Inquisition in Rome and conducted trials of heretics. When Pope Paul IV died in 1559, a mob attacked "his most cherished institution, liberating its prisoners and burning its records."[1] This is the building where Galileo was found guilty in 1633 for claiming that the earth revolved around the sun, contrary to church tradition that the earth didn't move.[2] The Inquisition was a mechanism for church authority in many parts of Europe, with a history more complex than its reputation for punishments, the cruelest of which was the burning of witches and heretics in public squares. Ironically, the Holy Office's provision for a defense attorney in heresy cases influenced sixteenth-century Roman trial procedure, while English courts as late as 1836 denied felons the right to counsel.[3] As wars in Europe weakened the church's secular power, the Holy Office became the most important ecclesiastical court, the powerful arbiter of doctrine—and careers.

In 1860, republican Italy annexed territories known as the Papal States, leaving a small area, subsequently called Vatican City, to the control of the pope. In 1870, as Italian nationalists occupied Rome, Pope Pius IX, without the protection of an army, summoned the First Vatican Council. He wanted to shore up the power of his office. Stricken with a childhood seizure disorder, Pius IX was subject to severe mood swings. His *Syllabus of Errors* "was grand in its crazy way—it took on science, secularism, materialism, relativism, democracy, freedom of speech, and the competency of all modern governments," writes Garry Wills.[4] This pope presented Vatican I with the doctrine of infallibility—that the pope cannot err when solemnly and definitively pronouncing on matters of faith and morality. When a group of concerned German bishops arrived for an audience, Pius withheld the papal ring for the customary kiss and literally showed them his foot, which one by one they stooped to kiss. The council's first vote on infallibility was 88 against, 62 for, with about 85 abstentions as bishops began leaving war-torn Rome. More dissidents left; the voting turned to a landslide. "There was something hollow about this victory, which prevented even the hardliners from showing true ebullience," notes Wills.[5]

It is generally accepted that infallibility has been invoked, explicitly, only once since 1870—when Pius XII in 1950 proclaimed Mary's bodily assumption into heaven. But the doctrine infused the papacy and Curia with a mentality of superiority. That elitism has fueled a continuing train of theologians caught between dissent and academic freedom.

"In certain cases the Holy Office will condemn a man's work, forbid him to publish it, and then forbid him to even say he has been forbidden," the renowned Vatican correspondent Robert Blair Kaiser wrote in 1963.[6] The French Jesuit Pierre Teilhard de Chardin was so reviled by the Holy Office for his vision of a spirituality in harmony with human evolution that his major works, which have reached millions of readers, were suppressed in his lifetime. Karl Rahner, who argued that theology should develop in the spirit of a time, and Yves Congar, who emphasized the role of laypeople in an evolving church, were marginalized in the 1950s by Pius XII, who had no use for their views. Pope John XXIII rehabilitated both men, allowing them to become vital influences at Vatican II.

Tensions between lockstep conformity and Pope John's vision of aggiornamento, or updating, crystallized at Vatican II on November 8, 1963. The German cardinal Joseph Frings denounced the secret tactics of the Holy Office as "a cause of scandal to the world." A thunder of applause erupted. "No one should be condemned," declared Frings, "without having been heard, without knowing what he is accused of, and without having the opportunity to amend what he can be reasonably reproached with." The cardinal called for the Curia, top-heavy with mostly Italian bishops, to give more jobs to laymen. One observer called it "the right speech by the right man at the right time."[7]

The secretary of the Holy Office, Cardinal Alfredo Ottaviani, spoke the next morning. Thick jowls shaking with anger, Ottaviani dismissed Frings's criticism as a product of ignorance; he defended the process of anonymous consultors, writing critiques and posing questions by mail to theologians who did not know the identity of their interrogators. If the questions were not clarified to the Holy Office's approval, the scholar was summoned to a hearing; his career hung in the balance. Each case got careful study, said Ottaviani. "In attacking the Holy Office, one attacks the pope himself, because he is its prefect," he asserted.

On the last day of Vatican II, Paul VI gave the Holy Office a new name, Congregation for the Doctrine of the Faith. "Love casts out fear," he said, suggesting that the encouragement of theologians would strengthen doctrine. But calcified habits of power do not easily fade. Paul handed Ottaviani the task of establishing new norms at the congregation, which a Belgian theologian quipped was "like asking the Mafia to reform the Mafia."[8] Ottaviani oversaw abolition of the *Index of Forbidden Books,* a holdover of sixteenth-century censoriousness that carried the possibility of excommunication for daring readers. As systemic change at the CDF dissolved, Ottaviani went to work on Paul VI, entreating him to be resolute on birth control. The cardinal's fingerprints mark that 1968 letter whose uproar so demoralized Paul that he wrote no other encyclical in his last ten years as pope. Ottaviani expired in 1979, a year after Pope Paul VI.

Father Joseph Ratzinger was an adviser to the German cardinal who rattled Ottaviani. As John Allen has written, Ratzinger's own essays of that period are laced with pejorative comments about "Roman theologians." In 1965 Ratzinger criticized the "all too smoothly functioning central teaching office which prejudged every question almost before it had come up for discussion."[9]

Ratzinger had become a deeply conservative thinker when John Paul appointed him prefect of the CDF in 1981. If the doctrinal battles he waged in marginalizing Hans Küng, Charles Curran, and the Liberation Theology advocates of Latin America, among others, left any regrets as the years passed, Ratzinger never showed it. He believed in the supremacy of truth articulated by the Holy See. "For Ratzinger, the church transcends history," wrote the Australian scholar Paul Collins. "It is the risen and ascended Christ who stands in spendour outside the world-process, both as saviour and as judge, who is his fundamental focus." The cardinal had a standing luncheon with John Paul every Friday the pope was in Rome. Sharing an apartment with his sister, Ratzinger relaxed by playing the piano. He governed the CDF as if it were a citadel, dispensing orders and investigations of religious scholars. Those who failed to clarify or change their positions knew the fate of Küng. Perhaps the most influential theologian in the Western world, Küng's vision of a church imbued with the evolutionary grace of Vatican II, unshackled from a Roman idea of superiority rooted in the infallibility doctrine, had cost him his license to teach Catholic theology. Küng—a priest, professor, traveling lecturer, and prolific writer in Tübingen—was not a Vatican-approved theologian.

Ratzinger's interview books with collaborators allowed him to reach many readers.[10] He turned down our interview request and thousands of others by journalists, even a scrupulous biographer like John Allen, who read his works in German. By shunning the spontaneous dialogue in which one defends his ideas, testing them through open discourse with others, Ratzinger stood behind official "truth," keeping the world's questions at bay. Küng bitterly called Ratzinger a "Grand Inquisitor," like Dostoyevsky's famous character in *The Brothers Karamazov*—a churchman whose dark view of human freedom collides with the morality of a Christ reappeared. In one of the most powerful scenes in Western literature, Jesus gives the Inquisitor a kiss of forgiveness, and then departs, leaving the world to reckon with those who possess the power to demand obedience of others.

The clergy sexual crisis drifted like a black cloud into Ratzinger's life in the late 1990s. The sign on the building still said *Palazzo del Sant' Uffizio*.

The Mexicans Take Their Case to Rome

José Barba had passed the Holy Office often as a young Legionary. He remembered the words of Father Maciel on a breezy day in early May of 1956 as they walked in a small group, wearing their black cassocks, after a mass audience with Pope Pius XII. "Let's hurry," Maciel chuckled cynically. "In this place they don't like me." In the fullness of time Maciel's words made sense: Cardinal Ottaviani would be among those in the Curia aware of his drug problems—Maciel would be suspended a few months later.

On October 7, 1998, José Barba and a canon lawyer from Mexico City flew to Rome. There they met Arturo Jurado Guzmán, who flew from California. Their goal was to file charges against Father Maciel for serious delicts, or crimes, as found in the Code of Canon Law. Barba had not set foot in Rome in forty years. Memories of Maciel cut against his pleasure at the beauty of Rome beheld anew. Ahead, two Swiss Guards stood at the entrance to the Palazzo del Sant' Ufficio like harlequins at a costume ball.

Arturo Jurado had carted his own psychological pain across four decades since leaving the Legion; his sexual encounters with Maciel had been much more numerous than Barba's. The fourth vow had produced years of bottled shame. Both men had grown children and viewed their failed marriages as on some level caused by Maciel's psychological cruelty. Jurado, fifty-eight, had a security clearance for the U.S. Department of Defense School of Languages in Monterey, California, where he taught military personnel and diplomats. He and Barba were representing the eight-man group that had contributed to the travel expenses of the Reverend Antonio Roqueñi, a canonist from the Mexico City archdiocesan tribunal.

Barba had reestablished contact with Juan Vaca in 1993. Amenábar's funeral in 1995 was the turning point in forging the group solidarity.

After the burial mass José Barba asked Father Alberto Athié about his homily quoting Amenábar: "I pardon Father Maciel, but at the same time, I ask for justice." The priest had not specified what Maciel was being pardoned for doing. Barba said that he, and others, wanted that justice while they were alive. Athié was sympathetic, but unwilling to speak with journalists.[11] In the spring of 1997, after *La Jornada*'s coverage, Athié—a vice president of Caritas, the Mexican bishops' national charity—met with Cardinal Norberto Rivera Carrera of Mexico City and revealed what Amenábar had told him about Maciel.

Rivera was cut in the mold of a John Paul prelate. As a critic of globalization for its effect on the poor, he had provoked the government of President Carlos Salinas; he also closed a seminary he considered too sympathetic to Liberation Theology. In 1997, Rivera was fifty-five, his name starting to appear as a *papabile,* a potential future pope. Rivera loathed media criticism of Maciel, who was the pope's ally and equally his own. Rivera had been Maciel's guest in Rome. After Athié had said his piece, Rivera told him that Maciel was the victim of a plot. Athié insisted that Amenábar had confirmed what the other men said. "It's a plot!" declared Rivera, showing Athié the door.

Athié was demoralized. He had given his word to a dying man to promote his cause for justice; now his own cardinal derided the truth as a conspiracy!

A priest in whom the white-haired Athié confided was in many ways his opposite. Antonio Roqueñi, a tall dark-haired canonist with an aristocratic confidence, did not suffer fools gladly. Born in 1934, raised in one of Mexico City's oldest neighborhoods near the Zocalo, or plaza, Roqueñi had been a student of the Jesuits. Like his father, he had earned a law degree. At twenty-four he decided to become a priest; he joined Opus Dei, the controversial religious movement begun in Spain in the 1930s, well known for its wealthy supporters, for cultivating people in power, and for the ascetic lifestyles of its most committed lay members.

In 1958, Roqueñi went to Rome on an Opus Dei scholarship to study canon law at the Angelicum. Ordained in 1963, he went to Madrid and spent eight years as a chaplain at an Opus Dei university; he also taught canon law. In 1977 Father Roqueñi returned to Mexico City, where the archbishop had invited him to work at the tribunal. He was a canonist and missed the work for which he had trained. "I don't share the criticisms of Opus Dei," Roqueñi later told Berry. "I entered Opus Dei freely and left it freely."[12]

Marriage annulments occupied most of his tribunal work; less than 1 percent of his cases involved wrongdoings by priests. After helping several women secure support payments for children sired by clerics, Roqueñi realized that too many Mexicans were ignorant of their canonical rights within the church, or afraid to demand them in the first place. He saw in them a mentality of foot soldiers obedient to military superiors rather than an identity as People of God.

When Roqueñi read the coverage of Maciel in *La Jornada*, he remembered Amenábar, who had once helped him secure an annulment for a mutual acquaintance. Roqueñi had liked the former college president, responding to him in the fraternal manner of priest to ex-priest. Amenábar had paid a visit to Roqueñi in 1994 to say that he was leaving for Spain; but his decline was all too apparent and he died before he could make the trip.

Roqueñi was well known in media circles for his clash with the papal nuncio, Archbishop Girolamo Prigione. He had watched approvingly in 1992 as Prigione helped negotiate the restoration of diplomatic relations between Mexico and the Holy See. That achievement fueled a swelling ego; Prigione tried to position himself as an overlord to the national bishops conference, earning "a well-deserved reputation as a controversial figure in Mexican religious and political affairs," by one scholar's account.[13] Roqueñi filed a canon law grievance on behalf of Mexican Catholics against the papal ambassador with the Secretariat of State in the Vatican, charging Prigione with abuse of his office. Though never adjudicated, the case was one factor among several that caused the Vatican to recall Prigione in 1997 and send a new nuncio in his place.

When Roqueñi read the ex-Legionaries' open letter to John Paul in the December 8, 1997, weekend magazine of *Milenio,* the words rang true. A producer of the Channel 40 documentary on Maciel suggested to José Barba that he meet Roqueñi. In late December the canonist had dinner with Barba and his friend José Antonio Pérez Olvera. As the two survivors laid out their story, Roqueñi was appalled. He offered to help them prepare a canonical case against Maciel. The irony of a priest who had risen through Opus Dei planning a canonical prosecution of the ultraorthodox Maciel was not lost on Roqueñi. But as he reflected, much later, "For me this was a matter of the law—church law."

For a canonical case to succeed, Roqueñi told them, they had to let Rome work without giving everything to the media. Heeding that advice, Barba and Saúl Barrales went to the residence of the new nuncio, Archbishop Justo Mullor García, delivering the original of their letter to the pope with the eight signatures. A nun allowed Barba to speak with Mullor by telephone from a parlor. "I promise your letter will reach the hands of the Holy Father," the papal ambassador told him.[14]

Spring drained into the summer of 1998 with no response. In July, Barba telephoned Mullor; they spoke nearly thirty minutes. The nuncio assured Barba he had delivered his letter to the pope. Mullor also told him that if he wanted a response from the church, they should stop speaking to the media. "The church has tribunals of her own," said Mullor, echoing the advice of Father Roqueñi.

After further research and planning, they went to Rome—Barba, Roqueñi, and Arturo Jurado. The canonical case had to be filed in the Vatican to have impact. Roqueñi knew they would need a canonist with experience before Vatican tribunals; he obtained a list of 130 canon lawyers accredited to the Signatura, the supreme court, and the Rota, an appellate court. Tribunals are also held in certain congregations of the Curia. Roqueñi arranged a procedural meeting with the Reverend Vicente Carcel Orti, the president of the Signatura. A short, stout Spaniard in his late sixties, Father Carcel received them cordially and listened closely as Roqueñi outlined the case, careful not to identify Maciel. Carcel remarked that such a charge ran the risk of being dismissed on an appeal by the accused—a sign to the Mexicans that they should find another tribunal. At Roqueñi's request, Carcel recommended several canonists at the Vatican, one of whom was named Martha Wegan. The meeting lasted thirty minutes.

The Mexicans were intrigued with the name Martha Wegan. Barba thought that a woman representing them might be jarring to Maciel. When they called, she agreed to see them that day. A native of Austria, Wegan was in her late fifties, with solid academic credentials and practical experience. She had an open, pleasant quality, and studied those who wished to be her clients, weighing the severity of the allegations. Wegan told them that she had represented a Canadian couple who wanted to extricate their son from the Legion of Christ; they believed the young man had been duped into joining a cult. Barba's interest quickened. The case was dismissed, she explained, because the Congregation for Religious and Secular Institutes, where it was brought, decided the son was old enough to make his own decision.

"You must accept what the Vatican says," Wegan insisted. She could introduce a case; but Vatican officials would decide whether the case had merit. Father Roqueñi nodded. He had sometimes been disappointed with the outcome of cases in which he had been involved; but the canons were church law.

The case against Maciel faced a steep procedural cliff. Four decades had passed since the investigation of the Carmelite visitators. There was a ten-year prescription, or statute of limitations, under canon law for sexual crimes by a cleric. Roqueñi wanted an approach known as *absolutionis complicis*. Juan Vaca, Arturo Jurado, and several others had received absolution from Maciel, as their confessor, after he sexually abused them. For a priest to absolve his own victim (covered by the more flexible term "accomplice") violated the sacrament of penance. This could be heard by the Congregation for the Doctrine of the Faith. For that delict, and other accused canonical crimes attributed to Maciel, there was no statute of limitations.

Wegan knew Cardinal Ratzinger and was on good terms with his staff. She had no privileged access but thought they would get a fair hearing. Barba and Jurado were satisfied. More important, so was Antonio Roqueñi. The two professors were surprised that her retainer of $400 was so small. "I work for the church," she said with a gentle smile.

Wegan secured an appointment with the Reverend Gianfranco Girotti, a Franciscan and one of Ratzinger's three secretaries, on October 17, 1998.

At St. Peter's Square, flocks of tourists were taking photographs at the fountains. A bittersweet feeling washed through Barba. Ahead was the Palazzo del Sant' Uffizio—forty-two years later. Wegan spoke with the Swiss Guards, who let them pass. As they entered the archway, Cardinal Ratzinger, his silver-white hair almost diaphanous in the warm sunlight, was talking with a man in the courtyard. Moments later they took an elevator to the office of Father Girotti.

Barba, Jurado, and Roqueñi were at ease with Girotti's native language, as was Wegan, so they conversed in Italian. Girotti asked few questions as the canonists outlined the case. Girotti listened patiently. Then, turning to Barba and Jurado, he said, in Spanish: *"Por qué ahora?"* Why now?

Wondering if those very words he had put in their letter to the pope had registered at some level, Barba told Girotti about the years they had spent unaware of how many in their group had been abused; he pointed to the pope's praise of Maciel in the big newspaper advertisements in 1994. More than that, Juan Vaca had written the Holy See as early as 1976, and to John Paul in 1978 and 1989. They had twice written the Holy Father as a group. Girotti seemed satisfied; the meeting turned to canonical matters required by the congregation.

"You must refrain from talking to journalists," said Father Girotti.

"But we have already done so," replied Barba. He explained that they had met with Sandro Magister, *L'espresso*'s religion correspondent, the week before, when they had no idea if a congregation would allow their case to be filed. Girotti understood that the allegations had been reported. He did not want media coverage of a canonical case: they must keep silence. They promised to do so.

Martha Wegan presented Girotti with a two-page statement of accusation that cited canon 977 ("the absolution of an accomplice in a sin against the Sixth Commandment . . . is invalid") and canon 1378 ("a priest who acts against the prescription of canon 977 incurs an automatic excommunication"). The final canon cited, 1362, involved prescription—issues of timely filing under a statute of limitation—which can be halted for "offenses reserved to the Sacred Congregation for the Doctrine of the Faith."

In essence, they accused Maciel of sacrilege, profaning the sacrament of confession. The case to excommunicate Maciel—have him declared a non-Catholic—was now in Ratzinger's domain.

They thanked Girotti and said good-bye. As they entered the hallway Cardinal Ratzinger stepped out of an elevator. Unaware of why they were there, he smiled in recognizing Martha Wegan. Wegan knelt. Ratzinger extended his hand and she kissed his ring in deference to a prince of the church.

Father Roqueñi knelt and kissed Cardinal Ratzinger's ring.

Arturo Jurado knelt and kissed the cardinal's ring.

José Barba knelt and kissed the ring. He was not, after all, mad at Ratzinger. The cardinal, clad in black, murmured thanks and stepped into his office, closing the door.

Buoyed by Girotti's receptivity, Barba and Jurado had another task in Rome. The two letters by Bishop Polidoro in Chile that the Legion had sent the *Courant* seemed to them a forgery. The bishop was in his nineties. In an effort to learn Polidoro's whereabouts, they visited the headquarters of the Franciscans, the bishop's religious order. The Reverend Gerald Moore gave them Polidoro's address and contact numbers in Santiago.

Barba and Jurado decided that Arturo would be the first-named complainant in the case. Thus, all correspondence would go to his Defense Department office in California, assuring a safe flow of mail. They left Rome with Father Roqueñi on a surge of optimism. Though clearly a Vatican loyalist, Martha Wegan had ignited the motor of ecclesiastical justice. Roqueñi was impressed with her expertise. In December, they sent a dossier of statements by members of the group, along with a statement by Dr. Gabriela Quintero, attesting to Amenábar's mental faculties in his final years.

Shortly after New Year's 1999, José Barba telephoned Wegan to check on the progress of the case. He was pleased with her assessment: Girotti seemed sympathetic. Maciel was "evasive"—the congregation was having trouble locating him. But Girotti had been disturbed by an edition of *L'espresso* with a three-page report by Sandro Magister on the Legionaries that discussed the accusations with fresh quotations from Barba.[15] The Mexican scholar sent word reminding Wegan and Girotti that he and Arturo Jurado had met with Magister just after arriving in Rome, more than a week before they were received at the CDF. They had spoken to no reporters since and would respect the agreement of silence.

Later that month John Paul II made his third papal visit to Mexico. The vast, adoring crowds welcomed him once more; bishops, clerics, and nuns turned out with exuberance. Maciel did not fly with the pope as on previous trips. "Maciel was nowhere in public," Professor Elio Masferrer Kan, a religious anthropologist and commentator in the Mexican press, said in 2001. A cardinal, ten archbishops, and a bishop formed the farewell committee. "In my opinion there were two reasons for Maciel's absence. First was the impact of the canon law case filed against him. The second has to do with his aloofness. . . . The hierarchy views him as a competitor who has broken with the structure of collegiality."[16]

In Rome, however, the Legion had found a niche in the collegial mores of the Curia by hosting conferences at its university, Regina Apostolorum; through its Catholic news service, Zenit, e-mailed free to subscribers; and by the pope's favorable view of the order. Maciel courted influential figures in the Curia at lavish dinners, among them Cardinal Ratzinger, Cardinal Angelo Sodano, the secretary of state and a strong ally since his years as nuncio to Chile, and Cardinals Pio Laghi, Roger Etchegaray of France, and Francis Arinze of Nigeria. "Even if they didn't like the Legion, it was a status symbol to be an honored guest there," recalled Glenn Favreau, who left the Legion in 1997.[17]

When such guests dined at Regina Apostolorum, Legionary brothers set the large table with fine china, crystal, and a cart with cocktails for Maciel's guests. "We lined up in the dining room like a perfect army, standing with our arms crossed, in silence," said Favreau. "Sometimes you'd wait half an hour. If it got much longer they'd let us talk." After dinner the Legion orchestra played Mexican and German songs for Ratzinger. As he rose to leave, the Legionaries left by the back door, ran around the building, and formed two lines in the driveway, applauding as Ratzinger entered his car, clapping until he was gone.

"For some cardinals Maciel would send his Mercedes," said Favreau.

"Although they come in for the usual criticisms, there is nothing besieged or sweated about the Legionaries," wrote Father Neuhaus.[18]

Events with their seminarians and priests are marked by a festive sense of delight, complete with ample wine and exuberant mariachi bands, reflecting a sheer joy in being invited to throw away their lives for Christ and his Church. . . . Some bishops complain that the Legionaries "steal" funding and priestly vocations from their dioceses, and there may be something to that, although one may wonder whether they are not enlisting people and resources that would otherwise go unlisted.

This pope has been very supportive of the Legionaries, as he has been supportive of the many other renewal movements that are lighting the fires of devotion to the new evangelization.

On February 20, 1999, barely a month after John Paul's trip to Mexico, Martha Wegan wrote her clients with encouraging news. The Congregation for the Doctrine of the Faith considered their grievance well founded, and had officially recorded it as a case in its tribunal.

"Such a delicate situation . . . "

As Barba, Jurado, and Roqueñi awaited further word from Rome, Father Athié was making his own effort. In his work for Caritas, the Mexican bishops' charity, Athié met with Archbishop Mullor. The new Vatican ambassador was repairing bonds with those who had despised his power-hungry predecessor. After dispensing with the items on their agenda, Athié, who would soon be visiting Rome as part of his job, told Mullor about his relationship with the late Fernández Amenábar. He unburdened himself of the frustration he felt at Cardinal Rivera's defense of Maciel as victim of a plot. The nuncio asked him to write down everything he had said, "without making any judgment," in a letter to Cardinal Ratzinger. Mullor asked for a copy of the letter, and told Athié to personally deliver the original to the cardinal on his trip.

Athié duly provided Mullor with a copy of the letter that he carried to Rome in June of 1999. During his stay of several weeks Ratzinger's office said he was too busy to meet with Athié. To leave the letter, he knew, ran the risk of receiving a pro forma response by mail, and that would achieve nothing. He wanted Ratzinger to read the contents. If he could not achieve that himself, Athié decided to entrust the document to someone who had the clout to see Ratzinger. On return to Mexico he met with a longtime friend, Bishop Carlos Talavera Ramírez of Coatzacoalcos, in the state of Veracruz, who was bound for Rome himself. Talavera, though no friend of Maciel's, declined our interview requests. Nevertheless, in separate conversations with Athié and Roqueñi the bishop gave an identical account of his meeting with the prefect of the CDF.

On reading the letter, Ratzinger asked Talavera if Father Athié was "trustworthy." He was indeed, replied the bishop.

It was a delicate matter, Ratzinger conceded. Father Maciel had done so much good for the church by bringing many young men into the priesthood. He wondered: was it "prudent" to raise the issue now?

"It was not so much a question as an answer," reflected Father Athié. "The bishop was hurt and upset, surprised and shocked by the answer."

Soon came the backlash.

Cardinal Rivera dismissed Father Roqueñi from the tribunal in Mexico City, where he had worked for twenty years. Athié lost his job with Caritas. In neither case was the reason officially linked to Maciel. As priests they had other options within the church and were expected to pursue them. Roqueñi went to work for a foundation. Athié took a sabbatical, studying at the Chicago Theological Union.

On Christmas Eve 1999, Martha Wegan wrote to Arturo Jurado:

I finally succeeded in speaking with Fr. Girotti. In fact, I spoke with him twice. But the result was not very good.

"For the time being" the matter is closed. They looked into the matter and confirmed to me that some people have lost their jobs, that the Cardinal of Mexico is the person who is, etc., etc.

Sad news, but on the other hand since this is such a delicate situation time should be allowed to play its role, and who knows what will happen later on.

It's my duty to inform you. . . . You can always telephone me or write to me, I'm at your disposal.

May the peace of Christmas fill your heart and your home now and through the New Year.

Wegan's reference—"the Cardinal of Mexico is the person who is, etc., etc."—stopped short of laying responsibility on Rivera for firing Athié and Roqueñi in retribution for their support of the men abused by Maciel. But Wegan was also leaving a door open to her clients in "such a delicate situation."

A lawyer to his bones, Roqueñi on March 1, 2000, wrote Ratzinger's secretary, Father Girotti, to say that the Congregation for the Doctrine of the Faith was not doing its job.

The fact is that more than seventeen months have gone by and the only notice that the claimants have, communicated by your attorney

[Martha Wegan], is that the matter is extremely delicate, that there are other related claims and that the judge [Ratzinger] is weighing the scandal that his judicial resolution would cause, if condemnatory to the one accused, or favorable to the claimants.

The claimants fear that, despite the accumulation of proof brought, up to this time, with respect to the illicit acts denounced, the file continues to be put off and there is no conclusion to the case.

Roqueñi expressed surprise that procedures "customary in any formal proceeding" had been ignored. "The legitimate authorities are bound by the rules of the church, putting to the side an arbitrary discretion in observing those rules, under no pretext."

Girotti was silent. No letter, not a word from a priest of the Word.

Rome, Again

On May 17, 2000, a prayer vigil was held at St. Peter's Square for the pope's celebration of the Jubilee for Priests. If the canonical case had made him a liability on the pope's visit to Mexico the year before, Maciel in Rome was in John Paul's good graces. Two months after turning eighty, a hale Maciel told the crowd: "Two feelings invade my spirit: on the one hand, the fear of violating the secrets of the soul, which are configured in a very personal relationship with Christ Jesus; and, on the other hand, the desire to publicly proclaim the marvels of the Lord, who, in His mercy elected us as priests to prolong in time His work of redemption and sanctification. . . . I also give thanks to the Holy Father John Paul II for the magnificent example he offers us each day in living his priesthood."[19]

In July, Barba traveled to Italy on vacation. He telephoned Martha Wegan in Rome regarding the standstill at the CDF. She suggested he speak directly to Ratzinger. After two years of being incommunicado with journalists, Professor Barba said he would rather meet with Father Girotti.

Wegan recommended that he pray to Saint Felicia, "an advocate for difficult cases." Barba, ever polite, was perplexed that a canonist would give such advice about a serious issue of church law. Wegan wore a colorful dress and accompanied the professor back to the great stone building that bore the letters *Palazzo del Sant' Uffizio*. They passed the Swiss Guards in their summer costumes. Father Girotti received them in a parlor with religious paintings.

After the exchange of courtesies, Barba said: "We want to be judged!"

"It is not you who have to be judged," said Girotti, "but *him*." The Franciscan remarked about the serious charges against Maciel; yet in his tone Barba detected an exasperation at having to talk about it all again.

"We gave our word to keep silent, but that ends now," announced Barba.

"Why?" Girotti frowned.

False rumors were circulating in Mexico that they had stopped talking to reporters because the Legion had bought them off. "We have suffered too much!"

Then Barba told Girotti about Ratzinger's remark to Bishop Talavera of Mexico, whether it was "prudent" to prosecute a priest who had done so much for the church.

Girotti folded his arms in a defense posture.

It had been two years since the papal ambassador to Mexico had advised Barba to work within the church tribunals, and now, with the ecclesiastical court caving in, he was astounded to hear Girotti suggest that the men *file a civil lawsuit against Maciel*.

That effectively was the end of the meeting.

Back in Mexico, Barba and his comrades renewed their dialogue with the authors and other members of the news media. Alejandro Espinosa meanwhile was hard at work on a memoir of his nightmare with Maciel.[20] Yet in all of this, the Congregation for the Doctrine of the Faith did not dismiss the accusations. The case simply sat there, entombed in the silence of an ecclesiastical court.

The Vatican Press Office denied that Cardinal Ratzinger said any of the words Bishop Talavera attributed to him in conversations with Roqueñi and Athié.[21]

Cardinal Rivera also made what can only be termed a "nondenial denial." In response to an inquiry Renner had made to him about his role, the cardinal wrote in an e-mail dated December 6, 2001, that he "was surprised" to be informed "that two Mexican priests . . . had lost their positions in the church because they said that I was displeased by the help they had given to the men who presented the complaints." He went on: "I say I was surprised, because that affirmation is totally false, since as far as I know the case of the 'Rev. Marcial Maciel' has not been presented in this Ecclesiastical Jurisdiction, and I do not know if the priests in question have in their personal capacity interested themselves in the case."

The cardinal knew perfectly well that the case had been presented in Rome, not in his "Ecclesiastical Jurisdiction."

Father Alberto Athié's demoralization was palpable when Renner interviewed him in a wood-paneled room at the Chicago Theological Union on a chilly April day in 2001. He had a white beard, snowy hair, and a quiet demeanor. Athié was uncomfortable discussing secrets of the church; but his reluctance melted as he revealed his own odyssey through the labyrinth. When asked about Ratzinger's handling of the canonical case, he said simply: "It is an immoral thing."[22]

PART THREE

Witnesses for the People of God

Chapter Twelve

RELIGIOUS DURESS

I'm now on an island that is beautiful to look at, caught in the early 19th century. . . . The base is small, which I like—I get to know everybody. The Air Force life gets better and better. The ministry is great, total hands on and no church bureaucracy to get in the way. I have little if anything to do with the institutional Catholic church and I have no interest in keeping it up. Sorry to make this short but I have to get ready to leave for Germany tonight. Military exercises never start at a normal time. . . . Peace,

—Thomas P. Doyle, to a friend, from the Azores, May 21, 1996

EXPLORING the flora and rock formations in his scuba gear was closer to mysticism than anything Father Doyle had experienced. He adored the sea fans, and the sheets of fish radiant with heavenly wonder. But the "institutional church" was his barnacle. Doyle pursued the free-floating ministry to abuse survivors through e-mail, and as time allowed, he advised attorneys suing the church.

Steve Rubino had used a phrase, "religious duress," in explaining why it took victims years to break their silence. Camden bishop James McHugh's November 3, 1994, statement—read aloud by some priests at Mass—deemed a class action suit Rubino had filed "a new type of terrorism against priests and bishops." The diocese eventually settled the twenty-five cases for $960,000 after Rubino's investigator filmed one of the priests, in Florida, supposedly infirm, driving his car.[1]

Doyle pondered "religious duress." Why *did* survivors stay silent so long? Why did bishops shelter sexual criminals, shun victims, or liken a lawyer to a terrorist from the pulpit? The concept sent him on a long research path. He used the term in testimony and in a scholarly essay that drew on his own field in hammering out an analysis.[2] Church law had evolved out of the Dark Ages as far-flung bishops forged local legislation. Harsh penalties for clerics who abused boys ran through that history like a red thread; pederasty was a serious concern to bishops at the sixteenth-century Council of Trent, which gathered because of Martin Luther's revolt. When canon law was codified in 1917, "clerics were protected against any kind of harm inflicted by the laity," wrote Doyle.[3] Canon 119 stated: "All the faithful owe reverence to clerics according to their various grades and offices, and they commit a sacrilege if they do real injury to a cleric." Another canon in the old code held that to summon a cleric before a civil court without ecclesiastical permission was to invite excommunication. Only the pope could grant permission for cardinals, bishops, and abbots to give court testimony.

The 1983 code eliminated such exemptions. Still, wrote Doyle,

> It has been traditionally taught that bishops are individually selected by the Holy Spirit who in turn inspires the Pope to appoint them . . . [as] direct descendants of the twelve apostles who were originally commissioned by Jesus Christ to lead the Church. . . . The common perception of the exalted state of bishops and priests is not simply "folk" theology. It is grounded in the Catholic Church's official theological teaching as well as its legal (canonical) discipline.[4]

For all of the Vatican II reforms, the Roman Curia had not changed much.

> Vatican functionaries are obliged to pronounce a solemn oath that they will always keep the "Pontifical Secret." . . . Hand in glove with the secrecy is a pervasive fear that any imperfections in the system or in its office holders will become publicly known. Honest mistakes, incompetence, negligence and intentional wrongdoing are all abhorrent to the higher leadership. All are denied, covered up and rationalized with equal zeal. The clerical world truly believes that it has been established by God and that its members are singled out

and favored by the Almighty. . . . Higher authority figures are
regarded with a mixture of fear and awe by all below them. The cir-
cles of power are closed, the tightest being among those existing
among bishops. . . . Secrecy provides a layer of insulation between
the one in authority and anyone who might be tempted to question
its exercise.[5]

The Spectacle of Hans Groer

In autumn 1994, Cardinal Hans Groer of Vienna sent the pope a pro
forma resignation letter on reaching the retirement age of seventy-five.
John Paul was happy for Groer to carry on. His predecessor, Cardinal
Franz König, had retired at eighty, a sign of John Paul's deference to the
man who was key in orchestrating his election as pope. Austrian Catholics
"felt there was no one who could speak for them with the same force and
eloquence" as König at Vatican II.[6] Our account builds on journalist
Hubertus Czernin's book about Groer.[7]

Born in 1919, Groer entered the minor seminary at fourteen, in Hollabrunn, forty miles north of Vienna, and went on to study theology at
the University of Vienna. Ordained in 1942, he did a stint of military
service, cut short by illness, and served three years as a parish priest. In
1946, he returned to Hollabrunn as prefect of studies and later religion
professor while completing his dissertation for a doctorate in theology
from the University of Vienna. He also immersed himself in the Legion
of Mary, an evangelistic movement of laypeople fostering prayer and pilgrimages. In 1970, König appointed Groer director of pilgrimages to a
Marian shrine at Roggendorf. His sermons drew large crowds; the village changed its name to Maria Roggendorf.

In 1974, Groer entered the Benedictine abbey of Gottweig, taking
the religious name Hermann, accompanied by eight followers from the
Legion of Mary. That impressed the abbot, Clemens Lashofer. Never in
the history of the nine-hundred-year-old abbey were so many candidates
accepted at the same time. Groer was fifty-four; Lashofer, thirty-three,
had grown up in the monastery (having entered at age ten). By 1980
some seventeen men inspired by Groer had joined the monastery. Groer
was their confessor and principal of the high school associated with the

abbey. Visitors, including bishops and nuncios, kept crowding the shrine to hear sermons by the slender monk with close-cropped hair.

In summer 1985, a monk who had been brought to the abbey by Groer revealed to Abbot Lashofer and two other monks that he had rebuffed Groer's sexual advances years earlier. Groer was supremely popular at the shrine. The situation, said Lashofer, was "sensitive." Any talk stayed within tightened circles of the abbey. In spring 1986, König had retired. With the archbishop's seat vacant, the nuncio in Vienna sent six names to Rome. Groer's was not on the list. Two cardinals—one an Italian and former nuncio to Austria, the other an Austrian at the Vatican Library—gave Groer's name to the Secretariat of State. Groer had credentials that the pope, who revered ascetics, would like.

Vienna is an important archdiocese. Austria, with a high level of education, was 80 percent Catholic. Catholics pay a tax for salaries of clergy and bishops. Polls showed most Austrians wanted a church with a more modern approach to sexual issues; yet they respected John Paul for his piety and support of human rights, especially in Poland.

Groer sailed through the Vatican vetting process. He was consecrated archbishop of Vienna on September 15, 1986. Ten days later John Paul met him for the first time at a private audience at the Vatican. In 1988, Groer was named a cardinal. Groer was König's opposite: a fundamentalist on church authority, a classic John Paul II appointee. To Christa Pongratz-Lippitt, an authority on the church in Austria, Groer seemed "terribly unsure of himself and easily hurt. He sometimes burst into tears when criticized by priests—totally unsuited to become a bishop."[8]

In summer 1988, another monk, Father Emmanuel Bauer, began talking in the abbey about a homoerotic atmosphere that had surrounded Groer. On a 1991 retreat other monks complained of the bitter sexual undertones of Groer's misuse of power. Abbot Lashofer, forty years a Benedictine now, forbade further discussion of Groer.

On March 6, 1995, Cardinal Groer issued a letter to be read at Mass, insisting that Catholics who remarried without an annulment should not receive communion. Groer also quoted Saint Paul's first letter to the Corinthians, chapter 6: "No fornicators, idolators, or adulterers, no sodomites . . . will inherit God's kingdom." The sodomy reference in German also meant "sexual abusers of boys." One week later the weekly magazine *Profil* received a letter from Josef Hartmann, thirty-seven, saying Groer incurred God's judgment for having molested him as a teenage seminarian. He called Groer "my mother, my father, my confessor, my lover."⁹ *Profil* asked Groer for a response. The cardinal said nothing to Hartmann's sworn affidavit. When the article appeared, Austria's bishops denounced "a conspiracy against the church,"¹⁰ while other men began calling the press with accounts of Groer groping and making advances on them years before. Seven of the seventeen men Groer had brought to the abbey accused him of molesting them.

Leading theologians called on the bishops to take a public stand.

Groer refused to respond.

Two auxiliary bishops (one of them, Christoph Schönborn, a Dominican theologian and a Ratzinger protégé) issued a statement reminding Austrians that priests had been slandered for homosexuality in the Nazi era and asked people to respect Groer's honor. On April 4, the bishops met to elect a conference president—and chose Groer, eight to seven. Two days later a Gallup poll found 69 percent of churchgoing Catholics wanted Groer to resign.¹¹ He did so, though only as president of the conference. On April 8, Father Bauer wrote to a bishop of having rebuffed Groer's overtures.

The bishop sent the letter to the pope and Cardinal Ratzinger. With no comment on the accusations, the Vatican on April 13 appointed Schönborn coadjutor bishop—Groer's designated successor. At the abbey, Lashofer faced monks complaining about Groer's molestations. As public outrage intensified, Groer issued a brief statement denying "the content and form of these defamatory and destructive criticisms."¹² By Palm Sunday a huge rift had opened between hard-liners supporting Groer and a mounting majority outraged by the stonewalling. Cardinal König, ninety, said the Vatican's selection process of bishops was out of touch. A stream of Catholics began going to government offices, officially resigning from the church. By refusing to pay the state tax supporting the church, they forfeited the right to receive sacraments. More than forty thousand left that year.¹³ In June, a group called We Are Church formed at Innsbruck with a platform of lay involvement in the selection of bishops, optional celibacy, a more equitable role for women, and greater tolerance on issues of human sexuality. In just a few weeks the petition drew five hundred thousand signatures, among 6 million

Catholics. "We have to be willing to listen," said König as We Are Church spread to Germany. He said he expected a married clergy one day, however inconceivable that was for "a pope from Poland."[14]

In June, Bishop Hansjörg Vogel of Basel, Switzerland, resigned, admitting that he had fallen in love with a woman and that she was pregnant. A poll found 90 percent of Swiss Catholics supporting a married clergy.

On September 14, Groer announced his resignation as archbishop of Vienna. He became the prior of the Maria Roggendorf abbey. In an interview with *Profil* he denounced the "character assassination" as "a put-up job."[15]

The pope issued a statement defending Groer against "violent attacks," thanking him for his "generous and faithful" service, accepting the resignation because of his age, seventy-five, with no mention of the sexual accusations.

The Groer events made fleeting news in America, where the bishops had balked at a request from the chairman of their own subcommittee on clergy sex abuse to pool data from all dioceses on the number of cases and financial losses. Although the U.S. bishops' conference had in 1992 expressed compassion for victims and pledged a resolute handling of priests, there was no actual policy. Inertia marked the standoff with the Vatican over the Americans' request for a streamlined process to laicize ("defrock") pedophiles.

John Paul wanted secret trials. No trial stopped Groer from returning to the shrine at Maria Roggendorf as prior, or second in command.

On January 3, 1998, the abbot of the Benedictine monastery at Gottweig, responding to internal pressure, admitted on radio that there were more accusations from the cardinal's past. In February, Vienna's Archbishop Schönborn went to Rome to be invested as a cardinal. On that happy occasion he was startled to learn that his scandal-tainted predecessor was there, meeting with the pope. Schönborn wanted Groer to admit his wrongdoing. The pope made no public comment; however, the Vatican dispatched Abbot Marcel Rooney, the head of the Benedictine Order, to investigate. John Paul was scheduled to make a pastoral trip to three Austrian cities in June; the Vatican had made no statement on why Groer left his position three years earlier.

The newly invested Cardinal Schönborn met with Cardinal Angelo

Sodano, who was secretary of state under John Paul. Sodano was a tough-minded Italian who as the nuncio in Chile during the Pinochet regime had taken a low-key approach to human rights abuses. Sodano recognized the importance of getting rid of Groer before the pope's trip, but he wanted it done delicately—Groer, after all, was a cardinal.

In early March, three other Austrian prelates joined Schönborn in a declaration stating their "moral certainty" that the allegations against Groer were "in essence correct." They admitted that the church was "burdened with the crippling suspicions that the reputation of a cardinal is more important than the well-being of the people." Schönborn asked Groer "to restrain for the moment" from ordaining priests or confirming children. But the ultraorthodox Bishop Kurt Krenn stood by Groer, telling the "so-called victims" to search their consciences.

On April 7, 1998, the pope, along with Austria's leading archbishops, including Schönborn, and Cardinals Sodano and Ratzinger, huddled in Rome to discuss Groer. A week later the papal embassy in Vienna released Groer's statement: "In the past three years numerous frequently inaccurate allegations have been made against my person. I ask God and humans for forgiveness if I have been guilty. It goes without saying that I am prepared to obey the Holy Father's request to give up my present sphere of activities."

On April 30, Groer and his longtime priest secretary left for Germany.

John Paul's trip to Austria did little to heal the breach. The crowds were smaller; a sense of betrayal because of the Vatican's inertia over Groer hovered like a bad cloud. John Paul did not reflect on the damage done by Groer. Rather, in a private meeting with Austria's fractured hierarchy, bishops who knew their credibility was damaged, he told them to not air grievances in public. He likened the church to a "house that has special rooms that are not open to all guests." The church needed "rooms for talks that require privacy." He assured them they were in his prayers.[16]

Soon thereafter, We Are Church leaders clashed with Ratzinger over their plans for an active role in a national conference of the Austrian church. Sensing a volatile atmosphere, Ratzinger retreated, permitting "the carefully circumscribed participation of members" in the gathering, provided they had no "official recognition."[17]

In a bastion of Catholic Europe, the Groer scandal exposed fault lines between a majority of laypeople espousing the Vatican II ideals of religious liberty, a national hierarchy swamped in religious duress, and a Vatican unable to acknowledge the disgrace of a man ill suited to be a cardinal. As John Paul left Austria, a priest remarked: "The pope is visiting a burning house, but instead of talking about the fire, he talks about the lovely flowers in front."[18]

The Vatican Intervenes in Arizona

On March 20, 1997, Archbishop Agostino Cacciavillan, the pronuncio in Washington, wrote to Bishop Anthony Pilla of Cleveland, then president of the U.S. bishops' conference:

> The Congregation for the Clergy has received numerous recourses, originating in the English-speaking world, from clerics who have been accused of sexual abuse or who have otherwise had their faculties removed, through the application of certain policies and procedures employed by many dioceses . . . [which] could be canonically null. . . . I would ask Your Excellency to provide [the congregation] with the most current copies of all your policies, procedures, or guidelines operative in this country on the national and archdiocesan level.

"Rome is arguing that the bishop should not be prosecutor, judge and jury," the Reverend Thomas J. Reese, a Jesuit sociologist and authority on the Vatican, said at the time.[19] American bishops, still resisting secret trials as cumbersome and an impediment in civil cases, were utilizing canon 1044, which allowed a bishop to remove a man from ministry for insanity or a "psychic defect." What, then, to do with him? "I know from my own visits," Bishop Anthony Bosco of Pennsylvania told the *Pittsburgh Post-Gazette*, "that the Vatican is very concerned about protecting the rights of priests."[20]

The prefect of the Congregation for the Clergy was Archbishop Darío Castrillón Hoyos, a native of Colombia. Born in 1925 in Medellin, Castrillón Hoyos taught canon law as a young priest, advancing into the hierarchy as a doctrinal purist. A blunt critic of drug lords, he also had no use for Liberation Theology. Of the Brazilian Father Leonardo Boff, whose writings caused Ratzinger to order him to keep silent for a year, Castrillón Hoyos said: "Boff will have to ask God to forgive him, and when God answers, then the pope and I will know whether to forgive him or not."[21] In 1996, John Paul called the Colombian to Rome. At the Vatican he dealt with issues involving diocesan priests, norms for preaching, and teaching catechism. In 1998 John Paul made him a cardinal. "For those seeking omens about what kind of pope Castrillón Hoyos would be," the writer John Allen drily noted, "the fact that he sleeps in the deathbed of Pius XII might offer a hint."[22]

The priest scandals in Ireland and North America had little impact on Colombia, reeling from civil war and drug gangsters. As his staff in Rome gathered diocesan policies, Castrillón intervened for a notorious priest in Arizona.

Robert Trupia, a graduate of the Los Angeles seminary, was ordained in 1973. At his first parish, in Yuma, Arizona, "he almost immediately began molesting eleven- and twelve-year-old altar boys in the rectory after Sunday services," the journalist Ron Russell would write.[23] In 1976, a lay brother named Ted Oswald helped several families report Trupia to the bishop. Trupia was packed off to Tucson, "where, astonishingly, he was assigned to teach sex education." Oswald sent the families' complaints to Tucson. The diocese destroyed them; the chancellor rebuked Oswald (who later became a priest) for making trouble.

Trupia courted Phoenix bishop James Rausch, a former general secretary of the bishops' conference. Rausch had unseemly secrets of his own. In 1979, Rausch was coming off a sexual relationship with a drug addict whom he sent to Trupia for counseling.[24] Trupia had sex with the young man, too. As vice chancellor for marriage annulments, Trupia helped the young man into recovery with a job at the chancery. Rausch made Trupia a monsignor; the bishop died in 1981. Trupia meanwhile was spending weekends at his old seminary in L.A. with high school boys considering a vocation. In 1982, a housekeeper found him in bed with a student. That news got him in trouble with Tucson's new bishop, Manuel Moreno, who let him off with a warning. The Los Angeles seminary was tolerant, too, until a 1988 sexual incident with another young man rendered Trupia persona non grata. In 1989, he went to Catholic University in Washington, D.C., to study canon law.

In early 1992, Trupia was back in Tucson as judicial vicar when the mother of an altar boy in Yuma reported him to the church and to police. Bishop Moreno called Cacciavillan, the papal ambassador in Washington, advising him of the situation. On April 1, the bishop and an aide asked Trupia to enter a treatment facility. Trupia refused. Calling himself "a loose cannon," he threatened to reveal that he had had a sexual relationship with the late Bishop Rausch, that the two of them and a *third* priest had had sex with the drug addict, who was then a teenager.[25] In exchange for shutting up, Trupia, forty-two, proposed his *retirement*, with pension, thus preserving his priestly status. Rejecting Moreno's request that he enter a hospital, Trupia returned to Washington. In a June 25 letter he told Moreno, "You have no right, either civilly or canonically or pastorally, to direct me . . . to seek evaluation." He stood on the "statute of limitations." In a follow-up letter he said he was not "in any way liable to penalty" under canon law.

Moreno wrote his testy canonist that he had put him on administrative leave "to protect the common good of Tucson while an investigation takes place." Trupia refused to get a psychiatric evaluation; Moreno suspended him. Trupia went to Rome. He filed an appeal at the Apostolic Signatura—the church's supreme court—challenging the Congregation for the Clergy's support of Moreno's suspension. Meanwhile, the Tucson diocese paid settlements to two of his victims.

A Vatican official wrote Bishop Moreno in May 1994: "Should Your Excellency wish to participate in this process as an interested party— which the Apostolic Signatura strongly recommends—you must choose another [Vatican-approved canonist] from the enclosed list." As he became the center of litigation involving eleven men who were abused as kids, Trupia wrapped himself in ecclesiastical law. "Until such time as the Apostolic Signatura has rendered a decision," Trupia instructed Moreno on July 27, 1995, "your latest mandate with its accompanying deadlines is moot and inoperative."

Trupia's canonical appeal cited a technicality, that Moreno had not conducted a sufficient canonical investigation in suspending him.[26] When attorney Lynn M. Cadigan, representing victims of Trupia and other priests, obtained the Vatican documents in discovery, she knew she had serious leverage. Tom Doyle, as a consultant, read the correspondence and saw in Trupia a man who, like a jailhouse lawyer, could cleverly manipulate the system.

The court barred key documents from public view. Michael Rezendes of *The Boston Globe* managed to see the entire file and reported that a 1997 letter from Castrillón Hoyos "ordered Moreno to reevaluate Trupia's proposal to be retired in good standing, and said the diocese must reimburse Trupia for legal expenses. The ruling made no mention of the sexual abuse allegations."[27] The *Globe* also reported that Castrillón advised Moreno "to entertain a proposal by Trupia . . . to retire as a priest in good standing and work as a consultant to other dioceses."[28]

Moreno appealed the Vatican decision, writing Castrillón Hoyos: "If I do this, and he commits an offense in that diocese, both this diocese and myself would be personally liable, not to mention the scandal that would be caused among the People of God and the harm that might result to an innocent party." Here was religious duress, with irony dripping like candle wax: a bishop who is threatened by blackmail over a dead colleague's sexual liberties appeals to Rome to withdraw its support for a pederast! With a $1,475 monthly pension from Tucson, Trupia got the Monterey, California, diocese to hire him as a consultant on annulments and canonical matters. He commuted from his flat in a Washington, D.C., suburb every other month.[29] In 2001, Yuma police arrested and briefly imprisoned Trupia, but dropped charges because of the statute of limitations. The Monterey diocese, however, decided to end his consultancy. The Tucson diocese agreed to a $14 million settlement with Cadigan's clients. When the *Monterey Herald* learned of Trupia's consulting agreement, the vicar general, Monsignor Charles G. Fatooh, resigned "with a heavy heart." Trupia was paying $1,100 a month rent at a condominium Fatooh owned in Maryland. According to the Tucson diocese, Castrillón Hoyos in 2003 had not replied to Moreno's 1997 plea about the danger Trupia posed. Trupia, eleven years after a suspension order, was still a priest, in a Roman sort of way.

Doyle in Dallas

I am now a redneck like the best. Have a beat up pickup truck. All I need is a beer gut, a baseball hat, a six-pack or two and a lobotomy. If the bishops thought I was out of their hair out here, they're wrong.

—Doyle, in a 1995 letter from the Azores

Sylvia Demarest was a plaintiff lawyer in Dallas, a city of big oil and big real estate, and one of America's fastest-growing dioceses. Demarest, who grew up in hardscrabble Cajun country, was a feminist given to jeans and cowboy boots. A relentless researcher, she approached discovery like a fencer with a foil. When she met Father Doyle at a 1993 canon law conference, he wore his Air Force uniform. She had legal actions under way against three priests and was building a database on clergy sex offenders. Two of her cases involved the Military Ordinariate, the church jurisdiction to which Doyle and other Catholic chaplains reported. "Those are good, stand-up guys," he told her.[30] Nevertheless, he agreed to help. After reading the documents she provided, Doyle realized that the tentacles of religious duress reached deeper than he had ever imagined.

One abuser, Robert Peebles, had arrived at a chaplains' orientation in late May 1982 at a house the Military Ordinariate owned on the New Jersey shore. With him was Kristopher Galland, fifteen, who had been one of his altar boys back in Dallas at affluent All Saints Parish. The youth slept in Peebles's room at the New Jersey house. Peebles had sex with him during the training period. Galland was the youngest of five children; his father traveled a lot. Peebles had taken him on camping trips "like a big buddy, getting me drunk and then having sex with me," Galland recalled.[31] Getting young guys drunk was how Bob Peebles made his moves on them. In New Jersey he told military priests that Galland was his nephew. Peebles was starting officer candidate school. Galland washed out of several schools in Dallas before graduating from a military academy. He didn't shake the drug and alcohol addiction till his thirties. By then he was angry.

In 1984, one of Galland's high school buddies, Mike Miglini, went to visit Chaplain Peebles at Fort Benning, Georgia. Miglini's mother had once sewn Peebles's scoutmaster uniform. Peebles plied him with beer and started crawling all over him; Miglini fled the room. Military police found him wandering on the base, partially clothed.

"But, in accord with deference patterns that shelter priests, the arresting officers did not notify Mike's parents or take him to the civil authorities," notes Garry Wills. "Instead, they placed him in the custody of another priest."[32] Miglini never spoke to his parents in the thirty-six hours before the base priest put him on a plane and called ahead to a priest at All Saints, who met him at the airport. At the parish his folks picked him up; he was too traumatized to tell what happened. The parish monsignor (who was also the diocesan chancellor) gave the parents a spare account of Peebles's error and asked them not to "bring scandal on the church." The parents sought help from a psychologist—who, unbeknownst to them, was on the diocesan payroll, counseling other aberrant priests, and soon began counseling Peebles. As the diocesan power structure closed in around the Miglinis, the parents agreed not to press charges, with the understanding that Bob Peebles would no longer function as a priest.

Documents that Demarest obtained in discovery in another case showed Doyle a deep hole of corruption. Peebles had molested three boys as a Dallas priest *before* he joined the Army. The diocese violated canon law in failing to investigate and sending him on to the military. Demarest cross-referenced a roster of chaplains from 1970 to 1982 with her database and found twenty priests who joined the military after church officials knew they had abused children. This was glum news for Doyle. Chaplains "are subject to the Uniform Code of Military Justice," he wrote in an analysis for Demarest. "A military commander does not, as a matter of course, notify a priest's ecclesiastical supervisor." Yet the Army bought the view "that a court martial would cause more harm than good." Peebles was not prosecuted.

Bob Peebles went back to Dallas; after a month of therapy he had a new parish. Fresh accusations arose. The diocese sent him to St. Luke Institute; he admitted to sexually abusing fifteen to twenty youngsters during his years as a priest. In an ecclesiastical equivalent of the golden parachute, the diocese helped Peebles petition Rome to be laicized, provided him with $22,000 for tuition at Tulane Law School, in New Orleans, and $800 a month for two years. Moreover, the diocese *never* reported him to the police. By the time the lawsuits were filed against him, the diocese, and the vicariate, Bob Peebles had become a lawyer in New Orleans, with the Louisiana State Bar Association unaware of his past. (Demarest eventually negotiated settlements for Galland and Miglini totaling $1.8 million.)

The Miglini family was unaware that another son, Tony, was among a group of boys at All Saints Parish with whom another priest, Rudolph Kos, used video games, booze, and pot to lure his sexual conquests.[33]

Born in 1945 in Louisville, Kos was four when his mother left the family. Raised by relatives and for a time by nuns in a Milwaukee orphanage, he was molested by an uncle. As a teenager he sought sex with boys in the neighborhood and molested one of his younger brothers.[34] Estranged from his siblings, he married a childhood friend and joined the Air Force; they never consummated the marriage but stayed together five years. She divorced him on discovering his love letters from several boys. Out of the military, he became a registered nurse. Working at Dallas's Methodist Medical Center in the pulmonary unit in the early 1970s, he befriended a fatherless eight-year-old boy with chronic asthma. He persuaded the boy's Russian mother to let him share parental duties, though without a legal status.[35]

When Kos applied to the Dallas seminary, the church wanted him to annul his marriage. Seminary officials contacted his ex-wife, who said he had a problem with boys. Nevertheless, Kos's annulment petition got rubber-stamp approval. "This case makes a travesty of the tribunal nullity procedure," Doyle wrote in analyzing the documents. Kos's ex-wife "was willing to give written testimony. . . . Had [she] been given the opportunity to challenge the decision there is no doubt that the canonical equivalent of a mistrial would have been declared."[36] His memo lends validity to Vatican complaints about church tribunals authorizing annulments without proper procedure—though not as a rationale for restricting bishops' ability to speedily remove proven child molesters.

The seminary Kos entered mirrored an institutional breakdown. The Reverend Joseph F. Wilson studied in the Dallas seminary from 1977 to 1986 and wrote:

> Under the influence of the vice rector in charge of the collegians there, the college wing of the seminary deteriorated dramatically, discipline eroded, sexually scandalous situations proliferated, and good men abandoned their vocations in disgust. That vice rector left the priesthood a year after I graduated—to "marry" the president of the Dallas Gay Alliance. . . . I actually had the experience of sitting through a lecture by Fr. Paul Shanley, the Boston priest who was recently arrested in California. As the public now knows, the Boston chancery office had a file of sixteen hundred pages on Fr. Shanley, including the diaries in which he described teaching kids

how to shoot up drugs and letters . . . protesting the lectures he gave
in which he actively promoted pedophilia as helpful and healthy. . . .
I was sitting behind the then bishop of Dallas, Thomas Tschoepe,
who laughed and joked his way through a truly vile presentation.[37]

Kos's "son" stayed with him periodically in the seminary and in the
rectory at All Saints, his first assignment. Kos had sex with him and
lured other All Saints youths with video games, gifts, and beer. In 1986,
Kos was sent to another parish. A priest who shared that rectory wrote
church officials: "There is an overnight guest in his room four nights out
of every week on the average." Monsignor Robert Rehkemper, the vicar
general, told Kos to stop having boys visit. In 1988, however, the bishop
promoted Kos to pastor of another parish. His young visitors concerned
the assistant pastor, Robert Williams. In July 1991, Father Williams got
Monsignor Rehkemper to meet with him and a therapist who treated
sex offenders. The therapist told the churchmen that Kos sounded like a
"classic, textbook pedophile."[38]

The church ordered Kos to begin therapy. In June 1992, with clergy
abuse making national headlines, Father Williams sent a twelve-page letter to the new bishop, Charles Grahmann, about the parade of boys
through Kos's room: "He would hold them tightly . . . and then rub
them against him, almost like they were a towel with which he was dry-
ing himself." Not until a victim actually complained, however, did
Bishop Charles Grahmann send Kos to St. Luke Institute for evaluation.
Grahmann refused to allow clinicians to use the device that measures
arousal patterns against slides on a screen. Kos ended up at the Servants
of the Paraclete treatment center in New Mexico in autumn 1992. He
returned to Dallas for Christmas break and molested another teenage
boy before heading back to his treatment in New Mexico.

By that time one of his victims at All Saints Parish had killed himself by gunshot and another one had contacted attorney Windle Turley.

Turley housed his law firm and handsome art collection in a large
building in downtown Dallas that bore his name. Turley was something
of a legend at the Texas trial bar; he had won multimillion-dollar claims
for victims' families in an airline crash and against automobile manufacturers for fuel tank flaws. In time, seven young men—along with the
parents of the dead one—became his clients against Kos and the dio-

cese; Sylvia Demarest was representing three of the survivors. Turley and Demarest joined forces on the Kos cases.

The diocese, meanwhile, had paid an out-of-court settlement to a family whose teenage girl was seduced by a third priest at All Saints Parish.

With a damning trail of internal documents, the attorneys suggested an $11 million settlement. "We would have taken a little bit less," said Turley later.[39] But Bishop Grahmann, stubborn as granite, backed church attorney Randal Mathis as they headed to trial. Dallas courts are much less sympathetic toward plaintiffs than courts in Houston or Beaumont, oil-patch cities with juries prone to awarding generous verdicts.

Rudy Kos was working as a paralegal in San Diego as the trial began.

When Tom Doyle flew to Dallas in June 1997 to testify, his tour of duty in the Azores was coming to an end. His new assignment would be Tinker Air Force Base in Oklahoma, a three-hour drive from Dallas, where his sister Kelly and her family lived. He would miss the island base, but was glad to be closer to family.

The issue of the Kos trial was institutional behavior: what does it take to trigger a church investigation? The diocese would argue that it had not known enough about Kos's pathology. If the evidence showed negligence, the jury could award punitive damages. Tom Doyle took the witness stand in his black clericals and collar, the gravitas of his rocklike persona softened by the tones of a reflective priest. After eliciting his opinion on Kos's annulment and Dallas's seminary standards, Turley asked: "Father, based on your study of this case . . . why in the world didn't they take action to remove this man before nineteen ninety-two?"

Doyle replied: "The question you're asking is, why are we sitting here today?"

"Exactly."

"I believe there was a fear of what would have been discovered had they confronted him," stated Doyle, "fear that the secrecy that is so much an important part of the ebb and flow of the Roman Catholic Church as an institution would have been violated."

Turley asked if the diocese showed "gross indifference" to the rights of children.

"I don't know what the proper word would be," Doyle answered, "but a defrauding, a stonewalling, and outright lying to the people."

"That is pure speculation!" fumed Mathis. "They're improper legal conclusions."

The judge overruled him.

"You started to say stonewalling?" resumed Turley.

"All of these issues were raised at one time or another, on a regular basis, to diocesan authorities, from the seminary authorities to the people in the chancery office," said Doyle. "And nothing happened, until one of these young men blew the whistle."

Each time the trial took a break, Demarest had trouble finding Doyle; he was huddling in empty conference rooms with the young plaintiffs and their families, apologizing for what they had endured, listening to their words in one of the most emotionally jarring experiences of his life.

When his two-day testimony was done, the room went quiet. The jury was removed. As court adjourned, the survivors and their parents waited for the judge to step down. They erupted in applause as Doyle left the witness box, applause rattling as if for a rock star, people crowding close to say thanks, and good-bye.

The trial wore on with heart-tearing testimony by the mother of the suicide victim. In counterpoint stood the surreal clericalism of Bishop Grahmann, with receding hairline and a craggy brow, utterly unable to gauge the tonnage of his words. In defending his decision *not* to remove Kos sooner, he said he had not read the twelve-page warning letter from the assistant pastor. "I stand by what I did. . . . In hindsight you may not agree with those decisions." What about the many "red flags" raised about Kos's behavior? parried Turley.

"They were yellow flags," Grahmann insisted.

As Demarest and Turley made their closing statements, Doyle's characterization of a "defrauding, stonewalling" diocese had powerful resonance. On July 24, 1997, the jury awarded $18.6 million in punitive damages and a staggering $101 million in compensation to the victims—$119.6 million total—with a handwritten note telling the Dallas diocese to make "significant changes [in] your policies. . . . Money alone can not atone for the damages to these plaintiffs. Please *admit* your guilt and allow these young men to get on with their lives." News of the record verdict made international headlines, signaling that the "American problem," as many in Rome viewed it, was far from over.

"Sometimes we are not alert, not on guard," Grahmann said in response. "We need to show the victims our deepest compassion."[40] But the jury's suggestion of atonement cut against habits of religious duress. Monsignor Rehkemper—the retired vicar general, who lived at All Saints, where Kos began his career, and who persuaded the Miglinis not to press charges against Peebles—stunningly told *The Dallas Morning News*: "No one ever says anything about what the role of the parents was in all this. They more properly should have known because they're close to the kids."[41]

Bishop Grahmann then held a closed meeting of advisers, including several high-powered attorneys who discussed persuading a Catholic appellate judge to rule that the trial judge had shown bias. Notes of the meeting found their way to investigative reporter Brooks Egerton, whose report in the *Morning News* caused the appellate judge to recuse himself.[42] The diocese scrambled to transfer its assets as a way to reduce its final liability. The shell game ended with a negotiated $30 million settlement.

Rudy Kos returned to Dallas, pleaded guilty to crimes with the younger victims, and began a long prison term. The Vatican appointed a coadjutor, Bishop Joseph Galante, to help rejuvenate the troubled Dallas diocese. But Bishop Grahmann refused to leave; no one in Rome ordered him to do so. Tension between the two bishops became an open secret, with the Dallas diocese a spectacular case of religious duress.

Chapter Thirteen

ORTHODOXY AND
DECEPTION

THE LEGION OF CHRIST is one of the new evangelical movements in the Catholic Church whose fundamentalism and organizational dynamics clash with the collegial spirit of Vatican II. Critics of the movements, especially ex-members, often call them cults. The Legion, though built on a cult of personality around Maciel, is seen by critics as actually more of a sect, a crooked branch off the trunk of true Catholicism that uses psychologically coercive and deceptive practices.

The most notable of the new movements is Opus Dei (Work of God), founded in Spain in 1928 by a priest named Josemaría Escrivá de Balaguer. Escrivá's origins share traits of Maciel's. A chronicler of Opus Dei writes of Escrivá at sixteen:

> *Repudiation of the father, identification with the mother and a nagging uncertainty about the future became the motivating forces of [his] growing spirituality. Gradually he laid aside the objects of his childhood to experiment with the* cilicio, *a barbed metal bracelet attached around the thigh, and the discipline, a braided whip-like instrument of penance.*[1]

Escrivá went into hiding during the Spanish Civil War; only after Franco's consolidation of power in the 1940s did Opus Dei begin to catch fire. Escrivá wanted to resurrect Catholic supremacy in Europe as a bulwark against any future persecution. He called for sanctification of the workplace, encouraging laypeople to lead holy lives in their occupations, advocating celibacy for those able to make the sacrifice. His full agenda, revealed gradually to entering members, called for a spiritual militia to achieve "in-depth penetration to protect and place the church at the summit of human activity."[2] Spain was an impoverished, if not broken, country in the 1940s and 1950s. Escrivá built Opus Dei by cementing ties with upper-echelon Franco supporters. The Jesuits had great influence over Franco and his core advisers, who made annual retreats for the Spiritual Exercises of Saint Ignatius. In 1944, Escrivá, though not a Jesuit, directed Franco's retreat.[3]

The disciplined Opus Dei members "resemble the Mormons in their penchant for private rites and secret societies, in their meticulous preoccupation with proper dress and circumspect manners, and—above all—in their cocksure attitude that they alone have found the form that Catholicism must take," Kenneth L. Woodward of *Newsweek* has written.[4] One of Opus Dei's lay celibates, Dr. Joaquín Navarro-Valls, a psychiatrist turned journalist, became spokesman for the Vatican and Pope John Paul. Opus Dei played a pivotal role in salvaging the Holy See's finances after the Vatican Bank scandal.[5] John Paul gave the movement unique status as a "personal prelature," allowing its members to operate under an Opus Dei bishop without regard to diocesan boundaries.[6] Like religious orders, Opus Dei answers only to the pope. In 1992, John Paul beatified its founder, just fifteen years after his death, a lightning-quick step toward sainthood. Escrivá became a saint in 2002, surpassing Pope John XXIII, a move demonstrating the politics of saint making, a boost to Opus Dei's influence in the church.[7]

The Legion of Christ, much smaller and not nearly as well known as Opus Dei, has a similar kind of messianic Hispanic spirituality and unswerving fidelity to the pope. Both groups believe in money and power to advance the aims of the church; they work hard to recruit orthodox Catholics and view each other as rivals. Opus Dei has 82,700 laypeople, 1,819 priests, and 16 bishops, with centers in sixty countries.[8] The Legion, with 500 priests and 2,500 seminarians in twenty countries,[9] has an affiliated organization, Regnum Christi (Kingdom of Christ), that claims "tens of thousands of lay men and women, as well as deacons and priests."[10] They are the Maciel's cadre for infiltrating and "re-Christianizing" existing Catholic organizations. Maciel claims the idea for Regnum Christi came to him in 1949. Several ex-Legionaries say he borrowed the "lay apostolate" idea from Opus Dei in the 1960s and took the name from a defunct European pious association.[11]

The infiltration strategy is rooted in Mexican history. In the 1930s, after the government crushed the Cristero Revolt, holdout Catholic rebels turned to terrorist tactics. In one village they cut off the ears of a man whose two daughters were socialist schoolteachers. Bishops, fearing retaliation from the government, worked with lay activists in a covert group called Las Legiones. With a secret oath of loyalty to the bishops, Las Legiones infiltrated the radical Catholic groups and purged the leaders.[12] Las Legiones' high command worked with a secret tier of secondary leaders in forming alternatives to socialist unions, and creating an organization of small landowners allied with capital and labor, called Sinarquismo, as a counterforce to communism and dictatorship, while strengthening the rights of Catholics.[13]

One lesson of Las Legiones was the value of stealth. No one learned it better than Father Maciel. The Legion has made a mission of converting Catholics to its cause as a counter to progressives in the church. Regnum Christi members are expected to obey orders and contribute money to the Legion. Recruitment is a top priority; so is disguising their goals to win recruits.

As Opus Dei followers read *The Way*, a collection of maxims by Escrivá, Regnum Christi members ponder *The Envoy*, a collection of Maciel's letters that circulates among his followers. "Unity is the supreme good," he advises, "as the Movement is a body and an army at the service of the Kingdom of Christ. . . . The director represents the authority of Christ the head, and the subject the redemptive obedience of Christ."[14] Twenty-five bound volumes of Maciel's letters are available to "the Movement." Manuals lay out in minute detail how to recruit young people, how priests should dress, how schools should be organized, prayers be said, and Regnum Christi meetings be conducted. Uniformity is so overarching that some Vatican wags call the Legionaries "the Stepford priests."

The control mechanisms drive men out of the Legion, complaining of a conspiratorial mentality. Peter Cronin, an Irish priest who left the

Legion after twenty years, called the training and recruitment of semi-narians in Connecticut "more characteristic of sects or cults." Cronin wrote a blistering critique of the Legion in a 1996 letter to a popular radio host in Ireland, Pat Kenny of RTE:

> *Numbers of recruits are important, seen as proof of the validity of the Legion and a way of impressing authorities in the Church. However, the screening process is minimal, and there is no true discernment of a vocation, of whether this way of life is good or healthy for the given individual. . . . Everybody has a vocation to the Legion until the Legion decides otherwise. Once the order gains access to a young person, all its powers of persuasion and attraction are trained on the unwitting target.[15]*

The younger the better, wrote Cronin, because "the immaturity of the candidate makes him vulnerable to brainwashing."

> *Brainwashing is brought about by a combination of different elements which influence and control the person with great effectiveness: for example, "spiritual direction" and "confession." Canon Law states that seminarians and religious should have complete freedom to choose a confessor and spiritual director. In the Legion . . . there is no freedom at all: all Legionaries have spiritual direction and confession with their superiors, in the novitiate, through their years of formation and even as priests. This is an aberration because it places the person completely in the control of the superior. It means that that superior who recommends or not a person for promotion to vows or orders or positions of responsibility in the order has access to [his] internal conscience. . . . Confession and spiritual direction are essentially tools in the hands of the Legion to brainwash the individuals to stay in the Legion.*

Cronin listed other traits, which the Legion vigorously denies: obsessive secrecy; systematic separation from family, the wider church, and society; viewing everyone outside the Legion with distrust; being encouraged to spy on others; letters opened and read by superiors; lockstep obedience to rules as divinely ordained; dissenters isolated, or banished "to some out of the way place (like the missions in Quintana Roo, Mexico) . . . When we joined the Legion we thought it was a mainstream order like the Dominicans, Franciscans, Jesuits. We were deceived. . . . It would take years before we would get the full picture."

In 1985, Cronin became a priest of the archdiocese of Washington, D.C. The archbishop (later cardinal), James Hickey, too powerful a figure for Maciel to manipulate, welcomed other Legion refugees. In his parish in Bethesda, Maryland, Cronin provided a self-styled "underground railroad" for other men leaving the Legion, scorned by the order. Cronin, who periodically sent out newsletters for former Legionaries, died of a heart attack in 1999, only fifty years old.

Paul Lennon, a leprechaun of a man who had been among the first eight teenagers recruited in Ireland, carried on Cronin's work. He was seventeen in 1961. Lennon was ordained in Rome in 1969, a swift advance in the Legion, but Maciel was eager to use the Irishman in taking the movement to the English-speaking world. The Legion "spirit and mystique" meant applauding whatever Maciel did, said Lennon, "his misgivings about Pope John XXIII's decision to summon an ecumenical council and criticisms of Catholic theologians he considered liberal. Anyone in church or state who didn't meet his approval was treated with disdain and sarcasm. The onlookers would laugh, fawning on his every opinion: 'Yes, of course, Nuestro Padre.' "

Lennon was grateful for his broad education in Spanish language and culture. In 1971, he was sent to Chetumal on the Yucatán Peninsula to establish a parish. In 1975 Maciel assigned him to establish a "School of Faith" in Mexico City, for bishops to send laypeople to be trained. He served there seven years until he ran into conflicts with Maciel over using the school to recruit members of Regnum Christi, rather than training laypeople for dioceses and bishops. The Legion sent him to an impoverished parish in Quintana Roo, in the Yucatán.

Lennon was despairing of the Legion when he attended a priests' retreat in 1984 in Maciel's hometown of Cotija. A friend had quit the Legion and become a "nonperson." Lennon rose in a community meeting, confronting Maciel about the harsh treatment of men who left the Legion. "Once they leave they are always the bad guys," Lennon complained. The audience was stunned that someone would contradict Nuestro Padre. Lennon stormed out of the meeting and for the first time in his life he stayed in a hotel. With money borrowed from friends, he flew to Mexico City and soon left for America. In 1985, he was accepted as a priest in Washington, D.C. In 1989, he left the priesthood. He obtained a master's degree in clinical counseling and began work as a family counselor in Alexandria, Virginia. Lennon founded the group Regain, an Internet-connected support group of those who say they have been burned by the psychologically coercive and abusive treatment of the Legion. The first conference was held in Dallas in June of 2002.[16]

Revolt in St. Paul

Lennon was particularly distressed with the way the Legion cultivated lay Catholics, using a façade of pious traditionalism to draw them in. Thus, the harshest critics of the Legion are not progressive Catholics but those who are staunchly conservative and conclude that the order violates basic standards of honest conduct. When one family member joins, the others become targets for recruitment in Regnum Christi. So it was with Bob and Mary Helmueller of St. Paul, Minnesota, who raised three sons and a daughter in their orthodox home. The couple was proud when John, their youngest son, entered the Legion seminary in Cheshire, Connecticut, in 1991. Mary soon agreed to lead a Regnum Christi group of a dozen women; she was flattered when a Legion priest told her that she was known as "the mother of Regnum Christi in St. Paul."

Regnum Christi has three levels. The first degree, or main level, constitutes the majority—men, women, even some non-Legionary priests and deacons—who meet regularly for prayer and reflection. Second-degree members commit themselves to "the Movement": couples and even families who will move, rather like missionaries, where they are most needed. Third-degree members, mostly women, are "consecrated" in "the Movement." They live in community, though not as a religious order, like nuns; they do not need a bishop's permission to move into a diocese, as nuns do. The consecrated women take directions from the Legion and Father Maciel.

Mary Therese Helmueller, a registered nurse, lived with her parents. She seldom missed daily Mass, a point not lost on the Legion priests who dropped by the house to say hello. Soon several consecrated women began visiting Mary Therese, who was unmarried and thus a potential recruit. "There was always this pressure," she recalled, "to think about going to Rhode Island"—where Regnum Christi had a training center.[17] She found them vague about what exactly they did. "I spent three hours with them in my living room and I still could not understand and they could not explain it." But the visitors were relentless, telling her she owed it to God to come with them.

She finally began to cry. One of them handed her a Kleenex and said, "See, you are fighting what God wants you to do." She recoiled at that, her gut instinct telling her that something about these people was just not right.

Steve Helmueller, one of her brothers, had worked as an administrator for six months at the Legion's Highlands School in Irving, Texas, followed by a year as an accountant in Orange, Connecticut. He declined to speak about what his mother and sister said were unhappy experiences working with the Legion. Two in the family—Mary Therese's father, Robert, and her married brother, Mark—kept their distance from Regnum Christi and the Legion. A retired electronics engineer, Bob Helmueller said tersely, "I never bought into that whole package."

Mary Therese and her mother ran a part-time travel agency in the home, arranging pilgrimages to Rome and to shrines approved by the church—Guadalupe in Mexico; Lourdes, France; Fatima, Portugal; and Knock, Ireland. In 1994—the fiftieth anniversary of Father Maciel's ordination—a large ordination of Legionaries was planned in Mexico. The family of a young man to be ordained asked the Helmuellers to handle the travel arrangements. The family said it was too expensive using the Legion's travel agency because each family member going to the ceremonies was assessed $200 to benefit the Legion. Mary Helmueller telephoned the headquarters in Orange. A priest told her that if she wanted to book families on the trip she must include the $200-per-person assessment. "We were willing to do it to cover cost only," said Mary Therese. "Their way was just a crime. We said, 'We will have nothing to do with it.'"

They had second thoughts about the Legion's way of operating. But with John studying for the priesthood in Connecticut, they did not make an issue of it, hoping the ticket billing had been a mere ethical lapse.

In early 1995, one Norma Peshard, a Mexican in Regnum Christi, telephoned Mary Therese: "You have been chosen by the Holy Father to participate in a project as a reporter for the Beijing Conference"—

an upcoming United Nations Conference on Women. Why would the pope invite her? Then she thought about her church activism, and the occasional articles she had written in conservative Catholic papers, which might have put her on a select list for recommendation by the Legionaries.[18]

Mary Therese Helmueller was an impassioned pro-life supporter. News reports suggested to her that the forthcoming U.N. conference in China would be "a major assault on family life." First lady Hillary Rodham Clinton was leading the American delegation; the Holy See, which had permanent observer status at the U.N., was sending a delegation headed by Mary Ann Glendon, a conservative Catholic who was a law professor at Harvard University. Norma Peshard told Mary Therese that she needed to go to Rome for a briefing by Vatican officials.

She approached a longtime friend, Al Matt, editor of *The Wanderer,* a fellow parishioner at St. Agnes. The beautiful baroque church with a bell tower over two hundred feet, topped by a fourteen-foot gold cross, was modeled after a monastery in Austria, whence many of the original parishioners had come. The parish was the spiritual home of *The Wanderer,* the ultraconservative Catholic weekly founded in 1867. Matt provided her with press credentials.

The next step on her journey was a retreat in the Regnum Christi house in Greenville, Rhode Island, where, she was told, women in the papal delegation would meet. Instead, what she found was a Holy Week retreat, with "a lot of pressure to enter the consecrated life." She again turned them down. She was getting more skeptical—and more curious. In August, at her own expense, she flew to Rome for the next stage of the briefing. "When I arrived at the Mother House of Regnum Christi I explained who I was and why I was there," she recounted. "The consecrated woman at the door replied, 'I'm sure the Holy Father would approve if he knew about it!' "

That answered her question about the alleged invitation from the Holy Father. *He knew nothing about it.* She asked questions of the consecrated women but could not get straight answers. "What terrified me," she explained, "was the mechanical way they spoke, a lot of hesitation . . . sometimes the answers would be avoided." During a meal, she was startled to see the women freeze in their places when Maleny Medina, the world head of the consecrated women, entered the dining hall.

"If they had a spoonful in their mouth they would stop chewing," she continued. "If they had their arm up it just stayed there. I was more and more convinced *this was a cult*. It just was not natural."

It soon became apparent there would be no training sessions or meetings with Vatican officials. Instead, the director, Maleny Medina, and a Legion priest from Spain gave the briefing for about eight women going to Beijing. The main purpose of the trip, she learned, was to recruit members for Regnum Christi among the many Catholic observers expected in Beijing. "The number one, important goal was *captivation*—a technique that includes attracting attention by smiling, flattery, and charm until you can actually recruit," she bristled.

She told them she was going as a reporter, and would associate herself with the pro-life groups. "I was told, '*No, you can't do that. They are too negative.*'" At that moment she felt disgust. Wasn't there something more important at the Beijing conference than recruiting for Regnum Christi? What about protecting the rights of the unborn, an agenda in which she believed?

She was not about to participate in a ridiculous project, born of a ruse. She felt emotionally and psychologically used. Wanting answers before she left Rome, she confronted the woman who had invited her, Norma Peshard. "She admitted that the Beijing project was '*the hook*' to get me consecrated," explained Helmueller. This was a recruiting technique in the Legion's quest to increase their numbers. After leveling with her, she said, Peshard warned her: "There will be serious repercussions if any of this is made public—and you know what I mean."

Helmueller took "repercussions" to mean that her brother John, who had yet to make final vows in the Legion, would be made to suffer.

Norma Peshard refused to be interviewed for this book.[19]

Mary Therese Helmueller left Rome, praying that her brother would find a way to escape the Legion of Christ. Back in St. Paul she gave an earful to her mother and the twelve women in the Regnum Christi group that had been meeting at the house. These women, most of whom had been friends before forming the group, had been having their own doubts. Instead of reading the letters of Father Maciel, which they found shallow, they had been turning to the Bible, papal encyclicals, and the catechism for group discussion.

They were also resisting the growth strategy of Regnum Christi.

Regnum Christi expects each cell to recruit new members in a five-step plan. Step one was to invite a potential recruit to a lecture or a meeting about "the Movement." Step two: developing "friendship." Step three: producing "trust." Step four: convincing the recruit how much "the Movement" means. Step five: the recruit "surrenders" to "the Movement"—in other words, closing the sale.

Cell leaders record the names of potential members and track the step-by-step process of "conversion."

The cell had met in the Helmuellers' cozy two-story home with a statue of the Virgin Mary in the backyard and images of Our Lady of Guadalupe and the Sacred Heart in the living room. Though conservative, the women accepted the changes of the Second Vatican Council but remained wedded to traditional devotions that had fallen into disuse in many places. They liked Regnum Christi's emphasis on such worship. When parishes began abandoning adoration of the Blessed Sacrament— a centuries-old devotion in which people pray for hours before the consecrated host, which they believe has become the body of Christ—these women organized their own worship schedules, despite the reluctance of overworked parish priests. Mary Helmueller organized a network of laypeople for round-the-clock adoration in her parish.

Though the women were middle and upper middle class, several were homeschooling their children. Joyce Nevins, wife of a pediatrician and mother of seven, had sent her children to parochial schools until 1995, when sex education was introduced. She withdrew her two youngest, then in the sixth and eighth grades, to teach them herself at home.

Sandy Stadtherr, the wife of an electronics equipment salesman and mother of four, was homeschooling her children too. Sandy had been "looking for a more structured discipline to aid me in my path to holiness" when someone invited her to a Regnum Christi "evening of reflection." She attended further meetings but was bothered that she could not get a straight answer to her questions about the meaning and purpose of Regnum Christi. She likened it to "childish games played to get one involved, *then we'll tell you more*." Sandy had attended several meetings around St. Paul when her friend Joyce Nevins invited her to the Helmuellers'. Sandy found the women there "friendly and openly kind," unlike those in "such rigid, structured meetings" she had found elsewhere.

But as women with many family obligations, no one was willing to devote the time "the Movement" expected of them. They met once a month instead of once a week. Mary estimated that she would need twenty-two evenings a month to follow Regnum Christi's direction. Very slowly, she came to the view that "the Movement" was subversive of the nuclear family, with men and women meeting separately, and kids in their own groups.

But for all of their doubts, Bob and Mary Helmueller felt they needed to support their son John as he studied for the priesthood in the Legionaries of Christ—which, after all, had Pope John Paul's blessing. "They knew there were problems within the Legion of Christ but had difficulty in coming to grips with the idea that Rome knew about this and would somehow approve it and even promote it," Mary Therese said of her parents. "I think everyone [in the family] was in a strange sort of denial."

Occasionally, leaders of Regnum Christi scolded Mary Helmueller and her group for not adhering to the agenda. Their tenuous ties to Regnum Christi frayed further when they read in *The Wanderer* in March of 1997 that Father Maciel had been accused of sexual abuse by former seminarians. Mary Therese said she tended to believe the allegations because "they weren't out for money or anything." She thought the statement made by the former priest Juan Manuel Fernández Amenábar a month before his death added to the credibility. But the report on Maciel was not a subject of great discussion among the group. They had already distanced themselves from the personality cult of Nuestro Padre.

Several members of the cell had made plans to attend the Regnum Christi convention, a "Family Encounter," in St. Louis at the end of May in 1997. For the Helmuellers it afforded a rare opportunity to see John.

About a thousand adults and children met in a downtown hotel for a weekend of lectures, workshops, and worship. The centerpiece was an inspirational address by Father Maciel. His arrival in the ballroom was preceded by a buildup worthy of a rock star. Several American women on the stage led the audience in a rhythmic chant: *"Nuestro Padre, we love you!"* Mexican women followed, striving to outdo the Americans with cheerleading in Spanish. The audience warmed up, Nuestro Padre appeared theatrically at the entrance to the ballroom, flanked by a phalanx of clerics. Holding his arms high as if in prayerful supplication and closing his eyes, he glided through a crowd of squealing, cheering young people trying to reach out to touch him.

He spoke in rapid Spanish to the enthralled crowd, with equally rapid translation into English by his American director, Father Anthony Bannon. He spoke of the boyhood memory of men killed for their faith, the bodies hanging in his hometown of Cotija. He spoke of his long struggle against foes of the church. He told parents how safe it was to send their sons to the Legion, where they would not find the dissent and homosexuality so rampant elsewhere.[20]

About fifteen minutes into Maciel's speech, Mary Therese Helmueller turned to her brother John and whispered: "He hasn't said anything." He replied: "You are right." Maciel rambled on for what seemed an eternity. When the Legionary chief was done, Mary Therese left the convention hall for a long walk and did not attend any more sessions.

Some parents were upset that their children, while attending "religion classes," were being drilled in Spanish chants and taught to greet Father Maciel by rushing forth to touch him. Joyce Nevins fired off a letter to one of the organizers, saying that "idolization" was out of place in a religious order.

> We have many discussions in our home regarding the inappropriate adulation given to superstar singers, actors and sportsmen. . . . Respect for humans is honorable because they are made in God's image. Endless practice of cheers and physical veneration of Father Maciel is fanatical and immature.

Adulation had reached such a point, Mary Therese said, that she had heard that "a blanket that was supposed to have been used by Father Maciel is being circulated among the Regnum Christi people to kiss."

The Helmueller group took comfort in one another's friendship and the quest for a firmer grounding in the faith, ignoring the rules of Regnum Christi. In autumn 1997, Bob Helmueller was diagnosed with colon cancer (he later recovered). Mary asked Sandy Stadtherr if she would take over the group. They maintained a tie to the Legion largely to preserve John Helmueller's road to ordination.

Juan Guerra, a Legionary priest from the order's academy in Edgerton, Wisconsin, asked Stadtherr if the group would organize a Regnum Christi service for the feast of Christ the King on November 23.

An obliging Sandy Stadtherr met with other Regnum Christi team leaders in her home. The wording of the invitations and advertising started the argument. Stadtherr wanted to state the time of the Mass; the others opposed it. They wanted to get people into church an hour earlier to hear testimonials about Regnum Christi. Sandy insisted that such an omission was deceptive, that the schedule had to be punctual "out of common courtesy and respect for people's time." The others told her: "You are not trusting divine providence"—a Regnum Christi tactic to squelch questions. Listening upstairs, her children later made it a joke. When their mother told them to do something they would chirp: "You are not trusting divine providence."

Stadtherr was appalled at the Regnum Christi leaders' "offensive, authoritative behavior." In many years of leadership in Catholic causes, she said, "I had never been part of such a hostile, uncooperative environment. I was so angry afterwards I cried for three days."

The morning after the meeting she called Father Guerra and told him she quit. When Mary Helmueller heard that, she called the priest and said they were all quitting.

About the same time that the St. Paul women were severing ties with Regnum Christi, John Helmueller was going through his own crisis inside the Legionaries. After eleven years he had taken vows that bound him to the order, yet he had not been ordained a deacon, the final step before becoming a priest. He had spent three years helping a priest as a vocational recruiter, looking for young men on the East Coast and in the Midwest to join the Legion. He was forbidden to contact his family without permission. At one point he was in a car one block away from his parents' home and was not allowed a quick visit.

The pressure was building on John: he wanted to leave the Legion, but not sacrifice his vocation to the priesthood. He asked his superiors for permission to talk to Bishop Robert Carlson of Sioux Falls, South Dakota, a friend of the family. Permission denied. He did, however, receive permission to join a pilgrimage to the shrine of Our Lady of Guadalupe in December 1999. His superiors did not know that Bishop Carlson was booked on the pilgrimage, which his mother and sister had arranged. Mary Therese booked them in adjoining seats on the flight from Dallas to Mexico City. Bishop Carlson immediately accepted him.

On return John Helmueller went straight to Sioux Falls. The bishop demanded, and received, his release from Legion of Christ. Bishop Carlson sent him to Mount St. Mary Seminary in Emmetsburg, Maryland, to finish his final two years of theology. On June 23, 2002, John Helmueller was ordained in Sioux Falls by Bishop Carlson, and now serves in that diocese. His framed photograph hangs in his parents' living room, and Mary, his mother, never refers to him as John anymore but always as Father John.

Schools to Make Money

The Helmuellers' struggle with the Legion is one variation on a theme of orthodoxy used to manipulate people. This too was the experience of Glenn Favreau, who in July 1987, as a twenty-three-year-old seminarian, was assigned as vice rector of a school in Santiago, Chile, called the Zambrano Institute.[21] Favreau had no experience as an educator; but the archdiocese had asked the Legion to take over the school, and the order needed people to run it.

The school, with an enrollment of twelve hundred from kindergarten through twelfth grade, was not for children of the elite and thus did not command a high priority for Legion resources. But Favreau was eager to make good. Reared in a pious French Canadian home in the Adirondacks region of upstate New York, he had spent a year in the diocesan seminary of Ogdensburg, New York, and a year at Niagara University before finding the Legion, which suited his idealism and conservative bent. At Zambrano he did financial administration, with no experience. One of his duties was to take 30 percent off the top of the school's monthly revenues and hand it over in cash in a satchel to a superior. That was the cut to support the Legion's work in Chile. The share was later reduced to 22 percent as a school that the Legion ran for upper-class children, which charged three to four times more tuition, began bringing in more revenue.

Schools for the wealthy are a major source of income for the Legion, according to two priests in a position to know.[22]

The profit-generating schools are mostly in Latin America, where wealthy families are willing to pay as much as $10,000 or more in tuition because the public schools are poor. Most parochial schools struggle at margins well below the norm of the Western democracies. The schools the Legion controls in the United States—about twenty-five—are smaller and barely break even, yet are still a source of recruitment for Legion seminaries and Regnum Christi. Two exceptions are the "language academies"—a girls' school in Warwick, Rhode Island, and the other, for boys, in Edgerton, Wisconsin—most of whose students come from Latin America. The tuition reportedly amounts to nearly $20,000 a year, though it costs the Legion $11,000 to $12,000 per child, according to a priest familiar with the inner workings. The Legion also runs a language academy in Dublin where students, mostly from Latin America, learn English. Two sons of the Mexican president, Vicente Fox, spent a year there.[23]

A priest knowledgeable about the finances estimated that the Legion needs to bring in roughly $60 million a year. About $30 million is required to sustain some four thousand priests, brothers, teachers, seminarians, and employees.[24] Another $30 million goes for services in Rome, for maintaining properties, for mortgages, and for capital expenditures for expansion, particularly in Latin America. The goal is for every operation to be self-sustaining.

Mexico provides the most money, primarily from people of great wealth and via fund-raising schemes set up by Regnum Christi. In 1997, Regnum Christi in Mexico began the Kilo Program. People buying groceries at several major supermarket chains are asked to donate money for the poor when they check out at the cashiers. The program, highly successful, was duplicated in Spain in 1998. In both countries the Kilo Program was established through groups that claim no formal association with Regnum Christi but are controlled by members of Regnum Christi.[25] The Spanish author and journalist Alfonso Torres Robles investigated an influential private organization of university alumni called IUVE. The Legionaries claimed no formal connection but acknowledged that their priests provided spiritual direction. Torres found that founders of IUVE in 1987 were members of Regnum Christi and IUVE's address was the same as the Legion's address in Madrid.[26]

The Legion faces a much harder task raising funds in Western Europe, North America, and Australia: the whole culture and history of the order is in collision with Western traditions of pluralism and democracy. An effort to establish a beachhead in Germany fizzled. Legion sights have now been reset on Poland. A seemingly bright launch in Ireland in the 1960s has sputtered to a near collapse. Vocations dried up, with Irish bishops quietly opposing Legion recruitment. In 2003, the Legion in Ireland had five priests, five professed religious, and twenty-five novices, most from Mexico, the United States, and Poland.[27]

The fund-raising base in the United States is the direct mail campaign operated from Hamden, Connecticut. The Legion buys mailing lists of people who subscribe to Catholic periodicals or belong to various Catholic organizations. The appeals are profitable but do not generate a huge flow considering the costs of printing and postage. What the mailings do give the Legion is a database of Catholics willing at least to donate something, if only $5 or $10. The Legion scans the zip codes of contributors and cross-references them with average-household income-lists of neighborhoods.

The strategy is to "bump up" a minor contributor in a wealthy neighborhood to a higher level of "planned giving." People willing to contribute to this second level are likely to be visited by a team, a priest and a brother. They ask whether the donors would be willing to give an annuity or other major gift to support the Legion. Six or seven of these two-man solicitation teams travel across the country, sizing up the wherewithal of the targeted contributors, noting what sort of home they have, the cars they drive. Their object is to enlist these people as "major givers" and to lead them into the ranks of Regnum Christi, where they will be prized as important assets, opening doors to still more people of influence. Whether the Legion is a cult, as certain of its disaffected followers allege, is perhaps less important than its role as a moneymaking machine in the spirit of Father Maciel.

Chapter Fourteen

THE LEGION'S
AMERICAN BATTLES

A s "MISUNDERSTANDINGS" shadowed Maciel in his early decades as a priest, so the Legion's latter years have been a trail of battles involving their schools in the United States. That is not to say that accusations of sexual abuse have been the concern. Rather, conflicts arose over *abuse of power*, born of the manipulative tactics of the founder. The diocese of Columbus, Ohio, threw out the Legionaries and Regnum Christi, while the Atlanta archdiocese has given "the Movement" carte blanche over the objection of skeptical pastors. The Legion's one American parish, in Sacramento, has been riven by religious duress. These conflicts hold a mirror on the Legion's spiritual corruption. Deceptions spun of the Mexican model collide with an American Catholicism nurtured by religious pluralism.

Mutiny in Atlanta

On September 13, 2000, stunned parents and crying children watched police officers remove a principal and three faculty from the Donnellan School in an affluent Atlanta neighborhood. Legion officials warned that the four would be arrested for trespassing if they tried to reenter the school.[1] Fired for "mutinous actions,"[2] the band of revolutionaries included a guidance counselor and the athletic director, who was pulled away from supervising a volleyball game.

In 1996 the archdiocese established the Archbishop Thomas A. Donnellan School, named for a late prelate, with its own board of directors, near the affluent Buckhead neighborhood. With a $7,400 tuition, Donnellan was competitive for a private school and an immediate success. Parents jumped in as volunteers. On Friday, January 8, 1999, Sister Dawn Gear, the principal and a driving force behind Donnellan, announced her resignation, cleaned out her desk, and left.

Her problems with the board over a long-range plan had crystallized in November; she had agreed to leave in June. A consultant hired by the board told her it was best not to wait. "We made an agreement with my salary and things like that," she told a reporter, much later. "The thing that really bothered me is that I was never able to speak to the parents and the faculty."[3]

A key figure in the maneuver was board member Frank Hanna III, a multimillionaire businessman well known in Georgia for Republican causes. Hanna, a leading member of Regnum Christi, introduced the staff to a Legionary priest, one Father John Hopkins, as the school's new "spiritual director."

The new principal, Angela Naples, had worked as Sister Gear's assistant. She was uneasy about the "swift, harsh" termination and board members she barely knew.[4] But Naples threw herself into the job. She mentioned to Hopkins that she would would be attending a summer workshop for new principals. He asked her to consider a monthlong workshop in Rome for new heads of schools. Rome, where she spent her honeymoon in 1994! Yes, she said.

In June, the archdiocese announced that Archbishop John F. Donoghue "has sold the assets of the Archbishop Thomas A. Donnellan School to The Donnellan School, Inc.,"[5] whose officers were Monsignor Edward Dillon, pastor of Holy Spirit Church; Father Hopkins; and Father Anthony Bannon, national director of the Legionaries of Christ. The archdiocesan newspaper explained: "The purchase price, just over $8.5 million, covers the amount of indebtedness by The Donnellan School to the Archdiocese of Atlanta. Approximately $1 million was paid at closing and the remaining $7.5 million was assumed as a loan from the archdiocese."

Though surprised, Angela Naples knew that Archbishop Donoghue had a keen interest in bolstering Catholic education. He had come to Atlanta in 1993, a former bishop of Charlotte. He was a canon lawyer who had worked under three successive cardinals in his native Washington, D.C. Naples wondered what the selling of her school meant. "Archbishop" was being dropped—henceforth, it would be the Donnellan School.

Naples and her faculty were confused further when Monsignor Ed Dillon—Angela's pastor and friend—and Hopkins complained about the press release from downtown. They said the article was wrong. "They denied the Legion of Christ was taking over," said Naples. The priests assured them the ownership transfer was a formality. When parents asked if Donnellan was now a Legion school, the priests said no, only that Hopkins, a Legion priest, was the chaplain.

Angela Naples went to Rome in July. She found not a workshop for new heads of schools, but training for women in Regnum Christi. She was given a headset to hear addresses translated from the Spanish. "The day was booked from the time you woke up till bedtime," she sighed. Discussion groups made her uncomfortable. "They pulled me aside and scolded me. It really puts you on the spot, sharing when you sinned or did wrong. . . . I was trying to be polite about it. I finally said, 'I am not going to share my spiritual feelings and thoughts!'"

Her husband, mother, and aunt visited Rome, and she skipped out early to join them for a long weekend, missing some of the sessions. "I kept saying, *I don't want to join Regnum Christi*," she said. "Sunup to sundown you are in these classes and it just wears on you." In week three, group leaders met the conferees, one at a time, about a "vocation" with Regnum Christi. "I told them it might go over in the Third World but it will never fly in Buckhead, Atlanta. You cannot shove things down people's throats. . . . They spoke of Maciel like he was right up there with the pope."

When school began that fall she appreciated Monsignor Dillon's attempts to improve her relationship with Hopkins. She felt a tension with the Legionary and wondered if he was displeased by her resistance to "the Movement." A problem arose when Hopkins began pressing the guidance counselor, Diane Stinger, for information on the parents and children with whom she dealt. Stinger refused to violate her standard of confidentiality, and Naples stood by her colleague.[6]

They began to see "consecrated women" and Legion seminarians visit Father Hopkins, organizing clubs for boys and girls. Diane Stinger's job was to work closely with the families; she complained that parents were in the dark about groups holding unofficial programs. At a boys' club meeting, Stinger heard a seminarian leading boys in chants: "Don't you want to be like Father Maciel?" *Yeah!* "Don't you want to be a hero like him?" *Yeah!*

The principal and guidance counselor went to the pastor, Monsignor Dillon, asking: "Are we a Legion school?"

"Over my dead body will we ever be a Legion school," he replied.

But parents and teachers were concerned that the Legion was taking over the school. Dillon told them not to worry. But people *were* worrying as they did Web searches and made phone calls to people in places where the Legion had schools. They heard complaints about manipulation to gain recruits for Regnum Christi. While the Legion emphasized the pursuit of holiness, a common complaint about their schools was piety taking precedence over learning, class time cut for students to attend Mass and retreats, and even to picket abortion clinics.

Not far away in Cumming, an Atlanta suburb, Regnum Christi members had launched a school called Pinecrest in 1993. Theresa Murray, whose daughter was in the third grade, complained that "books never got opened—they were too busy praying the rosary." She withdrew her child when the girl came home and said she wanted to commit suicide so she could see Jesus.[7]

From a suburb of Cincinnati the Atlanta parents heard how the Legion took over a school started in 1996 by traditionalist Catholics for whom parochial schools were too liberal. Parents accepted the Legion's help to teach religion. Three members of Regnum Christi—without making their allegiance known—joined the five-member board of directors. On March 21, 1997, the board voted three-to-two to turn over the school, Royalmont Academy in Mason, Ohio, to the Legion. The two dissenting members quit. "They have the attitude that if you are not a Regnum Christi mother, you are not properly formed . . . you can't be on the board," said Lisa Bastian, a business writer and one of many parents effectively shut out.[8] Another parent, Maggie Picket, complained: "We were never told this was [to be] a Legion school."[9]

"They have pictures of the Holy Father all over the place, and it's hard to tell people what is wrong with [the Legionaries]," said Colleen

Kunnuth. Her husband, Dr. Art Kunnuth, had been board president before the Legion took control "to slurp up money" and recruit kids "all over the place," she said.[10]

One of the first Legion schools, the Highlands in Irving, Texas, grew out of a small homeschooling program in the 1980s. In the early 1990s, Legion priests got involved. With the backing of a wealthy businessman, it grew to over four hundred students on a thirty-five-acre wooded campus adjoining the University of Dallas, a Catholic institution of the diocese. Bishop Charles V. Grahmann gave his support when the school agreed to follow diocesan education principles. But a rocky start led to several staff turnovers and a split that resulted in a competing school.

Ruth Lasseter worked at Highlands with her husband, Rollin, who has a doctorate in English from Yale and served as curriculum adviser. She was stunned when the school imposed an outdated curriculum from Mexico. "We were completely duped," she said. "Everything had to be approved through [Legion headquarters in] Cheshire."

In Atlanta, by the summer of 2000, teachers and parents at Donnellan saw the Legion consolidating control, though the board would not admit it. Teachers, uneasy about the direction and top-down secrecy, met with concerned parents on a Sunday morning in August off the school premises. Board members called the unauthorized meeting a "mutinous action."[11] The tap dance about school identity ended on September 5 when Angela Naples was summoned to Dillon's rectory. The pastor and Father Hopkins wanted her signature on a document that said: "Angela recognizes that the school is, and has been since June of 1999, associated with the Legionaries of Christ, and indeed, through the members of the corporation, *under the ultimate control of the Legionaries of Christ*."[12] The document forbade her

> *making any statements to anyone, including but not limited to any employee, student, parent or other person associated with the school, that is negative with regard to the Legionaries of Christ (or any member thereof). It also involves taking appropriate proactive steps to prevent anyone associated with the School from engaging in such negative conduct, and immediately informing Msgr. Dillon, in writing, of any such negative or detrimental actions or statements by any employees of the school.*

There it was—her very own vow of silence—like those binding all Legionaries. Dillon and Hopkins badgered her to sign the abridgment of her contract. She begged for time to review it with her husband or an attorney. They refused. Reduced to tears, she was allowed to call Ian Lloyd-Jones, a member of the parents association. He arrived shortly, reviewed the document, advised her not to sign, and suggested to the priests that they reframe it more positively. She withheld her signature and after a four-hour ordeal was allowed to go home.[13]

On September 9, Monsignor Dillon presided at the wedding of Diane Stinger's daughter at the parish church. "They used him and he did not see it," remarked Stinger ruefully. "Angela was like a daughter to him. I know he was hurt by this." Dillon was not present when the iron fist came down four days later. Angela Naples, Diane Stinger, Emily Deubel (the middle school coordinator), and Emily's husband, the school coach, Michael Deubel—alleged ringleaders—were fired. With police present they had to leave on the spot, with the school community given no explanation.

In response to parents' complaints, Archbishop Donoghue sent a letter disclaiming any responsibility for decisions made by an independent board of directors.[14] He endorsed the Legionaries of Christ in "the work of our holy church." About a third of the faculty resigned after the firings.[15] The student body was halved by the spring, to about two hundred.[16]

In less than two weeks dissatisfied parents raised $250,000 to start their own school, the Atlanta Academy. Angela Naples, Diane Stinger, and the Deubels were the first ones hired to run the new school, which found a home in a Methodist church. With the school at capacity with 145 students in 2003, the board was looking at land where they planned to build a new school.

Naples, Stinger, and the Deubels filed civil suits against the Donnellan School, Dillon, and Hopkins for breach of contract, emotional stress, and defamation. They reached an out-of-court settlement in October 2001, a week before trial, for a lump-sum award from Donnellan of $375,000.

The Legionaries and their Regnum Christi surrogates found a home in Atlanta with the support of Archbishop Donoghue, who imposed a gag order in a March 26, 2001, directive: "School, parish or archdiocesan agency personnel will not call, invite or speak with any person from any news agency without the approval of the Vice-Chancellor."

The archbishop put Lloyd Sutter, a deacon, retired lawyer, and father of a Legion seminarian, in charge of training parish catechists, those who teach religion in parishes to children who do not attend parochial schools. That amounts to more than 90 percent in greater Atlanta. Sutter denied being a member of Regnum Christi. "Almost all his friends are," a former coworker said. The Legion and Regnum Christi are providing alternative religious education programs in Atlanta parishes. "They had a father-daughter dance at our parish and they didn't say anything about it being sponsored by Regnum Christi," a source said. "They asked people to write checks to the 'home and family fund' and no one knows what that is." The source complained that many people mistakenly thought that the money raised would go to the parish rather than Regnum Christi.[17]

Alarmed at the trend, the Atlanta Council of Priests invited a representative of the Legionaries to explain their programs; the Legion refused and Archbishop Donoghue would not order them to cooperate.[18]

"It always appears to me that their mode here is the ends justify the means," said Monsignor Terry Young, the council president. "They say their teachers are all certified, when some are not even college graduates." Some fine people are in Regnum Christi, he said. "But in dealing with them, you never have the feeling that they are really free. The Legion has to approve everything."[19]

Father William Hickey, pastor of St. Brendan in Cumming, where the Legion's Pinecrest Academy is located, was more blunt: "Regnum Christi is not allowed to meet here. It doesn't feed the parish needs. They cause a lot of friction."[20]

Déjà Vu in Naples, Florida

In 1998 members of Regnum Christi opened a school in Naples, Florida, promoting the "Legion's educational philosophy" to families who had been homeschooling their children. Dan Anderson was impressed. A detective sergeant who supervised violent crime investigations, Anderson wanted his four kids to get a traditional Catholic education. He joined Regnum Christi as the school took shape.

"Unless you have been involved with Regnum Christi, and experienced the propaganda writings that accompany it, it is almost impossible to understand," he explained. Anderson sat across from Gerald Renner at a picnic table on a warm day in May 2002. His son Zach was practicing with his soccer team on an adjoining field in a sports park in the family-friendly town. Anderson had a sheaf of documents, his paper trail on Royal Palm International Academy. The school was founded by Carol Moore, a member of Regnum Christi and daughter of Jack Donohue, one of Naples's wealthiest citizens.

Anderson, who had given trial testimony many times in eighteen years of law enforcement, reviewed his dossier in a cool tone, marshaling the facts. In 1998, he became president of the Parents' Forum, an association that distributed Christmas gifts to migrant worker families, and food to the poor, disseminated the school newsletter, and did fund-raising. That year, the student body grew from thirty students to nearly 120.

Patrick Scott Smith, a businessman who chaired the three-member school board, volunteered as principal until an educator could be found. In January 1999, Smith visited Rome and met with Maciel, whom he found to be "a warm person, very charismatic."[21] He met Maciel again in Atlanta in late October, reiterating that Royal Palm needed an educator to run the school. In May 2000, Maciel sent Catalina Nader of Mexico, a "consecrated woman" of Regnum Christi.

When school began that fall, Catalina Nader began "forcefully adopting guidelines established by the National Consultants for Education," said Anderson. The NCE is based at Legion headquarters in Orange, Connecticut, and is "especially helpful when the Legion is unable to secure local diocesan approval to run a Legion school," the detective explained. Naples is part of the diocese of Venice. A diocesan spokesperson said the school "has no status."[22]

Teachers complained that Nader required that she review each piece of communication they had with parents, restricted their after-school access to the building, and forbade them from meeting with parents without her being present. Those orders stirred a stew of discontent. Nader summoned teachers, individually and in groups of two, questioned them about their activities, accused them of undermining the school's mission, and threatened to fire several of them.

Nader denied Dan Anderson's request for a roster of families to distribute to the school community. She told him to halt Forum activities until the school moved to a proposed new site. She changed the wording of his memorandum, explaining why the Forum was suspended, and distributed it in his name, without his signature or his permission.

Anderson saw that she was trying to limit interaction between families so they wouldn't question the changes she was making. That led to "the feeling that parents were no longer welcome at the school—that we should mind our own business," he said. Meanwhile, the local Regnum Christi cell was starting to crack. "Individual members began questioning their faith," said Anderson. "The teachings of the Legion and Father Maciel began to overwhelm them. They saw blind faith, untiring devotion to the Movement, secretive meetings . . . and they did not like it."

Two women who left Regnum Christi (and asked that their names not be used) were appalled that personal matters they confided to a Legion priest during spiritual counseling were shared with Regnum Christi "team leaders." Although it wasn't a direct violation of sacramental confession, it came close, like confession with a group of people knowing your sins. One woman had nightmares as a result.

"The whole façade came tumbling down," said Anderson, as people began doing research on the Internet, learning about the accusations against Maciel and the disputes involving other Legion schools, and having telephone conversations with people in Atlanta, where wounds were still fresh.

In Naples the school board split in a bitter dispute. Two of its three members fired Smith as chairman at a hastily called meeting of which he was unaware. They sued him for reneging on a promise to donate nearly $1 million to the school and for self-dealing by acquiring ten acres of land, in the name of a trust he controlled, on which a proposed new school was to be built.[23] Smith accused the board of illegally removing him as chairman and claimed that he acquired the land for the school because the school could not afford it.[24] He reneged on his promised payment, he said, when the Legion of Christ demanded transfer of the land to the order itself at no consideration. A mediation followed, with Royal Palm getting the land, and Smith was paid for his $3.5 million investment.[25]

The board dismissed Anderson as president of the Parents' Forum after he called an emergency meeting to discuss school issues off premises. In an echo of Atlanta, school officials said the meeting was "unauthorized."

Anderson told the assembly that many parents had complained to him that the school had "become a secretive, carefully controlled institution." Soon thereafter six teachers resigned, saying that "the conditions under which we have been working are atrocious." They respected "the Legion's right to run a school the way they see fit, however, we in good conscience cannot continue to be associated with this institution."

As in Atlanta, the unhappy parents and teachers set up their own school, Sacred Heart Academy. A story about the rift that appeared in the *Naples Daily News* included a defense from Jay Dunlap, the Legion spokesman in Connecticut.[26] Parents knew from the start what the school was all about, he said. He blamed the problems on Smith and his "self-dealings that jeopardized the school's legal status as well as the tax-exempt status." Smith, he said, "orchestrated a campaign to discredit the school."

Dunlap attacked Smith in a letter to Anderson,[27] to which the detective sent a blistering reply: "To suggest that I, as well as others, would have interrupted our lives to such an incredible degree, fractured friendships, left a school that at one point was the focal point of our lives . . . for the benefit of a board dispute is insulting and ludicrous."[28]

The new school collapsed for a lack of financial support. Smith moved to Raleigh, North Carolina, where he established a new business.[29] "When the pope stated, 'If you are what you should be you will set the whole world ablaze,' he echoed my own sentiments," reflected Anderson. "I believed in what the Legion espoused. I was energized by the thought of being a part of the reevangelization of the Catholic faith. I do not subscribe to the implementation of their plan. Deception and other improprieties should never be a mainstay of any mission of Christ."

Pope John Paul's endorsements are a huge boon to the Legion's school marketing. If the pope is with them, how can they be bad? The Legion got its schools in Atlanta, Cincinnati, Dallas, and Naples, Florida, with a steamroller that left many in a rubble. The Legion was targeting areas, particularly in the South, with growth potential because of weak parochial schools. Deep splits opened among parents at Cypress Heights Academy in Baton Rouge, Louisiana, and Rolling Hills Academy in San Antonio, Texas, in the summer of 2003 after Regnum Christi took control and dislodged those not "properly formed." In the world of the Legion, the same story can be expected to repeat again and again.

Backlash in Columbus

The pope's endorsement makes bishops and leaders of Catholic universities hesitant to challenge "the Movement" even when they see through the Legion–Regnum Christi pious façade. Some bishops quietly refuse to allow the Legion to operate in their dioceses. Confronting Regnum Christi is another matter. Laypeople can go wherever they want without episcopal approval.

One bishop took decisive action against the Legion and Regnum Christi. James A. Griffin, who has degrees in both canon law and civil law, has been bishop of Columbus, Ohio, since 1983. One of his parishes, St. Francis de Sales Church in Newark, Ohio, experienced the infiltration tactics of a Regnum Christi cell when a member of "the Movement," Rhett A. Young, was engaged as principal of the parish school. Young had been principal of Royalmont Academy, the Regnum Christi school in Cincinnati. He replaced the St. Francis parish school principal, who left abruptly, for the 2002–03 academic year. Certain parents in the parish, aware of how Regnum Christi operates, realized that several women, newly arrived, were popping up in key positions in parish organizations. As questions percolated, the pastor, Father Dean Mathewson, bristled at suggestions of anything sinister. In a six-page letter to parishioners on May 28, 2002, he defended Young as a well-qualified educator and the unanimous choice of a search committee. He acknowledged that Young was a member of Regnum Christi and had previously been at a Legion school, but pointed out that the Legionaries were fully sanctioned by the pope himself.

> By no means are these groups a "cult," or "groupies" as some in this parish have uncharitably and falsely alleged. I repeat, anyone who tells you that the members of Regnum Christi are "cultic" or "groupies" or any such thing are either ignorant of the facts or are deliberately spreading falsehoods. I call upon anyone who may be starting or repeating these and similar false rumors to cease.

Mathewson raised a familiar defense of the Legion—that the emergence of a new order "has almost always been accompanied by misunderstandings, suspicion, fear, and even deeply uncharitable and misguided opposition from fellow Catholics."

The pastor's letter failed to staunch his flock's concerns. "You could tell there was something unusual going on," said Julie Kohl, a mother of two.[30] School assemblies began eating into class time. "For the first couple of weeks they were praying so much the kids didn't get their lunch." Four teachers resigned. Parents were barred from observing a program for teenagers in the church basement. Teenagers who did not participate in night and weekend activities of the teen group were denied confirmation. "There are secret meetings all the time," Julie Kohl complained.

"They are like a cult . . . tight-lipped," said her husband, Tyler. "It is all so underhanded."

Parishioners peppered Bishop Griffin's office with letters and phone calls. Accompanied by the diocesan chancellor and his schools superintendent, Griffin made "an extraordinary visitation" to St. Francis on September 16, 2002.[31] He met with parishioners, parish council members, the finance committee, and the school board. On October 8, the bishop ordered the pastor and parishioners to collaborate on a "parish mission statement" for diocesan approval. He ordered the school to follow principles of the Ohio Catholic School Accrediting Association. "Parents are to be welcome and involved in all programs involving their children," the bishop directed. Then he dropped the hammer:

Effectively immediately, Regnum Christi meetings are not to be held on parish property. There is already an agreement with the provincial of the Legionaries of Christ such that their priests are not to be active in any way in the Diocese of Columbus; thus, the Legionaries of Christ are not to be used as advisers to the school or the parish. They are not to be involved in the school or in any school activities. Neither the school nor the parish is to be used as a recruitment tool for any program sponsored by the Legionaries of Christ or Regnum Christi. Programs for young people or adults sponsored by Regnum Christi are not to be operated through the parish or promoted through parish channels, including the bulletin. No one employed by the parish may use their position to promote the activities of Regnum Christi.

Effective October 15, 2002, the ban on the Legion and Regnum Christi applied to all of the parishes, facilities, and organizations in the diocese of Columbus.[32] Griffin's principled response stands out in high relief from the capitulation of Archbishop Donoghue in Atlanta, who gave free rein to the Legion and left his pastors to deal with the consequences.[33]

Beyond Culture

The Legion's problem goes beyond image, beyond culture, beyond conservatism. One would think that if ever there was a place for the Legion to find a niche, it would be in a parish of Mexican Americans, especially one named Our Lady of Guadalupe. That is what Bishop William Weigand of Sacramento apparently thought when he invited the order to take over the parish. The Legion does not usually do parish work, but an invitation from a bishop is rare. In September 2000 two Legion priests were assigned to Guadalupe parish, which was founded in 1958 by the growing numbers of Mexican immigrants in northern California, most of them farmworkers. The parish had given active support to Cesar Chavez in the struggle to gain decent working conditions for farmworkers. In 1978, Pope John Paul II declared it "the national shrine of all Hispanics and Mexican Americans in Northern California."[34]

The Society of Our Lady of Guadalupe was the oldest lay organization of Latino Catholics in the diocese. Many of its members had built up the parish. Guadalupanos served as lay ministers of the Eucharist and made weekly breakfasts and luncheons to raise money. Without explanation, the Legionary priests expelled them from the kitchen and refused to allow them to serve as Eucharistic ministers.[35]

"This has been our church for over forty years and priests have come and gone but this order has been especially rude, dismissive and abusive of our . . . Mexican community," said Maria Morales Gonzalez, a mother of three and longtime parishioner, who helped organize a protest.[36] Things got worse when parents complained that the new pastor, Irish-born Father John Monaghan, asked their teenaged children sexually intrusive questions in confession.

One boy said the priest asked if he had ever slept with a boy. He answered yes. The priest asked if he liked it. "It was a slumber party," the boy said. "Are you gay?" retorted the priest.[37] Answer: no.

Monaghan told a local newspaper it was a "cultural misunderstanding." In Quintana Roo, Mexico, where he had served twenty-four years, he said "adolescents tend to speak out about sexual issues during confessions"—he thought it would be the same among Mexican American children. The diocese embraced "cultural differences" in his defense.[38]

Two former Legionary priests—one Irish, the other Mexican—who served in Quintana Roo consider "cultural misunderstanding" a bogus excuse. "I never asked sexually explicit questions in the confessional. That is his personal hangup or obsession, not necessarily abusive but weird," commented Paul Lennon, the former Legion priest. A parish priest in a Texas border town who had once worked in the same place as Monaghan said, "Personally I think that's sick. You do not ask those questions. You often help a little bit to get kids to feel comfortable talking to them but I do not think we ordinarily ask this type of questioning."[39]

Throughout 2001, dissatisfied parishioners kept pressure on the diocese. Morales and others organized a boycott of a diocesan fund-raising drive. Six hundred parishioners signed a demand that the Legion be ousted from Guadalupe. Monaghan was sent back to the Yucatán, but replaced by another Legionary from Mexico, Father Salvador Gomez, who admitted mistakes had been made. He said he would do "anything I have to do to reach peace and harmony."[40]

Gomez made good on his promise to restore peace.[41] He allowed the Guadalupanos to have their own Mass once a month, but did not let them back in the kitchen. The parish reverted to an old rule, "Father knows best." The parish council the diocese had promised was never established. No parish financial statements were issued after the Legionaries took charge.

The Legion got what it wanted: a base on the West Coast after subduing lay activists. In the California capital, where no Catholic university exists, the order has set its sights on establishing the University of Sacramento[42] on two hundred county-owned acres of a defunct Air Force base. "They hope to have a campus of five thousand undergrads and two thousand graduate students by 2006 or 2007," said Paul Hahn, Sacramento County development director,[43] who was helping the Legion look for a place to lease temporarily for a graduate school in downtown Sacramento.

On May 27, 2003, the Legion announced a thirty-year plan to turn a large part of its Regnum Christi training center in Thornwood, New York, in Westchester County, into a university.[44] The Legion plans to build the campus on 165 of the 264 acres it acquired from IBM for $33.4 million in 1996. The acquisition proved controversial in 1997 when the Legion's secret public relations plans to neutralize opposition to zoning changes—including pressuring politicians—were leaked to local media.[45]

The order has a toehold in higher education in America, having opened in 1999 a graduate school, the Institute for Psychological Sciences, in Arlington, Virginia, "dedicated to the development and promotion of approaches to psychology founded in the Catholic vision of the human person."[46] It offers a master's of science and doctoral degrees in clinical psychology. Its president is a Legion priest, the Reverend Richard Gill, and the founding dean is Dr. Gladys Sweeney, a Regnum Christi member who was formerly on the staff at Johns Hopkins School of Medicine. Seventeen students comprised the starting class.

The Legion's ambitions depend, bluntly, on whether they can find enough rich people who believe that Maciel is a living saint and the Legionaries an authentic order of educators. Put another way, they need wealthy people blind to the Legion's history and internal dynamics. Universities provide the order with a powerful moneymaking machine in America and a base for "captivation"—the Legion's expression—of idealistic conservative Catholics, the younger the better.

The bishops of the United States could save the church a long migraine headache and more bad publicity by following the example of Bishop Griffin of Columbus, Ohio, who saw through the Legion's pietistic façade and took action based on common sense. Or they can follow the route of Archbishop Donoghue of Atlanta, who was willing to be bamboozled. If the bishops have learned anything at all from the disasters of the child molestation scandal, it is that the only way to confront immoral power in the church is by insisting on values of honesty, charity, and an open flow of information—lessons lost on Maciel, Regnum Christi, and the Legionaries of Christ.

Chapter Fifteen

A VATICAN

OF NAKED TRUTHS

O N JANUARY 4, 2001, Pope John Paul appeared in Rome at a cere-mony marking the sixtieth anniversary of the Legion's founding. He told twenty thousand people: "With special affection, I greet your beloved founder, Father Marcial Maciel, and extend to him my heartfelt congratulations."

Later that year Lieutenant Colonel Doyle transferred to Ramstein, Germany, the largest U.S. base outside America. Through his legal work he had become friends with A. W. Richard Sipe, an authority on clergy sexual behavior. "Tom's absolutely right about religious duress," said Sipe. "He suffers from all this. I think it's also purified him, making him go to the essence of his priesthood. He's one of the 'dogs of truth'—as the Dominicans are called."[1] Newly assigned to Ramstein, Doyle was troubled that an Irish Legionary had been scheduled to speak by some civilian members of the community. He attended the lecture, which was a rather authoritarian exposition of the Catholic catechism, but prom-ised the lay organizers that this would be the last time a Legionary would visit Ramstein while he was there.

At Christmas 2001, he sent an e-mail to his ever-lengthening list of contacts: "It's hard for me to estimate what progress has been made in the area of ecclesiastical enlightenment. Surely there must be some in leadership roles . . . who appreciate the pain of the survivors and the crying need for institutional honesty—but where?"

On May 18, 2001, the pope signed a secret decree giving the Congregation for the Doctrine of the Faith authority over six canonical crimes, including "absolution of an accomplice,"[2] the charge filed in 1998 against Maciel. Publicized in December, the decree ordered American bishops to inform the CDF if a priest was accused. Ratzinger's congregation could hold a secret tribunal or allow the diocese to hold a trial. The CDF would rule on laicization cases. "The judicial process protects the rights of victims," Archbishop Tarcisio Bertone, secretary of the CDF, stated, "the ecclesial community which [has] suffered scandal and damage, and the rights . . . of those accused."[3] But as John Thavis of Catholic News Service reported:

> One bishop well-informed on the issue, who asked not to be named, said the secrecy demanded by the norms gives the appearance of a "cover-up" by the church. He said the norms were too legalistic and ignored the pastoral needs raised by pedophilia cases. He questioned whether victims would find an all-priest tribunal an acceptable forum.

In America, the number of active pedophiles being recycled by bishops had fallen dramatically because of litigation, media coverage, and the survivors' movement; nevertheless, many priests with past offenses remained on the job as the tide of lawsuits continued.

Pope John Paul's decree came, coincidentally, two months after a shocking *National Catholic Reporter* account of sexual abuse of African nuns by priests in the sub-Sahara. The Curia had ignored five internal reports by sisters' superiors. In many of the AIDS-ravaged countries, "young nuns are sometimes seen as safe targets of sexual activity," wrote John Allen and Pamela Schaeffer.[4] "In a few instances . . . priests have impregnated nuns and then encouraged them to have abortions." In 1995, a nun who was a physician and the author of an internal report had briefed Cardinal Eduardo Martínez, prefect of the Congregation for Religious, telling him how the vicar general of one African diocese had said, "Celibacy in the African context means a priest does not get married but does not mean he does not have children."

A Vatican spokesman said: "We are working on two fronts: training of people and finding a solution to individual cases."[5]

On January 6, 2002, *The Boston Globe* began the series that set off a global chain reaction. Overnight, Tom Doyle was deluged with calls from journalists and TV producers. Survivors he knew well were popping up on CNN, while the press excavated cover-up patterns. In January, Ireland's Conference on Religious and the national government announced a $110 million settlement to abuse survivors of church-run training schools from 1940 through 1970. A producer at RTE, Irish public television, asked Doyle's assistance on a documentary about Ireland's hierarchy sheltering sex offenders well into the 1990s. Doyle began reading documents.

"I think I have lost my sanity," Doyle quipped in an e-mail to friends.[6]

> If I responded in the affirmative to everyone who wants a piece of me I would need a month crammed into a week. I honestly never, ever thought that what I have to offer or what I have done is anything like it's made out to be. . . . I am getting 7–9 calls a night. It has taken up every bit of my time and I find myself getting irritable late at night. I end up working hard all day with one crisis on the base after another. In one week—2 deaths, 2 suicide attempts, casualties from the war [in Afghanistan] plus all the counseling. . . . Anyway, that's my rant for tonight. I am going to bed.

Now he watched as scandal-battered bishops dramatized his theory of clericalism, an elite caste unaccountable to laypeople, in a media narrative. On March 8, Anthony O'Connell quit as bishop of Palm Beach, Florida—the second consecutive bishop there to resign for having sex with a minor years earlier. On March 17, *The Hartford Courant* unearthed documents showing that Cardinal Edward Egan of New York, as the bishop of Bridgeport, "allowed several priests facing multiple accusations of sexual abuse to continue working for years." On March 23, Bishop Robert Lynch of St. Petersburg admitted his diocese paid $100,000 to resolve a sexual harassment claim against the bishop by a layman who had been his former spokesman. Lynch, a former general secretary of the N.C.C.B., denied the accusations.[7] Rome said nothing. Lynch stayed on the job.

Survivors were functioning like the chorus in a Greek tragedy, warning that a moral order had been broken. As a clamor rose in Boston for

Cardinal Law's resignation, John Paul told him to stay on. Protestors picketed outside Boston's cathedral when the cardinal said Mass. Doyle felt anger more than sorrow toward Law. Cardinal Rivera of Mexico City defended Law as the victim of "a campaign of media persecution . . . against the entire church" like that of "Nero . . . in Nazi Germany and in communist countries."[8]

In his annual letter to priests on Holy Thursday, March 21, John Paul stated:

> We are personally and profoundly afflicted by the sins of some of our brothers who have betrayed the grace of ordination in succumbing even to the most grievous forms of the "mysterium iniquitatis" at work in the world. . . . [A] dark shadow of suspicion is cast over all the other fine priests who perform their ministry with honesty and integrity. . . . The Church shows her concern for the victims and strives to respond in truth and justice to each of these painful situations.[9]

"Mystery of evil" telegraphed John Paul's abstract view of a crisis that since 1985 had gotten little of his attention. At eighty-two, hobbled with Parkinson's disease, a slumped back, tilted neck, and sunken lower lip, his very person seemed a sign of the systemic ills. He had censored any discussion of celibacy as a factor in the crisis. Since midcentury a hundred thousand men worldwide had left the priesthood—more than the number who had entered. A stream of studies on psychological problems in clerical life had appeared since a psychiatrist gave a paper at a 1971 Vatican bishops' synod.[10] A tradition of ignoring sexual reality had allowed the priesthood to become a huge closet for gay men, many of whom scoffed at celibacy. Women were a greater threat, as John Paul made clear in his 1992 letter barring them from the priesthood.

In 2002, statements by Vatican officials exposed a moral myopia in the Roman Curia (from the Latin *covir*, "man together").[11]

Cardinal Castrillón Hoyos presented John Paul's letter at a news conference. As reporters asked questions of spokesman Joaquín Navarro-Valls, the cardinal jotted notes. When given the podium, he said: "The language [English] used is interesting. This by itself is an x-ray of the problem."[12] Ignoring the questions, he read a statement. The crisis stemmed from "pan-sexuality and sexual licentiousness." Three percent of U.S. priests had "tendencies" toward such abuse and only 0.3 percent were actual pedophiles, he insisted, citing incomplete data from the Chicago archdiocese.[13]

"I would like to know the statistics from other groups and the penalties the others have received and the money the others have paid to victims," he remarked, praising the pope's conferring of authority on the CDF. He emphasized that the Vatican had also expanded the statute of limitations under canon law for such crimes to ten years after a victim's eighteenth birthday—an important concession especially in developing countries with no age of consent. He defended the secret canonical norms to avoid "a culture of suspicion." Church laws must deal "with internal matters in an internal way." Now he was on a roll, declaring: "The church has never ignored the problem of sexual abuse, above all among its sacred ministers, even before it was on the front pages."

Tom Doyle derided Castrillón's "pansexuality" remark in an *Irish Times* op-ed piece.[14] "There is a solid principle in political science that says the governing elite of an organization will eventually think *it is* the organization," he wrote.

> *The hierarchy is facing off with a faithful who have thrown off the infantile bonds of clerical control and grown up. They are demanding accountability and honesty. . . . As one U.S. victim, Peter Isely, said, "The dioceses spend tens of millions of dollars on the highest-priced lawyers and hired the best public relations firms to fight us. And what did we have? All we had was the truth."*

The following week, the bishop of Ferns, covering County Wexford, Ireland, resigned. Bishop Brendan Comisky had shown great lenience to one of Ireland's worst pedophiles, Father Sean Fortune, who committed suicide in 1999 before trial. Writing again in *The Irish Times*, Doyle gave one his strongest statements on record:

> *Priests express their embarrassment to appear in public dressed in clerical garb. The pope is "personally and profoundly" afflicted and worries that the acts of the abusers will taint all men of the cloth. The truth is that most people couldn't care less about their pain and embarrassment. . . . Something is wrong and that wrong can't be sandpapered away by emotional expressions of personal hurt or*

self-righteous expressions of rage at the abusers. It is precisely *this clerical narcissism that produced the crisis in the first place.*[15]

In articles and on television, conservatives were blaming the crisis on gay priests. The gay clergy subculture *was* a factor, for within the priesthood a small strand of regressive homosexuals had preyed on a disproportionate number of victims. But survivors' groups were quick to point out that many of their members were women. No one had complete data. The greater problem was the bishops' pathology of lying and John Paul's failure to confront the sexual secrecy honeycombed through ecclesiastical governing. The Roman Catholic hierarchy showed no maternal grace. Bishops and cardinals, lacking children of their own, had coddled child molesters in a weird parody of incest. Conservatives failed to see how John Paul's litmus test for selecting bishops, like his campaign against "dissident" theologians, stemmed from a notion of faith as obedience that was blind to the psychodynamics behind the church's state of sin.

Cardinal Karol Wojtyla's experience of a free society ended in his adolescence, with a brief revival of civil freedom during his early studies in Rome. Then, at fifty-eight, he vaulted from communist Poland to the throne of Europe's last fully functioning monarchy. The Vatican has no parliament or independent judiciary. John Paul's belief in moral absolutes served him well as the Soviet empire fell. His governance of the church was hostile to the spirit of an evolving, open church after Vatican II. The church that prevailed over communist tyranny would maintain authority through its structures. A sexual underworld inside the castle was a force that he, a virgin monarch, could only perceive as scattered sins, not the hungry worms of structural decay.

March 28 saw the resignation of Juliusz Paetz, the sixty-seven-year-old archbishop of Poznan, Poland, forced out by Cardinal Sodano, the secretary of state. Paetz denied reports that he had sexually abused seminarians, which Vatican investigators had confirmed *the previous November*. Paetz claimed the Vatican made no accusation against him, nor subjected him to a trial. "Not everyone understood my genuine openness and spontaneity toward people," he told a Polish Catholic news agency.[16]

"Members of the papal court dare not tell the pope the whole truth about the scandals (because that's the way it is around a king: they only tell him what he wants to hear)," wrote Robert Blair Kaiser, an author with seasoned knowledge of the Vatican.[17] Paetz had been part of the papal household in the early 1990s. "I have run into two priests in the last two days who knew Paetz when he was working in the Vatican," continued Kaiser, in his "Rome Diary" e-mail:

> One said, "He was always on the make." The other said he'd been propositioned by Paetz, twice. Paetz was finally banned by the rector of his own seminary for making continual advances on the young men there who were training for the priesthood. "And we cannot tell the Holy Father about Paetz today," said one source of mine inside the Vatican. "The news would kill him."

Having foreclosed dialogue on celibacy, birth control, and a priestly role for women, John Paul aborted reform prospects when the church needed them most. As the sexual underworld proliferated, the papal yes-men included the likes of Cardinal Rivera of Mexico, who protected Maciel; Groer, whose personal corruption embodied sexual secrecy; and Law, who in 1997 scorned the Catholic Theological Society of America as "a wasteland" for questioning the church's teaching office, the magisterium.[18] These prelates emulated John Paul's response to sexual corruption: keep quiet, deny, apologize if necessary, and when in doubt, attack the messenger.

"Convinced that they know the truth—whether in religion or in politics—enthusiasts may regard lies for the sake of this truth as justifiable," the philosopher Sissela Bok has written.[19] "They may perpetrate so-called pious frauds to convert the unbelieving or strengthen the conviction of the faithful. They see nothing wrong in telling untruths for what they regard as a much 'higher' truth." Catholic hierarchs perpetrated many pious frauds, as when Cardinal Ratzinger gave Father Maciel a womb that protected him from justice. That immunity begs scrutiny of the high guardian of religious "truth."

Paul Collins and the Attack on History

That Ratzinger controlled the court of last resort for priests fighting laicization struck Paul Collins as ironic. "The CDF's caution has some merit, I hate to say," remarked Collins. An Australian authority on the papacy, he was visiting New York as the scandal escalated.[20] "Many priests are hurting, afraid that a false accusation might put them in jeopardy," he continued. Collins had just published *The Modern Inquisition*, a study of Catholic thinkers who had been punished by Ratzinger.[21]

Born in 1940, Collins grew up in a working-class suburb of Melbourne. As an altar boy in neo-Gothic churches he felt "the experience of divine transcendence. . . . Nothing replaces the pristine and youthful experiences of spirituality and faith, especially when they are conveyed through the medium of fine music and good liturgy."[22] He joined the Missionaries of the Sacred Heart. In 1977, after a decade of parish work, Collins went to Harvard, earning a master's of divinity. "My chronology makes me a classic product of Vatican II," he wrote. "The theology I learned was open to development and change, and the Church I inhabited as a young man embraced renewal and looked outward towards the world not as hostile, evil territory, but as a place permeated by the grace of God, as well as by the effects of sin."[23]

Returning to his homeland, Collins earned a Ph.D. in history at Australian National University. He found his métier as a writer and religion editor for the Australian Broadcasting Corporation. Witty and professorial, Collins was also a priest deeply engaged in his church. In 1987 he wrote for *Commonweal* about John Paul's travels:

> *A close examination of the Australian trip shows that images—settings and groups with whom the pope identified (handicapped, youth, aborigines, workers, politicians)—were more important than what he said. Certainly, this visual approach is part of the Catholic tradition, for it conjures up the sacramental nature of the church— persons, actions, and experiences that symbolically make present the power and reality of God. . . . People see him, especially on television, as an accessible and human figure who stands for justice and a return to traditional values. . . . Local leadership, bishops, and communities fade into insignificance. The pope has given a new lease on life to the papal monarchy.[24]*

In 1997, Collins published his fourth book, *Papal Power*, a melding of history, theology, and polemics. After modest sales in Australia and Britain (there was no American edition), the CDF targeted the book for investigation, a striking departure, it seemed, since Collins was a journalist-historian. Andrew Greeley, a sociologist, had never been so prosecuted for his high-profile criticism of the birth control letter. Instead, Ratzinger sacked Curran, a theologian, from Catholic University.

In fact, the CDF had tightened the censorship coils in 1995, ordering Bishop Peter Smith of England to withdraw his approval of a study guide for Catholic teenagers. A reactionary group issued a pamphlet accusing the author of heresy. Smith ignored a summons to the CDF. As Robert Blair Kaiser later reported,[25] Smith was in Rome in early 1998 with other English bishops to visit the pope. Ratzinger entered the room before the meeting and said: "Which of you is Peter Smith?"

Bishop Smith raised his hand.

"I want to see you in my office right after this," ordered the cardinal.

Shortly thereafter, Smith went to the Palace of the Holy Office. The cardinal took the copy of *Roman Catholic Christianity* and slammed it on the desk. *"This book will not do!"* He slammed the book again, repeating his words. Invoking his authority in canon law, he ordered the bishop to remove his official approval of the text for Catholic teenagers. "And you are not to tell anyone that it is I who have given you this order!"

With a hundred thousand copies pulled from circulation in schools, the author, Clare Richards, a married mother of two, lost substantial income. Bishop Smith removed his approval of the text, but in a public statement praised Clare Richards as a "very faithful, practicing Catholic, highly respected in her profession."

"The Holy Office may have changed its name, but the ideology underpinning it has survived," Collins, unaware of the dispute, wrote in *Papal Power.* "This body has no place in the contemporary Church. It is is irreformable and should be abolished."[26] Collins cited John Henry Newman, the nineteenth-century English cardinal, who famously wrote of doctrine that "to live is to change." Cardinal Frings of Germany echoed Newman's idea at Vatican II in calling for reform of the Holy Office.[27]

Collins scored Ratzinger's 1990 global "Instruction" to theologians, telling them to respond with "submission of will and intellect" to his office,[28] as undercutting the development of doctrine. The letter "effectively destroys theology as a discipline. The papacy alone is the judge of theological truth."

John Paul "distorts the *traditionally* understood structure of the church," Collins continued, by abandoning "the collegial nature of authority. . . . Absolutism is not the norm in the Church. And always there has been the *sensus fidelium,* the acceptance or rejection, by the Catholic people, of the Church's teaching."[29]

Collins traced that unchecked power to the 1870 conciliar decree on infallibility, after which twenty dissenting theologians in German-speaking universities were excommunicated and many of the bishops who disagreed with the doctrine did not speak about it.[30] Collins drew a link with the 1968 birth control encyclical, which most theologians considered "an exercise of the ordinary magisterium [teaching office]. But the problem is that John Paul II clearly thinks that it is infallible."[31]

The pope had shot off rockets of confusion in telling bishops that "the charism of infallibility" could also come from statements by Ratzinger's teaching office. In an analogy to pregnancy, Collins insisted: "A definition is either infallible or it is not." But "infallible" had been salted into the papal letter barring women priests without formally invoking the doctrine. Collins's criticism of "creeping infallibility" shaped his argument about power. "Abusive sexuality is a symptom," he wrote. "The abuse of power occurs most where it is most centralized— at the top of the hierarchy."[32] *Papal Power* called for a new Vatican Council to restore balance between pope and church.

In January 1998, Collins learned in a letter from his superior in Rome that the CDF was investigating *Papal Power. Who* had reported the book was a secret. But Collins had tangled on a TV panel with Melbourne archbishop George Pell, a member of the CDF. Later, when a reporter asked if he had recommended a probe, Pell said: "No, not really." He told another journalist, "Paul Collins certainly has a case to answer."[33]

The CDF secretary, Archbishop Tarcisio Bertone, asked Collins's superior in Rome to "provide the needed clarifications for submission to the judgment of this Congregation." Bertone the canon lawyer included a critique by an anonymous consultor, who accused Collins of "quoting like-minded theologians, but failing to cite those who oppose and refute them"; Collins denied "true and binding Revelation," misunderstood infallibility, and rejected the primacy of the pope over the church.

"Years before, Hans Küng had advised me that the only way to keep the Vatican honest in any dispute was to go public immediately," noted

Collins.[34] He wrote his superiors in Rome to say he would not respond unless his accusers were named. He also wanted the book assessed by independent scholars. Realizing that would not happen under CDF rules, Collins gave the documents to the media and posted them on the Web site of the Association for the Rights of Catholics in the Church. He wrote a ten-page letter to Bertone justifying his "attempts to deal with the major structural issues facing the Catholic Church. . . . We are dealing with historical facts."

One year later, Ratzinger wrote Collins's superior. Several concerns were no longer mentioned; but the CDF wanted Collins to write an article "clarifying" other issues for the congregation to vet before publication. Collins, fed up with the shadowboxing, was writing his book on the CDF, which included a chapter on his own experience. In 2001, as it was published,[35] Paul Collins left the priesthood after thirty-three years. He brooded about the Vatican view of "permissiveness and commercialism" in Western countries, and the championing of "elitist enclaves"[36] like Opus Dei and the Legionaries of Christ.

The Roman Spring of 2002

Vatican officials fed the abuse scandal by showing their distance from reality. "Civil society has the obligation to defend its own citizens," Bertone told an Italian journal in March 2002. "But it must also respect the 'professional secrecy' of priests."[37]

"If a priest cannot confide in his bishop because he is afraid of being denounced," said the canonist, "it would mean that there is no more freedom of conscience." Bertone would allow a bishop to conceal sexual crimes, which is exactly what caused the crisis.

Italy's legal system had no sweeping discovery powers like those in common-law countries. A search of Italian newspapers made on our behalf found nineteen scattered reports of child-molesting clerics; Italy's legal system had no force of civil cases building against the church, as in the English-speaking countries with common-law provisions for major discovery power. Bertone, the prosecutor of theologians, conformed to an emergent Vatican view of the American church as victim of a witch hunt because of the media.

On Easter Sunday, Tom Doyle, wearing a coat and tie, looking drawn, appeared by satellite from Germany on *Meet the Press*. "The American bishops have changed their attitude toward these allegations because of what's happened over the past seventeen years," he told NBC's Tim Russert. "It's two shotguns, one on either side of their collective heads. One side is the press, and the other side is the legal system."[38]

In mid-April, Pope John Paul II summoned the American cardinals to Rome.

On April 19, as the cardinals began leaving for their summit, thirty-eight-year-old Mark Serrano went back to Mendham, New Jersey, a green suburb of New York, to meet with eight other men whose childhood years had been plundered by Father Jim Hanley. A graduate of Notre Dame, Serrano had a wife and children, and a good business in Virginia. Traumatic memories stalked him. His parents, who lived in the home where they raised seven kids, joined other parents at a gathering near St. Joseph's Parish.[39]

Hanley, sixty-five, a suspended priest, lived on a church pension thirty miles away.

Monsignor Kenneth Lasch, the pastor, had arranged for three former altar boys to meet with the Morris County prosecutor in 1993. It was too late to prosecute Hanley; but the men filed civil suits against the Paterson diocese. As Lasch learned the scope of Hanley's sexual depravity, he encouraged others to sue the church. "At times I felt as if my whole life was just keeping the parish intact because of Hanley," sighed Lasch, who lived in the rectory that had been Hanley's hothouse.

Serrano, who settled his lawsuit in 1987, broke the secrecy clause in 2002 with press interviews that led to network TV programs. His boyhood friend Bill Crane called from Oregon. "I sat in my living room holding my wife's hand, watching television, and I heard my story come from your mouth." Other men called, connecting across the years.

Thus began the first gathering of a large group victimized by the same priest. "Today is about healing," said Serrano. "We've got to speak about the injustice in the church." Hanley had shown each boy pornographic magazines, wearing down defenses, advancing to oral sex. "People need to know details, the sensation of semen in my pants and having to flee from that rectory—but not being able to tell my parents," said Serrano.

"At eleven years old I weighed forty-five pounds," said Bill Crane, now a strapping six feet, who had six siblings. "Hanley said, 'You must be lifting weights.' . . . He made me feel like an only child. We all thought that we were alone." The priest "fell in love with me, absolutely." His bewildered mother had tried to comfort him as he sobbed in his room at night. In 1982, Hanley left the parish to detox from alcoholism. Out of high school in a fog of confusion, Billy Crane joined the navy. On a base in Scotland he told his chaplain about Hanley; the priest said, Don't scandalize the church. He started riding a bike, "five hundred miles a week to sedate myself so I could sleep at night." Later he sedated himself with alcohol, until his wife got him into recovery.

Crane's twin, Tommy, hid what happened to him for years too. "It's like the whole community was anesthetized," he said. "Who am I supposed to trust?"

"In my twenties," said Serrano, "I couldn't go to Mass without seeing the image of the priest and thinking of Hanley's genitals. It angers me that I can't take the good things of being a Catholic and share it with my kids."

"What that man did permeates every level of your life," said Steve Holenstein, a computer network administrator. "With your children, in the marital bed—it's a spiritual shipwreck. . . . I'm four years older than you guys. I wish I could have stopped him."

His voice choked. *"By the grace of God—I'm here!"*

"It's been a long, lonely seventeen years," said Mark's mother, Pat, eyes welling. "Sharing these stories helps us get on with our lives as religious people, as a faith-filled people. I knew you guys when you played in my pool. . . . I'm proud of all of you."

Her words captured a spirit of the close-knit parish and the bonds formed as the men went about their lives. There was, too, the sad dignity of Monsignor Lasch, listening to the sinned against, atoning for the church by his presence.

"To all of you," said Tommy Crane, "I love you for being here."

The Cranes, with six children, and the Serranos, with seven, were among the largest families in the parish. Pat and Lou Serrano remained active in St. Joe's. The Cranes left the Catholic Church; several family members moved to the Pacific Northwest.

"Today I got part of my youth back," said Bill Crane.

Bishop Frank Rodimer of Paterson had agreed to attend the final session and hear the men. In removing Hanley without telling police, Rodimer saved him from jail.

For years Bishop Rodimer rented a beach house on the New Jersey shore with a Camden priest, Peter Osinski. Starting in 1984, Osinksi brought a boy whose family he had befriended. For twelve years Osinski and the boy slept down the hall from Rodimer. The boy grew up and filed charges. Steve Rubino sued Rodimer for failing to stop Osinski. The bishop paid a settlement of $250,000 with Paterson diocesan funds.

Rodimer entered the parish conference room to a bevy of TV cameras and reporters besides the survivors. Rodimer, portly with silver hair, had blue eyes full of caution. He sat opposite eight of the men and a poster with their childhood photographs. Serrano had reported Hanley to the bishop as an undergraduate. Now, he pointed to photographs of the boys. "Seventeen years ago I came to you as a young man. You were the highest authority I knew. You told me Father Hanley apologized and wouldn't endanger anyone and you had to take him at his word."

Rodimer had recycled other perpetrators and publicly apologized. Now, lips pursed, he gazed into the media lights and the survivors' anger.

"Justice means truth and openness," said Serrano. "Unlock your vaults, release the files and documents on these cases."

"I will never set foot in a Catholic church again," said Holenstein, voice cracking.

"Frank," said Tom Crane, dripping scorn. "Hanley's a pedophile, collecting a pension, and he took away my faith."

Bishop Rodimer nodded, grimacing.

"You're responsible," continued Tom. "What are you going to do?" Crane pointed to a photograph of a sweet-faced kid. "That's *me*."

Mark Serrano cut in. "The clergy have been protected! Peter Osinski was your friend. You knew about pedophiles! That man had sex with that child under your roof!"

Rodimer's face flushed red.

Tom Crane brought up Hanley: "This man belongs behind bars."

The bishop frowned. "What are you proposing?"

"Your question troubles me," said Serrano. "Where is your moral indignation?"

"Then I don't get it," said Rodimer. "What do you want?"

People groaned. Serrano demanded that the diocesan paper run a photograph of Hanley, saying: *Wanted, Recent Victims of Jim Hanley.*

"I don't have the right to put him behind bars," said Rodimer. "I've never had to go through anything like this. . . . I knew this was going to be tough. I've got a thousand different emotions. . . . I'm approaching the age of retirement. I do know in the time given to me I will use it to make sure what happened to you won't happen to others."

Rodimer agreed to offer help to any victims at the first parish Hanley served.

Serrano said: "Have you ever tried to reach the victim of Peter Osinski?"

"I can't discuss that," the bishop said flatly.

As he rose to leave, Rodimer told S.N.A.P.'s David Clohessy that he wanted "to learn more about your group."

"Seek out survivors!" said Mark Serrano.

"I will try," said Rodimer. "Thank you."

The session had lasted forty-five minutes.

Several weeks later Rodimer announced he would repay the $250,000 to the Paterson diocese for his role in the lawsuit involving the imprisoned Father Osinski.

Division at the Top

An army of journalists followed the eight cardinals to Rome for their summit with John Paul—Bernard Law of Boston, Roger Mahony of Los Angeles, Edward Egan of New York, Anthony Bevilacqua of Philadelphia, Adam Maida of Detroit, Francis George of Chicago, Theodore McCarrick of Washington, D.C., and William Keeler of Baltimore.

In June they would meet in Dallas to adopt a youth protection charter. "Zero tolerance" was the mantra from survivors, who wanted all offenders removed from the clergy.

On April 23, at the Apostolic Palace, the cardinals with red caps gathered with bishops and men of the Curia in a semicircle facing Pope John Paul, sitting in a chair, wearing a white cassock with a cross around his neck, his work hours sharply reduced by Parkinson's disease.

The pope read from a prepared text: "The Church herself is viewed with distrust." The men around him loved the church—baptizing infants, performing weddings, celebrating the Word in churches aglow at Christmas and Easter—yet now in the twilight of a papacy what they loved was stained. "The abuse which has caused this crisis is by every standard wrong and rightly considered a crime by society," John Paul declared. "It is also an appalling sin in the eyes of God. To the victims and their families, wherever they may be, I express my profound sense of solidarity and concern.

"A generalized lack of knowledge," he continued,

> and also at times the advice of the clinical experts led bishops to make decisions which subsequent events showed to be wrong. You are now working to establish more reliable criteria to ensure that such mistakes are not repeated. At the same time . . . we cannot forget the power of Christian conversion, that radical decision to turn away from sin and back to God, which reaches to the depths of a person's soul and can work extraordinary change.

Then he said: "People need to know that there is no place in the priesthood and religious life for those who would harm the young"—his strongest statement yet. But how did that square with the "power of conversion" to turn away from sin and back to God? Should repentant pedophiles not be laicized? Was there a papal absolute?

The pope's only other meeting with the group was for lunch the next day.

They worked elsewhere in the palace, amidst the ornate frescoes of the Sala Bologna. Cardinal Sodano, the secretary of state, presided. Each cardinal gave an opening statement. A chastened Law apologized to his colleagues. After curial members spoke they got into the give-and-take on policy, and a surreal schism surfaced.

The Curia wanted church authority made clear. The media-battered Americans wanted to show Catholics back home that they had a plan, that reform was at hand.

Bertone, who had helped Ratzinger sanitize the Maciel case, joined Castrillón Hoyos in demanding language on "dissent" and "ambiguous pastoral practices." Cardinal Francis Stafford, a former archbishop of Denver, now in the Curia, wanted affirmation of the 1968 birth control letter.

The American cardinals had a backlog of offenders, some in prison, some not; they wanted a way to laicize them, quickly. Bertone and Castrillón opposed such latitude: the CDF held that power.[40] They worked through the second day on language for a joint statement at a news conference scheduled that night on CNN. Bertone and Castrillón wrote a draft in Italian, McCarrick and Bishop William Skylstad of Spokane wrote in English. Soon three English texts were circulating with the sketchier Italian draft as they raced against time to express the agenda for serious reform.

The communiqué released to skeptical journalists at 10 P.M. showed the internal divisions. Though McCarrick was normally at ease before the cameras, he had trouble explaining why there was no mention of laypeople in the communiqué. The basic points were: Celibacy is "as a gift of God to the Church." Pastors must promote "correct moral teaching" and "reprimand individuals who spread dissent." The Vatican would conduct a visitation of U.S. seminaries; U.S. bishops would hold a day of prayer and penance (recommended by Ratzinger) for "the conversion of sinners and the reconciliation of victims." The Americans would agree on a national policy and get Vatican approval. The U.S. bishops would "recommend a special process" to expel a priest who was "notorious" for "the serial, predatory, sexual abuse of minors."

As the spectacle worsened in Rome, Tom Doyle was traveling in America, briefing prosecutors, meeting with survivors, and giving interviews to the media. On April 22, he caught a cab to the ABC News complex in New York. There, José Barba and Arturo Jurado were eager to meet him after e-mail exchanges. They had just been interviewed by correspondent Brian Ross for a *20/20* report on Maciel. Doyle walked in wearing khaki pants, a blazer and tie. "I've never felt more embarrassed about being a priest," he muttered to Berry.

They approached him. Barba said: "It is an honor to meet you, Father Doyle."

Doyle shook hands. "I want to apologize for what the Catholic Church has done to you men."

"But Father Doyle," said Barba gently, "we do not blame you for Father Maciel or Cardinal Ratzinger."

After his interview, Doyle caught a cab for the airport.

Ross had been in Rome the week before. Maciel refused to talk. Ratzinger's office said he was not granting interviews. Not to be put off,

Ross and his television crew went one morning to the cardinal's apartment building, which can be seen through an arch just off St. Peter's Square on the opposite side from his office. An ice cream vendor had set up shop under a shade tree just across from the cardinal's door in the small piazza. A large Mercedes pulled up and as the cardinal came down the steps to his car, Ross approached him. Ratzinger smiled. Ross mentioned Maciel's name, saying, "There's a question of whether you—"[41] The camera inched closer.

Ratzinger scowled. "Come to me when the moment is given." He slapped the reporter on the hand. "Not yet."

"Excuse me," said Ross. "Well, we tried to ask you a question."

Ratzinger left in the Mercedes, leaving an unforgettable image behind.

A Fractured Landscape

With the Vatican effectively handing crisis management back to the bishops, a *USA Today* poll found that 87 percent of Catholics surveyed wanted bishops who had concealed child molesters to step down. Only the pope can remove a bishop, and John Paul was in no condition or hurry to execute such changes. The U.S. Conference of Catholic Bishops (U.S.C.C.B.) hired a Madison Avenue public relations firm, R. F. Binder, which specialized in corporate damage control. Central to the script for Dallas was the decision (which some bishops had opposed) that put four survivors before the assembled body. In those choking accounts, the human impact of the crisis permeated the hushed room of 325 bishops. Seven hundred reporters watched by closed circuit in the pressroom in an environment of overpowering emotion. The news marathon unfolded as S.N.A.P. leaders David Clohessy, Barbara Blaine, Peter Isely, and Mark Serrano spoke to journalists in the lobby while the bishops upstairs used parliamentary debate to enact a youth protection charter. Each diocese would draft a policy, form a review board to investigate accusations, and cooperate with law enforcement. The U.S.C.C.B. appointed Oklahoma governor Frank Keating, a former FBI agent and prosecutor, to lead a National Review Board of prominent laypeople and produce a report on causes of the crisis with recommendations for reform. One clause in the youth protection charter sent flares to Rome: "For even a single act of sexual abuse of a minor—past, present, or future—the offending priest or deacon will be permanently removed from ministry."

In the weeks that followed, bishops began removing priests with past offenses—well more than three hundred by year's end.[42] Rome would not say how many priests filed canonical protests at the CDF. But as complaints arose about priests abruptly removed for fleeting encounters years in the past, the opinion pendulum was swinging away from sympathy for survivors toward a beleaguered majority of good priests who were feeling the stress and the deep embarrassment of the scandal in their ranks. The inadequacy of the canonical system to cope with the range of issues showed when thirty-five-year-old Father John Bambrick accused a fellow priest, Anthony Eremito, a hospital chaplain in Texas, of having repeatedly abused him as a teenager. Bambrick protested to Cardinal Edward Egan, Eremito's archbishop. Egan suspended Eremito, who denied the allegations and hired as a canonist a cleric formerly assigned to the papal staff. Bambrick was hit with a canonical grievance for violating Eremito's right to privacy. "Surreally, I was charged under the same canon 1717 used on perpetrators," he said. Bambrick's bishop cleared him after a secret inquiry; Egan's review board refused to let him testify against Eremito.

In October, U.S. canonists went back to Rome for more negotiations on Vatican approval of the norms that would give their youth protection charter the force of law. Bertone and Castrillón Hoyos wanted greater specificity in defining "sexual abuse" to protect clerics claiming wrongful removal—an understandable concern, yet grossly out of balance with reality: the clerical system had sheltered hundreds of guilty men while trampling on the rights of their victims. Opinions proliferated about whether gay men should be de facto excluded from seminaries, evading the greater issue of how to attract well-grounded heterosexuals. Avoiding questions about a clerical culture warped by sexual secrecy, the Vatican with its storied beauty was ever ready to welcome shell-shocked pilgrims visiting from the New World.

A Priest in Time

Voice of the Faithful held its first conference in Boston on July 20 of that year. In five months VOTF had gone from twenty-five people meeting in the basement of a suburban parish to nineteen thousand supporters in forty states. Its goal was to support survivors, and good priests, and push the church to make structural change. Some forty-two hundred people gathered for workshops and lectures. That night Tom Doyle received the first Priest of Integrity award. Wearing a blue blazer, red tie, and the ever-ready khaki trousers, he stood at the podium, gazing out at the cavernous auditorium.

"What we have experienced in our lifetime is a disaster the horror of which is perhaps equaled by the bloodshed of the Inquisition but which certainly makes the indulgence scam that caused the Reformation pale by comparison," he began, to a scatter of chuckles. "The deadliest symptom is the unbridled addiction to power. . . . We, you, are not onlookers whose main duties are to pay and obey. The church's most vital members are not those wearing elaborate robes, but the marginalized, the hurting, the rejected."

He entreated them to withhold money from those who abused power. "There is no longer room for timidity or fearful deference to the very structures that have betrayed us," he declared. "This sexual abuse nightmare has caused so many of us to question everything about our church and to even wonder if the Lord cared. . . . God is alive and well in the church and you are the proof. Your response to his promptings through this tragedy is perhaps the most eloquent and convincing proof that he cares."

As the audience rose in applause, people flooded the stage. S.N.A.P. founder Barbara Blaine handed him a bouquet of roses; David Clohessy gave him a bear hug.

He left the stage, shaking hands, hugging those he knew and some he did not.

At fifty-seven he had traveled far from the priesthood of his youth. He was a radical now—from the Latin *radix,* meaning "root, first thing"—full of love for his people, a man with a fire in his soul.

EPILOGUE

O N JANUARY 11, 2001—one week after Pope John Paul celebrated Maciel's ministry at the Legion's sixtieth anniversary—José Barba and Arturo Jurado flew from Mexico City to Santiago, Chile. They were determined to find Bishop Polidoro Van Vlierberghe, whose name appeared on two letters the Legion had sent *The Hartford Courant* in 1996 as proof of Maciel's innocence. Bishop Polidoro, one of the visitors in the 1950s Vatican investigation, had never interviewed them. The 1956 and 1996 letters struck them as phony. The Legion circulated the Polidoro letters to show Maciel as the victim of a plot.

They found the ninety-two-year-old bishop living in a convent connected to the Church of Our Lady of Luján in a rundown section of Santiago known as Nuñoa. The bishop's nurse and personal assistant, a woman named Irene, allowed a visit on the morning of January 13. The bishop sat in a wheelchair, partially blind in one eye, though mentally alert. He received them with great courtesy. The walls of his quarters had photographs of his relatives, and one of Father Maciel embracing Pope John Paul II. "The bishop and his nurse-assistant told us the two letters were absolutely false," said Barba. "Irene pointed out to us that the bishop used an entirely different kind of stationery with a letterhead and never signed them without his seal."[1] When Barba and Jurado asked if the bishop would sign a statement to that effect, Irene said he would need the approval of a longtime adviser, Juan Ruiz, and his lawyer, Sergio Novoa.

Shortly afterward, they met with Ruiz and Novoa, who remarked that Polidoro had always used an old manual typewriter. The 1996 letter was typed on an electric machine, did not have Polidoro's letterhead, and lacked his customary seal. The bishop carefully dated his letters. The older letter had no date. Moreover, on the given date of the second letter, December 12, 1996, Bishop Polidoro had been in the hospital with a pulmonary infection, and had been convalescent all that month.

But Ruiz and Novoa wanted no trouble for Bishop Polidoro. They were willing to answer a church inquiry about the documents but would offer no written statements. Failing to persuade them otherwise, Barba and Jurado left Chile.

Back in Mexico, Barba consulted a lawyer, Rafael Garcia-Zuazua, who had been supportive of their quest to expose Maciel. Garcia-Zuazua engaged a lawyer in Santiago, Osvaldo Valenzuela, to file a civil action that sought a ruling on the authenticity of the letters. Valenzuela drafted a complaint, said Garcia-Zuazua.[2] His initial telephone conversations with the Santiago lawyer "were long and very sharp on the issues." Then the Chilean reported back to say that the judge found Polidoro "did not remember" meeting Barba and Jurado. He would not allow a proceeding to continue. Despite many requests, the Santiago lawyer refused to send copies of any court documents, nor did he bother collecting the second half of his $2,500 fee. "It smelled fishy," said Garcia-Zuazua.

Pope John Paul made his fifth trip to Mexico in late summer 2002 to preside at the canonization Mass of Juan Diego, the Indian peasant reputed to have seen the apparition of Our Lady of Guadalupe. The accusations against Maciel had become a news event in Mexico, especially after the ABC 20/20 report with Ratzinger slapping the reporter's hand, and footage showing a stooped John Paul giving a fraternal kiss to Father Maciel. Maciel did not fly on the papal plane to Mexico, as he had on earlier trips. Curial members planning the trip recognized the chief Legionary as a media liability.

The Legionaries of Christ nevertheless played a central role in the logistical planning for the trip. In Mexico, students from Legion schools worked as volunteers in the press office. When the beatification Mass began, unbeknownst to most members of the news media, Maciel entered the Guadalupe basilica and took a place among ecclesiastical dignitaries on the altar behind the pope.[3]

José Barba and his comrades had been giving interviews to reporters in the months before the trip, keeping the pressure on Maciel and the church. Barba was sixty-two now, and the years of trying to get justice had left few glimmers of hope. When an abortion-rights group called Catholics for a Free Choice invited him to participate in press conferences that fall in Rome and Geneva on clergy sex abuse, he accepted. The October 8, 2002, event in Rome had little impact, though while there Barba decided to call Martha Wegan, the canon lawyer, and invite her to dinner.

Their grievance at the Palace of the Holy Office hung in canonical limbo, not dismissed, more like frozen in time. On October 13, they walked from Wegan's apartment to a restaurant near Campo dei Fiori, which has a statue of a sixteenth-century philosopher who was burned at the stake for heresy. "She told me that perhaps it was better for eight innocent men to suffer than thousands of people losing their faith," said Barba.[4] "She had said something like that in nineteen ninety-nine, when we were trying to get an answer about our case."

He replied in no uncertain terms that he did not agree with her.

In fact, he thought it an astounding statement, telling himself it was not something she made up, more likely a rationale communicated to her by Ratzinger and Girotti, the CDF secretary.

They arrived at the restaurant. "Much to my surprise, she said that Cardinal Sodano interfered with Ratzinger in his handling of Maciel," continued Barba. "She said it was difficult to understand, but insisted that it was true."

Sodano, the secretary of state, was the papal nuncio to Chile during the years of Augusto Pinochet's dictatorship. Sodano might be seen as an ecclesiastical version of Henry Kissinger, a practitioner of realpolitik who befriended the Pinochet family. In 1999, with Chile a restored democracy, Sodano petitioned the British government for leniency when Pinochet, an aging senator for life (immune from Chilean prosecution), was under house arrest in London after his indictment in Spain for human rights abuses.

Sodano's pressuring Ratzinger to go easy on Maciel would be consistent with his political character. Maciel had cultivated Sodano during his time as nuncio in Chile. Sodano's relationship to Pinochet was undoubtedly complex, given the nuncio's ties to bishops in opposition to the regime. The Pinochet dictatorship welcomed Maciel and the Legionaries into Chile during those dark years. The Legion flourished by ministering to the wealthy and powerful, the backbone of Pinochet's support. When Pope John Paul went to Chile in 1987 he met with opposition leaders and the poor. "He said an evening Mass in the stadium that Pinochet had used as a slaughterhouse," wrote Jonathan Kwitney.[5]

> He declared what the packed throng was already thinking: that the stadium was a "a place of competitions, but also of pain and suffering in times past." Every politically infused reference was cheered. The crowd interrupted occasionally with chants of "Freedom" or "End to the dictatorship."

Kwitney credits John Paul's visit as a force in paving the way, eighteen months later, for the plebiscite that led to a restoration of democracy.

Why did such a pope champion a man like Maciel?

John Paul saw the Legionaries as a sign of Catholic restoration in Latin America, akin to Opus Dei in Spain. The pope whose concept of church was fired in the crucible of resisting communism found a triumphal force in the militant spirituality of Opus Dei and the Legion, their cultivation of traditional Catholics, their ability to raise funds, and their stance against moral relativism. In Maciel, the pope saw a figure inspiring young men to be priests. John Paul grossly misread Maciel's character.

The Legion is a development of a Hispanic church with influence and numbers visible in Rome. In Latin America the tensions between wealth and poverty, freedom and repression, Spanish and Indian cultural patterns are vast. The Legion's catering to the rich is a crass appeal to a society unwilling to reckon with the great disparities. As Protestant evangelicals cut into the patterns of Latin Catholicism, the Legion and Opus Dei vie for power in an aristocratic church, leaving Jesuits, Dominicans, and Franciscans to take care of the poor. The Legionaries have far less influence in English-speaking countries steeped in traditions of pluralism and concern for the less privileged.

José Barba made a final trip to Rome in November 2002 in the company of his Mexico City canonist, Father Roqueñi. Barba had the Polish translation of a letter addressed to the pope, asking that the Maciel case be reopened; he had it personally delivered to John Paul's closest assistant, Bishop Stanislaw Dziwisz.

In Rome, Barba and Roqueñi made a final attempt to see Father Girotti, hoping to get some insight on the chance of reviving the grievance at the CDF. Girotti had moved to a new position, at the Apostolic Penitentiary, the department of the Curia that handles extraordinary cases of priests abusing the sacraments and cases not resolvable in church courts. The penitentiary's exceptionally secret work is conducted in the Palazzo della Cancelleria, an elegant building near Campo dei Fiori, several miles from Vatican City. The men arrived at eight-thirty in the morning, asking to see Girotti. A young priest who received them assumed they had an appointment and ushered them into a waiting room. Momentarily, Girotti appeared, short, dark-haired, wearing glasses, and invited them into his office.

Father Roqueñi asked why he had not replied to his long letter of 1999 regarding the failure to apply canon law in the Maciel matter.

Girotti shrugged, as if to say, *I receive so many letters . . .*

Barba pressed him for an explanation on the tabling of the case against Maciel. Girotti said that he should not have gone to journalists. Barba reminded him that they had spoken to no one for two years after filing the grievance and that the *L'espresso* article of 1999 had dealt with past matters, not the case itself. Father Roqueñi insisted that a magazine article had nothing to do with a canonical proceeding anyway. "This is a matter of the law."

Girotti smiled, and said nothing.

Barba gave him a Spanish translation of the letter to Dziwisz. He read it. "And so," said Girotti, "what do you want?"

They asked him to give the letter to Cardinal Ratzinger. He nodded. That would be easy enough to do; but Girotti no longer had any role in the case.

The emptiness of the moment was overwhelming. Girotti showed no emotion. With nothing more to say, they left.

In the marbled hallway they encountered an elderly priest with gray hair. He greeted them with a kind tone and in the spontaneous pleasantries expressed his delight at meeting Mexicans! He loved Mexico. He had gone to a gathering of the Legionaries of Christ. He called them *"bravisima gente!"*—very good people. Gratuitously, the priest grumbled: "The scandal in the U.S. is the work of Jews and Freemasons."

Barba and Roqueñi introduced themselves and were amazed to learn that this voluble Italian was Archbishop Luigi De Magistris, prefect of the Apostolic Penitentiary—Girotti's boss. Barba asked if they might briefly speak with him and he invited them into his office. The penitentiary room was huge, with high ceilings, few pieces of furniture, filing cabinets, an enormous desk with a manual typewriter—and no computer. "I am glad you are the major penitentiary," Barba said with aplomb, "because I have been excommunicated."

"Why?" said the archbishop.

As a young man, explained Barba, he was a member of a religious order and had lied to visitators from the Vatican. Technically, that failure to be truthful about Maciel could constitute his excommunication as a Catholic. With the solid presence of Roqueñi by his side, Barba told Archbishop De Magistris the history of Maciel. The old man's face froze. When Barba was done, the prefect of the Apostolic Penitentiary said: "But I am not the person to whom you should go."

The case had already gone to Cardinal Ratzinger, explained Father Roqueñi. "What happened?" asked the penitentiary prefect.

"*Nothing!*" they said in unison.

Roqueñi gave more background. He finally said, "They made a mistake going to the press."

"In my time, we used to say dirty laundry must be washed at home," said De Magistris. "I can assure you, what you have told me enters here"—he put a finger to one ear—"and stays here"—he touched the other ear.

A few minutes later they stepped into a mild Roman morning. Barba was infuriated by the archbishop's blaming the abuse scandal on Jews and Freemasons. He had Jewish friends and Jewish students. What a vile remark!

Father Roqueñi said simply: "They don't care."

Nuestro Padre Speaks

In July of 2003, Maciel released a memoir of sorts, *Christ Is My Life*, as told to a journalist who directs Zenit, the news agency in Rome sponsored by the Legionaries. The new book carries forward the aggrandizing history of Maciel as recounted in Father Villasana's booklet that was distributed in the 1990s to Regnum Christi members. In the new work, Maciel presents himself as a "formator," a priest whose speciality has been the forming of young men who become priests. It is not surprising that he fails to mention the charges of sexual abuse directed against him by his own former seminarians, and thus provides no explanation for the "conspiracy" of those who brought charges against him at the Vatican. Maciel does say that "a new, very grave calumny, drug addiction," was a force behind the Vatican investigation of the 1950s. Maciel's tone—gentle, cerebral, with many citations of scripture—is consistent with the way the Legion has long presented him: as a living saint. "I think the secret to working with adolescents is to believe you can trust them," he reflects.

> *They are open to the great ideals of life: they have huge reserves of generosity, and they will respond eagerly to what you ask of them— as long as you give them a motivating ideal. . . . Our experience has been very positive, though it is not easy work, especially because adolescents are extremely malleable, for good and for evil, and there are many other alternatives available that can easily lead them astray.*[6]

The Church Beyond John Paul

The paradox is awesome. The pope who championed freedom from political dictatorships turned a cold shoulder to human rights within the church—a paradox all the more striking when weighed against John Paul's line of public apologies, calling on Catholics to acknowledge terrible passages in our history. No pope in centuries has been so visionary as to insist that "the Church should become more fully conscious of the sinfulness of her children, recalling all those times in history when they departed from the spirit of Christ and his Gospel and, instead of offering to the world the witness of a life inspired by the values of faith, indulged in ways of thinking and acting which were truly forms of counter-witness and scandal."[7]

John Paul began making amends to Jews, notably in a first-ever papal visit to a synagogue in 1986. He established diplomatic ties between the Vatican and Israel in 1993, and in 1998 issued a document on the Holocaust, *We Remember*. He later visited the Holocaust memorial Yad Vashem and the Wailing Wall in Jerusalem. In a memorandum to his cardinals in spring 1994, the pope outlined a greater concept of "confessions of sin" than anyone in the Curia had ever imagined. "Up to that point," wrote the Vatican correspondent Luigi Accattoli,

> *in more than fifteen years of his pontificate, Pope John Paul had acknowledged at least forty instances of sins and errors. He had already spoken, directly or indirectly, about responsibility for the treatment of Galileo, the Jews and Muslims . . . Luther, the Indians; the injustices of the Inquisition, the Mafia, racism; religious integralism, schism and the papacy, wars and injustice, and the treatment of the Blacks. After the issuance of the memorandum, there would be papal pronouncements on the Crusades, dictatorships, women, religious wars, and Rwanda.*[8]

John Paul's call for "purification of the historical memory" may be one of his greatest legacies. To "confess" the sins of history is more than a gesture of intellectual honesty; it implies a standard of justice. For most of his life in Poland justice was subverted to ideology and a state-controlled economy propped up by disinformation. John Paul's insistence on facing the past flowed out of the struggle of those years to see human suffering not merely as a consequence of sin, but of ideology that trampled on individual dignity.

His myopia on the church's corruption suggests the kind of hubris we associate with kings in Shakespearean drama, coupled with a tragic naïveté about sexual intimacy. Instead of squarely facing the sexual revolution inside the priesthood, asking why so many good men left and others refused to enter, John Paul sanctioned the punishment of scholarly priests and intellectuals who asked the hard questions and argued for honesty and structural change.

The church's system of justice is laden with contradictions. In 2002 Archbishop George Pell of Sydney was accused of molesting a young man decades earlier in a youth camp when Pell, a seminarian, was barely out of adolescence himself. The Australian church, in its outreach policy to victims, honored the accuser's request for anonymity. Pell strongly proclaimed his innocence, took leave of his duties as prelate, and had an attorney for the closed church tribunal. A non-Catholic judge agreed to serve as an independent jurist. But the secret proceeding could not guarantee its cloaked standards. Before the hearing, information on the accuser's arrest record made it into the media, feeding suspicion that the church had leaked material to damage the man's reputation. In a strange twist on the tactics used by Ratzinger's congregation (of which Pell himself was a member), the man's identity was a secret though his checkered past was publicized. In the end, the judge ruled that the allegations could not be substantiated, thereby acquitting Pell. The judge also made a point of saying that the accuser did not seem untruthful. The result was a weird quasi-vindication of the man who made the complaint, but not his complaint. Archbishop Pell affirmed his dignity in a proceeding that many people thought unfair. In that he shared an ironic station with Paul Collins, who asserted his dignity over the CDF, though at the cost of leaving the priesthood. Pell has since become a cardinal.

"A power structure that is accountable only to itself will always end by abusing the powerless," James Carroll, the author of *Constantine's Sword,* has written. "Even then, it will paternalistically ask to be trusted to repair the damage."[9]

The Roman Catholic Church desperately needs a separation of powers. The canonical courts are hardly independent. The church has no oversight mechanism to remove bishops or priests who grossly betray the trust of the faithful, much less a selection process for bishops that takes laypeople into account. The most immediate task for the next pope is to embrace the politics of collegiality born of Vatican II, allow a fearless introspection of celibacy and the priesthood, and open the church to faithful dialogue on theology and doctrine.

The parish is the heartbeat of Catholicism. The place of the Word harks back to the earliest Christian communities, the pulse of the Holy Spirit extending in time. The abuse of power in this papacy has done incalculable damage to pastors, local priests who preach the Word in what they say *and choose not to say*—about birth control, theological justice, and the celibacy law, especially. Most Catholics do not believe the church on these matters. Ratzinger's demand for "submission of will" to Rome cannot coexist with the *sensus fidelium,* "the sense of the faithful." As the novelist Flannery O'Connor wrote: "It's our business to try to change the external faults of the Church—the vulgarity, the lack of scholarship, the lack of intellectual honesty—wherever we find them and however we can."[10]

When a Vatican prefect crushes the fair exchange of ideas, pastors in far-flung pulpits will replace "submission of will" with their own sense of the gospel. They have been doing it under this papacy—and others—for years. How many priests preach against birth control when they know that the overwhelming majority of the faithful ignore the church teaching? For that matter, the same applies to homosexuality. The notion that homosexual people are inclined toward "an intrinsic moral evil" (as the Vatican would have it) is unimaginable coming from Jesus's lips. If gay people, as many studies attest, cannot choose their sexual orientation, then a true theology must begin with the question of free will, and reckon with how our understanding of sexuality has evolved. If people are homosexual "through no fault of their own" (to use the American bishops' phrase in a 1976 pastoral letter), would Jesus deny them intimacy?

We might also ask how Jesus would reckon with what has happened to the priesthood. At one level, the church's crisis is a politically incorrect scandal, for it challenges assumptions of diversity with serious questions about moral behavior. Political correctness turns on the idea that society carries a debt to the harshly marginalized and should make atonement with justice. There is a crucial distinction between homosexual priests who embody genuine Christian witness and the gay priest culture that arose in the 1970s, cynical about celibacy, riddled with hypocrisy and narcissistic behavior. We have not as a society come to terms with what it means when a victimized minority (*some* bishops and priests who are gay) gains power, creates cliques, and uses clericalism to harass heterosexual seminarians, cover up promiscuity, and extend its patterns of deception to blanket those who have sex with youths. Reports of priests with pornographic gay Web sites are symptomatic of a subculture subversive to the good of the church. That agenda has victimized priests, gay and straight, who live the vows. The same holds for clerics who regularly abused their trust with women.

We raise these matters with reluctance. The gay clergy issue cannot be easily reported without offending just about everyone. Many conservatives blame *"the gays"* for a crisis with many tangled roots; gay liberationists cry homophobia at any whisper of criticism. We should be clear about both sides of this harsh paradox. Condemning homosexuality as a moral disorder heaps incalculable harm on good people who happen to be gay, on those they love, and on their families. To condemn people on the basis of *how* they express physical love presupposes a moral wisdom to which the Roman Catholic hierarchy, as evidenced by its disgraceful internal standards, simply cannot lay claim. The journey toward a renewed understanding of sexual ethics has only just begun. By the same token, we must be honest about the damage done by the hypocrisy of gay clericalism.

It is hard to imagine a rejuvenated priesthood without optional celibacy. "You can kick out ephebophiles, but the system is constantly producing others to fill their shoes," Richard Sipe has said, "by favoring those who are emotionally immature and reject women."[11] The arrival of married priests should not be seen as a panacea—families come with all kinds of baggage. Nevertheless, the spread of husbands, wives, and children in rectory life will give ministry a different sacred essence than the celibate world with sexual secrecy. Imagine a church with a lineage of theologians similar to family lines of rabbis.

That said, the Catholic Church in the prism of mass media has become the postmodern bête noir, the big powerful religion that many people love to hate—homophobic, antifeminist, the church with all those rules about sex. Yet the mainstream Christian churches are struggling with issues of homosexuality and moral standards based on scripture. Lost in this media lens is the church of parish councils, Catholic Worker Houses, apostolates that help the poor and teach the young, and the many priests who extend a sacramental imagination, Sunday after Sunday, that makes our big wobbly tent both human and divine. Custodians of orthodoxy should look around the tent and recognize that celibacy—a church law that could be changed with the stroke of a papal pen—has driven from the priesthood too many good people. This sprawl of humanity—radicals at either end, the great mass of us in the center—lumbers on, seeking serenity in the sacraments and the better angels of our nature in the liturgy. The church as a force of good stems from its own diversity, shaped by an ethos of forgiveness and redemption in the gospels. Catholicism by its nature is about inclusion.

The power structure of the church is quite a different matter, as Frank Keating, the former Oklahoma governor, learned while serving as chairman of the bishops' National Review Board. Keating resigned in May of 2003 after accusing some bishops of acting like members of the Cosa Nostra, a remark that riled Cardinal Mahony of Los Angeles as he dealt with a legal quagmire. The board was still working on its report as Keating reflected on his stormy tenure:

> *Some say the scandal is blown out of proportion . . . victims exaggerate . . . it's not fair to the Church . . . it's an example of anti-Catholic bias . . . other churches are plagued by sexual abuse allegations, too . . . and on and on.*
>
> *The problem with this is that it's false. The American Catholic Church faces a seismic upheaval, and the Catholic lay community is angry and getting angrier. Dioceses are paying huge sums of lay money to settle cases. Recently, the attorney general of Massachusetts—himself a Catholic—writing of the Boston archdiocese, declared that the mistreatment of children there was "so massive and so prolonged that it borders on the unbelievable." A Phoenix bishop was arrested for a hit-and-run death. The archbishop of Milwaukee resigned following revelation that he used diocesan funds to pay off a boyfriend.*
>
> *The lay community is justifiably incredulous.*[12]

Far away in Rome, Pope John Paul rewarded several men who personified the Vatican's corrosive secrecy. Tarcisio Bertone—the canon lawyer under Ratzinger who sheltered Maciel, while endorsing "professional secrecy" for clergy—became the archbishop of Genoa. In October 2003, John Paul elevated him to the College of Cardinals. Bertone, like Ratzinger, refused our interview requests, in keeping with the vow of pontifical secrecy.

Another newly named cardinal, Archbishop Julián Herranz, was the one member of Opus Dei in charge of a Vatican office; he chaired the Pontifical Council for the Interpretation of Legislative Texts. Herranz was, in effect, the Vatican's attorney general. During an April 2002 speech at Catholic University in Milan, Herranz criticized the press for its "tenacious, scandalistic style" in reporting on clergy abuse. The canonist echoed other curial members in complaining of "an unjust climate of suspicion and ambivalence toward priest . . . in which certain 'media' give voice to any charges whatsoever." With an alarming leap of logic Herranz spoke of "the concrete form of homosexuality that is pedophilia." Herranz echoed Bertone in upholding the mind-set that has brought such disgrace upon the church: "The rapport of trust and the secrecy of the office inherent to the relationship between the bishop and his priest collaborators, and between priests and the faithful, must be respected."[13]

John Paul was growing more frail as church leaders and pilgrims flocked to Rome for the twenty-fifth-anniversary celebration of his pontificate in mid-October of 2003. The pope elevated his longtime personal assistant, Bishop Stanislaw Dziwisz (for whom José Barba had his final letter translated into Polish), to archbishop. John Paul also named the head of the papal household, Bishop James M. Harvey, an archbishop.

Harvey's elevation came despite a *Dallas Morning News* revelation that a U.S. priest, Monsignor Daniel Pater, had been promoted with Harvey's support in the Vatican diplomatic corps despite information from church officials in Cincinnati that he had sexually abused a thirteen-year-old girl ten years earlier. The church paid the victim an out-of-court settlement in 1995, yet Pater moved up the ladder as a diplomat for the Holy See. He was serving in India when the investigation by Reese Dunklin of the *Morning News* led to his diplomatic resignation and return to the United States. Bishop Harvey "is one of the most powerful Americans at the Vatican and one of the few people of any nationality with daily access to the pope," wrote Dunklin.[14] As the newspaper reported: "The Vatican knew the status of the case."

> *The man who alerted Bishop Harvey about the Pater case is the Rev. Lawrence Breslin, pastor of the Cincinnati Archdiocese church where the abuse had taken place. He was formerly a top official of the Pontifical North American College, a seminary in Rome to which U.S. bishops send some of their most promising priest candidates.*
>
> *Monsignor Breslin said he first told his friend about the matter in 1995. Bishop Harvey, he said, responded that higher-ranking officials in the Vatican state department knew the priest "had some problems in the states, and it'd pass over."*
>
> *"I told this man, 'It's not going to pass over,'" Monsignor Breslin said.*

He recalled that during their second conversation, in 1999, Bishop Harvey said one restriction had been placed on Monsignor Pater because of the abuse: He would never be promoted to an ambassador post.

"I wasn't surprised, but I think they should have sidelined him," said Monsignor Breslin, who has publicly criticized his own archbishop's handling of other abuse cases in the Cincinnati area. "He'd almost have to murder somebody."

"That's the Vatican," he added. "It's hard to get fired over there."

Bishop Harvey said he did not remember many details of his talks with Monsignor Breslin.

In fall 2003 John Paul also removed the seventy-eight-year-old Archbishop Luigi De Magristris from the Apostolic Penitentiary, without making him a cardinal, and in his place installed Cardinal J. Francis Stafford, an American. "Some speculated that his fall was a consequence of De Magistris' outspokenness; although he doesn't give interviews, he is known within the Holy See for privately expressing candid views," wrote John Allen. "When De Magistris was a judge for the Congregation for the Causes of Saints, he voted against the beatification of Josemaria Escriva, the founder of Opus Dei."[15]

De Magistris had been a protégé of the late Cardinal Ottaviani, who put up great resistance to Vatican II reforms and pushed Pope Paul VI to renounce birth control devices. Ottaviani's ghost pervades the Roman Curia yet today. "I am an old policeman guarding the gold reserves," Ottaviani told an Italian journalist with the council in its final session. "If you tell an old policeman that the laws are going to change, he will realize that he is an old policeman, and he will do everything he can to prevent them from changing. . . . Once the new laws have become the Church's treasure, an enrichment of her gold reserves, there is still only one principle: loyalty in the Church's service. But this service means loyalty to her laws—like a blind man. Like the blind man that I am."[16]

If the Vatican's blindness to sexual reality continues under a new pope indifferent toward structural reform, the church will see a continued loss of numbers and declining credibility in the countries on which it relies for financial support.

As John Paul leaves the stage, the extraordinary achievements that ensure his role as one of our greatest popes must be weighed against the human suffering wrought by internal corruption on his watch. However great his goodness, he will be also be remembered as a conflicted pope, a man who failed to apply his own "purification of the historical memory" to sexual realities in the priesthood. His tragic naïveté left him unable to look inside the Roman Curia, the bishops, and the culture of the priesthood with the intelligence he brought to bear in diplomacy.

Further, justice is that virtue which gives everyone his due.
—Augustine, *City of God*

GLOSSARY

OF CHURCH TERMS

Sources: Richard P. McBrien, ed., *The HarperCollins Encyclopedia of Catholicism* (HarperSanFrancisco, 1995); Thomas J. Reese, *Inside the Vatican* (Cambridge, Mass.: Harvard University Press, 1996); Matthew Brunson, ed., *Catholic Almanac* (Huntington, Ind.: 2002); Donald Attwater, ed., *A Catholic Dictionary,* 3rd ed. (1958; reprinted 1997, TAN Books and Publishers, Rockford, Ill.).

Archbishop: The title of a bishop who heads an *archdiocese,* a territorial jurisdiction that includes a leading city. Typically an archbishop heads a *province* that includes *suffragan* dioceses, but he has only limited control over them. The title of archbishop is also given to a prelate who heads an important Vatican office or is of ambassadorial rank. Also see BISHOP, CARDINAL, DIOCESE.

Bishop: A bishop with jurisdiction over a diocese is known as an *ordinary.* He may be assisted by one or more *auxiliary* bishops, and sometimes by a *coadjutor bishop,* an assistant with the right of succession. The Catholic Church considers a bishop as one raised "to the fullness of the priesthood," and as a successor to the apostles. A bishop is answerable only to the pope, who is bishop of Rome.

Cardinal: A member of the Sacred College of Cardinals, which elects the pope and advises the pope when asked. Archbishops of some of the most important cities—for example New York, Chicago, and Los Angeles—and those who hold important positions at the Vatican are typically made cardinals. The pope may appoint as cardinal a priest of distinction who is not a bishop. At one time laymen were also made cardinals, but that is no longer the case.

CDF: The Congregation for the Doctrine of the Faith, known formerly as the Holy Office of the Inquisition. One of nine congregations of the Vatican, it is charged with promoting and safeguarding faith and morals. It may also act as a tribunal, or church court, on occasion, and has jurisdiction over cases involving priestly sexual abuse. Cardinal Joseph Ratzinger has been the powerful head of the CDF for most of the pontificate of John Paul II.

Chancellor, Diocesan: A notary by law, the chancellor organizes and authenticates official church documents and in some dioceses may be delegated broad powers; most are ordained priests but in some places lay men and women and religious sisters have been appointed to this position.

Chancery: More colloquially, the "bishop's office," which has charge of secretarial duties related to running a diocese.

Curia, Diocesan: The offices that assist the bishop in the government of his diocese, including those of the vicar general, chancellor, tribunal judges, and others who act with the bishop's authority. The way dioceses are organized varies.

Curia, Roman: From Latin *covir,* "men together." The offices that act with the pope's delegated authority in governing the church. Known as dicasteries, they are comprised of the Secretariat of State, nine congregations, eleven councils, three tribunals, and several other offices.

Dicasteries: See CURIA, ROMAN.

Diocese: A territory established by the pope and governed by a bishop, also known as a *see.* Several dioceses may make up a *province,* centered around an *archdiocese* and headed by an *archbishop,* who has limited supervisory responsibility for the dioceses. Each bishop is answerable to the pope and is obligated to meet the pope on an *ad limina* visit every five years and report on the status of his diocese. Priests ordained for a diocese are commonly called *secular* priests and are not bound by vows, unlike members of religious orders. See also RELIGIOUS ORDERS.

Encyclical: A formal pastoral letter (literally, "circular letter") from the pope to the whole church on social, moral, doctrinal, or disciplinary issues.

Episcopate, Episcopacy: From the Greek word for "overseer." A reference to the office of a bishop, the reign of a bishop, or the body of bishops of a particular country.

Holy See: The pope, the Roman Curia, and all who assist the pope in Rome in governing the church as its universal pastor.

HumanaeVitae: Meaning "Of Human Life," the controversial 1968 encyclical of Pope Paul VI that upheld the teaching that artificial contraception is immoral.

Laicization: The process of returning an ordained cleric to the lay state; more commonly and loosely referred to as "defrocking," although that term is not recognized in canon law.

Magisterium: The pastoral teaching office and authority of the church embodied in the pope and the bishops, who define what is authentic for a common understanding of the faith. Sometimes used as a synonym for the hierarchy.

Monsignor: An honorary title bestowed by the pope, at the request of a bishop, on a priest who has distinguished himself. Outside the United States, the title "monsignor" ("my lord") often refers to a bishop.

Novitiate: A place where new candidates *(novices)* spend at least one year of instruction before being admitted to a religious community of men or women.

Nunciature: The diplomatic headquarters of a papal ambassador. See PAPAL REPRESENTATIVES.

Nuncio: See PAPAL REPRESENTATIVES.

Oblates: From Latin *oblatus,* "offered." Men or women who offer themselves in service to certain religious communities, usually a monastery.

Papal Representatives: There are two kinds of papal emissaries to other countries. A *nuncio* (Italian, "messenger"), who has the rank of ambassador, is sent to countries that have formal diplomatic relations with the Holy See. The nuncio also serves as the pope's liaison to that nation's bishops. An *apostolic delegate* is assigned to countries that do not have formal relations with the Holy See, as was the case in the United States before 1984; he is assigned only to the nation's bishops. (Until recently, a nuncio who was not the dean of the diplomatic corps in the country to which he was assigned was called a *pronuncio*.)

Prefect: From Latin *praefectus,* "one set over." Commonly used title for various administrators, such as the prefect of a congregation in the Roman Curia or the prefect of studies in a college.

Prelates: High-ranking ecclesiastics, including bishops, archbishops, and cardinals. Some priests in the United States who are given the honorary title of "monsignor" are considered "honorary prelates." See also MONSIGNOR.

Pronuncio: See PAPAL REPRESENTATIVES.

Religious Orders: Communities of men and women who take vows of poverty, chastity, and obedience and live in accordance with the rules and particular purpose of the order (such as missionary work, teaching, preaching, and nursing). Such orders may be of diocesan right, answerable to a local bishop, or pontifical right, answerable to Rome.

U.S. Conference of Catholic Bishops: The bishops act on matters of mutual interest through their conference based in Washington, D.C., which is headed by a general secretary and staffed by priests, laypeople, and members of religious orders. Its policies are prescribed by the bishops, who meet semiannually, and directed by an elected administrative board of bishops. It evolved from an organization first formed in 1919, reorganized in 1966 following Vatican Council II, and reconstituted in its present form in 1997.

Vatican: Where the pope resides, an independent city-state in Italy recognized as sovereign in international law since 1929. An area of almost one square mile, it includes the Basilica of St. Peter, its piazza, the papal apartments, residences of various prelates, offices, five museums, gardens, and an astronomical observatory. Often used as shorthand to refer to the central government of the church, as "Washington" is used to refer to the U.S. government.

Vatican Council II: A gathering of the world's Catholic bishops in Rome in four sessions between October 11, 1962, and December 8, 1965, the twenty-first such assembly in the history of the church and the first since Vatican Council I in 1870. Pope John XXIII summoned the council in 1959, not to condemn heresy or define doctrine as many previous councils had done, but to promote worldwide peace and unity and make the church relevant in the modern world. Council fathers issued sixteen documents, defining "the church in the modern world," authorizing the use of vernacular language rather than Latin in the liturgy, opening the way to friendly relations with Protestant and Eastern Orthodox churches and non-Christian religions, condemning anti-Semitism, and instituting various internal church reforms.

Vicar General: Deputy of a diocesan bishop or of a superior general of a religious order, who can act in place of the bishop or superior.

NOTES

PROLOGUE

1. Jason Berry first interviewed Vaca by telephone in 1994. Gerald Renner met with Vaca for extensive interviews in 1996 and early 1997, and again in 2001, with continuing interviews in person and by telephone with both writers in 2002–03.
2. Eugene Kennedy, *Re-Imagining American Catholicism* (New York: Vintage, 1985), 9.
3. Vaca's Oct. 20, 1976, letter to Maciel was in Spanish; he provided an English translation to assist Bishop McGann.
4. GR telephone interview with Félix Alarcón, June 25, 2002; interview with Vaca, Port Jefferson, N.Y., Aug. 12, 2002.
5. Gerald Renner and Jason Berry, "Head of Worldwide Catholic Order Accused of History of Abuse," *Hartford Courant*, Feb. 23, 1997.
6. Ibid.
7. Donald Cozzens, *The Changing Face of the Priesthood* (Collegeville, Minn.: Liturgical Press, 2000), 107.
8. Jason Berry, *Lead Us Not into Temptation: Catholic Priests and the Sexual Abuse of Children* (New York: Doubleday, 1992).
9. Jason Berry, "A Conflicted Attitude Toward Gays," *Los Angeles Times,* Aug. 1, 1999.
10. Andrew M. Greeley and Conor Ward, "How Secularised Is the Ireland We Live In?" *Doctrine and Life* 50, no. 10 (December 2000): 581; Tom Inglis, *Moral Monopoly: The Rise and Fall of the Catholic Church in Modern Ireland* (Dublin: University College Dublin Press, 1998).
11. These extra "vows," as the Legionaries universally refer to them, are privately made formal promises, not vows as defined and regulated in church law. To be canonically binding, the vows would have to be approved by the Congregation for Religious, which reports it has never sanctioned them.
12. Albert Camus, *The Rebel* (London: Penguin, 1969), 19.
13. The Millenari, *Shroud of Secrecy: The Story of Corruption Within the Vatican* (Toronto: Key Porter Books, 2000), 46. After the original edition, in Italian, the pseudonymous clerical author identified himself as Luigi Marinelli.
14. "The Homosexual Network's Death-Grip on the Roman Catholic Church," *Ad Majorem Dei Gloriam,* spring/summer 2000 (Roman Catholic Faithful, Inc., P.O. Box 109, Petersburg, IL 62675-0109, www.rcf.org). See also Enrique T. Rueda, *The Homosexual Network: Private Lives and Public Policy* (Old Greenwich, Conn.:

Devon Adair, 1982), and Paul Likoudis, *AmChurch Comes Out* (Petersburg: Roman Catholic Faithful, 2002).

15. Blaise Pascal, *Pensées: Thoughts on Religion and Other Subjects* (New York: Washington Square Press, 1965), 104.

CHAPTER 1. TO BE A PRIEST

1. Henri Fesquet, *The Drama of Vatican II: The Ecumenical Council, June, 1962–December, 1965* (New York: Random House, 1967), 5.

2. JB interviews with Tom Doyle by telephone, June 2002; in Dallas, Tex., July 16–17, 2002; in Frankurt, Germany, Nov. 11, 2002; and continuing telephone interviews and e-mail. Unless otherwise noted, the information on Doyle is drawn from these sessions.

3. Austin Flannery, ed., *Vatican Council II: The Conciliar and Post Conciliar Documents* (Northport, N.Y.: Costello Publishing, 1981). See *Lumen Gentium* (Dogmatic Constitution of the Church), Chapter II, "The People of God."

4. Family genealogy courtesy of Sharon N. Doyle, Madison, Wisc.

5. JB interview with Kelly Doyle Tobin, Dallas, May 24, 2002.

6. Daniel Pilarczyk of Cincinnati, in Donald Cozzens, *The Changing Face of the Priesthood* (Collegeville, Minn.: Liturgical Press, 2000), 3–4.

7. Tim Pat Coogan, *Wherever Green Is Worn* (London: Hutchison, 2000); Charles Morris, *American Catholic* (New York: Times Books, 1997); John Cooney, *The American Pope: The Life and Times of Francis Cardinal Spellman* (New York: Times Books, 1984); Tess Livingstone, *George Pell* (Sydney: Duff and Snellgrove, 2002); Alan Gill, *Orphans of the Empire* (Sydney: Random House Australia, 1988).

8. Pope Paul VI, *Sacerdotalis Caelibatus* ("The Celibacy of the Priest"), in *The Papal Encyclicals 1958–81* (Ann Arbor: Priam Press, 1990), 203–21.

9. Robert Blair Kaiser, *The Politics of Sex and Religion* (Kansas City: Sheed and Ward, 1985).

10. JB telephone interview with Eugene Kennedy, July 12, 2002.

11. On Cody's investment of $2 million, see David A. Yallop, *In God's Name* (New York: Bantam, 1984), 188. General biographical material: Michael Tacket and Howard A. Tyner, "Cardinal Cody Dies of Coronary," *Chicago Tribune,* Apr. 25, 1982.

12. Eugene Kennedy, *Cardinal Bernardin* (Chicago: Bonus Books, 1989), 134.

13. Andrew M. Greeley, *The Making of the Popes 1978: The Politics of Intrigue in the Vatican* (Kansas City: Andrews and McMeel, 1979), 89.

14. See www.DailyCatholic.org, "Cardinal Pio Laghi," Aug. 30, 1999; James Conaway, "Messenger from the Vatican," *Washington Post,* Feb. 9, 1984.

15. Penny Lernoux, "Blood Taints Church in Argentina," *National Catholic Reporter,* Apr. 12, 1985; Penny Lernoux, *People of God: The Struggle for World Catholicism* (New York: Viking, 1989), 71; Ann Rodgers-Melnick, "Bishop Calls Laghi Charges 'Nonsensical,' Former Nuncio Aided His Activist Brother," *National Catholic Reporter,* Aug. 29, 1997.

16. The *Sun-Times* investigation by William Clements, Gene Mustain, and Roy Larson covered months of reporting and began in Sept. 1981, continuing through the cardinal's death in 1982. For a comprehensive account of forces behind the coverage, see John Conroy, "Cardinal Sins," *Chicago Reader,* June 5, 1987. See also Robert J. McClory, "Catholics Rally Behind Cody," *National Catholic Reporter,* Sept. 25, 1981.

17. Christopher Winner, "Vatican Delegates Letter Dismays Diocesan Press," *National Catholic Reporter,* July 3, 1981.
18. Garry Wills, "The Greatest Story Ever Told," *Columbia Journalism Review,* Jan./Feb. 1980.
19. Thomas J. Reese, S.J., *A Flock of Shepherds: The National Conference of Catholic Bishops* (Kansas City: Sheed and Ward, 1992), 6.
20. Thomas J. Reese, S.J., *Archbishop: Inside the Power Structure of the American Catholic Church* (San Francisco: Harper & Row, 1989), 4.
21. Richard A. Schoenherr and Lawrence A. Young, *The Catholic Priest in the United States: Demographic Investigations* (Madison: Comparative Religious Organization Studies Publications, University of Wisconsin, 1990); Tom Inglis, *Moral Monopoly: The Rise and Fall of the Catholic Church in Modern Ireland* (Dublin: University College Dublin Press, 1988), 211–13.
22. Wilton Wynn, *Keeper of the Keys* (New York: Random House, 1988), 90–91.
23. Peter Hebblethwaite, *Pope John Paul II and the Church* (Kansas City: Sheed and Ward, 1995), 16–18.
24. Jonathan Kwitney, *Man of the Century: The Life and Times of Pope John Paul II* (New York: Henry Holt, 1997), is the most authoritative account of the pope's role in bringing down the Eastern bloc.
25. Lernoux, *People of God,* 81.
26. John L. Allen Jr., *Cardinal Ratzinger: The Vatican's Enforcer of the Faith* (New York: Continuum, 2000), 116.
27. Joseph Cardinal Ratzinger with Vittorio Messori, *The Ratzinger Report: An Exclusive Interview on the State of the Church,* trans. Salvator Attanasio and Graham Harrison (San Francisco: Ignatius Press, 1986), 30.
28. Robert Nugent, ed., *A Challenge to Love: Gay and Lesbian Catholics in the Church* (New York: Crossroad, 1984), xi–xii.
29. Paul Collins, *The Modern Inquisition: Seven Prominent Catholics and Their Struggles with the Vatican* (New York: Overlook, 2002), 131.
30. Nugent, *Challenge to Love,* 257.
31. Sacred Congregation for Religious, "Careful Selection and Training of Candidates for the States of Perfection and Sacred Orders" (February 2, 1961), *Canon Law Digest* 5 (1962): 452–86.
32. Michael Rezendes, "Ariz. Abuse Case Names Bishop, 2 Priests," *Boston Globe,* Aug. 20, 2002.

CHAPTER 2. EVIDENCE OF THINGS UNSAID

1. Investigative staff of *The Boston Globe, Betrayal: The Crisis in the Catholic Church* (Boston: Little Brown, 2002), 142–43.
2. Robin Washington, "Ex-Classmates Contradict Cardinal Law's Deposition," *Boston Herald,* Aug. 21, 2002.
3. Jim Castelli, *The Bishops and the Bomb: Waging Peace in a Nuclear Age* (New York: Image, 1983).
4. Garry Wills, "A Tale of Two Cardinals," *New York Review of Books,* Apr. 26, 2001.
5. "Frequently Cited Church Statistics," Center for Applied Research in the Apostolate, Georgetown University, 2001; Richard Schoenherr and Lawrence Young, *Full Pews and Empty Altars* (New York: Oxford, 2002). An interpretation of data from the

Annuarium Statisticum Ecclesiae (Libreria Editrice Vaticana, 2000), available on the Web site www.ewtn.com, draws a rosier picture of vocations by focusing on the growing numbers of seminarians and priests in Africa and Asia, without offering historical context.

6. Paul J. Isely, "Child Sexual Abuse and the Catholic Church: An Historical and Contemporary Review," *Pastoral Psychology* 45, no. 4 (1997); Vern L. Bullough, "The Sin Against Nature and Homosexuality," in Vern Bullough, ed., *Sexual Practices in the Medieval Church* (Buffalo: Prometheus Books, 1982), 59.

7. John Boswell, *Christianity, Social Tolerance, and Homosexuality* (University of Chicago Press, 1980), 216.

8. James A. Brundage, *Law, Sex and Christian Society in Medieval Europe* (University of Chicago Press, 1988), 219.

9. Thomas P. Doyle, "Roman Catholic Clericalism, Religious Duress, and Clerical Sexual Abuse" *Pastoral Psychology* 51, No. 3 (January 2003).

10. Jason Berry, *Lead Us Not into Temptation,* 189.

11. James P. Hanigan, *Homosexuality: The Test Case for Christian Ethics* (Mahwah, N.J.: Paulist Press, 1988).

12. A. W. Richard Sipe, *Sex, Priests and Power: Anatomy of a Crisis* (New York: Brunner/Mazel, 1994), 140–41.

13. For an in-depth analysis of the *L.A. Times* poll, see Andrew Greeley, *Priests in the Pressure Cooker: The Sociology of a Profession Under Attack* (Chicago: University of Chicago Press, 2004).

14. Donald Cozzens, *The Changing Face of the Priesthood* (Collegeville, Minn.: Liturgical Press, 2000), 107.

15. George Weigel, *The Courage to Be Catholic* (New York: Basic, 2002), 82.

16. See John Allen Jr., *Cardinal Ratzinger* (New York: Continuum, 2000), 198–200, on gay clergy in Rome.

17. Alison O'Connor, *A Message from Heaven: The Life and Crimes of Father Sean Fortune* (Dingle, Ireland: Brandon, 2000), 18.

18. Berry, *Lead Us Not,* 244–48. See also Michael Rose, *Goodbye! Good Men: How Catholic Seminaries Turned Away Two Generations of Vocations* (Cincinnati: Aquinas Publishing, 2002). Rose cites compelling case studies, but his book is a polemic without the balance of fair-minded journalism. For a thoughtful examination of homosexuality, among other issues, in one religious order, see Peter McDonough and Eugene C. Bianchi, *Passionate Uncertainty: Inside the American Jesuits* (Berkeley: University of California Press, 2002).

19. Berry, *Lead Us Not,* 263.

20. Marie Rohde, "Former Rector Admits Abuse of 7 Students," *Milwaukee Journal,* Feb. 18, 1994.

21. John Rivera, "Archdiocese Lists 6 Accused of Child Abuse," *Baltimore Sun,* Aug. 21, 2002.

22. Rose Marie Arce and David Firestone, "Church Deals with AIDS—Among Priests," *New York Newsday,* Sept. 16, 1990.

23. Berry, *Lead Us Not,* 88.

24. Berry, *Lead Us Not,* 90.

25. Ellen Barry, "Priest Treatment Unfolds in Secretive World," *Boston Globe,* Apr. 3, 2002.

26. Michael Harris, *Unholy Orders: The Tragedy of Mount Cashel* (Toronto: Viking, 1990), 240; George B. Griffin, "Bishop Places Kane on Leave," *Worcester Telegram &*

Gazette, Apr. 24, 1993; Kathleen A. Shaw, "Northbridge Man Wants Monsignor Prosecuted," *Worcester Telegram & Gazette,* May 22, 2002.

27. David W. Chen, "Priest Ousted from Long Island Church Panel Defends Its Work," *New York Times,* Apr. 19, 2002.

28. Rita Ciolli, "Diocese Strips Placa of Duties," *Newsday,* June 14, 2002.

29. Kathleen A. Shaw, "Priest May Have Lied About Ph.D.," *Worcester Telegram & Gazette,* Aug. 9, 2002.

30. Robert Limoges went to the monastery, Valerie Pullman to St. Luke.

31. James F. McCarty, "The Churchman at Scandal's Heart," *Cleveland Plain Dealer,* July 21, 2002.

32. Michael Peterson, Thomas P. Doyle, F. Ray Mouton Jr., *The Problem of Sexual Molestation by Roman Catholic Clergy: Meeting the Problem in a Comprehensive and Responsible Manner* (1985). The document appears on several Web sites, including www.thelinkup.com, www.survivorsnetwork.org, and the *National Catholic Reporter,* www.natcath.org. See also *Lead Us Not,* 98–102.

33. Investigative staff, *Betrayal,* 33.

34. Eugene Kennedy, *Re-Imagining the Catholic Church* (New York: Vintage, 1985).

35. JB telephone interview with Eugene Kennedy, July 26, 2002.

36. Berry, *Lead Us Not,* 112.

37. Kristen Lombardi, "Cardinal Sin," *Boston Phoenix,* Mar. 23, 2001.

38. Globe staff, "Church Allowed Abuse by Priest for Years," *Boston Globe,* Jan. 6, 2002; Matt Carroll, "A Revered Guest; a Family Left in Shreds," *Boston Globe,* Jan. 6, 2002.

39. Correspondence in the Geoghan and Shanley cases appears in the appendix to the *Globe* staff's book *Betrayal* and on the newspaper's Web site, www.Globe.com.

40. Investigative staff, *Betrayal,* 96.

CHAPTER 3. EXILE AND RENEWAL

1. Cardinal Ratzinger's letter appears in, among other works, Jeannine Gramick and Pat Furey, eds., *The Vatican and Homosexuality* (New York: Crossroad, 1988), 1.

2. Jason Berry, *Lead Us Not into Temptation,* 239–42.

3. Jonathan Friendly, "Catholic Church Discussing Priests Who Abuse Children," *New York Times,* May 4, 1986.

4. Andy Rodriguez, "Priest Pedophilia Called Church's Biggest Problem," *National Catholic News Service,* May 2, 1986.

5. JB telephone interview with Eugene Kennedy, July 16, 2002.

6. Jason Berry, "Sending the Bishops a Message," *Baltimore Sun,* Nov. 4, 1989.

7. Alex Friederich, "Breaking the Silence: Monk's Seduction of Santa Catalina Student Led to an Affair That Shattered Her Faith," *Monterey County Herald,* June 23, 2002.

8. Jason Berry, "Survivors Connect to Heal, Raise Voices," *National Catholic Reporter,* Nov. 8, 2002.

9. See chapter 12 in Berry, *Lead Us Not.*

10. *Brooks v. Maher,* Superior Court, San Diego County, Calif., no. 529114.

11. Mark Brooks, sworn statement, May 21, 1999.

12. Mark Brooks, e-mail to JB, Sept. 15, 2002.

13. "Editorial: Pedophilia Problem Needs Tackling," *National Catholic Reporter,* June 7, 1985.

14. Carl M. Cannon, "The Priest Scandal," *American Journalism Review* 24, no. 4 (May 2002).

15. Cannon e-mail correspondence and telephone interview with JB, Oct. 21, 2002.

16. Carl M. Cannon, "The Church's Secret Child Abuse Dilemma," *San Jose Mercury News,* Dec. 30, 1987.

17. "USCC Pedophilia Statement," Feb. 9, 1988 (Washington, D.C.: U.S. Catholic Conference).

18. Glenn F. Buntin, Ralph Frammolino, and Richard Winton, "Archdiocese for Years Kept Claims of Abuse from Police," *Los Angeles Times,* Aug. 18, 2002.

19. Rev. Thomas P. Doyle, O.P., J.C.D., "Report to the Canonical Affairs Committee of the NCCB on Action Items One and Two Concerning the Laicization and Dismissal of Priests Who Have Sexually Abused Minors," Apr. 20, 1989 (unpublished).

20. United States Conference of Catholic Bishops, Ad Hoc Committee on Sexual Abuse, *Restoring Trust: A Pastoral Response to Sexual Abuse: Efforts to Combat Clergy Sexual Abuse Against Minors,* Chronology (Washington, D.C.: June 2002).

21. JB interview in Rome, Nov. 26, 2002.

22. Canon Law Society of Great Britain and Ireland, *The Code of Canon Law: In English Translation* (London: Collins Liturgical Publications, 1983), 324.

23. Bishop Quinn was deposed by attorneys Jeffrey R. Anderson and William M. Crosby on May 26, 1995, in Cleveland. *Laura Livingston et al. v. Diocese of Cleveland,* State of Ohio, County of Cuyahoga, Court of Common Pleas, case no. 93-257621.

24. Peter Hebblethwaite, *Pope John Paul II and the Church* (Kansas City: Sheed and Ward), 76.

25. JB telephone interview with Jeffrey Anderson, June 4, 2002. Statement of Facts, *John T. Doe et al. v. Diocese of Winona et al.,* C6-89-012659, State of Minnesota, County of Winona, 10th Judicial District.

26. JB interview with Sylvia Demarest, Dallas, May 23, 2002.

27. Jason Berry, "Immunity: A Haven for Sensitive Files Too?" *Cleveland Plain Dealer,* June 17, 1990, and *Lead Us Not,* 290.

28. See Michael Harris, *Unholy Orders; The Report of the Archdiocesan Commission Enquiry into the Sexual Abuse of Children by Members of the Clergy* (St. John's Archdiocese, 1990), also referred to as the Winter Commission report; Berry, *Lead Us Not,* Chapter 18.

29. JB telephone interview with Barry M. Coldrey, Apr. 7, 2003.

30. Barry M. Coldrey, *Religious Life Without Integrity* (Thornbury, Australia: Tamanaraik Press, 1988), 37–39.

CHAPTER 4. A TIME OF SOLIDARITY

1. Charles Sennott, *Broken Trust* (New York: Scribner's, 1992).

2. Ibid., 326.

3. Eric MacLeish, in conversation with JB, Chicago, Mar. 18, 2002.

4. Investigative staff of the Boston Globe, *Betrayal* (Boston: Little Brown, 2002), 47.

5. Carl M. Cannon, "The Priest Scandal," *American Journalism Review* 24, no. 4 (2002).

6. Jonathan Kwitney, *Man of the Century* (New York: Henry Holt, 1997), 592.

7. Jason Berry, "Listening to the Survivors: Voices of the People of God," *America,* November 13, 1993.

8. Barbara Blaine, unpublished manuscript, 1989. She published a shortened version, "Abused by Priest, She Sought Healing," *National Catholic Reporter*, Nov. 3, 1989.

9. Jason Berry, "A Dark Journey of the Soul, *Chicago Tribune Magazine*, Feb. 11, 2001.

10. Blaine, unpublished manuscript.

11. *S.N.A.P. News*, Oct. 1992.

12. JB interviews with David Clohessy, 1990, 1991, 2002. See also Virginia Young, "Memory Prompts Abuse Suit Against Priest," *St. Louis Post-Dispatch*, Nov. 24, 1991, and Frank Bruni, "Am I My Brother's Keeper," *New York Times Magazine*, May 12, 2002.

13. Hilary Stiles, *Assault on Innocence* (Albuquerque: B&K Publishers, 1988).

14. JB telephone interview with Barbara Blaine, Oct. 26, 2002.

15. Andrew M. Greeley, *Confessions of a Parish Priest* (New York: Simon & Schuster, 1986), 179.

16. Andrew M. Greeley, *Love Affair: A Prayer Journal* (New York: Crossroad, 1993), 26–27.

17. Andrew M. Greeley, "Church Time Bomb: Pederast Priests," *Chicago Sun-Times*, July 13, 1986.

18. Andrew M. Greeley, "Catholic Church Must Clean Out the Pedophile Priests," *Chicago Sun-Times*, Dec. 19, 1989.

19. Andrew M. Greeley, *The Making of the Popes 1978; 1979*.

20. For an extensive account of the conflict between Greeley and Bernardin, see John Conroy, "Cardinal Sins," *Chicago Reader*, June 5, 1987.

21. Andrew M. Greeley, "Hardball Not the Answer," *Chicago Sun-Times*, June 2, 1991.

22. Berry, *Lead Us Not into Temptation*, 346.

23. Andrew M. Greeley, "A Special Prosecutor Needed on Pedophilia," *Chicago Sun-Times*, Oct. 20, 1991.

24. Eugene Kennedy, *Cardinal Bernardin*, 247.

25. D. J. R. Bruckner, "Chicago's Activist Cardinal," *New York Times Magazine*, May 1, 1983.

26. William Grady, "Court Rejects New Bid to Open Priests' Files," *Chicago Tribune*, Mar. 24, 1993.

27. Andrew M. Greeley, *Furthermore! Memories of a Parish Priest* (New York: Forge, 1999), 92–93.

28. Michael Hirsley, "Priests' Sex Charges Cost Archdiocese $1.8 million," *Chicago Tribune*, Jan. 24, 1993, and "$6 Million Deficit for Archdiocese," *Chicago Tribune*, Feb. 5, 1993; Daniel J. Lehmann, "Archdiocese Awash in Red," *Chicago Sun-Times*, Feb. 5, 1993.

29. Judy Tarjanyi, "Woman Who Says Priest Abused Her Seeks Apology," *Blade*, January 3, 1993.

30. Florence Shinkle, "Sins of the Fathers," *St. Louis Post-Dispatch*, Feb. 21, 1993.

CHAPTER 5. POPE JOHN PAUL II BREAKS HIS SILENCE

1. Jonathan Kwitney, *Man of the Century*, 639.

2. "Press Release, Servants of the Paraclete, Inc., (The Very Rev.) Liam J. Hoare, S.P., Servant General (CEO), Re: Settlement of Minnesota and New Mexico Litigation," *Priestly People* 8, no. 6 (Dec. 1993), 5.

3. Douglas Todd, "Bishop Denies Sex Abuse in Letter," *Vancouver Sun*, Jan. 8, 1991. The two other members of his order, Br. Glen Doughty and Fr. Harold McIntee, were convicted for sexual indecencies with minors.

4. Lisa Hobbs Birnie, "Sins of the Father," *Saturday Night* (Toronto), Feb. 1994.

5. Jean Barman, "Taming Aboriginal Sexuality: Gender, Power and Race in British Columbia, 1850–1900," *BC Studies,* no. 115/116 (autumn/winter 1997/1998), 237.

6. Cindy Wooden, "O'Connor Statement," Catholic News Service, Mar. 11, 1993; see *National Catholic Reporter,* Mar. 19, 1993.

7. James Franklin, "US Dioceses Lack Policy for Cases of Sex Abuse," *Boston Globe,* July 12, 1992. Comments by Cincinnati archbishop Daniel Pilarczyk are a case in point: "Pastoral experience, illuminated by increasing medical and sociological knowledge about the roots of this disordered behavior, has helped us see areas in which the action of the church and its leadership can improve. . . . Until recently, few in society and the church understood the problem well."

8. Cindy Wooden, "O'Connor Statement."

9. Kwitney, *Man of the Century,* 640.

10. Mary Kenny, *Goodbye to Catholic Ireland: How the Irish Lost the Civilization They Created* (Springfield, Ill.: Templegate, 2000), 308–9.

11. Barry Coldrey, "Memorandum by Congregation of Christian Brothers Holy Spirit Province," Select Committee on Health First Report, Appendix 10, Feb. 1998.

12. Alan Gill, *Orphans of the Empire: The Shocking Story of Child Migration to Australia* (Sydney: Random House Australia, 1998), 6. The author generously provided insight on statistics in a March 6, 2003, e-mail to Berry, stating that the "consensus of opinion is that about 10,000 'orphaned' children were sent to Australia between 1920 and 1967 when the traffic ceased."

13. Suzanne Fournier and Ernie Crey, *Stolen from Our Embrace: The Abduction of First Nations Children and the Restoration of Aboriginal Communities* (Vancouver/Toronto: Douglas & McIntyre, 1998), 107.

14. Mary Raftery and Eoin O'Sullivan, *Suffer the Little Children: The Inside Story of Ireland's Industrial Schools* (New York: Continuum, 2001), 262. On the ill-preparedness of the Christian Brothers for dealing with children, see p. 266; also Barry M. Coldrey, "The Distinctive Catholic Problem over Child Migration from Britain and Malta to Australia After World War II," *The Occasional Papers of the Independent Scholars Association of Australia (Victoria Chapter)* 1, no. 3 (Dec. 2002).

15. Raftery and O'Sullivan, *Suffer the Little Children,* 265–66.

16. David Cairns, "Church to Hear Abuse Claims," *Standard* (Australia), Feb. 1, 1994.

17. Glenn Conley, "Pope Sacks Priest in Abuse Case," *Herald Sun,* Melbourne ed., Nov. 20, 1993. The priest, Gerald Ridsdale, was found guilty on May 27, 1993, of thirty counts of indecent assaults on ten boys in an eight-year period.

18. George Weigel, *Witness to Hope: The Biography of John Paul II* (New York: HarperCollins, 1999), 657.

19. Eileen Welsome and Dennis Domrzalski, "Ex-Priest-Turned-Counselor Accused in Lawsuit," *Albuquerque Tribune,* Apr. 1, 1993.

20. Eileen Welsome, "Founder Didn't Want Molesters at Paraclete," *Albuquerque Tribune,* Apr. 2, 1993.

21. Weigel, *Witness to Hope.*

22. JB telephone interview with Pio Laghi, Nov. 25, 2002.

23. George Weigel, *The Courage to be Catholic: Crisis, Reform, and the Future of the Church* (New York: Basic Books, 2002), 149.

24. Ibid., 124–25.

25. Ibid., 123.

26. John Thavis and Cindy Wooden, "Pope: Accept Church Teachings Fully," *Criterion,* Indianapolis archdiocesan newspaper, Mar. 26, 1993.

27. JB interview with Robert Mickens, Rome, Nov. 19, 2002.

28. "Vatican Mandates New Fidelity Oath," *National Catholic Reporter,* Mar. 17. 1989.

29. Adam J. Maida, "The Selection, Training, and Removal of Diocesan Clergy," *Catholic Lawyer* 33, no. 1 (Feb. 1990).

30. As this book goes to press, there is no definitive tabulation on the number of victims or perpetrators. In a Mar. 20, 1993, article in *America,* "How Serious Is the Problem of Sexual Abuse by Clergy?" Andrew M. Greeley used the data on priests removed from the Chicago archdiocese as a baseline in projecting national estimates of 2,500 priest abusers and 100,000 victims. Laurie Goodstein, "Train of Pain in Church Crisis Leads to Nearly Every Diocese, *New York Times,* Jan. 12, 2003, found 1,200 perpetrators from dioceses. The *Times* study, while valuable, did not include religious order priests or speculate on a figure for victims. The most extensive database on perpetrators of which we are aware is that of Dallas attorney Sylvia Demarest, who claimed 2,100 clerics as this book went to press. The National Review Board was gathering data on perpetrators through 2003.

31. Florence Shinkle, "The Sins of the Fathers," *St. Louis Post-Dispatch,* Feb. 21, 1993.

32. JB telephone interview and e-mails with Ann Rodgers-Melnick, Mar. 2003.

33. Ann Rodgers-Melnick, "Vatican Clears Priest, Wuerl Rejects Verdict," *Pittsburgh Post-Gazette,* Mar. 21, 1993.

34. JB interview with Msgr. Brian Ferme, Lateran University, Rome, Nov. 27, 2002.

35. Rodgers-Melnick, "Vatican Clears Priest."

36. Ann Rodgers-Melnick, "Hospital That Evaluated Priest Attacks Vatican," *Pittsburgh Post-Gazette,* Mar. 23, 1993.

37. Ann Rodgers-Melnick, "Petition Suspends Vatican Verdict on Cipolla," *Pittsburgh Post-Gazette,* Mar. 25, 1993.

38. Ann Rodgers-Melnick, "Molestation Suit Settled with Church," *Pittsburgh Post-Gazette,* October 1, 1993; "Banned Priest Says Mass on TV," Feb. 18, 1994.

39. Ann Rodgers-Melnick, "Diocese Targets Ousted Priest," *Pittsburgh Post-Gazette,* Aug. 7, 2000.

40. Ann Rodgers-Melnick, "Rare Sanction Imposed on Priest," *Pittsburgh Post-Gazette,* Nov. 16, 2002.

41. JB telephone interview with Barry Coldrey, Mar. 31, 2003.

42. Jerry Filteau, "Special U.S. Church Law on Clergy Sex Abuse Extended," Catholic News Service, Dec. 31, 1998. John Thavis, "In U.S., Sex Abuse Norms Expected to Apply Only to Religious Priests," Catholic News Service, Jan. 11, 2002.

43. Douglas Todd, "O'Connor Appeal Dropped After Healing Circle," *Vancouver Sun,* June 18, 1998.

44. Craig McInnes, "Rape Charges Dropped Against B.C. Bishop," *Globe and Mail,* June 18, 1998.

CHAPTER 6. MEMORIES OF THE CARDINAL

1. JB interview with Stephen Rubino, Margate, N.J., Apr. 18, 2002. See also Christopher McDougall, "The Cross Examiner," *Philadelphia Magazine,* June 2002.

2. JB interview with Stephen Rubino, Margate, N.J., Nov. 29, 1993.
3. Gustav Niebuhr, "Bishops' Panel to Address Sexual Abuse by Clergy," *Washington Post,* June 18, 1993.
4. David Briggs, "Pope Names Panel to Study Dismissal of Abusive Priests," Associated Press, June 22, 1993.
5. Ron Russell, "Cardinal Coverup," *Los Angeles New Times,* May 2, 2002.
6. Milo Geylin, "The Catholic Church Struggles with Abuse over Sexual Abuse," *Wall Street Journal,* Nov. 24, 1993.
7. JB interview with Greg Flannery, Cincinnati, Nov. 25, 1993.
8. Jan Crawford, "Lawyer Doubted Accuser Would Recall Bernardin," *Chicago Tribune,* Jan. 14, 1994.
9. Jason Berry, "Sudden Recall: Memories Delayed or Imagined?" *National Catholic Reporter,* Dec. 3, 1993.
10. Quotations from Cardinal Bernardin are verbatim from a videotape of the news conference.
11. Marilyn Vise, "Group Asks for End to Attacks," *Belleville News-Democrat,* Nov. 16, 1993.
12. Eugene Kennedy, *My Brother Joseph: The Spirit of a Cardinal and the Story of a Friendship* (New York: St. Martin's Griffin, 1998), 116.
13. See David E. Kepple, "Carroll Grads Recall Harsham 3 Questioning Priest's Behavior," *Dayton Daily News,* Nov. 20, 1993, and "Archdiocese Wants Sources to Step Forward Regarding Abuse," Nov. 21, 1993.
14. Joe Robertson, "Cardinal Compassion," *Daily Southtown,* Nov. 20, 1993.
15. Jan Crawford, "Bernardin's Accuser Has Potential Problem," *Chicago Tribune,* Feb. 9, 1994; Michael Hirsley and Jan Crawford, "Bernardin Accuser Recants," Mar. 1, 1994.
16. JB telephone interview with Denis Ventriglia, Mar. 26, 2003.
17. Tony Bartelme, "Secret Sins," *Charleston Post and Courier,* Apr. 28, 2002. See also Schuyler Kropf, "Hopwood Faces More Accusations," *Charleston Post and Courier,* Dec. 29, 1993, and "Hopwood Resigns His Parish," Dec. 30, 1993.
18. A. W. Richard Sipe, "Priest Sex Abuse Case Stirs Political Storm in Ireland," *National Catholic Reporter,* Dec. 2, 1994.
19. Stephen Kurkijian and Michael Rezendes, "Settlement in Minnesota and Retraction Cited," *Boston Globe,* Mar. 22, 2002. The *Globe* reported that the settlement was "less than $100,000."
20. Brooks gave an affidavit on behalf of the defendant in *Roman Catholic Bishop of San Diego v. Robert Kumpel,* Superior Court of San Diego, GIC 783810. The affidavit also appears on the Web site of the Roman Catholic Faithful, an ultraconservative group, at www.rcf.org.
21. Andrew M. Greeley, *I Hope You're Listening, God: A Prayer Journal* (New York: Crossroad, 1997), 64.

Chapter 7. Evangelism by Stealth

1. Jonathan Kwitney, *Man of the Century* (New York: Henry Holt, 1997), 259.
2. Melinda Henneburger, "Vatican's Influence Is in Vision, Not Details," *New York Times,* Apr. 22, 2002.
3. Vincent A. Yzermans, *Journeys* (Waite Park, Minn.: Park Press, 1994), 234–35.

4. James Patrick Shannon, *Reluctant Dissenter: An Autobiography* (New York: Crossroad Publishing Company, 1998), 113.
5. The N.C.C.B. was originally known as the National Catholic Welfare Council. It has since been renamed the U.S. Conference of Catholic Bishops.
6. Kenneth Briggs, *Holy Siege: The Year That Shook Catholic America* (New York: HarperCollins, 1992), 10–15, 337–43.
7. Gerald P. Fogarty, *American Catholic Biblical Scholarship* (San Francisco: Harper & Row, 1989), 296.
8. Gerald Renner, "Church Leaders Meet Pope," *Hartford Courant*, Mar. 9, 1989.
9. Ibid.
10. Ibid.
11. Gerald Renner, "Vatican Cardinal Denounces U.S. Television," *Hartford Courant*, Mar. 11. 1989.
12. Ibid.
13. James J. LeBar, *Cults, Sex and the New Age* (South Bend, Ind.: Our Sunday Visitor Press, 1989), 288.
14. GR telephone interview with Joop Koopman, October 18, 2002.
15. Gerald Renner, "Catholic Legionaries Expand Base in State," *Hartford Courant*, Mar. 25, 1996.
16. Gerald Renner, "Novices Accuse Catholic Order of Intimidation, Unnecessary Pressure," *Hartford Courant*, June 10, 1996.
17. In June of 2003, as this book was being completed, the Legion placed on its Web site, www.legionaryfacts.org/escape.html, a strange disavowal from Joseph Williams that his night flight from the seminary was not due to unhappiness with the Legion. His disavowal astonishes Jeffries, who said it "is a complete distortion of the facts" and must have been made under Legion pressure due to his brother.
18. Gerald Renner, "Order's Leader Withholds Comment on Allegations," *Hartford Courant*, June 11, 1996.
19. Bannon to GR, unpublished.
20. Gerald Renner, "Archdiocese Fears Backlash over House," *Hartford Courant*, Mar. 13, 1992.
21. Gerald Renner and Constance Neyer, "Archbishop Rejects Church's Plan to Adopt Soup Kitchen," *Hartford Courant*, Dec. 27, 1993.

CHAPTER 8. MYTH OF THE FOUNDER

1. David Willey, *God's Politician: Pope John Paul II, the Catholic Church and the New World Order* (New York: St. Martin's, 1992), 26–27.
2. Henry Bamford Parkes, *A History of Mexico* (Boston: Houghton Mifflin, 1938), 112.
3. Enrique Krauze, Mexico, *Biography of Power: A History of Modern Mexico, 1810–1996* (New York: HarperCollins, 1997), 496.
4. George Weigel, *Witness to Hope* (New York: HarperCollins, 1999), 282.
5. Penny Lernoux, *People of God* (New York: Viking, 1989), and John Allen, *Cardinal Ratzinger* (New York: Continuum, 2000), have detailed accounts of Ratzinger's treatment of liberation theology intellectuals. On the Legion in Argentina, see Olga Wornat, *Nuestra Santa Madre: Historia pública y privada de la iglesia católica Argentina* (Buenos Aires: Eddiciones B, 2002). Interviews with ex–Legion members provide insight on the order's role in Chile.

6. Alfonso Torres Robles, *La Prodigiosa adventura de los Legionarios de Cristo* (Madrid: Foca, 2001), 15.
7. "Biographies of Blesseds," www.ewtn.com/library/MARY/bios95.htm#valencia.
8. See www.cotija.com.
9. J. Alberto Villasana, *Perspectives on a Foundation* (Legion of Christ, 1991), 12.
10. Jesús Colina interviews Marcial Maciel, *Christ Is My Life* (Manchester, N.H.: Sophia Institute Press, 2003), 3.
11. Villasana, *Perspectives,* 1.
12. Legion flyer, "Teacher of Her Children in the Faith," soliciting donations for "the Cause of Canonization of Maura Degollado Guizar"; also see Web site, http://www.catholic-forum.com/saints/candidates/prot1990.htm.
13. Villasana, *Perspectives,* 14.
14. GR interview with Father Peter Cronin, former Legionary priest, in Silver Spring, Md., Oct. 30, 1996.
15. GR interview with Glenn Favreau, Plattsburgh, N.Y., Dec. 28, 2001.
16. Br. George Busto of the Oratorians in Brooklyn, N.Y., said in a May 6, 2003 interview with GR about Saint Philip Neri: "The story is true. It is told whenever his life is related."
17. GR telephone interview with Fr. Rogelio Orozco, Jan. 23, 2003.
18. GR telephone interview with Juan Vaca, Jan. 24, 2003.
19. "Fr. Marcial Maciel y Cotija," www.cotija.com, translated from the Spanish.
20. Torres, *Prodigiosa adventura,* 16.
21. Parkes, *History of Mexico,* 105.
22. Krauze, *Mexico,* 34.
23. Peter Steinfels, "Proof (or Not) of Saintly Existence," *New York Times,* July 20, 2002; Stafford Poole, *Our Lady of Guadalupe: The Origins and Sources of a Mexican National Symbol* (Tuscon: University of Arizona Press, 1995); David A. Brading, *Mexican Phoenix* (New York: Cambridge, 2001).
24. Krauze, *Mexico,* 72.
25. David C. Bailey, *!Viva Cristo Rey!: The Cristero Rebellion and the Church-State Conflict in Mexico* (Austin and London: University of Texas Press, 1974), 54–55, 68.
26. Jim Tuck, *The Holy War in Los Altos: A Regional Analysis of Mexico's Cristero Rebellion* (Tucson: University of Arizona Press, 1982), 44.
27. Bailey, *!Viva Cristo Rey!,* 246 ff.
28. Ibid., 281.
29. Ibid., 286–88.
30. Pius XI, *Acerba Animi.*
31. "Biographies of Blesseds" (see note 7).
32. Ibid.
33. Krauze, *Mexico,* 496.
34. Villasana, *Perspectives,* 14.
35. Roderic Ai Camp, *Crossing Swords: Politics and Religion in Mexico* (New York: Oxford University Press, (1997), 164.
36. "Fr. Maciel y Cotija" (see note 19).
37. Villasana, *Perspectives,* 24.
38. Ibid., 26.
39. Maciel repeats the stories of his heroics in the interview book *Christ Is My Life,* 19 ff.
40. Villasana, *Perspectives,* 31.
41. *Legionaries of Christ: 50th Anniversary* (Horizons Institute, 1991), 23.

42. The seminary authorities "did not look kindly on my desire to form a new congregation," Maciel says in *Christ Is My Life*, 21.

43. GR telephone interview with Fr. Orozco. Orozco is the only one of the original group to be ordained. He left the Legion in 1945 to be a parish priest.

44. Villasana, *Perspectives*, 58.

45. Colina and Maciel, *Christ Is My Life*, 24.

46. Ibid., 25.

47. Villasana, *Perspectives*, 63.

48. JB interview, Mexico City, Nov. 1996. See also Gerald Renner and Jason Berry, "Head of Worldwide Catholic Order Accused of History of Abuse," *Hartford Courant*, Feb. 23, 1997.

49. Villasana, *Perspectives*, 66–67.

50. Ibid., 67.

51. The number of original seminarians is variously given as twelve or thirteen. Fr. Orozco, who was one of them, insists it was twelve, as in the original photograph. The Legion booklet says thirteen.

52. *Legionaries*, 34.

53. Ibid., 25.

54. JB interviews with former Legionaries, Mexico, 1996.

55. Villasana, *Perspectives*, 81.

56. JB interview in Mexico in 1996 with ex–Legion member who chose to remain anonymous.

57. Torres, *Prodigiosa adventura*, 24–26; for Vasquel's baseball venture, see Michael M. Oleksak and Mary Adams Oleksak, *Beisbol: Latin Americans and the Grand Old Game*, 2nd ed. (New York: McGraw Hill/Contemporary Books, 1996).

58. Krauze, *Mexico*, 425.

59. Torres, *Prodigiosa adventura*, 26.

60. JB interview with José Barba, Mexico City, Nov. 2, 1996.

61. *Legionaries*, 28.

62. James Brodrick, S.J., *The Origin of the Jesuits* (Toronto: Loyola University Press, 1986), 95.

63. *Legionaries*, 28; Maciel gives a different account in *Christ Is My Life*, 39, saying the minister needed the recommendation of a cardinal of the Roman Curia.

64. *Legionaries*, 29.

65. Barrett McGurn, *A Reporter Looks at the Vatican* (New York: Coward-McCann, 1962), 92.

66. A summary of the press accolades heaped on Pius XII after he died, on Oct. 5, 1958, is found in a booklet, *The 1958 Rome Story*, researched by Gerald Renner and published in April 1959 by the Bureau of Information, National Catholic Welfare Conference, Washington, D.C.

67. John Cornwell, *Hitler's Pope: The Secret History of Pius XII* (New York: Viking Penguin, 1999), 271–72.

68. *Legionaries*, 28.

69. In *Christ Is My Life*, 40, Maciel's story changes. Here is no mention of a beatification, only a "ceremony."

70. See www.catholic-forum.com/saints.

71. Anne O'Hare McCormick, *Vatican Journal: 1921–1954* (New York: Farrar, Straus and Cudahy, 1957), 129–32.

72. Torres, *Prodigiosa adventura,* 19; the Legion history mistakenly refers to Güell as a marquis rather than a count.

73. *Legionaries,* 30–31.

74. GR interview with Juan Vaca, Holbrook, N.Y., July 16, 2002.

75. Torres, *Prodigiosa adventura,* 24.

76. *Legionaries,* 31.

77. Colina and Maciel, *Christ Is My Life,* 46.

78. *Legionaries,* 31.

79. McGurn, *Reporter,* 55.

80. Peter Hebblethwaite, *Paul VI: The First Modern Pope* (New York/Mahwah: Paulist Press, 1993), 147.

81. *Legionaries,* 32.

82. Ibid.

83. Torres, *Prodigiosa adventura,* 20.

84. GR telephone interviews with Dominguez in Oct. 1996 and on Sept. 3, 2002.

Chapter 9. The War Against Internal Enemies

1. The advertisement, entitled "Felicita S.S. Juan Pablo II al Padre Marcial Maciel," appeared on the same day in the newspapers.

2. Alfonso Torres Robles, *La Prodigiosa adventura de los Legionarios de Cristo* (Madrid: Foca, 2001), 48–50, 228–29.

3. Ronan O'Neill, "Sex Abuse and the Vatican," *Magill,* September 1998.

4. Ibid.

5. According to multiple Legionary sources. An internal Legion memo obtained by the authors, dated June 6, 1999, shows plans to rent a helicopter for Nuestro Padre in Colombia for two days for $700. On the cost of the Concorde see Larry Gelbart, "The Future Is Past," op-ed page, *New York Times,* Apr. 26, 2003.

6. JB interview with José Barba, Mexico City, Nov. 1, 1996. Gerald Renner and Jason Berry, "Head of Worldwide Catholic Order Accused of History of Abuse," *Hartford Courant,* Feb. 23, 1997.

7. JB interview with José Barba, Dallas, June 27, 2002; Rome, November 13, 2002.

8. Eric Hanson, *The Catholic Church in World Politics* (Princeton: Princeton University Press, 1987), 93.

9. JB interview with Arturo Jurado, Mexico City, Nov. 2, 1996.

10. José Barba Martin, "The Reasons for My Silence," *L'espresso,* Feb. 1, 2003. The article was written at the editorial invitation of *Prometo,* a Mexican cultural magazine, which then refused to publish it. Sandro Magister, the religion editor of *L'espresso,* arranged for its publication in Italy. The English translation was done by Paul Lennon.

11. May 1, 1952, letter from Legionary student to Flora Barragán de Garza, courtesy of José de Cordoba.

12. Paul Lennon, e-mail to Jason Berry, Feb. 1, 2003.

13. Arturo Jurado, memo to authors for *Hartford Courant* report, Jan. 2, 1997.

14. JB interview with Alejandro Espinosa Alcalá, Mexico City, Nov. 3, 1996.

15. Garry Wills, *Why I Am a Catholic* (Boston and New York: Houghton Mifflin Company, 2002).

16. See "flagellation" in Richard P. McBrien, ed., *The HarperCollins Encyclopedia of Catholicism* (HarperSanFrancisco, 1995), 532.

17. Fernando Pérez Olvera, written statement to Jason Berry, Sept. 30, 1996, for *Hartford Courant*.
18. Ibid.; see *Hartford Courant*, Feb. 23, 1997.
19. JB interview with José Antonio Pérez Olvera, Nov. 3, 1996, Mexico City: José Antonio Pérez Olvera, Dec. 18, 1994, letter to Jason Berry.
20. JB interview with Alejandro Espinosa Alcalá, Mexico City, Nov. 3, 1996.
21. JB interview with Saúl Barrales Arellano, Mexico City, Nov. 7, 1996.
22. Saúl Barrales Arellano, notarized statement for the *Hartford Courant*, Mexico City, Jan. 31, 1997.
23. GR interview with Vaca, Port Jefferson, N.Y., Aug. 19, 2002.
24. Barba, "The Reasons for My Silence."
25. Félix Alarcón to José Barba, Aug. 4, 1997.
26. Ibid.
27. JB interview with José Barba, Mexico City, Nov. 12, 2002.
28. Barba, "The Reasons for My Silence."
29. Dolantin is the name of a highly addictive narcotic made by Hoechst Marion Roussel in Belgium. The drug, which is meant for acute pain, is also known by other names, such as meperidine, Demerol, and pethidine, according to information from the Thomas Jefferson University Medical School in Philadelphia.
30. Jurado memo.
31. *Legionaries of Christ* (Horizons Institute, 1991), 23.
32. GR telephone interviews with Federico Dominguez, Oct. 1996 and Sept. 3, 2002.
33. JB background interview with confidential source, Mexico City.
34. GR interview with Vaca, Feb. 18, 2003.
35. "Ballestrero, Anastasio Alberto Cardinal," *Encyclopaedia Britannica* (2003), Encyclopaedia Britannica Premium Service.
36. Document provided by the Legion, through its law firm of Kirkland & Ellis, to *The Hartford Courant*, Dec. 20, 1996.
37. Thomas J. Reese, S.J., *Inside the Vatican* (Cambridge: Harvard University Press, 1996), 76.
38. There is no published literature regarding addiction and electroshock therapy, says retired New Jersey physician David Canavan, M.D., who developed and ran the program that is the national model for handling physicians with addiction problems. This does not mean insulin shock therapy has not been done. Psychiatrists long thought addiction was secondary to depression, and shock therapy is a standard for depression. Modern thinking is that addiction is depressive in its own right: get rid of the addiction, and the depression will subside.

CHAPTER 10. THE LEGION'S DEFENSE OF FATHER MACIEL

1. In 2002, the Tribune Company, which owns the *Chicago Tribune*, purchased the Times Mirror chain and its media properties, including the *Hartford Courant*.
2. *The Official Catholic Directory*, 2000 ed. (New Providence, N.J.: P. J. Kenedy & Sons).
3. *The Hartford Courant* reported on Mar. 17, 2002, that secret court documents revealed that Egan, as bishop of Bridgeport, had allowed several priests facing multiple accusations of sexual abuse to continue working for years.
4. Stephanie Summers to GR, in a reflection on how the story developed.

5. Lennon e-mail to GR and others, on Fernández Amenábar, Feb. 7, 2002; Lennon e-mail to JB, Feb. 26, 2003.

6. Juan Manuel Fernández Amenábar, personal declaration, Jan. 6, 1995. Amenábar's statement says: "I have asked Mr. Alejandro Espinoso Alcalá, Mr. José Antonio Pérez Olvera, Mr. José Barba Martín and Mr. Arturo Jurado Guzmán, using the verbal and gestural means of communication at my command, to express this declaration of mine in writing." Although the document is not signed by a notary public, the information conforms to what Dr. Gabriela Quintero recounted in her interview and notarized statement, based on her years of dialogue with Amenábar and on his diary, which she read before it was stolen from his room.

7. Ibid.

8. JB interview with Dr. Gabriela Quintero Calleja, Mexico City, Nov. 8, 1996.

9. GR interview with the Rev. Alberto Athié, Chicago, Apr. 16, 2001.

10. Gerald Renner and Jason Berry, "Head of Worldwide Catholic Order Accused of History of Abuse," *Hartford Courant,* Feb. 23, 1997.

11. For a detailed account of the accusations against Barba et al., see Gerald Renner and Jason Berry, "Legion Calls Macial's Accusers Disgruntled Conspirators," *Hartford Courant,* Feb. 23, 1997, sidebar to main story, accessible in the archives on the *Courant*'s Web site, www.ctnow.com.

12. Owen Kearns, L.C., "Collateral Damage from Abusers in Collars," *National Catholic Register,* Nov. 11–Nov. 17, 2001.

13. Documents provided by the Legionaries' law firm, Kirkland & Ellis, to *The Hartford Courant,* Dec. 20, 1996.

14. GR interview with Dominguez, Nov. 15, 1996.

15. The attorney James Basile sent copies of the letters.

16. "Barred from Practice for Writing Articles on Pope's Final Illness," *New York Times,* Dec. 13, 1958; Paul I. Murphy with R. René Arlington, *La Popessa* (New York: WarnerBooks, 1983), 21.

17. GR telephone interview with Michael Massing, Aug. 30, 2002.

18. Authors' interview with José Barba, New Orleans, May 3, 2003.

19. "No Sexual Abuse Ever Took Place," letters to the editor, *Hartford Courant,* Mar. 2, 1997.

20. Ibid.

21. "Legionaries Founder Accused of Sex Abuse," *National Catholic Reporter,* Mar. 7, 1997.

22. "Maciel Denies Sexual Abuse Allegations," *National Catholic Reporter,* Mar. 14, 1997.

23. Salvador Guerrero Chiprés, "Acusan a líder católico de abuso sexual de menores," *La Jornada* (Mexico City), Apr. 14–17, 1997.

24. Kevin Sullivan and Mary Jordan, "Reluctant Mexican Church Begins to Question Its Own: For First Time, a Bishop Acknowledges Pedophilia Cases," *Washington Post,* Apr. 17, 2002.

25. Sandro Magister, "Eran 50 mila giovani e forti," *L'espresso,* Jan. 21, 1999.

26. See www.legionaryfacts.org.

27. Richard John Neuhaus, "Feathers of Scandal," *First Things,* Mar. 2002. Elsewhere in the essay, Neuhaus discusses the canon law case that Barba et al. filed in Rome in 1998, which we cover in chapter 11.

28. In the same article, Neuhaus writes of the Boston scandal as "grist for the mills of

liberals pressing for married priests. . . . And, of course, [legal proceedings] feed the media mill." He goes on: "Stories about Catholic priests have a certain cachet—and, for trial lawyers, a promise of cash—that is usually lacking in other cases." *First Things* championed Philip Jenkins, author of *Pedophiles and Priests: Anatomy of a Contemporary Crisis* (New York: Oxford, 1996), a work based entirely on secondary sources, which argues that media coverage of the early 1990s was a construction fueled by liberal Catholics. Jenkins's essay "The Uses of Clerical Scandal" appeared in the Feb. 1996 issue of *First Things*.

29. Katharine Q. Seelye, "Relentless Moral Crusader Is Relentless Gambler, Too," *New York Times,* May 3, 2003.
30. Gerald Renner and Jason Berry, "Pope Taps Accused Priest for Assembly," *Hartford Courant,* Oct. 23, 1997.
31. "La acusación al padre Marcial Maciel llega al Vaticano," *Milenio Semanal,* Dec. 8, 1997.

CHAPTER 11. IN THE VATICAN COURTS

1. John Tedeschi, *The Prosecution of Heresy: Collected Studies on the Inquisition in Modern Italy* (Binghamton: Center for Medieval and Renaissance Studies, State University of New York, 1991), 23.
2. In 1979 Pope John Paul II conceded that the church had erred in its treatment of Galileo.
3. Tedeschi, *Prosecution of Heresy,* 8.
4. Garry Wills, *Papal Sin* (New York: Doubleday, 2000), 74.
5. Ibid., 249–56.
6. Robert Blair Kaiser, *Pope, Council and World* (New York: Macmillan, 1963), 223.
7. John Allen, *Cardinal Ratzinger* (New York: Continuum, 2000), 65.
8. Paul Collins, *The Modern Inquisition: Seven Prominent Catholics and Their Struggles with the Vatican* (New York: Overlook, 2002), 18.
9. Allen, *Ratzinger,* 66.
10. One of the more spirited exchanges can be found in Joseph Cardinal Ratzinger, *Salt of the Earth: The Church at the End of the Millennium: An Interview with Peter Seewald,* trans. Adrian Walker (San Francisco: Ignatius Press, 1996).
11. GR interview with Athié, Apr. 16, 2001, Chicago. See also Jason Berry and Gerald Renner, "Sex-Related Case Blocked in the Vatican," *National Catholic Reporter,* Dec. 7, 2001.
12. JB interview with Antonio Roqueñi, Mexico City, Mar. 3, 2001.
13. Roderic Ai Camp, *Crossing Swords: Politics and Religion in Mexico* (New York: Oxford University Press, 1997), 230.
14. Authors' interviews with Barba and Jurado, New Orleans, Feb. 10, 2001.
15. Sandro Magister, "Eran 50 mila giovani et forti," *L'espresso,* Jan. 21, 1999.
16. JB interview with Elio Masferrer, Mexico City, Mar. 2, 2001.
17. JB telephone interview with Glenn Favreau, May 1, 2003.
18. Richard John Neuhaus, *Appointment in Rome: The Church in America Awakening* (New York: Crossroad, 1999), 110.
19. "Passion for the Priesthood: Testimony Given by Fr. Marcial Maciel, L.C., Saint Peter's Square, Prayer Vigil of the Jubilee for Priests, Vatican City, May 17, 2000," www.legionofchrist.org.
20. *El Legionario* by Alejandro Espinosa (Mexico City: Editorial Grijalbo, 2003).

21. *National Catholic Reporter,* Dec. 7, 2001. The comment was given to John Allen, the paper's Vatican correspondent, who assisted in preparation of the Dec. 7 article.
22. GR interview with Athié; *National Catholic Reporter,* Dec. 7, 2001.

CHAPTER 12. RELIGIOUS DURESS

1. David O'Reilly, "Camden Diocese Agrees to Settle Sex-Abuse Suit," *Philadelphia Inquirer,* Mar. 14, 2003; JB interview with Rubino.
2. Thomas P. Doyle, O.P., J.C.C., "Roman Catholic Clericalism, Religious Duress, and Clergy Sexual Abuse," *Pastoral Psychology* 51, no. 3 (January 2003).
3. Ibid., 219.
4. Ibid., 218.
5. Ibid., 221.
6. Robert Blair Kaiser, *Pope, Council and World* (New York: Macmillan, 1963), 75, 149–150.
7. Hubertus Czernin, *Das Buch Groer: Eine Kirchenchronik,* 2nd ed. (Klagenfurt, Austria: Wieser Verlag, 1998). Professor Ingrid Shafer of the University of Science and the Arts of Oklahoma provided a translation and summary of relevant sections. Verbatim quotations not taken from the book are indicated in subsequent footnotes.
8. JB e-mail correspondence with Christa Pongratz-Lippitt, May 19, 2003.
9. Christa Pongratz-Lippitt, "Cardinal Silent over Sex Abuse Charges," *Tablet,* Apr. 1, 1995.
10. Christa Pongratz-Lippitt, "Death of Cardinal Groer," *Tablet,* Mar. 29, 2003.
11. Roland Prinz, "Cardinal Accused of Sexual Abuse Quits Leadership Post," Associated Press, Apr. 6, 1995.
12. Christa Pongratz-Lippitt, "Cardinal's Stance Puts Church in Turmoil," *Tablet,* Apr. 15, 1995.
13. "Dialogue for Austria," *Radio National Encounter with Margaret Coffee,* Australian Broadcasting Corporation, Dec. 16, 2001.
14. Ingrid Shafer, "Petition Drive Moves to Germany," *National Catholic Reporter,* Aug. 25, 1995.
15. Christa Pongratz-Lippitt, "Accused Cardinal Is Appointed Prior," *Tablet,* Aug. 10, 1996.
16. "Pope Ticks Off Austrian Bishops over Quarrels." *Examiner* (Dublin), June 19, 1998.
17. John L. Allen Jr., "Austria's Catholic Revolution," *National Catholic Reporter,* Oct. 30, 1998.
18. Ibid.
19. Ann Rodgers-Melnick, "Vatican Eyes U.S. Bishops' Rules on Priestly Sex Abuse," *Pittsburgh Post-Gazette,* June 29, 1997.
20. Ibid.
21. John L. Allen Jr., *Cardinal Ratzinger* (New York: Continuum, 2000), 160.
22. John L. Allen Jr., *Conclave: The Politics, Personalities, and Process of the Next Papal Election* (New York: Doubleday Image, 2002), 163.
23. Ron Russell, "Mahony's Cronies," *Los Angeles New Times,* June 13, 2002.
24. Michael Rezendes, "Ariz. Abuse Case Names Bishop, 2 Priests," *Boston Globe,* Aug. 20, 2002.
25. Ibid.
26. In brief, Trupia claimed that Moreno's suspension was penal in nature and canonically invalid because the bishop did not conduct the preliminary canonical investiga-

tion according to canons 1717–31, which give the bishop the authority to remove the accused from office pending the outcome of a criminal investigation. In fact, Moreno had conducted the investigation through other sources. Moreno defended his decision, stating that it was "administrative" rather than penal, which he had every right to make for the good of the people.

27. Rezendes, "Ariz. Abuse Case."
28. Sacha Pfeiffer and Michael Rezendes, "Skeptics Sit on Panel for Clergy Abuse Policy," *Boston Globe*, Oct. 24, 2002.
29. Alex Friedrich and Royal Calkins, "Diocese Official Leaves Post," *Monterey Herald*, Feb. 14, 2003.
30. JB interview with Sylvia Demarest, Dallas, June 11, 2002.
31. JB interview with Kristopher Galland, Dallas, June 14, 2002.
32. Garry Wills, *Papal Sin* (New York: Doubleday, 2000), 175–76.
33. Todd J. Gillman, "Siblings Say Father Kos Abused Boys," *Dallas Morning News*, Dec. 26, 1993.
34. Dan Michalski, "Innocence Lost," *D* (magazine of Dallas/Forth Worth), Sept. 1995.
35. JB telephone interview with attorney Tahara Merritt of Dallas, May 28, 2003.
36. Thomas P. Doyle to Sylvia Demarest, *Does v. Dallas, Rudy Kos,* memorandum on annulment procedures, Dec. 14, 1995.
37. Joseph F. Wilson, "The Enemy Within: MTV Is Not the Problem," in Paul Thigpen, ed., *Shaken by Scandals: Catholics Speak Out About Priests' Sexual Abuse* (Ann Arbor: Servant Publications, 2002), 32–33.
38. Anne Belli Gesalman, "Early Concerns over Priest Cited in Sex-Abuse Suit," *Dallas Morning News,* July 20, 1993; Michalski, "Innocence Lost."
39. JB interview with Windle Turley, Dallas, June 14, 2002.
40. Ed Housewright, "Bishop Says Abuse Victims 'Need Our Sincere Apology,'" *Dallas Morning News,* July 12, 1997.
41. Sam Howe Verhovek, "Sex Abuse Victims Angered by a Monsignor's Remark," *New York Times,* Aug. 11, 1997.
42. Brooks Egerton, "Catholic Judge Steps Down from Dallas Diocese Case," *Dallas Morning News,* Aug. 23, 1997.

CHAPTER 13. ORTHODOXY AND DECEPTION

1. Robert Hutchison, *Their Kingdom Come: The Secret World of Opus Dei* (New York: St. Martin's Press, 1997), 43–44.
2. Ibid., 53.
3. Joan Estruch, *Saints and Schemers: Opus Dei and Its Paradoxes* (New York: Oxford, 1995), 131.
4. Kenneth Woodward, *Making Saints* (New York: Touchstone, 1990), 384.
5. Hutchison, *Their Kingdom Come,* 221 ff.
6. James Martin, S.J., "Opus Dei in the United States," *America,* Feb. 25, 1995.
7. Frank Bruni, "Validating Opus Dei, the Pope Makes Its Founder a Saint," *New York Times,* Oct. 7, 2002.
8. Opus Dei communication office, New Rochelle, N.Y., April 22, 2003.
9. See www.legionofchrist.org.
10. See www.regnumchristi.org.

11. Founded in 1934 by the bishop of Laibach, Austria, and others.
12. Servando Ortoll, "Catholic Organizations in Mexico's National Politics (1926–42)" (Ph.D. diss., Columbia University, 1986), 195.
13. Ibid., 195–96.
14. Letters quoted are from documents provided to Regnum Christi members not available outside "the Movement."
15. Peter Cronin's letter of Oct. 23, 1996, to Pat Kenny can be found on the Web at www.regainnetwork.org.
16. Regain's web site is www.regainnetwork.org.
17. GR interviews by telephone and e-mail and at the Helmueller home in St. Paul, Minn., Feb. 22, 2003.
18. Mary Therese Helmueller to Mary Ann Glendon, April 16, 2002.
19. Norma Peshard did not respond to a request for an interview made through Mater Ecclesiae, the consecrated women's center in Greenville, Rhode Island.
20. GR telephone interview with Ruth Lasseter, June 1, 2003.
21. GR interviews with Favreau in Plattsburgh, N.Y., Dec. 28, 2001; Irving, Tex., June 28–30, 2002; and in telephone conversations and e-mail.
22. One is a priest who held a high position in the Legion and the other is a priest still in the Legion, both of whom requested anonymity.
23. Patsy McGarry, "Back to the Future in Rome," *Irish Times,* Jan. 11, 2003.
24. Financial informants (see note 22).
25. Alfonso Torres Robles, *La prodigiosa adventura de los Legionarios de Cristo* (Madrid: Foca, 2001), 148–49.
26. Ibid., 143–44.
27. McGarry, "Back to the Future."

CHAPTER 14. THE LEGION'S AMERICAN BATTLES

1. Gerald Renner, "Turmoil in Atlanta," *National Catholic Reporter,* Nov. 3, 2000.
2. Deposition of board member Martin Gatins, Mar. 27, 2001, in the case of *Angela Sarullo Naples v. The Donnellan School, Inc., Monsignor Edward J. Dillon and Father John Hopkins,* Fulton County State Court, Ga.
3. Gayle White, "School Dispute Puts Religious Order in Spotlight," *Atlanta Journal-Constitution,* Oct. 28, 2000.
4. GR interview with Naples in Atlanta on May 2, 2002, as well as interviews by telephone and e-mail, supplemented by court documents.
5. Kathi Stearns, "New Donnellan School Ownership Announced," *Georgia Bulletin,* June 17, 1999.
6. GR interviews with Stinger in Atlanta, Oct. 2, 2000, and May 2, 2002, as well as by telephone and e-mail, supplemented by court documents.
7. Renner, "Turmoil in Atlanta."
8. GR telephone interview with Lisa Bastian, Mar. 20, 1997.
9. GR telephone interview with Maggie Picket, Mar. 20, 1997.
10. Renner, "Turmoil in Atlanta."
11. Deposition of Martin Gatins.
12. *Complaint of Angela Sarullo Naples, plaintiff, v. The Donnellan School, Inc.; Monsignor Edward J. Dillon and Father John Hopkins,* Sept. 29, 2000, Fulton County State Court, Ga.

13. Ibid.

14. Renner, "Turmoil in Atlanta."

15. Gayle White, "School Dispute."

16. Deposition of Martin Gatins.

17. GR telephone interview with parish worker who did not want to be identified for fear of losing the job, Sept. 30, 2002.

18. Council of Priests, minutes of meeting, Mar. 19, 2003.

19. GR telephone interview with Msgr. Young, June 6, 2003.

20. GR telephone interview with Fr. Hickey, June 5, 2003.

21. GR telephone interview with Patrick Smith, Dec. 14, 2000.

22. GR telephone interview with Sr. Roberta Schmidt, C.S.J., education director, Mar. 18, 2003.

23. *Royal Palm International Academy vs. Patrick S. Smith, Jane E. Smith, and Robert Sorrentino, trustee, Sorrentino Florida Land Trust,* Circuit Court, Collier County, Fla., Nov. 9, 2000.

24. *Patrick S. Smith vs. Carol Moore, Dr. James J. Crandall, Jack Donohue, Royal Palm International Academy, the Legion of Christ, and National Consultants for Education, Inc.,* Circuit Court, Collier County, Fla., Nov. 3, 2000

25. Rachel Bott, "Change in Leadership Fractures Naples Catholic School Community," *Naples Daily News,* Dec. 17, 2000.

26. Ibid.

27. Jay Dunlap to Dan Anderson, Jan. 15, 2001.

28. Dan Anderson to Jay Dunlap, Jan. 19, 2001.

29. Beth Francis, "Alzheimer's: Smith Is Business Mind Behind Potential Alzheimer's Cure Venture," *Naples Daily News,* July 1, 2001.

30. GR telephone interview, Sept. 18, 2002.

31. Bishop Griffin to Fr. Mathewson and parishioners of St. Francis, Oct. 8, 2002.

32. See http://saintjosephcathedral.org.

33. In the diocese of Calgary, in northwest Canada, Bishop Fred Henry faced the concerns of parents at a private Catholic school called Clearwater Academy. People complained of being deceived into believing the school was autonomous, only to learn it was a Regnum Christi–Legionaries joint venture. They accused Regnum Christi members of shielding their true purpose. Henry ordered the Legion out of the diocese and appointed a commission of three priests and two women to investigate. The commission's May 31, 2001, report said that the Legion and Regnum Christi offer "a style and type of direction for a segment of the faithful that answers reasonable and worthwhile needs"; however, they agreed with disaffected parents who felt "hoodwinked" and they criticized "a perception of secrecy surrounding the activities of the movement that is unnecessary, unfortunate and correctable." The commission thought the shortcomings could be overcome. It said the school board, "realizing the ramifications of 'truth in advertising,' is dedicated to openly communicating this important link [to Regnum Christi and the Legion] to all prospective students and parents." It suggested closer ties between the school and the bishop, who should appoint a board member and a part-time chaplain not in the Legion. The commission found "a joyful and peaceful environment" at the school, and felt Legion priests should be permitted to visit the diocese several times a year to minister to Regnum Christi members, with the diocese approving each visit. The commission noted "a certain rigidness" in Regnum Christi. The strict division by gender "encourages an antiquated approach to reality

and may encourage sexism especially with respect to women's role in society and the church. . . . In some few isolated cases, attitudes of elitism and superiority are evident in its members' attitudes toward non-member and non-Legion priests; perhaps, some of the Latin American flavor of the order is inappropriate in our culture."

34. Jennifer Garza, "A Church Divided," *Sacramento Bee,* Mar. 2, 2002.
35. Robert V. Scheide, "Our Lady of Infinite Division," *Sacramento News and Review,* July 4, 2002.
36. Maria Morales Gonzalez, in a letter rallying supporters to a press conference on June 8, 2001, to protest what they called the "Legionaire's disease" afflicting their church.
37. Scheide, "Our Lady of Infinite Division."
38. Ibid.
39. Lennon e-mail, June 24, 2002; Mexican priest who did not want to be named, e-mail, Aug. 7, 2002.
40. Garza, "A Church Divided."
41. GR telephone interview with Maria Morales Gonzalez, May 13, 2003.
42. Terri Hardy, "Mather Eyed for Catholic College," *Sacramento Bee,* Nov. 8, 2002. The Legion counts two European universities, in Rome and Madrid, seven in Mexico, and one in Santiago, Chile.
43. GR telephone interview with Hahn, May 8, 2003.
44. Jay Dunlap, "New University Seeks Permit to Build," www.legionariesofchrist.org /eng/index.phtml.
45. Robert Marchant, "Catholic Move to Block Foes," *White Plains (N.Y.) Reporter-Dispatch,* Apr. 5, 1997.
46. See www.ipsciences.edu

Chapter 15. A Vatican of Naked Truths

1. JB telephone interview with A. W. Richard Sipe, Sept. 12, 2002.
2. "Vatican Norms Governing Grave Offenses, Including Sexual Abuse of Minors" was posted on the *National Catholic Reporter* Website (www.natcath.org) by John L. Allen Jr., Nov. 22, 2002. The document, which is officially called a *papal motu proprio,* was titled "Defense of the Most Holy Sacraments."
3. John Thavis, "Doctrinal Congregation Takes Control of Priestly Pedophilia Cases," Catholic News Service, Dec. 5, 2001.
4. John L. Allen Jr. and Pamela Schaeffer, "Reports of Abuse," *National Catholic Reporter,* Mar.16, 2001.
5. Steve Pagani, "Report: Priests, Missionaries Sexually Abuse Nuns," Reuters, Mar. 20, 2001.
6. Doyle e-mail to JB, Apr. 16, 2002.
7. Elizabeth Hamilton and Eric Rich, "Egan Protected Abusive Priests," *The Hartford Courant,* Mar. 17, 2002. George Weigel, *The Courage to Be Catholic* (New York: Basic Books, 2002), 11–12.
8. Rivera interview with the Italian Catholic journal *30 Giorni,* translated. See John L. Allen Jr., "U.S. Media in Anti-Plot Says Mexican Prelate," *National Catholic Reporter,* July 19, 2002.
9. John Thavis, "In Letter to Priests, Pope Says Clergy Sex Abusers Betray Priesthood," Catholic News Service, in *Denver Catholic Register,* Mar. 27, 2002.
10. The psychiatrist Conrad Baars presented a paper to the 1971 Synod of Bishops at the

Vatican, "The Role of the Church in the Causation, Treatment and Prevention of the Crisis in the Priesthood." Eugene Kennedy and Victor Heckler produced a study for the American bishops in 1972, *The Catholic Priest in the United States: Psychological Investigations.* Doyle's "Religious Duress" essay in *Pastoral Psychology* contains a bibliography of similar works. See also A. W. Richard Sipe, *Sex, Priests and Power: Anatomy of a Crisis* (New York: Brunner/Mazel, 1995).

11. Eugene Kennedy, e-mail and conversation with JB, June 5, 2003.

12. John Allen, "Vatican Defends Church's Handling of Sexual Abuse Allegations," *National Catholic Reporter,* Mar. 29, 2002; Thavis, "Letter to Priests."

13. Allen, "Vatican Defends." Castrillón Hoyos drew the percentage estimate from Philip Jenkins's *Pedophiles and Priests: Anatomy of a Contemporary Crisis* (New York: Oxford, 1996). The Chicago study, conducted in 1992, was a decade old. Jenkins's book, based entirely on secondary sources, argued that the early 1990s crisis was a construction of the news media keying off dissident liberal Catholics.

14. Thomas Doyle, "They Still Don't Get It and Probably Never Will," *Irish Times,* Mar. 22, 2002.

15. Thomas Doyle, "Bishops Must Be Held Accountable," *Irish Times,* June 4, 2002.

16. John Tagliabue, "Sex Charges Claim Polish Archbishop," *New York Times,* Mar. 29, 2002.

17. Robert Blair Kaiser, "Rome Diary 43 / 30 March 2002," http://justgoodcompany.com/RomeDiary.

18. Peter Steinfels, *A People Adrift: The Crisis of the Roman Catholic Church in America* (New York: Simon & Schuster), 247.

19. Sissela Bok, *Lying: Moral Choice in Public and Private Life* (New York: Vintage, 1999), 7.

20. Authors' interview with Paul Collins, New York, Sept. 23, 2002.

21. Originally published as *From Inquisition to Freedom: Seven Prominent Catholics and Their Struggle with the Vatican* (Sydney: Simon & Schuster Australia, 2001).

22. Collins, *The Modern Inquisition* (New York: Overlook, 2002), 210.

23. Ibid., 211.

24. Paul Collins, "The Peripatetic Pope: Papal Visits Are a Mixed Blessing," *Commonweal,* Sept. 11, 1987.

25. Robert Blair Kaiser, "Rome Diary 13 / 9 December 1999," http://justgoodcompany.com/RomeDiary.

26. Paul Collins, *Papal Power* (London: Fount, 1997), 7.

27. John Henry Newman, *An Essay on the Development of Christian Doctrine* (Notre Dame, Ind.: University of Notre Dame Press, 1989), 40.

28. Collin, *Papal Power,* 17.

29. Ibid., 29.

30. Ibid., 116.

31. Ibid., 105–6.

32. Ibid., 215.

33. Collins, *The Modern Inquisition,* 219.

34. Ibid., 222.

35. The Australian and U.K title is *From Inquisition to Freedom: Seven Prominent Catholics and Their Struggle with the Vatican.*

36. Paul Collins, "Reasons for Resignation," Mar. 2001, Association for Rights of Catholics Web site: http//arcc-catholic-rights.org/collins2001a.htm.

37. John Allen Jr., *National Catholic Reporter,* Mar. 29, 2002, quotes from Bertone's interview in *30 Giorni.*
38. NBC News, *Meet the Press,* transcript, Mar. 31, 2002, courtesy of NBC.
39. For accounts of Mark Serrano and the Mendham gathering, see Jason Berry, "The Priest and the Boy," *Rolling Stone,* June 20, 2002, and "Survivors Connect to Heal, Raise Voices," *National Catholic Reporter,* Nov. 8, 2002.
40. John Allen, "Catholic Vatican Summit Produces Flawed Document," *National Catholic Reporter,* May 10, 2002.
41. Brian Ross, reporter, and Rhonda Schwartz, producer, "Eight Men Accuse High Catholic Church Official Father Marcial Maciel of Sexual Abuse When They Were Children," ABC News, *20/20,* Apr. 26, 2002.
42. In what Associated Press calls a "conservative count," 325 accused priests resigned, retired, or were removed from ministry in calendar year 2002. GR telephone interview with Rachel Zoll, AP religion writer. The *New York Times* puts the count at 432; see Laurie Goodstein, "Trail of Pain in Church Crisis Leads to Nearly Every Diocese," *New York Times,* Jan. 12, 2002.

EPILOGUE

1. José Barba interview with the authors, May 3, 2003, New Orleans.
2. GR telephone interview with Garcia Zuazua and e-mail exchange, Aug. 27, 2002.
3. John Allen, "The Word from Rome," weekly e-mail, *National Catholic Reporter,* Aug. 9, 2002.
4. Barba interview, May 3, 2003, New Orleans.
5. Jonathan Kwitney, *Man of the Century* (New York: Henry Holt, 1997), 563.
6. Jesús Colina interviews Marcial Maciel, *Christ Is My Life* (Manchester, N.H.: Sophia Institute Press, 2003), 172.
7. Luigi Accattoli, *When a Pope Asks Forgiveness: The Mea Culpa's of John Paul II,* trans. by Jordan Aumann, O.P. (Boston: Pauline Books, 1998), 69. The letter is called *Tertio Millennio Adveniente.*
8. Ibid., 56.
9. James Carroll, *Toward a New Catholic Church: The Promise of Reform* (Boston: Houghton Mifflin, 2002), 15.
10. Robert Ellsberg, ed., *Flannery O'Connor: Spiritual Writings* (Maryknoll, N.Y.: Orbis Books, 2003), 83.
11. Jason Berry, "Fathers and Sins," *Los Angeles Times Magazine,* June 13, 1993.
12. Frank Keating, "The Last Straw: Quitting the Bishops' Review Board," *Crisis,* Oct. 2003.
13. John L. Allen Jr., "Curial Official Blasts U.S. Media Coverage," *National Catholic Reporter,* May 17, 2002.
14. Reese Dunklin, "Vatican Elevated Abusive Priest." *Dallas Morning News,* Aug. 30, 2003.
15. John L. Allen Jr., "The World from Rome," www.natcath.org, Oct. 10, 2003.
16. Mario von Galli, *The Council and the Future* (New York: McGraw-Hill, 1966).

ACKNOWLEDGMENTS

THE WORK that led to this book began in 1996 with a joint assignment at *The Hartford Courant,* thanks to the then editor, David Barrett, and the managing editor, Clifford Teutsch. We appreciate the careful attention that Teutsch, Stephanie Summers, and Claude Albert gave to editing our report published in February of 1997. Staff writer Helen Ubiñas graciously translated several documents. Gerald Renner also wishes to thank Bernard Davidow, a tireless editor of features and news, for his constant encouragement and many courtesies both before and after Renner's retirement from the *Courant* in April of 2000.

The *National Catholic Reporter* has been in the forefront of covering the church for many years and has been an important outlet for both of us. To publisher Tom Fox, editor Tom Roberts, and the former managing editor Pamela Schaeffer, we appreciate the support for articles that developed into chapters of this book. We owe a special debt to John L. Allen Jr., the newspaper's Vatican correspondent and a distinguished writer, for his professional generosity and peerless insight into the affairs of the Holy See. Thanks as well to *NCR*'s Boston correspondent, Chuck Colbert.

We are most grateful to the Fund for Investigative Journalism, in Washington, D.C., its board members, and the director, John Hyde, for a timely research grant, and for the assistance provided, through the Fund, by Lisa Romero, communications librarian, associate professor of library administration, University of Illinois at Urbana-Champaign.

To literary agent Deborah Grovesnor of Bethesda, Maryland, major thanks.

It has been a pleasure to work with Frederic Hills, our editor at the Free Press; his fine copy editor, Chuck Antony; and his colleagues, especially Martha Levin, Carisa Hays, Cassie Dendurent, Paul O'Halloran, Robert Niegowski, and Andrea Au.

Father Thomas Doyle was unstinting in his generosity despite the demands made on his time for interviews in person, by telephone, and by e-mail. His sister Kelly Doyle Tobin graciously shared family memories, as did his cousin Sharon Doyle, with the family genealogy.

Professor José de Jesús Barba Martin has been a diligent guide through the labyrinth of the Legion of Christ; we admire his tenacity and thank him for his goodwill.

There are others who took courageous stands, without whom this book would never have been written: the Reverend Félix Alarcón, Saúl Barrales Arellano, Alejandro Espinosa Alcalá, Arturo Jurado Guzmán, Fernando Pérez Olvera, José Antonio Pérez Olvera, Juan Vaca, and the late Juan Manuel Fernández Amenábar.

Many people provided information from within the church, particularly in Rome, who asked not to be identified. We thank them for leading us to the right questions. Three canon lawyers who spoke on the record were of great assistance: Monsignor Brian Ferme, an Australian, the dean of the canon law faculty at the Pontifical Lateran University in Rome; Monsignor Kenneth Lasch, the pastor of St. Joseph Parish in Mendham, New Jersey; and the Reverend Antonio Roqueñi of Mexico City.

We are especially grateful for what we learned from Father Alberto Athié, Isaac Chute, the late Father Peter Cronin, Federico Dominguez, Kevin Fagan, Glenn Favreau, Tony Fernandez, Rollin and Ruth Lasseter, Paul Lennon, Father Rogelio Orozco, and Rafael Garcia-Zuazua.

We also thank Detective Sergeant Dan Anderson, Lisa Bastian, Melissa Cook, Diane Dougherty, Barbara Felix, Sue Greve, the Helmueller family, Tyler and Julia Kohl, Colleen Kunnuth, Susan McDermott, Maria Morales, Theresa Murray, Angela Naples, Gerry Neely, Dr. Henry and Lisa Perez, Maggie Picket, Rex and Maurine Smith, Diane Stinger, Patricia Swanson, Indra Turnbull, and David and Sue Youngerman.

Veteran correspondent and author Robert Blair Kaiser, who covered Vatican II for *Time* and writes for *Newsweek*, was most generous in guiding us to sources. Other correspondents in Rome who helped include Robert Mickens of the English Catholic weekly magazine the *Tablet*; David Willey of the BBC; Judy Harris; Sandro Magister of *L'espresso*; Peggy Polk of Religion News Service; Eduardo Lliteras, who reports for

Milenio and other Mexican publications; Philippa Hitchen of Vatican Radio; and Delia Gallagher of *Inside the Vatican*.

Flavio Viscardi was invaluable as a researcher into sexual abuse reporting in the Italian press, and for providing translations. Thanks also to Fabrizio Tonello.

Ann Rodgers-Melnick, religion reporter for the *Pittsburgh Post-Gazette,* went far beyond courtesy to share her experiences reporting a complicated canon law case. In reading our manuscript she offered many insightful comments. In like measure, we wish to thank Joe Rigert, a distinguished investigative reporter, recently retired from the *Star-Tribune* in Minneapolis.

For assistance in understanding texts in Spanish, thanks to Blanca Anderson, Mary Frances Berry, and Paul Lennon. For translation assistance, Nela Garcia-Zuazua. For translation from German—and for her own reporting on events in Austria and Germany—thanks to Professor Ingrid Shafer of the University of Arts and Sciences of Oklahoma.

The Austrian journalist and *Tablet* correspondent Christa Pongratz-Lippitt was generous in providing research on Cardinal Groer.

Among other colleagues who facilitated our research we are particularly grateful to Carl Cannon, now a White House correspondent for the *National Journal*.

Two journalists who have since died were of great assistance, in different ways: Richard Baudouin, a courageous editor at the *Times of Acadiana*, and Jonathan Kwitney, one of the finest investigative reporters of his generation, author of an excellent biography of Pope John Paul II.

In more or less alphabetical order, we wish to thank these colleagues: ABC News, correspondents Bill Blakemore and Brian Ross; chief investigative producer Christopher Isham; senior producers Rhonda Schwartz and Richard Harris; producers Jill Rackmill and Madeline Sauer. Associated Press, Rachel Zoll. *The Boston Globe,* Ellen Barry, Matt Carroll, Michael Paulson, Sacha Pfeiffer, Michael Rezendes, Walter V. Robinson, Stephen Kurkjian, and Charles Sennott. *The Boston Herald,* Robin Washington. *The Boston Phoenix,* Kristen Lombardi. *Canadian Press,* correspondent and author Darcey Henton. *Catholic New Times* in Toronto, editor Ted Schmidt. Catholic News Service, David Gibson and John Thavis. The *Chicago Tribune,* Todd Lighty and Elizabeth Taylor. *The* Cleveland *Plain Dealer,* James McCarty. *The Dallas Morning News,*

Brooks Egerton and Rod Dreher. *Dayton Daily News,* Vince McKelvey. *Los Angeles Times,* Gary Spiecker and Glenn Bunting. *Milwaukee Journal Sentinel,* Marie Rohde and Meg Kissinger. *Newsday,* Carol Eisenberg. *The New York Times,* Sam Dillon. *The New Orleans Times-Picayune,* Lolis Elie, James Gill, Bruce Nolan, and at *Gambit Weekly,* Clancy DuBos and Michael Tisserand. Religion News Service, Peggy Polk. *Rolling Stone,* Bill Tonelli. *San Francisco Weekly,* Ron Russell. *Vancouver Sun,* Douglas Todd. *The Wall Street Journal,* Jose de Cordoba. *The Washington Post,* Alan Cooperman and Caryle Murphy. *The Worcester Telegram & Gazette,* Kathleen Shaw.

In Mexico City, we wish to thank Ciro Gomez Legura of *Milenio;* Professor Elio Masferrer Kan, a religious anthropologist at Escuela Nacional de Antropologia e Historia, who helped explain the complex politics of the Mexican hierarchy; and for gracious hospitality, Willie Frehoff Evers and Victoria Miranda Frehoff.

Paul Collins, on a visit from Australia to New York, went out of his way to meet with us and in a wide-ranging interview gave leads and rare insights. The editor of our Australian edition, Matthew Kelly at Hodder-Headline, was of great assistance in facilitating research from across the world. Paul Collins, Barry M. Coldrey, Alan Gill, and researcher Bernard Barrett, with Broken Rites, all went more than the scriptural extra mile in fielding questions via the Internet. Thanks also to journalist Chris McGillion for timely assistance. Jason Berry is indebted to Chris MacIsaac for providing research materials through the early 1900s.

We profited greatly by the wide-angle lens that Andrew Greeley, Eugene Kennedy, A. W. Richard Sipe, and Garry Wills provided on the Catholic Church through their books and articles, and in responses in our varied inquiries.

A special thanks to the Reverend Raymond Schroth, S.J.

The Reverend Thomas J. Reese, S.J., and the Reverend Vincent O'Keefe, S.J., shared their personal knowledge on how the Vatican works, and doesn't work, in the interregnum between popes. Brother Hugo Rieping, O.S.B., of Mount Angel Abbey Library, St. Benedict, Oregon, provided helpful background on Abbot Gregorio Lemercier of the Monastery of the Resurrection in Santa Maria Ahuacatitlán, near Cuernavaca. The Reverend Bruce Williams, O.P., provided helpful guidance.

Among the attorneys who facilitated our research, we thank Jeffrey

Anderson of Minneapolis; William Crosby of Cleveland; Sylvia Demarest and Windle Turley of Dallas, and their assistants, respectively, Trish McLelland and Barbara Louisell; Simon Kennedy of County Wexford, Ireland; Roderick "Eric" MacLeish of Boston; Tahara Merritt of Dallas; Stephen Rubino of Margate, N.J.; Arch Stokes of Atlanta; Denis Ventriglia of Charleston, S.C.; and the late Bruce Pasternack of New Mexico.

Special thanks to the remarkable leaders of S.N.A.P., Barbara Blaine, David Clohessy, Laura Barrett, Peter Iseley, Mark Serrano, Mark Brooks, Mary Grant, Lyn Hill Hayward, among others; to the founder of Linkup, Jeanne Miller, and those who continue her work, including Sue Archibald and Reverend Gary Hayes, and the many others who are bringing new light to the church.

For background on Ireland we are especially obligated to the work of Mary Raferty of RTE (Irish National TV), who produced the groundbreaking documentary series *States of Fear* in 1999 and *Cardinal Sins* in 2002. She is also coauthor of *Suffer the Little Children*. We thank also Aoife Rickard, of RTE's *Prime Time*, and independent producer Mark Day of Vista, California. Thanks also to Deirdre Valdon at the *Irish Times*.

John Shepherd, assistant archivist, American Catholic History Collection at the Catholic University of America, and his aide, Heather Morgan, went out of their way to assist in research into records of the Montezuma Seminary; Shepherd called attention to a noteworthy unpublished doctoral dissertation we otherwise would not have known about: Servando Ortoll, "Catholic Organizations in Mexico's National Politics (1926–42)," Columbia University, 1986.

We thank medical doctors Louis Keller and Lawrence J. Mellon for pinning down the nature of the drug Dolantin through the Thomas Jefferson University Medical Center in Philadelphia.

An invaluable resource was Connecticut's statewide library catalogue on the Internet, which lists holdings in public, university, seminary, and special libraries. Lauren Rosato of Norwalk, representing Lexpress International, most graciously provided translation services.

Philip Braun of New Orleans provided superb research assistance.

For various forms of assistance: Robert Bell, Stephen Brady of Roman Catholic Faithful, the Reverend David Boileau, the Reverend Frank Coco, S.J., Rob Couhig, Dan Devine, Mark Dowie, Ludwig Ring-Eifel, Max Holland, Jeffrey Gillenkirk, Caitlin Kelly, Steve and Juile Knipstein,

Michael Massing, Avia Morgan, Michael and Linda Mewshaw, Ray Mouton, Adam Nossiter Mimi Nothacker, Thomas Powers, June Rosner, Joe Sanford of Pelican Pictures, Henri Schindler, Tom Smith, Peter Steinfels, the Reverend Bruce Teague, Roberta Wilk, Gerard and Mathilde Wimberly, Christine Wiltz.

Jacquelyn Renner gave the manuscript in progress a critical reading and two of the Renners' computer-literate children assisted, Mary X. Yordon lending her skill in computer graphics and Jack applying his wizardry in overcoming several technical complexities.

Lastly, profound thanks to Melanie McKay, who brought her background as an English professor to bear on many readings of this work and gave valuable editorial advice.

Jason Berry and Gerald Renner

INDEX

University of Sacramento, 272
U.S. Conference of Catholic Bishops, 23,
    26–27, 30, 32–33, 57, 63, 66, 99, 111,
    125, 151, 200, 230
  Doyle, et al. report to, 44–52, 62, 65, 68,
    79, 98, 99
  national review board of, 7, 291–92,
    304–5

Vaca, Juan, 1–6, 141–45, 149, 160, 164,
    165, 166, 169, 174, 175, 181–82, 183,
    184, 185, 187, 210, 213
Valeri, Cardinal Valerio, 180, 181, 184,
    195
van der Kolk, Bessel, 113
Vatican Bank, 125, 244
Vatican embassy, Washington, D.C., 9,
    20–30, 32, 41, 43–44, 47, 53–54, 59,
    98
  as nunciature, 27, 46, 99
  as secret files depository, 69–70
Vatican I (First Vatican Council), 206
Vatican II (Second Vatican Council), 9,
    13–14, 15–16, 27, 28, 33, 34, 35, 60,
    65, 75, 82, 109, 126, 127–28, 135, 144,
    168, 172, 207, 208, 226, 232, 252, 279,
    281, 282, 302, 307
Ventriglia, Denis, 119–20
Vienna, Austria, case, 227–32
Villasana, J. Alberto, 154–56, 160,
    299–300
Vlazny, Archbishop John, 121

Vogel, Bishop Hansjörg, 230
Voice of the Faithful (VOTF), 292–93

Walsh, Edmund A., 151
Warren, Chet, 75–78, 88, 120
Washington Post, 73, 200
Weakland, Archbishop Rembert G., 32, 35
We Are Church, 129–30, 231
Wegan, Martha, 212–15, 217, 218–20, 296
Weigand, Bishop William, 271
Weigel, George, 6, 97, 98–99, 147, 202–3
Welsh, Bishop Thomas, 58
Wempe, Michael, 111
Whealon, Archbishop John F., 126–28,
    130, 132, 133, 139
Whiteley, John, 78
Wiesner, Bishop Gerry, 105
Wilgress, Sarah, 60, 120–21
Williams, Robert, 239
Williams, Joseph, 137
Wills, Garry, 24, 206, 236
Wilson, Joseph F., 238–39
Woodward, Kenneth L., 244
Wuerl, Bishop Donald, 98, 101–4
Wynn, Wilton, 26

X, Father, 64–66

Young, Terry, 265
Young, Rhett A., 269

Zambrano Institute, Santiago, Chile, 256

ABOUT THE AUTHORS

JASON BERRY has produced an award-winning film documentary based on *Vows of Silence*. His previous books include the highly praised *Lead Us Not into Temptation* and *Up from the Cradle of Jazz*, a history of New Orleans music. He was the recipient of an Alicia Patterson Fellowship for reporting on political demagogues, and a Guggenheim Fellowship for a history of jazz funerals. He writes for many publications and appears often on national television. He lives in New Orleans and is a 1971 graduate of Georgetown.

GERALD RENNER (1932–2007) was a veteran journalist at *The Hartford Courant*, where he was a staff writer specializing in religious news, issues, and trends. Later a freelancer, he was the recipient of a Templeton Prize for religion writing from the Religion News Association, a John Hancock Award for deadline reporting, and several investigative reporting awards from the Connecticut Society of Professional Journalists. Before joining the *Courant*, Renner was editor and director of Religion News Service in New York and a vice president of the National Conference of Christians and Jews. He lived in Norwalk, Connecticut, and was a 1959 graduate of Georgetown.